From:

To:

Ludden Library ILL
Laramie County Community Colleg
1400 E College Drive
Cheyenne, WY 82007

LIBRARY MAIL

CAESAR

III

LCL 402

CAESAR

ALEXANDRIAN WAR
AFRICAN WAR
SPANISH WAR

WITH AN ENGLISH TRANSLATION BY

A. G. WAY

HARVARD UNIVERSITY PRESS
CAMBRIDGE, MASSACHUSETTS
LONDON, ENGLAND

First published 1955
Reprinted 1964, 1978, 1988, 1997, 2001

LOEB CLASSICAL LIBRARY® is a registered trademark
of the President and Fellows of Harvard College

ISBN 0-674-99443-4

Printed in Great Britain by St Edmundsbury Press Ltd,
Bury St Edmunds, Suffolk, on acid-free paper.
Bound by Hunter & Foulis Ltd, Edinburgh, Scotland.

CONTENTS

GENERAL INTRODUCTION

THE three works contained in this volume, though
commonly ascribed by the MSS. to Caesar, are
nowadays generally regarded as of uncertain authorship; and though any detailed presentation of the
evidence would occupy too much space, some brief
discussion of the problem seems called for.

Even as early as the beginning of the second century of our era there were doubts about their
authorship [1]; and certainly the unity of their theme
and the fact that they all three virtually formed a
continuation of the Civil Wars may easily account
for the early tradition that Caesar wrote them.

Now the style of *de Bello Alexandrino* is, as Klotz [2]
demonstrated in great detail, very similar to the style
of the eighth, and last, book of the Gallic Wars,
which is very commonly attributed to Hirtius. The
opening chapter of this eighth book contains the
following sentence [3]:

> ' I have tacked a supplement to the Com-
> mentaries of our great Caesar on the operations
> in Gaul . . . and his last work (*i.e.* the Civil
> Wars), which was left unfinished from the

[1] Suetonius : *Life of Caesar* (Holland's Translation) : ' For
of the Alexandrine, African and Spanish Wars, who was the
writer it is uncertain ; while some think it was Oppius, others
Hirtius, who also made up and finished the last of the Gallic
War.'

[2] *Cäsarstudien* (1910), pp. 180–204.

[3] As translated by H. J. Edwards : Loeb Classical Library.

vii

operations at Alexandria onwards, I have completed as far as the conclusion, not indeed of civil discord, of which we see no end, but of Caesar's life.'

This certainly appears to confirm what seems likely on stylistic grounds, namely that, if it was Hirtius who completed the Gallic Wars, it was Hirtius also who wrote *de Bello Alexandrino*. If he did so, his knowledge of the campaign was second-hand; for later in the same chapter he says:

'For myself, I had not the fortune ever to take part in the Alexandrian and the African campaign.' [1]

Was he then also the author of *de Bello Africo* and *de Bello Hispaniensi*? His words—'as far as the conclusion of Caesar's life' may indeed be so interpreted. The internal evidence, however, seems strongly against this theory, and suggests, on the contrary, that the three works are the independent productions of three separate hands, none of which was Caesar's own.

For anyone who reads the Latin text carefully must surely be forcibly struck by certain idiosyncrasies of style peculiar to one of the books, but not apparent in either of the other two. Thus, to cite but one example, the author of *de Bello Hispaniensi*—quite apart from his quotations from Ennius—constantly employs the adverb *bene* as a

[1] He goes on to remark that these two campaigns are partially known to him from conversations with Caesar; and as he may well have had access to Caesar's note-books, it does not seem impossible that he was the author of *de Bello Alexandrino*.

mere intensive particle, as in the recurrent phrase
bene magna pars; while the author of *de Bello Africo*
has a passion for the word *interim*, and can seldom
think of any alternative with which to introduce a new
chapter. Neither of these foibles is common in the
other work, nor do they occur to any extent in *de
Bello Alexandrino*.

Accordingly, though many scholars nowadays are
disposed to accept Hirtius as the author of *de Bello
Alexandrino*, few still contend that he wrote the other
two works, at any rate in the form in which they have
come down to us. The claims of Asinius Pollio and of
Sallust to the authorship of *de Bello Africo* have
each had a brief vogue. Possibly, however, as Bouvet
has recently suggested,[1] both the *de Bello Africo*
and *de Bello Hispaniensi* which we possess are in
reality no more than rough drafts prepared at the
request of Hirtius by two separate soldiers who
fought in the respective campaigns; and had he
survived, Hirtius would have worked up this ' copy '
into more effective literary form.

The manuscripts on which the text of these three
works is based are in the main the same as those
which contain the Civil Wars; and most of them are
far inferior to those which contain only the Gallic
Wars. The most important are:

Laurentianus Ashburnhamiensis   x–xi century
Lovaniensis [2] .   .   .   . xi century
Mediceus Laurentianus   .   . xi–xii century

---

[1] *César : La Guerre d'Afrique* (1949): Introduction,
p. xix. The suggestion, as Bouvet points out, was originally
made by Nipperdey.

[2] This MS. breaks off abruptly in chapter 33 of *de Bello
Africo.*

Ursinianus	.	.	.	.	xi–xii century
Riccardianus	.	.	.	.	xi–xii century
Thuaneus	.	.	.	.	xi century
Vindobonensis	.	.	.	.	xii century
Neapolitanus	.	.	.	.	xii–xiii century

Their relations to one another have already been discussed by Peskett in his Introduction to the Civil Wars in this series.

For *de Bello Alexandrino* and *de Bello Africo* the text which these MSS. afford is reasonably sound; but for *de Bello Hispaniensi* it is far otherwise. Rice Holmes was perhaps not overstating the case when he wrote:[1]

> 'Bellum Hispaniense is the worst book in Latin literature; and its text is the most deplorable. The language is generally ungrammatical and often unintelligible. The copyists performed their tasks so ill that in the forty-two paragraphs there are twenty-one gaps and six hundred corrupt passages, which Mommsen and lesser men have striven with an industry worthy of a better cause to restore.'

In these circumstances the task of producing a readable translation has proved no easy one; the less so since this series allows little scope for explanatory notes. Hence, though I have generally adhered to the MS. reading wherever it seemed reasonably satisfactory, I have not hesitated in many places to adopt conjectural emendations, so as to produce as continuous and intelligible a rendering as possible. The more important departures from the text I have

[1] *The Roman Republic :* vol iii, p. 298.

indicated, with due acknowledgements, in brief footnotes below the Latin.

In view of the independent character of these three military monographs, linked together though they are by a common theme, it has seemed best to give to each a separate introduction of its own; and, in the case of *de Bello Alexandrino*, to include a brief summary of the concluding chapters of *Civil Wars*, Book III, of which it is a continuation. A separate index of personal and place names contained in each work has been placed at the end of the book, followed by a combined subject index and six maps. Certain problems which are too unwieldy for footnotes—mainly topographical, sometimes controversial—are discussed in four appendixes.

Among various other works and editions which have proved helpful, acknowledgement is due in particular to Rice Holmes' *The Roman Republic*, Bouvet's *La Guerre d'Afrique* and Klotz's *Kommentar zum Bellum Hispaniense*. Unfortunately the recent edition in the Budé series—*Guerre d'Alexandrie* by J. Andrieu (1954)—reached me only when my own final proofs were being revised: hence only the briefest references to it have been possible.

BIBLIOGRAPHICAL ADDENDUM
(1987)

Translation

Jane F. Mitchell, *Caesar, The Civil War together with The Alexandrian War, The African War, and The Spanish War by other Hands* (Penguin Books), Harmondsworth 1967

Lexicons

S. Preuss, *Vollständiges Lexicon zu den pseudocäsarianischen Schriftwerken*, 1884 (repr. 1964)
H. Merguet, Jena 1886 (repr. Hildesheim 1963)

General

K. Barwick, 'Caesars Commentarii und das Corpus Caesarianum,' *Philol.* Suppl. xxxi (1938)
M. Gelzer, *Caesar, Politician and Statesman*, trans. P. Needham, Blackwell, Oxford 1968 (of 6th ed., Wiesbaden 1968)
J. Kroyman, 'Caesar und das *Corpus Caesarianum* in der neueren Forschung: Gesamtbibliographie 1945–1970,' *ANRW* I.3 (1972) 457–487, Berlin
H. Gesche, *Caesar, Ertäge der Forschung*, Darmstadt 1976

CHRONOLOGY OF THE ALEX-ANDRIAN, AFRICAN AND SPANISH WARS

(The dates are given according to the official calendar, which, before Caesar reformed it in 46 B.C. by inserting two intercalary months between November and December, was approximately two months ahead of the solar reckoning.)

48 B.C.

9 August. Battle of Pharsalus : Cn. Pompeius Magnus flees to Egypt.

September. Pompeius murdered in Egypt.

October. Caesar reaches Alexandria.

October 48—March 47. Caesar engaged in operations in and around Alexandria.

December. Pharnaces routs Domitius Calvinus at Nico-polis.

47 B.C.

March. Battle of the Nile : Caesar defeats the Egyptians.

27 March. Enters Alexandria in triumph.

June.[1] Leaves Alexandria for Syria.

29 July. Enters Pontus.

2 August. Defeats Pharnaces at Zela.

September. Embarks for Italy and Rome.

17 December. Reaches Lilybaeum in Sicily.

---

[1] The date is entirely conjectural. The average estimate seems to be some time in June (Holmes, *The Roman Republic*, vol. III, p. 204 'about the 7th of June'. Andrieu, *Guerre d'Alexandrie*, p. 83, 'at the end of June'). But L. E. Lord, in an article entitled *The date of J. Caesar's departure from Alexandria* (Journal of Roman Studies, vol. 28, pp. 19–40), argues in favour of an earlier date and repudiates the later traditions of Caesar's dalliance with Cleopatra.

CHRONOLOGY OF THE WARS

47 B.C.

  25 December. Embarks for Africa.
  28 December. Disembarks at Hadrumetum.
  29 December. Encamps at Ruspina.

46 B.C.

  26 January. Leaves Ruspina and moves to the heights to the East of Uzitta.
  26 January—3 April. Operations at Uzitta and Aggar.
  4 April. Caesar marches to Thapsus and begins to invest it.
  6 April. Battle of Thapsus.
  12 April. Cato commits suicide.
  13 June. Caesar embarks at Utica for Sardinia.
  25 July. Arrives at Rome.
  December. Reaches Spain.
  December–January. Operations at Corduba. Caesar lays siege to Ategua.

45 B.C.

  19 February. Ategua surrenders to Caesar.
  5 March. Engagement near Soricaria.
  17 March. Battle of Munda.
  12 April. The head of Cn. Pompeius brought to Hispalis.
  September. Caesar returns to Rome.

(Certain minor operations—chiefly those which are mentioned in the Latin text out of chronological sequence—are dated individually in the margin of the translation.)

THE ALEXANDRIAN WAR

INTRODUCTION

THE battle of Pharsalus, fought in August 48, was a crushing defeat for the Pompeians, but not finally decisive. Fifteen thousand men were said to have perished: more than twenty-four thousand to have been captured. Their field army was indeed shattered; but both leader and cause yet survived.

There were several quarters of the Roman world where resistance might be renewed successfully in the name of senatorial government: the province of Africa, where King Juba of Numidia was a formidable, if exacting, supporter of the Pompeians, and where, since Curio's defeat in the previous year, Caesar's prestige had ebbed; Spain, where Pompey's name still stood high, while Caesar's cause had suffered from the prolonged misgovernment of his deputy, Q. Cassius; and, closer at hand, Egypt, an independent kingdom whose rulers were indebted to Pompey for past services and so might be expected to succour him now.

But Egypt—important to Rome as a prolific source of corn—was now faced with a constitutional crisis. The late king, Ptolemy Auletes, had been expelled in 58 but reinstated three years later by Gabinius, acting in the interests of the triumvirs— Caesar, Pompey and Crassus—who were still awaiting payment for this service. An unofficial Roman army of occupation, comprising many soldiers who had once served under Pompey, still remained in the country. In 51 Ptolemy had died, bequeathing

3

his throne jointly to his elder son—a mere boy—
and his eldest daughter, Cleopatra, and urging the
Senate in his will to ensure that its terms were
faithfully observed. Nevertheless, Cleopatra had
been driven out by the young king's regents, only
to raise an army in Syria, return at its head, and
confront her brother at Pelusium.

In such a situation Pompey's arrival was hardly
opportune. To the young king's unscrupulous
regents, menaced as they were by Cleopatra and
her adherents, his motives were obscure. Had he
in mind to win over the Roman occupation troops
and conquer the country? And anyway, was not
Caesar's cause now for them the better risk? Thus
possibly they argued; and, untroubled by scruples,
accordingly contrived his murder, the treacherous
character of which shocked the whole world and
gave to Pompey the status of a martyr.

Three days later Caesar arrived to find his foremost rival thus destroyed. But others remained:
prompt action was advisable both in Asia, whither
Domitius had already been despatched, and in
Africa, to crush the remnants of his opponents.
However, the seasonal winds off Alexandria prevented any immediate departure; and he might
utilise the interval by settling the dispute over the
royal succession and collecting the moneys long
owing to the triumvirs. But if he argued thus he
failed to take into account two factors: first, the
natural feelings of the Egyptians and the resentment they might show at his official interference in
their domestic affairs; and secondly, the charms of
Cleopatra. Of these two important factors the former
is duly mentioned by Caesar himself, whereas the

INTRODUCTION

latter is studiously glossed over in *de Bello Alexandrino*. Yet what other reason can account for Caesar's strange inaction between March, when he made himself master of Alexandria and Egypt, and June, when at last he left for Syria to conduct a whirlwind campaign against Pharnaces ? Where later writers [1] shed a lurid light, Hirtius observes a discreet silence.

In literary merit *de Bello Alexandrino*, though in general a plain and somewhat pedestrian tale, is the best of the three works. If it never soars to the heights, it never sinks to the depths of *de Bello Hispaniensi*. The subject matter is well arranged, and Caesar's victory at Zela provides an effective climax. The facts presented seem reasonably accurate and undistorted by party bias.[2] The style is neither so terse nor so lively as Caesar's ; but it is neat, free from affectations, and above all clear. Though the narrative tends sometimes to monotony, yet the author is not without a sense of the dramatic and is at pains on occasion to work up the reader's interest before a climax.[3] Nor is he a mere purveyor of facts : though there are very few speeches he not infrequently speculates on motives. His tendency in this respect is to suggest alternatives from which the reader may make his own choice ;[4] and where he does commit himself, his judgment does not always ring true.[5]

---

[1] *e.g.* Suetonius : *Life of Julius Caesar*, ch. 52.
[2] At any rate he does not appear in chapters 21 and 40 to underestimate Caesarian losses.
[3] *e.g.* chapter 16.   [4] *e.g.* chapters 43 and 63.
[5] *e.g.* chapter 24, where he suggests that Caesar's motive in releasing the young king was merely to enhance his own prestige, and makes no attempt to reconcile this attitude with the earlier policy described in *Civil Wars* III, ch. 109.

5

SUMMARY OF THE NARRATIVE IN CIVIL WARS

BOOK III

SUMMARY OF THE CIVIL WARS

(The reason for including the above summary has been stated in the General Introduction, p. xi.)

ANALYSIS OF THE BOOK

8

ANALYSIS OF THE BOOK

DE BELLO ALEXANDRINO

1 BELLO ALEXANDRINO conflato Caesar Rhodo atque
ex Syria Ciliciaque omnem classem arcessit; Creta
sagittarios, equites ab rege Nabataeorum Malcho
evocat; tormenta undique conquiri et frumentum
mitti, auxilia adduci iubet. Interim munitiones
cotidie operibus augentur atque omnes oppidi
partes, quae minus esse firmae videntur, testudinibus
ac musculis aptantur;[1] ex aedificiis autem per
foramina in proxima aedificia arietes immittuntur,
quantumque aut ruinis deicitur aut per vim recipitur
loci, in tantum munitiones proferuntur. Nam
incendio fere tuta est Alexandrea, quod sine contig-
natione ac materia sunt aedificia et structuris ac
fornicibus continentur tectaque sunt rudere aut
pavimentis. Caesar maxime studebat ut, quam
angustissimam partem oppidi palus a meridie
interiecta efficiebat, hanc operibus vineisque agendis
ab reliqua parte urbis excluderet, illud spectans
primum ut, cum in duas partis esset urbis divisa acies,
uno consilio atque imperio administraretur, deinde ut
laborantibus succurri atque ex altera oppidi parte

---

[1] *So MSS.*: temptantur *Nipperdey, perhaps rightly.*

---

[1] A people of Arabia Petraea.
[2] This seems to be the meaning of *pavimentum* here: elsewhere it is used only of floors.

THE ALEXANDRIAN WAR

1 WHEN the Alexandrian war flared up, Caesar summoned every fleet from Rhodes and Syria and Cilicia; from Crete he raised archers, and cavalry from Malchus, king of the Nabataeans,[1] and ordered artillery to be procured, corn despatched, and auxiliary troops mustered from every quarter. Meanwhile the entrenchments were daily extended by additional works, and all those sectors of the town which appeared to be not strong enough were provided with shelters and mantlets; battering-rams, moreover, were introduced from one building into the next through holes, and the entrenchments were extended to cover all the ground laid bare by demolitions or gained by force of arms. For Alexandria is well-nigh fire-proof, because its buildings contain no wooden joinery and are held together by an arched construction and are roofed with rough-cast or tiling.[2] Caesar was particularly anxious that, by bringing to bear his siege-works and pent-houses, he should isolate from the rest of the city that narrowest part of the town which was most constricted by the barrier of marshland lying to the south; his object being first that, since his army was divided between two sectors of the city, it should be controlled by a single strategy and command; secondly, that if they got into difficulties in one sector of the town, assistance

auxilium ferri posset, in primis vero ut aqua pabuloque abundaret, quarum alterius rei copiam exiguam, alterius nullam omnino facultatem habebat; quod utrumque large palus praebere poterat.

2 Neque vero Alexandrinis in gerendis negotiis cunctatio ulla aut mora inferebatur. Nam in omnis partis, per quas fines Aegypti regnumque pertinet, legatos conquisitoresque dilectus habendi causa miserant magnumque numerum in oppidum telorum atque tormentorum convexerant et innumerabilem multitudinem adduxerant. Nec minus in urbe maximae armorum erant institutae officinae. Servos praeterea puberes armaverant; quibus domini locupletiores victum cotidianum stipendiumque praebebant. Hac multitudine disposita munitiones semotarum partium tuebantur; veteranas cohortis vacuas in celeberrimis urbis locis habebant, ut quacumque regione pugnaretur integris viribus ad auxilium ferendum opponi possent. Omnibus viis atque angiportis triplicem vallum obduxerant—erat autem quadrato exstructus saxo neque minus XL pedes altitudinis habebat—quaeque partes urbis inferiores erant, has altissimis turribus denorum tabulatorum munierant. Praeterea alias ambulatorias totidem tabulatorum confixerant subiectisque eas rotis funibus iumentisque obiectis derectis plateis in quamcumque erat visum partem movebant.

---

[1] A much disputed passage. I assume that Caesar already occupied two separate sectors of the city south of Cape Lochias, and these he now intended to join up into one by securing the ground immediately to the south, adjoining the marshy depression.

[2] Or possibly ' along the straight streets.'

and support could be brought from the other sector.[1] But above all his object was to secure himself abundance of water and fodder; of which, as regards the former, he had but a scanty supply, and, as regards the latter, no stocks whatever; and the marsh-land could afford him bountiful supplies of both.

2   Not indeed that this occasioned any hesitation or delay on the part of the Alexandrians in concerting their measures. They had in fact despatched emissaries and recruiting officers throughout the entire length and breadth of the territory and kingdom of Egypt for the purpose of holding a levy, and had conveyed into the town a large quantity of weapons and artillery and mustered a countless host. In the city too, no less, vast arms factories had been established. They had, moreover, armed the adult slaves, and these the wealthier owners furnished with their daily food and pay. This numerous force they deployed to guard the fortifications of outlying areas; while they kept their veteran cohorts unemployed in the most frequented quarters of the city so that, no matter in what district fighting occurred, they could be thrown in as fresh and lusty reinforcements. All the streets and alleys were walled off by a triple barricade, built of rectangular stone blocks and not less than forty feet high; while as for the lower quarters of the city, these were fortified with very lofty towers, each ten stories high. Besides these there were other towers which they had contrived—mobile ones of the like number of stories; and these, being mounted on wheels with ropes and draught animals attached, they moved along the level [2] streets to any area they saw fit.

CAESAR

3 Urbs fertilissima et copiosissima omnium rerum apparatus suggerebat. Ipsi homines ingeniosi atque acutissimi quae a nobis fieri viderant ea sollertia efficiebant ut nostri illorum opera imitati viderentur, et sua sponte multa reperiebant unoque tempore et nostras munitiones infestabant et suas defendebant. Atque haec principes in consiliis contionibusque agitabant: populum Romanum paulatim in consuetudinem eius regni occupandi venire. Paucis annis ante A. Gabinium cum exercitu fuisse in Aegypto; Pompeium se ex fuga eodem recepisse; Caesarem venisse cum copiis, neque morte Pompei quicquam profectum quo minus apud se Caesar commoraretur. Quem si non expulissent, futuram ex regno provinciam; idque agendum mature: namque eum interclusum tempestatibus propter anni tempus recipere transmarina auxilia non posse.

4 Interim dissensione orta inter Achillan, qui veterano exercitui praeerat, et Arsinoen, regis Ptolomaei minorem filiam, ut supra demonstratum est, cum uterque utrique insidiaretur et summam imperi ipse obtinere vellet, praeoccupat Arsinoe per Ganymeden eunuchum, nutricium suum, atque Achillan interficit. Hoc occiso sine ullo socio et custode ipsa omne imperium obtinebat; exercitus Ganymedi traditur. Is suscepto officio largitionem

---

[1] A supporter of Pompeius who in 55 B.C., as governor of Syria, restored Ptolemy Auletes to the throne of Egypt. See ch. 43 below for his death in Illyricum.

[2] Presumably a reference to *Civil Wars* III, ch. 112.

[3] Though in the Latin text I have retained the unfamiliar spelling given by all the MSS., in translation I have adopted the more common form.

3　Highly productive and abundantly supplied as it was, the city furnished equipment of all kinds. The people themselves were clever and very shrewd, and no sooner had they seen what was being done by us than they would reproduce it with such cunning that it seemed it was our men who had copied their works. Much also they invented on their own account, and kept assailing our entrenchments while simultaneously defending their own. In their councils and public meetings the arguments which their leaders kept driving home were as follows: ' the Roman people were gradually acquiring a habit of seizing that kingdom; a few years earlier Aulus Gabinius [1] had been in Egypt with an army; Pompeius too had resorted thither in his flight; Caesar had now come with his forces, and the death of Pompeius had had no effect in dissuading Caesar from staying on among them. If they failed to drive him out, their kingdom would become a Roman province: and this driving out they must do betimes; for cut off as he now was by storms owing to the season of the year, he could not receive reinforcements from overseas.'

4　Meanwhile a quarrel had arisen—as related above [2] —between Achillas, who commanded the veteran army, and Arsinoe, the younger daughter of king Ptolemaeus; [3] and with each party plotting against the other and anxious to obtain the supreme power for himself, Arsinoe, acting through the eunuch Ganymedes, her tutor, struck the first blow and killed Achillas. After his murder she herself exercised complete control without any consort or guardian, while the army was entrusted to Ganymedes. On undertaking this duty the latter in-

15

in militem auget; reliqua pari diligentia administrat.

5 Alexandrea est fere tota suffossa specusque habet a Nilo pertinentis, quibus aqua in privatas domos inducitur, quae paulatim spatio temporis liquescit ac subsidit. Hac uti domini aedificiorum atque eorum familiae consuerunt: nam quae flumine Nilo fertur adeo est limosa ac turbida ut multos variosque morbos efficiat; sed ea plebes ac multitudo contenta est necessario, quod fons urbe tota nullus est. Hoc tamen flumen in ea parte erat urbis quae ab Alexandrinis tenebatur. Quo facto est admonitus Ganymedes posse nostros aqua intercludi; qui distributi munitionum tuendarum causa vicatim ex privatis aedificiis specubus ac puteis extracta aqua utebantur.

6 Hoc probato consilio magnum ac difficile opus aggreditur. Intersaeptis enim specubus atque omnibus urbis partibus exclusis quae ab ipso tenebantur, aquae magnam vim ex mari rotis ac machinationibus exprimere contendit: hanc locis superioribus fundere in partem Caesaris non intermittebat. Quam ob causam salsior paulo praeter consuetudinem aqua trahebatur ex proximis aedificiis magnamque hominibus admirationem praebebat, quam ob rem id accidisset; nec satis sibi ipsi credebant, cum se inferiores eiusdem generis ac saporis aqua dicerent

---

[1] This is generally taken to be the Canal (see map).

creased the soldiers' bounty and performed the rest of his functions with consistent thoroughness.

5   Practically the whole of Alexandria is undermined with subterranean conduits running from the Nile, by which water is conducted into private houses; which water in course of time gradually settles down and becomes clear. This is what is normally used by the owners of mansions and their households; for what the Nile brings down is so muddy and turbid that it gives rise to many different diseases: yet the rank and file of the common sort are perforce content with the latter, inasmuch as there is not one natural spring in the whole city. The main stream in question,[1] however, was in that quarter of the city which was held by the Alexandrians. This circumstance suggested to Ganymedes the possibility that the water supply could be cut off from our troops; who, posted as they were in various quarters of the town to guard our entrenchments, were using water drawn from conduits and cisterns in private buildings.

6   This plan being once approved, Ganymedes embarked upon a serious and difficult task. Having first blocked up the conduits and sealed off all quarters of the city occupied by himself, he then made haste to draw off a vast quantity of water out of the sea by means of mechanical water-wheels; and this he steadily poured from higher ground into Caesar's area. For which reason the water drawn from the nearest buildings was a little more brackish than usual, and occasioned no little wonder among men as to why this had come about. Nor could they quite believe the evidence of their own ears when their neighbours lower down said that the water they were using was of the same kind and

uti atque ante consuessent, vulgoque inter se conferebant et degustando quantum inter se differrent aquae cognoscebant. Parvo vero temporis spatio haec propior bibi omnino non poterat, illa inferior corruptior iam salsiorque reperiebatur.

7 Quo facto dubitatione sublata tantus incessit timor ut ad extremum periculi omnes deducti viderentur atque alii morari Caesarem dicerent quin navis conscendere iuberet,[1] alii multo gravius extimescerent, quod neque celari Alexandrini possent in apparanda fuga, cum tam parvo spatio distarent ab ipsis, neque illis imminentibus atque insequentibus ullus in navis receptus daretur. Erat autem magna multitudo oppidanorum in parte Caesaris, quam domiciliis ipsorum non moverat, quod ea se fidelem palam nostris esse simulabat et descivisse a suis videbatur: at mihi si[2] defendendi essent Alexandrini neque fallaces esse[3] neque temerarii, multa oratio frustra absumeretur; cum vero uno tempore et natio eorum et natura cognoscatur, aptissimum esse hoc genus ad proditionem dubitare nemo potest.

8 Caesar suorum timorem consolatione et ratione minuebat. Nam puteis fossis aquam dulcem reperiri posse adfirmabat: omnia enim litora naturaliter aquae dulcis venas habere. Quod si alia esset

---

[1] *The MSS. are divided between* iuberent *and* iuberet.
[2] ut mihi *MSS.*: at mihi si *Madvig.*
[3] essent *MSS.*: esse *Nipperdey.*

taste as they had previously been accustomed to; and they were openly discussing the matter amongst themselves and, by tasting samples, learning how markedly the waters differed. However, in a short space of time the water nearer the contamination was entirely undrinkable, while that lower down was found to be relatively impure and brackish.

7   This circumstance dispelled their doubts, and so great was the panic that took hold upon them that it seemed that they were all reduced to a most hazardous plight, and some asserted that Caesar was being slow in giving orders to embark. Others were much more seriously alarmed, on the ground that, in making their preparations for a withdrawal, it was impossible to keep the Alexandrians in the dark, being as they were so short a distance away from them; and with their foes on top of them and pursuing them, no chance was afforded them of retreating to their ships. There was, however, a large number of townsfolk in Caesar's sector, whom Caesar had not evacuated from their homes, because they openly affected loyalty to our side and appeared to have deserted their own folk. Yet, as far as I am concerned, had I now the task of championing the Alexandrians and proving them to be neither deceitful nor foolhardy, it would be a case of many words spent to no purpose: indeed when one gets to know both the breed and its breeding there can be no doubt whatever that as a race they are extremely prone to treachery.

8   By encouragement and reasoning Caesar allayed his men's alarm, declaring that sweet water could be found in wells and trenches, inasmuch as all sea-shores naturally possessed veins of sweet water.

litoris Aegypti natura atque omnium reliquorum,
tamen, quoniam mare libere tenerent, neque hostes
classem haberent, prohiberi sese non posse quo
minus cotidie navibus aquam peterent vel a sinistra
parte a Paratonio vel a dextra ab insula, quae
diversae navigationes numquam uno tempore adversis ventis praecluderentur. Fugae vero nullum esse
consilium non solum eis qui primam dignitatem
haberent, sed ne eis quidem qui nihil praeterquam
de vita cogitarent. Magno negotio impetus hostium
adversos ex munitionibus sustinere; quibus relictis
nec loco nec numero pares esse posse. Magnam
autem moram et difficultatem ascensum in navis
habere, praesertim ex scaphis; summam esse contra
in Alexandrinis velocitatem locorumque et aedificiorum notitiam. Hos praecipue in victoria insolentis
praecursuros et loca excelsiora atque aedificia occupa-
turos: ita fuga navibusque nostros prohibituros.
Proinde eius consili obliviscerentur atque omni
ratione esse vincendum cogitarent.

9   Hac oratione apud suos habita atque omnium
mentibus excitatis dat centurionibus negotium ut
reliquis operibus intermissis ad fodiendos puteos
animum conferant neve quam partem nocturni
temporis intermittant. Quo suscepto negotio atque
omnium animis ad laborem incitatis magna una

---

¹ The places referred to are much disputed and have not
been marked on Map 2. Strabo mentions a Παραιτόνιον,
but it lay some 130 miles W. of Alexandria—too far, it seems,
to be intended here. As for the island, Pharos itself hardly
lay on their right: perhaps either the Delta is intended or
some otherwise unknown island near Canopus.

But if the nature of the sea-shore of Egypt was different from all others, none the less, since they held unfettered command of the sea, while their enemies had no fleet, they could not be prevented from seeking water daily in their ships, either from Paratonium on their left, or the island on their right [1]—voyages which, being in opposite directions, would never be prevented by contrary winds at one and the same time. As for retreating, there was no sound policy in that, not merely for those who held the chief responsibility, but not even for those whose sole concern was for their own lives. They were hard put to it to contain the enemies' frontal attacks from their entrenchments: once abandon those and they could be no match for them either in vantage ground or numbers. Moreover, boarding ships, especially from pinnaces, involved considerable delay and difficulty; while set against this the Alexandrians had the greatest mobility and knowledge of the ground and buildings. These people above all, overweening as they became in victory, would dash ahead and seize the higher ground and the buildings and thus prevent our men from retreating and gaining their ships. Accordingly, they should put that policy out of their minds and reflect that, at all costs, they must win the day.

9 Having harangued his men to this effect and put fresh heart into them all, he briefed his centurions as follows: they were to interrupt their other tasks and turn their attention to digging wells, continuing without any cessation all through the night. Whereupon, the business being once undertaken with unanimous enthusiasm for the task, in the course of

nocte vis aquae dulcis inventa est. Ita operosis Alexandrinorum machinationibus maximisque conatibus non longi temporis labore occursum est. Eo biduo legio XXXVII. ex dediticiis Pompeianis militibus cum frumento, armis, telis, tormentis imposita in navis a Domitio Calvino ad litora Africae paulo supra Alexandream delata est. Hae naves Euro, qui multos dies continenter flabat, portum capere prohibebantur; sed loca sunt egregia omni illa regione ad tenendas ancoras. Hi cum diu retinerentur atque aquae inopia premerentur, navigio actuario Caesarem faciunt certiorem.

10 Caesar, ut per se consilium caperet quid faciendum videretur, navem conscendit atque omnem classem se sequi iussit nullis nostris militibus impositis, quod, cum longius paulo discederet, munitiones nudare nolebat. Cumque ad eum locum accessissent, qui appellatur Chersonensus, aquandique causa remiges in terram exposuissent, non nulli ex eo numero, cum longius a navibus praedatum processissent, ab equitibus hostium sunt excepti. Ex his cognoverunt Caesarem ipsum in classe venisse nec ullos milites in navibus habere. Qua re comperta magnam sibi facultatem fortunam obtulisse bene gerendae rei crediderunt. Itaque navis omnis quas paratas habuerant ad navigandum propugnatoribus instruxerunt Caesarique redeunti cum classe occurrerunt. Qui duabus de causis eo die dimicare

---

[1] Identified by some with a promontory about 8 miles W. of Alexandria.

that one night a great quantity of sweet water was discovered. Thus the laborious machinations and supreme efforts of the Alexandrians were countered by a few hours' work. In the course of the following day the Thirty-Seventh legion, part of the surrendered remnants of Pompeius' troops, after being embarked by Domitius Calvinus with corn, arms, weapons and artillery, made the coast of Africa a little beyond Alexandria. An East wind, which blew continuously for many days, prevented this fleet from gaining harbour; but the ground throughout all that area gives excellent hold for anchors. And as they were weather-bound for a long time, and hard put to it for lack of water, they informed Caesar by means of a fast boat.

10   In order to take some personal decision as to what he thought ought to be done, Caesar boarded a ship and ordered his whole fleet to follow him. He did not embark any of our troops, since, as he was going somewhat too far afield, he was loth to leave our entrenchments unmanned. On their arriving at that place which is called Chersonensus,[1] and putting the rowers ashore to fetch water, some of their number, bent on plunder, advanced rather too far from the ships and were picked up by enemy cavalry. From them the enemy learned that Caesar himself had arrived with his fleet, without any troops on board. This intelligence prompted the belief among them that fortune had put in their way a great opportunity for scoring a success. Accordingly, they manned with combat troops all the ships they had got in readiness for sailing, and encountered Caesar as he was returning with his fleet. Now there were two reasons why Caesar was loth to fight an action that

23

nolebat, quod et nullos milites in navibus habebat et
post horam X. diei res agebatur, nox autem allatura
videbatur maiorem fiduciam illis, qui locorum notitia
confidebant; sibi etiam hortandi suos auxilium
defuturum, quod nulla satis idonea esset hortatio
quae neque virtutem posset notare neque inertiam.
Quibus de causis navis quas potuit Caesar ad terram
detrahit, quem in locum illos successuros non
existimabat.

11 Erat una navis Rhodia in dextro Caesaris cornu
longe ab reliquis collocata. Hanc conspicati hostes
non tenuerunt sese, magnoque impetu IIII ad eam
constratae naves et complures apertae contenderunt.
Cui coactus est Caesar ferre subsidium, ne turpem in
conspectu hostium contumeliam acciperet, quamquam, si quid gravius illis accidisset, merito casurum
iudicabat. Proelium commissum est magna contentione Rhodiorum; qui cum in omnibus dimicationibus et scientia et virtute praestitissent, tum
maxime illo tempore totum onus sustinere non
recusabant, ne quod suorum culpa detrimentum
acceptum videretur. Ita proelium secundissimum
est factum. Capta est una hostium quadriremis,
depressa est altera, duae omnibus epibatis nudatae;
magna praeterea multitudo in reliquis navibus propugnatorum est interfecta. Quod nisi nox proelium
diremisset, tota classe hostium Caesar potitus esset.
Hac calamitate perterritis hostibus adverso vento

day: he had no troops on board; and it was now after the tenth hour as the matter now stood, and on the other hand nightfall would, he thought, inspire greater confidence in the enemy, who were relying on their local knowledge. In his own case, also, he would be denied the advantage of encouraging his men, since no encouragement was quite to the point where it was impossible to single out for comment either bravery or slackness. For these reasons Caesar withdrew to land what ships he could, at a point where he supposed that the enemy would not follow them.

11 There was one Rhodian ship on Caesar's right wing stationed far apart from the rest. As soon as the enemy caught sight of it they could not restrain themselves, and four decked ships and several open ones dashed madly towards it. This vessel Caesar was obliged to succour, to prevent the disgrace of sustaining rough treatment in full view of the enemy; though, if any serious mischance should overtake its crew, he reckoned they would deserve it. Battle was joined, with hard fighting on the part of the Rhodians; and though in every fray they had excelled both in seamanship and valour, on this present occasion above all they bore the whole brunt unflinchingly, lest it should seem their fault if any defeat were sustained. And so a highly successful action was fought. One enemy quadrireme was captured, a second was sunk, and two stripped of all their marines; in addition, a large number of combat troops was killed aboard the other vessels. If night had not put an end to the action, Caesar would have become master of the entire enemy fleet. This catastrophe utterly demoralised the enemy, and

leniter flante navis onerarias Caesar remulco victricibus suis navibus Alexandream deducit.

12 Eo detrimento adeo sunt fracti Alexandrini, cum iam non virtute propugnatorum, sed scientia classiariorum se victos viderent, ut vix ex aedificiis defendi posse se confiderent, quibus et superioribus locis sublevabantur,[1] et materiam cunctam obicerent, quod nostrae classis oppugnationem etiam ad terram verebantur. Idem, postea quam Ganymedes in concilio confirmavit sese et eas quae essent amissae restituturum et numerum adaucturum, magna spe et fiducia veteres reficere navis accuratiusque huic rei studere atque inservire instituerunt. Ac tametsi amplius CX navibus longis in portu navalibusque amiserant, non tamen reparandae classis cogitationem deposuerunt. Videbant enim non auxilia Caesari, non commeatus supportari posse, si classe ipsi valerent; praeterea nautici homines urbis et regionis maritimae cotidianoque usu a pueris exercitati ad naturale ac domesticum bonum refugere cupiebant et quantum parvulis navigiis profecissent sentiebant; itaque omni studio ad parandam classem incubuerunt.

[1] *This clause is faulty as it stands in the MSS., which read—* quibus et superioribus locis sublevabantur, ut ex aedificiis defendi possent. *I have adopted Dinter's conjecture.*

---

[1] The contrast here appears to lie between combat crews (*propugnatores*, practically synonymous perhaps with the Greek term *epibatae*), whose function was that of marines, and navigating crews (*classiarii* = fleet personnel, sailors, as distinct from marines). Caesar had no marines on board, whereas the Alexandrians had; so that, though Caesar doubtless improvised boarding parties from such sailors as could be spared, he had to rely mainly upon superior seamanship to ram or cripple his opponents' ships.

Caesar returned to Alexandria with his victorious
fleet, towing the merchant-ships against a gentle
head wind.

12 So shattered were the Alexandrians by this
reverse—for they saw that now it was not the bravery
of combat troops but the seamanship of sailors that
had caused their defeat [1]—that they scarcely trusted
their ability to defend themselves from the buildings,
from which, as well as from their higher positions,
they derived support,[2] and used all their timber in
building barricades, fearing as they did that our fleet
would attack them even ashore. Nevertheless, after
Ganymedes had declared in the council that he would
not only make good the losses they had sustained but
also increase the number of their ships, their hopes
and confidence ran high and they began to repair
their old ships and to devote greater care and more
earnest attention to this matter. And though they
had lost more than a hundred and ten warships in the
harbour and docks,[3] yet they did not abandon the
idea of re-equipping their fleet. They saw in fact
that neither troop reinforcements nor supplies could
be conveyed to Caesar if they themselves had a strong
fleet; apart from which the men of the city and the
coastal district, seamen as they were and trained as
such from boyhood by daily practice, were anxious to
resort to this their natural and native gift, and were
aware how successful they had been with their humble
little vessels. Consequently they threw themselves
whole-heartedly into the task of equipping a fleet.

[2] Or perhaps *ut superioribus locis* should be read, the sense
being ' which, as being more elevated sites, had proved their
mainstay.'

[3] These losses are briefly alluded to in *Civil Wars* III,
ch. 111.

13 Erant omnibus ostiis Nili custodiae exigendi portorii causa dispositae; naves veteres erant in occultis regiae navalibus, quibus multis annis ad navigandum non erant usi: has reficiebant, illas Alexandream revocabant. Deerant remi: porticus, gymnasia, publica aedificia detegebant, asseres remorum usum obtinebant; aliud naturalis sollertia, aliud urbis copia sumministrabat. Postremo non longam navigationem parabant, sed praesentis temporis necessitati serviebant et in ipso portu confligendum videbant. Itaque paucis diebus contra omnium opinionem quadriremis XXII, quinqueremis V confecerunt; ad has minores apertasque compluris adiecerunt et in portu periclitati remigio quid quaeque earum efficere posset idoneos milites imposuerunt seque ad confligendum omnibus rebus paraverunt. Caesar Rhodias navis VIIII habebat—nam decem missis una in cursu litore Aegyptio defecerat—, Ponticas VIII, Lycias [1] V, ex Asia XII. Ex his erant quinqueremes et quadriremes decem, reliquae infra hanc magnitudinem et pleraeque apertae. Tamen virtute militum confisus cognitis hostium copiis se ad dimicandum parabat.

14 Postquam eo ventum est ut sibi uterque eorum confideret, Caesar Pharon classe circumvehitur

---

[1] Lycias or licias *MSS.*: ⟨Syrias . . . Ci⟩ licias *Schneider.*

---

[1] This is somewhat difficult to reconcile with chapter 1, where Syria and Cilicia, as well as Rhodes, are specifically mentioned, and with the statement in *Civil Wars* III, ch. 106, where it is said that Caesar arrived at Alexandria with ten warships from Rhodes and a few from Asia. Could the missing Rhodian galley be after all the one described in chapter 11? Even so, unless the requisition for additional Rhodian ships had not so far been complied with, the figure

13   There were guardships posted at all the mouths of the Nile to levy customs dues, and in secret royal dockyards there were old ships which had not seen service afloat for many years. These last they proceeded to repair, while the guardships they recalled to Alexandria. There was a shortage of oars: the roofs of colonnades, gymnasia and public buildings were dismantled, and their beams made to serve as oars. In one case it was natural ingenuity that helped to bridge the gap, in another the city's resources. In fine it was no lengthy voyaging for which they were preparing; but perceiving that the conflict must take place in the harbour itself they obeyed the dictates of the moment. In a few days, therefore, they surprised everyone by completing 22 quadriremes and 5 quinqueremes, to which they added a considerable number of smaller, open craft; and then, after trying out in the harbour by rowing what each of them could do, they manned them with suitable troops and prepared themselves at all points for the conflict. Caesar had 9 Rhodian ships (10 had been sent, but one had been lost during a voyage, on the coast of Egypt), 8 Pontic, 5 Lycian and 12 from Asia.[1] These included 10 quinqueremes and quadriremes, while the rest were smaller craft and most of them un-decked. None the less, though informed of the enemies' forces, Caesar proceeded with his preparations for an action, confident in the valour of his troops.

14   Now that the stage was reached when each side was self-confident, Caesar sailed round Pharos[2]

of 9 remains a difficulty. The total of 34 tallies with the dispositions in ch. 14, below.
    [2] *i.e.* from the Great Harbour to the Eunostos Harbour.

adversasque navis hostibus constituit: in dextro
cornu Rhodias collocat, in sinistro Ponticas. Inter
has spatium CCCC passuum relinquit, quod satis
esse ad explicandas navis videbatur. Post hunc
ordinem reliquas navis subsidio distribuit; quae
quamque earum sequatur et cui subveniat constituit
atque imperat. Non dubitanter Alexandrini classem
producunt atque instruunt: in fronte collocant
XXII, reliquas subsidiarias in secundo ordine constituunt. Magnum praeterea numerum minorum
navigiorum et scapharum producunt cum malleolis
ignibusque, si quid ipsa multitudo et clamor et
flamma nostris terroris adferre possent. Erant inter
duas classis vada transitu angusto, quae pertinent
ad regionem Africae—sic enim praedicant, partem
esse Alexandreae dimidiam Africae—satisque diu
inter ipsos est exspectatum ab utris transeundi
fieret initium, propterea quod ei qui intrassent et
ad explicandam classem et ad receptum, si durior
accidisset casus, impeditiores fore videbantur.

15 Rhodiis navibus praeerat Euphranor, animi magnitudine ac virtute magis cum nostris hominibus quam
cum Graecis comparandus. Hic ob notissimam
scientiam atque animi magnitudinem delectus est
ab Rhodiis qui imperium classis obtineret. Qui ubi
cessare [1] Caesarem animum advertit, ' Videris mihi,'
inquit, ' Caesar, vereri, si haec vada primis navibus

_____
[1] Caesaris *MSS.*: cessare Caesarem *Hoffmann.*

with his fleet and drew up his ships facing the enemy. On his right wing he posted the Rhodian ships, on his left the Pontic ones, leaving a gap of 400 paces between them—a distance which he regarded as adequate for deploying his vessels. Behind this line he arranged his remaining ships in reserve, deciding which should follow each of the former vessels and which ship each should support, and giving orders accordingly. Nor were the Alexandrians hesitant to bring up and array their fleet; posting 22 ships in front, and the remainder in a second line in reserve. Besides these they brought up a large number of smaller craft and pinnaces, equipped with incendiary missiles and combustibles, in the hope that sheer numbers and the shouts and flames might have some effect in intimidating our men. Between the two fleets lay shoals with a narrow intersecting channel (these shoals belong to the region of Africa—in fact they say that half Alexandria is part of Africa); and for quite a long time there was a pause among the actual combatants as they waited to see which side was to begin the passage, inasmuch as it seemed that those who once entered the channel would be more restricted both in deploying their fleet and, if things fared badly, in withdrawing.

15 The commander of the Rhodian squadron was Euphranor, a man who in point of personality and bravery deserved comparison with our people rather than with the Greeks. Thanks to the great fame which his professional skill and forceful personality enjoyed, the Rhodians chose him to command their fleet. When he perceived Caesar's hesitation, he said: ' It seems to me, Caesar, that you are afraid

31

intraris, ne prius dimicare cogaris quam reliquam
classem potueris explicare. Nobis rem committe:
nos proelium sustinebimus—neque tuum iudicium
fallemus—dum reliqui subsequantur. Hos quidem
diutius in nostro conspectu gloriari magno nobis et
dedecori et dolori est.' Caesar illum adhortatus
atque omnibus laudibus prosecutus dat signum
pugnae. Progressas ultra vadum IIII Rhodias navis
circumsistunt Alexandrini atque in eas impetum
faciunt. Sustinent illi atque arte sollertiaque se
explicant; ac tantum doctrina potuit ut in dispari
numero nulla transversa hosti obiceretur, nullius
remi detergerentur, sed semper venientibus adversae
occurrerent. Interim sunt reliquae subsecutae.
Tum necessario discessum ab arte est propter
angustias loci, atque omne certamen in virtute
constitit. Neque vero Alexandreae fuit quisquam
aut nostrorum aut oppidanorum, qui aut in opere aut
in pugna occupatum animum haberent, quin altissima
tecta peteret atque ex omni prospectu locum specta-
culo caperet precibusque et votis victoriam suis ab
dis immortalibus exposceret.

16   Minime autem par erat proeli certamen. Nostris
enim pulsis neque terra neque mari effugium dabatur
victis, omniaque victoribus erant futura in incerto;
cum illi, si superassent navibus, omnia tenerent, si
inferiores fuissent, reliquam tamen fortunam peri-

that, if you once sail into these shoals with your leading flotilla, you may be forced to fight before you can deploy the rest of your fleet. Leave it to us: we shall bear the brunt of the fighting—we won't let you down—until the others can come up with us. Certainly for these fellows to go on boasting yonder in our sight is a sore disgrace and mortification to us.' Caesar offered him encouragement and paid him every tribute of praise, and then gave the signal for battle. Four Rhodian ships advanced beyond the shoals to be at once surrounded and attacked by the Alexandrians. The Rhodians bore up and by skill and dexterity deployed their line; and of such powerful effect was their training that despite the odds not one of them exposed its broadside to the enemy, not one had its oars swept away, but they always met the oncoming foe head-on. Meanwhile the remaining ships came up with them. Then through lack of sea room skill had perforce to be sacrificed and the whole struggle devolved on courage. And indeed there was not one man in Alexandria, either of our troops or of the townsfolk, whose attention was bespoken with either work or fighting, but he made for the loftiest roof-tops and from out of all the vantage points chose one from which to view that spectacle, and besought the immortal gods with prayers and vows to grant victory to his side.

16   The issues involved in the struggle were by no means equal. On our side no chance of escape either by land or sea was presented in the event of repulse and defeat, while victory would in no way settle the question; whereas in their case, if their fleet should gain the upper hand, they would hold all the cards, while if they were beaten, it would still be left to

clitarentur. Simul illud grave ac miserum videbatur, perpaucos de summa rerum ac de salute omnium decertare; quorum si qui aut animo aut virtute cessisset, reliquis etiam esset cavendum, quibus pro se pugnandi facultas non fuisset. Haec superioribus diebus saepenumero Caesar suis exposuerat, ut hoc maiore animo contenderent, quod omnium salutem sibi commendatam viderent. Eadem suum quisque contubernalem, amicum, notum prosequens erat obtestatus, ne suam atque omnium falleret opinionem, quorum iudicio delectus ad pugnam proficisceretur. Itaque hoc animo est decertatum, ut neque maritimis nauticisque sollertia atque ars praesidium ferret, neque numero navium praestantibus multitudo prodesset, neque electi ad virtutem e tanta multitudine viri virtuti nostrorum possent adaequare. Capitur hoc proelio quinqueremis una et biremis cum defensoribus remigibusque, et deprimuntur tres, nostris incolumibus omnibus. Reliquae propinquam fugam ad oppidum capiunt; quas protexerunt ex molibus atque aedificiis imminentibus et nostros adire propius prohibuerunt.

17 Hoc ne sibi saepius accidere posset, omni ratione Caesar contendendum existimavit ut insulam molem-

them to try their luck again. At the same time it seemed a grievous shame that the supreme issue and the salvation of all should be decided by the rival exertions of so few; and if any one of these wavered in purpose or courage, the others too, who had had no chance of fighting to defend themselves, would have to look out for themselves. These considerations Caesar had repeatedly explained to his men in recent days, that they might fight with the greater resolution because they saw that the safety of all was entrusted to themselves. It was by these same arguments too that every man, as he escorted his messmate, friend or acquaintance, implored him not to prove false to the estimate which not only he himself had formed of him, but all those others likewise, to whose decision he owed it that he was now going forth as one of the chosen combatants. Consequently such was the resolute spirit with which the battle was contested that the Alexandrians, albeit a maritime and seafaring folk, derived no assistance from their dexterity and skill, nor did they benefit from their superiority in number of ships, nor could their men, though chosen for their bravery from so vast a multitude, match the bravery of our men. In this battle one quinquereme and a bireme were captured with their combat crews and rowers, and three were sunk, all our ships being unharmed. The rest of their ships fled to the nearby town, where the townsmen, from stations on the moles and adjacent buildings, protected them and prevented our men from approaching at all close.

17   To prevent the possibility of this kind of thing occurring to him too frequently, Caesar thought that he ought at all costs to make an effort to gain control

que ad insulam pertinentem in suam redigeret potestatem. Perfectis enim magna ex parte munitionibus in oppido et insulam et urbem uno tempore temptari posse confidebat. Quo capto consilio cohortis X et levis armaturae electos, quosque idoneos ex equitibus Gallis arbitrabatur, in navigia minora scaphasque imponit; alteram insulae partem distinendae manus causa constratis navibus aggreditur, praemiis magnis propositis qui primus insulam cepisset. Ac primo impetum nostrorum pariter sustinuerunt: uno enim tempore et ex tectis aedificiorum propugnabant et litora armati defendebant, quo propter asperitatem loci non facilis nostris aditus dabatur, et scaphis navibusque longis quinque mobiliter et scienter angustias loci tuebantur. Sed ubi primum locis cognitis vadisque pertemptatis pauci nostri in litore constiterunt atque hos sunt alii subsecuti constanterque in eos qui in litore aequo institerant impetum fecerunt, omnes Pharitae terga verterunt. His pulsis custodia portus relicta navis ad litora et vicum applicarunt seque ex navibus ad tuenda aedificia eiecerunt.

18 Neque vero diutius ea munitione se continere potuerunt, etsi erat non dissimile atque Alexandreae genus aedificiorum, ut minora maioribus conferantur, turresque editae et coniunctae muri locum obtinebant, neque nostri aut scalis aut cratibus aut reliquis

---

¹ According to *Civil Wars* III, ch. 112, Caesar had already seized Pharos and placed a garrison in it; but this may have been only the eastern tip, where the lighthouse stood, commanding the entrance to the Great Harbour.

of the island [1] and the mole extending to it. For as his entrenchments in the town were in the main completed, he was confident that a simultaneous attempt could be made against both island and city. Having formed this plan, he embarked in smaller craft and pinnaces ten cohorts, some picked light-armed troops and such of his Gallic cavalry as he deemed suitable; and, to distract the enemy garrison, he launched an attack with decked ships upon the other side of the island, offering large rewards to the first to capture it. At first the islanders held off our troops' attack, simultaneously fighting back from the roofs of buildings, and with equal success defending the beaches with armed parties—and there the roughness of the ground did not afford our troops an easy approach—and guarding the narrow waters with pinnaces and five warships displaying both speed and skill. But as soon as our men had become acquainted with the ground and tried out the shallows, a few got a footing on the beach, others followed in their wake, and a determined attack was launched upon those of the enemy who were drawn up against us on the level foreshore; whereupon the men of Pharos all turned tail. Following their rout the enemy abandoned their defence of the harbour, brought their ships to the built-up area by the water-front, and hastily disembarked to defend the buildings.

18   They could not, however, hold on so very long with the defences these afforded, though the buildings were of a type not unlike those of Alexandria—to employ a flattering comparison—with a continuous line of lofty towers taking the place of a wall; and our troops had not come equipped with ladders or

37

rebus parati venerant ad oppugnandum. Sed terror
hominibus mentem consiliumque eripit et membra
debilitat; ut tum accidit. Qui se in aequo loco ac
plano pares esse confidebant, idem perterriti fuga
suorum et caede paucorum XXX pedum altitudine in
aedificiis consistere ausi non sunt seque per molem in
mare praecipitaverunt et DCCC passuum intervallum
ad oppidum enataverunt. Multi tamen ex his capti
interfectique sunt; sed numerus captivorum omnino
fuit sex milium.

19 Caesar praeda militibus concessa aedificia diripi
iussit castellumque ad pontem, qui propior erat
Pharo, communivit atque ibi praesidium posuit.
Hunc fuga Pharitae reliquerant; artiorem[1] illum
propioremque oppido Alexandrini tuebantur. Sed
eum postero die simili ratione aggreditur, quod his
obtentis duobus omnem navigiorum excursum et
repentina latrocinia sublatum iri videbatur. Iamque
eos qui praesidio eum locum tenebant tormentis ex
navibus sagittisque depulerat atque in oppidum
redegerat et cohortium trium instar in terram exposuerat—non enim pluris consistere angustiae loci
patiebantur—; reliquae copiae in navibus stationem
obtinebant. Quo facto imperat pontem adversus
hostem praevallari et, qua exitus navibus erat fornice
exstructo, quo pons sustinebatur, lapidibus oppleri

---

[1] fortiorem or certiorem *MSS*.: artiorem *Vielhaber*.

wicker screens or any other equipment for assault. But panic robs men of their sense and reason and palsies their limbs; and so it happened then. The very men who on level and unbroken ground were confident they were a match for us, none the less, utterly demoralised now by the flight of their fellows and the slaughter of a few, did not venture to take up a position on buildings thirty feet high, but at various points along the mole dived into the sea and swam the intervening 800 paces to the safety of the town. Many of these, notwithstanding, were captured or killed; indeed, the number of captives amounted all told to six thousand.

19   After granting his soldiers leave to plunder, Caesar ordered the buildings to be demolished. Near the bridge—the one closer to Pharos—he fortified a redoubt, and posted a garrison there. This bridge the inhabitants of Pharos had abandoned in their flight; while the other one, which was narrower and closer to the town, was guarded by the Alexandrians. However, on the next day he attacked it from a similar motive, because the possession of these two bridges seemed likely to do away with all the sallies and sudden forays of the enemies' ships. And by now he had dislodged the members of its garrison with artillery and arrows shot from his ships, had driven them back into the town, and put ashore approximately three cohorts—the confined space would not afford a footing for more—while the rest of his forces remained at their posts aboard the ships. At this stage he ordered the bridge to be screened by a rampart on the side facing the enemy, and the opening for the passage of ships—formed by an arch which supported the bridge—to be filled up and

atque obstrui. Quorum altero opere effecto, ut
nulla omnino scapha egredi posset, altero instituto
omnes Alexandrinorum copiae ex oppido se eiecerunt
et contra munitiones pontis latiore loco constiterunt,
eodemque tempore quae consueverant navigia per
pontis ad incendia onerariarum emittere ad molem
constituerunt. Pugnabatur a nobis ex ponte, ex
mole; ab illis ex area, quae erat adversus pontem, et
ex navibus contra molem.

20   In his rebus occupato Caesare militesque hortante
remigum magnus numerus et classiariorum ex longis
navibus nostris in molem se eiecit. Pars eorum
studio spectandi ferebatur, pars etiam cupiditate
pugnandi. Hi primum navigia hostium lapidibus
ac fundis a mole repellebant ac multum proficere
multitudine telorum videbantur. Sed postquam
ultra eum locum ab latere eorum aperto ausi sunt
egredi ex navibus Alexandrini pauci, ut sine signis
certisque ordinibus, sine ratione prodierant, sic
temere in navis refugere coeperunt. Quorum fuga
incitati Alexandrini plures ex navibus egrediebantur
nostrosque acrius perturbatos insequebantur. Simul
qui in navibus longis remanserant scalas rapere
navisque a terra repellere properabant, ne hostes
navibus potirentur. Quibus omnibus rebus perturbati milites nostri cohortium trium quae in ponte

blocked with stones. The latter task being completed, so that not a single pinnace could come out, and the former one being under way, all the Alexandrians' forces burst out of the town and took post in a fairly open position over against our fortifications of the bridge; while at the same time they drew up near the mole the vessels which they had been in the habit of sending out under the bridges to set fire to our transports. And so the battle proceeded, with us fighting from the bridge and the mole, and with them from the area facing the bridge and from their ships opposite the mole.

20   While Caesar was occupied with this situation, and as he was encouraging the troops, a large number of rowers and seamen left our warships and suddenly landed on the mole. Some were inspired by their anxiety to watch the fray, others also by the desire to take part in it. They began by driving back the enemy vessels from the mole with stones and slings, and it seemed that their heavy volleys of missiles were having great effect. But when a few Alexandrians ventured to disembark beyond that point, on the side of their unprotected flank, then, just as they had advanced in no set order or formation and without any particular tactics, so now they began to retire haphazardly to the ships. Encouraged by their retreat, more of the Alexandrians disembarked and pursued our flustered men more hotly. At the same time those who had stayed aboard the warships made haste to seize the gang-planks and ease the ships away from land, to prevent the enemy from gaining possession of them. All this thoroughly alarmed our troops of the three cohorts which had taken post on the bridge and the tip of the mole;

ac prima mole constiterant, cum post se clamorem exaudirent, fugam suorum viderent, magnam vim telorum adversi sustinerent, veriti ne ab tergo circumvenirentur et discessu navium omnino reditu intercluderentur munitionem in ponte institutam reliquerunt et magno cursu incitati ad navis contenderunt. Quorum pars proximas nacta navis multitudine hominum atque onere depressa est, pars resistens et dubitans quid esset capiendum consili ab Alexandrinis interfecta est; non nulli feliciore exitu expeditas ad ancoram navis consecuti incolumes discesserunt, pauci allevatis scutis et animo ad conandum nisi ad proxima navigia adnatarunt.

21　　Caesar quoad potuit cohortando suos ad pontem ac munitiones continere, eodem in periculo versatus est; postquam universos cedere animadvertit, in suum navigium se recepit. Quo multitudo hominum insecuta cum irrumperet neque administrandi neque repellendi a terra facultas daretur, fore quod accidit suspicatus sese ex navigio eiecit atque ad eas quae longius constiterant navis adnatavit. Hinc suis laborantibus subsidio scaphas mittens non nullos conservavit. Navigium quidem eius multitudine depressum militum una cum hominibus interiit. Hoc proelio desiderati sunt ex numero legionariorum militum circiter CCCC et paulo ultra eum numerum classiarii et remiges. Alexandrini eo loco castellum magnis munitionibus multisque tormentis confirma-

and as they heard the clamour behind them, and saw the retreat of their comrades, and sustained a heavy frontal barrage of missiles, they feared they might be surrounded in rear and have their retreat entirely cut off by the departure of their ships; and so they abandoned the entrenchment they had begun at the bridge, and doubled frantically to the ships. Some of them gained the nearest ships, only to be capsized by the weight of so many men; some were killed by the Alexandrians as they put up a forlorn and bewildered resistance; some proved luckier in reaching ships at anchor cleared for action, and so got away safely; and a few, holding their shields above them and steeling their resolution to the task, swam off to ships near by.

21 So long as by words of encouragement Caesar was able to keep his men at the bridge and its emplacements, he too was involved in the same danger; but when he perceived that they were all retreating, he withdrew to his own vessel. As a large number of men followed him and kept forcing their way aboard it, and as no opportunity was afforded either of navigating it or easing it off shore, anticipating what actually happened he dived from the vessel and swam to those ships which were hove to farther off. From them he sent pinnaces to the help of his men who were in difficulties, and saved not a few. His vessel was in fact capsized by the large number of troops, and foundered with the men on board. In this battle the losses among the legionary troops amounted to approximately 400, with a slightly larger number of seamen and rowers. The Alexandrians reinforced the redoubt there with strong entrenchments and many pieces of artillery and

runt atque egestis ex mari lapidibus libere sunt usi postea ad mittenda navigia.

22 Hoc detrimento milites nostri tantum afuerunt ut perturbarentur, ut incensi atque incitati magnas accessiones fecerint in operibus hostium expugnandis. In proeliis cotidianis, quandocumque fors obtulerat, procurrentibus et erumpentibus Alexandrinis, manum conserendi potestate facta multum proficiebat Caesar voluntate optima[1] et ardentibus studiis militum; nec divulgata Caesaris hortatio subsequi legionum aut laborem aut pugnandi poterat cupiditatem, ut magis deterrendi et continendi a periculosissimis essent dimicationibus quam incitandi ad pugnandum.

23 Alexandrini cum Romanos et secundis rebus confirmari et adversis incitari viderent neque ullum belli tertium casum nossent quo possent esse firmiores, ut coniectura consequi possumus, aut admoniti a regis amicis qui in Caesaris erant praesidiis, aut suo priore consilio per occultos nuntios regi probato legatos ad Caesarem miserunt, ut dimitteret regem transireque ad suos pateretur: paratam enim omnem multitudinem esse, confectam taedio puellae, fiduciario regno, dominatione crudelissima Ganymedis, facere id quod rex imperasset; quo si auctore in Caesaris fidem amicitiamque venturi essent, nullius periculi timorem multitudini fore impedimento quo minus se dederent.

[1] Alexandrinis manum comprehendi multum operibus et *MSS. I have adopted Dinter's conjecture.*

[1] *viz.* by Arsinoe to Ganymedes (*cf.* ch. 33) : others, however, interpret the phrase as meaning ' the kingdom, by rights Ptolemy's, held in trust by others '. Andrieu, omitting the comma after *puellae*, renders ' dégoûté de l'autorité fictive d'une jeune fille.'

removed the stones from the sea, subsequently making free use of the opening to despatch their vessels.

22   This reverse, so far from dismaying our troops, fired and stimulated them to carry out large-scale sallies in the course of storming the enemy's defence-works. Every day encounters took place, and whenever a chance offered itself and the Alexandrians burst out in a frontal sally and gave Caesar an opportunity of engaging battle, he achieved considerable success, thanks to the excellent morale and ardent enthusiasm of his troops ; nor could his widespread words of encouragement keep pace with the legions' exertions or their eagerness for fighting, so that they had to be deterred and held back from the most hazardous encounters rather than be spurred on to fight.

23   The Alexandrians saw that the Romans were heartened by successes and stimulated by reverses, nor were they aware of any third vicissitude of war which could make them yet more steadfast. And so, whether it was they were warned by the king's friends who were in Caesar's camp, or whether they were acting on some previous plan of their own made known to the king by secret despatches and approved by him, —we can only guess at their motive—they sent envoys to Caesar requesting him to release the king and allow him to go over to his own side. ‘ The whole population ’, they said, ‘ being tired and wearied of the girl, of the delegation of the kingship,[1] and of the utterly remorseless tyranny of Ganymedes, were ready to do the king's bidding ; and if, at his instance, they were to enter into a loyal friendship with Caesar, then no danger would intimidate or prevent the population from submitting.’

24   Caesar etsi fallacem gentem semperque alia
cogitantem, alia simulantem bene cognitam habebat,
tamen petentibus dare veniam utile esse statuit,
quod, si quo pacto sentirent ea quae postularent,
mansurum in fide dimissum regem credebat, sin, id
quod magis illorum naturae conveniebat, ducem ad
bellum gerendum regem habere vellent, splendidius
atque honestius se contra regem quam contra con-
venarum ac fugitivorum manum bellum esse gestu-
rum.   Itaque regem cohortatus ut consuleret regno
paterno, parceret praeclarissimae patriae, quae
turpibus incendiis et ruinis esset deformata, civis
suos primum ad sanitatem revocaret, deinde con-
servaret, fidem populo Romano sibique praestaret,
cum ipse tantum ei crederet ut ad hostis armatos
eum mitteret, dextra dextram tenens dimittere
coepit adulta iam aetate puerum.   At regius animus
disciplinis fallacissimis eruditus, ne a gentis suae
moribus degeneraret, flens orare contra Caesarem
coepit ne se dimitteret: non enim sibi regnum ipsum
conspectu Caesaris esse iucundius.   Compressis pueri
lacrimis Caesar ipse commotus celeriter, si illa sen-
tiret, fore eum secum adfirmans ad suos dimisit.
Ille, ut ex carceribus in liberum cursum emissus, adeo
contra Caesarem acriter bellum gerere coepit ut

24   Though Caesar was well aware that they were a deceitful race, always pretending something different from their real intentions, yet he decided that it was expedient to satisfy their plea for clemency, since, if their demands in any way reflected their feelings, then he believed the king would remain loyal when released; but if, on the other hand, they wanted to have the king to lead them with a view to waging the war—and that was more in keeping with their character—then he thought there would be greater honour and distinction for him in waging war against a king than against a motley collection of refugees. Accordingly, he urged the king to take thought for the kingdom of his fathers, to have pity on his most illustrious country, shamefully scarred as it was by fire and desolation, to recall his citizens to sanity first and then to preserve them therein, and to prove his loyalty to the Roman people and to Caesar, inasmuch as Caesar himself had such faith in him that he was sending him to join an enemy under arms. Then, grasping his right hand in his own, Caesar made to take leave of the boy—already grown to manhood. But the royal mind, schooled in all the lessons of utter deceit, was loth to fall short of the customary standards of his race; and so with tears he proceeded to beseech Caesar to the opposite effect not to send him away: his very kingdom, he declared, was not more pleasing to him than the sight of Caesar. Checking the lad's tears, albeit not unmoved himself, Caesar declared that, if that was the way he felt, they would speedily be reunited, and so sent him back to his people. Like a horse released from the starting-gate and given his head, the king proceeded to wage war against Caesar

lacrimas quas in colloquio proiecerat gaudio videretur profudisse. Accidisse hoc complures Caesaris
legati, amici, centuriones militesque laetabantur,
quod nimia bonitas eius fallaciis pueri elusa esset.
Quasi vero id Caesar bonitate tantum adductus ac
non prudentissimo consilio fecisset.

25   Cum duce assumpto Alexandrini nihilo se firmiores
factos aut languidiores Romanos animadverterent
eludentibusque militibus regis aetatem atque in-
firmitatem magnum dolorem acciperent neque se
quicquam proficere viderent, rumoresque exsisterent
magna Caesari praesidia terrestri itinere ex Syria
Ciliciaque adduci, quod nondum auditum Caesari
erat, commeatum, qui mari nostris supportabatur,
intercipere statuerunt. Itaque expeditis navigiis
locis idoneis ad Canopum in statione dispositis navibus insidiabantur nostris commeatuque. Quod ubi
Caesari nuntiatum est, universam classem iubet
expediri atque instrui. Praeficit huic Tiberium
Neronem. Proficiscuntur in ea classe Rhodiae
naves atque in his Euphranor, sine quo nulla umquam dimicatio maritima, nulla etiam parum feliciter
confecta erat. At fortuna, quae plerumque eos
quos plurimis beneficiis ornavit ad duriorem casum
reservat, superiorum temporum dissimilis Euphra-
norem prosequebatur. Nam cum ad Canopum

---

[1] The father of the Emperor Tiberius.

so energetically that the tears he had shed at their conference seemed to have been tears of joy. Not a few of Caesar's officers and friends and many of the centurions and soldiers were delighted at this turn of events, inasmuch as Caesar's over-generosity had, they felt, been made fun of by the deceitful tricks of a boy. As if indeed it was merely generosity and not the most far-sighted strategy which had led him to do it!

25   Having got themselves a leader, the Alexandrians observed no greater degree of resolution in themselves or of listlessness in the Romans; in addition, the fun which the soldiers made of the king's youthfulness and irresolution caused great resentment, and they saw they were making no headway. As, moreover, rumours were current that large reinforcements for Caesar were on their way overland from Syria and Cilicia—intelligence which had not yet come to Caesar's ears—they decided to intercept a convoy of supplies which was being conveyed to our troops by sea. Accordingly they stationed some lightly armed vessels on guard at suitable points near Canopus, and lay in wait for our ships and supplies. When Caesar was informed of this he ordered his entire fleet to be got ready and equipped, putting Tiberius Nero [1] in command. Included in this fleet when it set out were the Rhodian ships, and aboard them Euphranor, without whom no naval action had ever been fought, and none even that was not a resounding victory. Fortune, however, very often reserves for a harsher fate those upon whom she has showered her most prolific blessings; and so too the fortune that now attended Euphranor was different from that of former times. For when they reached

49

ventum esset instructaque utrimque classis con-
flixisset et sua consuetudine Euphranor primus
proelium commisisset et quadriremem hostium per-
forasset ac demersisset, proximam longius insecutus
parum celeriter insequentibus reliquis circumventus
est ab Alexandrinis. Cui subsidium nemo tulit, sive
quod in ipso satis praesidi pro virtute ac felicitate eius
putarent esse, sive quod ipsi sibi timebant. Ita,
qui unus ex omnibus eo proelio bene rem gessit, solus
cum sua quadriremi victrice perit.

26   Sub idem tempus Mithridates Pergamenus,
magnae nobilitatis domi scientiaeque in bello et
virtutis, fidei dignitatisque in amicitia Caesaris,
missus in Syriam Ciliciamque initio belli Alexandrini
ad auxilia arcessenda, cum magnis copiis, quas
celeriter et propensissima civitatium voluntate et sua
diligentia confecerat, itinere pedestri, quo coniungitur Aegyptus Syriae, Pelusium adducit:[1] idque
oppidum firmo praesidio occupatum Achillae propter
opportunitatem loci—namque tota Aegyptus maritimo accessu Pharo, pedestri Pelusio velut claustris
munita existimatur—, repente magnis circumdatum
copiis multiplici praesidio pertinaciter propugnantibus et copiarum magnitudine, quas integras

---

[1] adducit, *the MSS. reading, is difficult. Davies proposed*
advenit : *Hoffmann* adductis, id oppidum . . .

---

[1] Son of a wealthy citizen of Pergamum who had been
adopted by Mithridates the Great, from whom he took his
name : another account made him out to be a natural son of
the latter.

[2] I assume here that something like *oppidanis* is to be
supplied as the noun defined by *propugnantibus*.

Canopus and each side had drawn up its fleet and entered the conflict, Euphranor, following his normal custom, was the first to join battle; but when he had holed and sunk one enemy quadrireme, he pursued the next one too far; and as the other ships were not quick enough in following his lead, he was surrounded by the Alexandrians. No one brought him assistance, either because they thought that, considering his courage and his good luck, he was quite able to take care of himself, or because they were afraid for their own sakes. And so the one and only man who was successful in that battle perished alone along with his victorious quadrireme.

26 Round about the same time Mithridates of Pergamum [1] approached Pelusium. A man of high standing in his own country and of great experience and valour in war, as well as a very loyal and valued friend of Caesar, he had been sent into Syria and Cilicia at the outbreak of the Alexandrian war to fetch reinforcements; and now, accompanied by large forces which he had speedily raised, thanks both to the very helpful attitude adopted by the states and to his own conscientious efforts, he arrived at Pelusium by the overland route which links Egypt with Syria. This town had been occupied by a strong garrison of Achillas on account of the tactical importance of the place; for Pharos and Pelusium are regarded as the keys, as it were, to the defence of the whole of Egypt, Pelusium guarding the overland approach, as Pharos defends the seaward one. Mithridates now suddenly surrounded it with large forces; and, despite the obstinate defence put up by its numerous garrison,[2] thanks both to the large number of fresh troops which he kept throwing in to

vulneratis defessisque subiciebat, et perseverantia constantiaque oppugnandi quo die est aggressus in suam redegit potestatem praesidiumque ibi suum collocavit. Inde re bene gesta Alexandream ad Caesarem contendit omnisque eas regiones per quas iter faciebat auctoritate ea quae plerumque adest victori pacarat atque in amicitiam Caesaris redegerat.

27 Locus est fere regionum illarum nobilissimus non ita longe ab Alexandrea, qui nominatur Delta; quod nomen a similitudine litterae cepit: nam pars quaedam fluminis Nili derivata [1] duobus itineribus paulatim medium inter se spatium relinquens diversissimo ad litus intervallo mari coniungitur. Cui loco cum appropinquare Mithridaten rex cognovisset et transeundum ei flumen sciret, magnas adversus eum copias misit, quibus vel superari delerique Mithridaten vel sine dubio retineri posse credebat. Quem ad modum autem optabat eum vinci, sic satis habebat interclusum a Caesare a se retineri. Quae primae copiae flumen a Delta transire et Mithridati occurrere potuerunt, proelium commiserunt festinantes praeripere subsequentibus victoriae societatem. Quorum impetum Mithridates magna cum prudentia [2] consuetudine nostra castris vallatis sustinuit; cum vero incaute atque insolenter suc-

---

[1] derivata inter se *MSS. Duebner deleted* inter se.
[2] *Some MSS. add the words* constantiaque virtutum et Alexandrinorum imprudentia.

---

[1] Apparently he marched south so as to cross the Nile south of the Delta.
[2] In antiquity the term ' Delta ' was also applied, in a restricted sense, to the southern apex of the triangle. The

replace the wounded and exhausted and to the stubborn and unremitting nature of his assault, he reduced it to submission on the same day he started to attack it, and then posted a garrison of his own in it. Whereupon, having achieved this success, he marched to join Caesar in Alexandria, peacefully subduing, meanwhile, and winning over to friendship with Caesar, by that authority which normally belongs to the victor, all those districts along his line of march.[1]

27   Not so very far from Alexandria lies what is perhaps the best known spot in those parts. It is called Delta, and took its name from its resemblance to the letter; for a certain section of the river Nile splits up into two channels which diverge gradually but are separated by a very wide interval at the coast, where the river joins the sea. When the king learned that Mithridates was approaching this spot,[2] and knew that he must cross the river, he despatched large forces against him, by which he believed Mithridates could either be beaten and destroyed, or else undoubtedly held in check. However, desirous as he was for his defeat, he was quite as content to cut him off from Caesar and hold him in check. The first of his forces to succeed in crossing the river from Delta and meeting Mithridates joined battle in eager haste to forestall those following up behind, and so rob them of the chance to participate in victory. Mithridates contained their attack with great discretion, fortifying his camp after our regular fashion; but when he saw them coming up to the entrenchments with a con-

battle must have taken place to the east of the Nile—according to Josephus at the Encampment of the Jews, identified by some with Tal-el-Jahoudieh about 17 miles north of Cairo.

cedere eos munitionibus videret, eruptione undique
facta magnum numerum eorum interfecit. Quod
nisi locorum notitia reliqui se texissent partimque in
navis quibus flumen transierant recepissent, funditus
deleti essent. Qui ut paulum ab illo timore se
recrearunt, adiuncti eis qui subsequebantur rursus
oppugnare Mithridaten coeperunt.

28   Mittitur a Mithridate nuntius Caesari qui rem
gestam perferret. Cognoscit ex suis eadem haec
accidisse rex. Ita paene sub idem tempus et rex
ad opprimendum Mithridaten proficiscitur et Caesar
ad recipiendum. Celeriore fluminis Nili navigatione
rex est usus, in quo magnam et paratam classem
habebat. Caesar eodem itinere uti noluit, ne navibus
in flumine dimicaret, sed circumvectus est eo mari,
quod Africae partis esse dicitur, sicuti supra demonstravimus; prius tamen regis copiis occurrit, quam is
Mithridaten aggredi posset, eumque ad se victorem
incolumi exercitu recepit. Consederat cum copiis
rex loco natura munito, quod erat ipse excelsior
planitie ex omnibus partibus subiecta; tribus autem
ex lateribus variis genere munitionibus tegebatur:
unum latus erat adiectum flumini Nilo, alterum
editissimo loco ductum, ut partem castrorum obtineret, tertium palude cingebatur.

---

   [1] See chapter 14. Apparently Caesar sailed W. to Chersonensus, to avoid fighting his way through the enemy-
occupied part of Alexandria, and then marched S.E., keeping
Lake Mareotis on his left.

   [2] There is wide disagreement about identifying this
position; but assuming that Mithridates marched N.W. to
join Caesar it seems reasonable to place it close to the western

temptuous recklessness, he made a general sally and killed a large number of them. And had not the remainder employed their knowledge of the district to find cover for themselves, and some retired to the ships in which they had crossed the river, they would have been completely wiped out. When they had recovered a little from the resulting panic, they joined forces with their comrades following up behind, and proceeded to a new attack on Mithridates.

28   A messenger was despatched by Mithridates to Caesar to bring him tidings of the action. The king learned of these same events from his own people. Accordingly at practically the same time the king set forth to crush Mithridates, and Caesar to relieve him. The king had recourse to the quicker method of transport, namely sailing up the river Nile, in which he had a large fleet in readiness. Caesar was unwilling to use the same route, so as not to fight a naval action in the river. Instead, he sailed round by that sea which is said to belong to part of Africa, as I have explained earlier.[1] Yet in spite of this he came up with the king's forces before the latter could attack Mithridates, and so rescued the victorious Mithridates with his army intact. The king had encamped with his forces in a naturally strong position,[2] since in itself the position was higher than the plateau which lay beneath it on all sides; moreover, on three sides it was covered by defences of diverse types: one side abutted the river Nile; a second ran along very high ground and formed one face of his camp; while the third was encircled by a marsh.

branch of the Nile about half-way between Cairo and Alexandria, but perhaps closer to the latter.

29   Inter castra et Caesaris iter flumen intercedebat
angustum altissimis ripis, quod in Nilum influebat,
aberat autem ab regis castris milia passuum circiter
VII. Rex cum hoc itinere venire Caesarem com-
perisset, equitatum omnem expeditosque delectos
pedites ad id flumen misit qui transitu Caesarem
prohiberent et eminus ex ripis proelium impar
inirent: nullum enim processum virtus habebat aut
periculum ignavia subibat. Quae res incendit dolore
milites equitesque nostros, quod tam diu pari proelio
cum Alexandrinis certaretur. Itaque eodem tempore equites Germani dispersi vada fluminis quae-
rentes partim demissioribus ripis flumen tranarunt,
et legionarii magnis arboribus excisis, quae longitudine utramque ripam contingerent, proiectis eis [1]
repentinoque aggere iniecto flumen transierunt.
Quorum impetum adeo pertimuerunt hostes ut in
fuga spem salutis collocarent; sed id frustra: namque
ex ea fuga pauci ad regem refugerunt paene omni
reliqua multitudine interfecta.

30   Caesar re praeclarissime gesta, cum subitum
adventum suum iudicaret magnum terrorem Alexandrinis iniecturum, protinus victor ad castra regis
pertendit. Haec cum et opere magno vallata et loci
natura munita animadverteret confertamque arma-
torum multitudinem collocatam in vallo videret,
lassos itinere ac proeliando milites ad oppugnanda

[1] eis *added by Nipperdey.*

29 Between the camp and Caesar's line of march ran a narrow river with very high banks, which flowed into the Nile and was some seven miles distant from the king's camp. When the king learned that Caesar was coming by this route, he despatched all his cavalry and a picked force of light-armed infantry to this river to prevent Caesar from crossing it and to engage at long range from its banks—an unfair engagement, for the spot could neither afford scope for valour nor involve cowardice in any risk. These tactics filled our infantry and cavalry with burning resentment at the thought that for so long their struggle with the Alexandrians should prove a drawn battle. And so, at the same time as scattered groups of German cavalry, looking for places to ford the river, swam across it at some points where the banks were lower, simultaneously the legionary troops, having felled lofty trees tall enough to reach from bank to bank, hurled them forward and crossed the river on a causeway hastily thrown on top. So terrified were the enemy by their attack, that they pinned their hopes of deliverance to flight: in vain, however; for few survived that rout to take refuge with the king, and practically all the remainder were killed.

30 After this most notable success Caesar forthwith pushed forward triumphantly to the king's camp, holding the view that his sudden approach would strike great terror into the hearts of the Alexandrians. But when he observed that this camp was strongly entrenched as well as protected by its natural position, and saw the serried mass of armed men posted at the rampart, he was unwilling to let his soldiers, weary as they were with marching and

57

castra succedere noluit. Itaque non magno intervallo relicto ab hoste castra posuit. Postero die
castellum, quod rex in proximo vico non longe a suis
castris munierat bracchiisque cum opere castrorum
coniunxerat vici obtinendi causa, Caesar aggressus
omnibus copiis expugnat, non quo id minore numero
militum consequi difficile factu putaret, sed ut ab ea
victoria perterritis Alexandrinis protinus castra regis
oppugnaret. Itaque eo cursu, quo refugientis
Alexandrinos ex castello in castra sunt milites insecuti, munitionibus successerunt acerrimeque eminus
proeliari coeperunt. Duabus ex partibus aditus
oppugnationis nostris dabatur: una, quam liberum
accessum habere demonstravi, altera, quae mediocre
intervallum inter castra et flumen Nilum habebat.
Maxima et electissima multitudo Alexandrinorum
defendebat eam partem, quae facillimum aditum
habebat; plurimum proficiebant in repellendis
vulnerandisque nostris, qui regione fluminis Nili
propugnabant: diversis enim telis nostri figebantur,
adversi ex vallo castrorum, aversi ex flumine, in quo
multae naves instructae funditoribus et sagittariis
nostros impugnabant.

31 Caesar cum videret milites acrius proeliari non
posse nec tamen multum profici propter locorum
difficultatem, cumque animum adverteret excelsissi-

---

[1] This interpretation assumes *qui . . . propugnabant* as the
subject of *proficiebant*; and the normal usage of *propugnare*
of defensive fighting seems to confirm it. The alternative—
omitting the comma after *nostris*—'they (the largest contingent of the Alexandrians) were the most successful in . . .
wounding our men who were fighting in the area of the Nile.'
seems hardly to agree with the tactical situation.

fighting, advance to attack the camp. Accordingly he pitched camp at no great distance from the enemy. In a nearby hamlet, not far distant from the king's camp, there was a fort which the king had built and linked with bastions to the main defences of his camp so as to hold the hamlet. This fort Caesar attacked and took by storm on the following day with all his forces; not that he thought it would be difficult to gain that objective by using a smaller number of soldiers, but in order that, with the Alexandrians thoroughly unnerved as a result, he might go straight on from that victory to attack the king's camp. And so, having chased the retreating Alexandrians from the fort into their camp, our troops carried on their charge right up to the fortifications, where they proceeded to fight at long range very briskly. On two sides our men were afforded an opening for assault: the first was the one which, as I have explained, allowed unimpeded approach; the second comprised the moderate-sized space between the camp and the river Nile. The largest and most carefully picked contingent of the Alexandrians was defending that side which afforded the easiest approach; but the defenders in the area of the river Nile were the most successful in repelling and wounding our men:[1] for the latter were being hit by missiles coming from opposite directions—from the rampart of the camp ahead of them, and from the river behind them, where many ships manned with slingers and archers were engaging our men.

1   Now Caesar saw that, while it was impossible for his soldiers to fight with any greater gallantry, yet little headway was being made on account of the difficulty of the ground; he also noted that the

59

mum locum castrorum relictum esse ab Alexandrinis, quod et per se munitus esset et studio partim pugnandi partim spectandi decucurrissent in eum locum in quo pugnabatur, cohortis illo circumire castra et summum locum aggredi iussit eisque Carfulenum praefecit, et animi magnitudine et rei militaris scientia virum praestantem. Quo ut ventum est, paucis defendentibus munitionem, nostris contra militibus acerrime pugnantibus, diverso clamore et proelio perterriti Alexandrini trepidantes in omnis partis castrorum discurrere coeperunt. Quorum perturbatione nostrorum animi adeo sunt incitati ut paene eodem tempore ex omnibus partibus, primi tamen editissimum castrorum locum caperent; ex quo decurrentes magnam multitudinem hostium in castris interfecerunt. Quod periculum plerique Alexandrini fugientes acervatim se de vallo praecipitarunt in eam partem quae flumini erat adiuncta. Horum primis in ipsa fossa munitionis magna ruina oppressis ceteri faciliorem fugam habuerunt. Constat fugisse ex castris regem ipsum receptumque in navem multitudine eorum qui ad proximas navis adnatabant demerso navigio perisse.

32   Re felicissime celerrimeque gesta Caesar magnae victoriae fiducia proximo terrestri itinere Alexan-

highest sector of their camp had been abandoned by
the Alexandrians, not only because of its natural
strength, but also because, in their eagerness in
some cases to fight, in others to look on, its defenders
had rushed down to the sector where the fighting was
going on; consequently he ordered some cohorts to
proceed thither, skirting the camp, and storm the
height, putting in command of them Carfulenus, a
man of exceptional personality and experience in the
field. When they arrived there our men fought with
the greatest gallantry against those few of the enemy
who were defending the entrenchment; whereupon
the Alexandrians, panic-stricken by the shouting and
fighting on both sides of them, began to rush about in
confusion hither and thither throughout the camp.
This utter bewilderment of theirs fired the spirits of
our troops to such a pitch that they captured the
camp almost simultaneously in all sectors, though its
highest point was the first to capitulate; and from
that point our men rushed down and killed a vast
multitude of the enemy in the camp. In their efforts
to escape this danger most of the Alexandrians
hurled themselves *en masse* from the rampart into the
area adjoining the river; the first of these were
crushed by their heavy fall in the actual trench of the
fortification, but the rest found it easier to escape.
It is established that the king himself fled from the
camp and then, after being taken aboard a ship along
with a large number of his men who were swimming
to the nearest ships, perished when as a result of the
numbers the vessel capsized.

32   This signal victory, the outcome of a most speedy
and successful action, filled Caesar with such confidence that he hastened with his cavalry to Alexan-

dream cum equitibus contendit atque ea parte
oppidi victor introiit quae praesidio hostium tenebatur. Neque eum consilium suum fefellit quin
hostes eo proelio audito nihil iam de bello essent
cogitaturi. Dignum adveniens fructum virtutis et
animi magnitudinis tulit: omnis enim multitudo
oppidanorum armis proiectis munitionibusque suis relictis, veste ea sumpta qua supplices dominantis
deprecari consuerunt, sacrisque omnibus prolatis
quorum religione precari offensos iratosque animos
regum erant soliti, advenienti Caesari occurrerunt
seque ei dediderunt. Caesar in fidem receptos
consolatus per hostium munitiones in suam partem
oppidi magna gratulatione venit suorum, qui non
tantum bellum ipsum ac dimicationem sed etiam
talem adventum eius felicem fuisse laetabantur.

33 Caesar Aegypto atque Alexandrea potitus reges
constituit quos Ptolomaeus testamento scripserat
atque obtestatus erat populum Romanum ne muta-
rentur. Nam maiore ex duobus pueris, rege, amisso
minori tradidit regnum maiorique ex duabus filiis,
Cleopatrae, quae manserat in fide praesidiisque eius;
minorem, Arsinoen, cuius nomine diu regnasse
impotenter Ganymeden docuimus, deducere ex regno

---

dria by the nearest overland route, and entered it triumphantly by that quarter of the town which was held by the enemy garrison. Nor was he mistaken in his own conclusion that, as soon as they heard of that battle, the enemy would cease to think any longer in terms of war. On his arrival he reaped the well-earned fruits of valour and magnanimity; for the entire population of townsfolk threw down their arms, abandoned their fortifications, assumed that garb in which suppliants are used to placate tyrants with earnest prayers, and brought forth all the sacred emblems by the sanctity of which they had been wont to conjure the embittered and wrathful hearts of their kings: even so did they hasten to meet Caesar on his arrival and surrendered themselves to him. Caesar took them formally under his protection and consoled them; then, passing through the enemy fortifications, he came to his own quarter of the town amid loud cheers of congratulation from his own troops, who rejoiced at the happy issue, not only of the war itself and the fighting, but also of his arrival under such circumstances.

33   Having made himself master of Egypt and Alexandria, Caesar appointed as kings those whose names Ptolemaeus had written down in his will with an earnest appeal to the Roman people that they should not be altered. The elder of the two boys—the late king—being now no more, Caesar assigned the kingdom to the younger one and to Cleopatra, the elder of the two daughters, who had remained his loyal adherent; whereas Arsinoe, the younger daughter, in whose name, as we have shewn,[1] Ganymedes had long been exercising an unbridled sway, he determined to remove from the realm, to

statuit, ne qua rursus nova dissensio, prius quam diuturnitate confirmarentur regibus imperia, per homines seditiosos nasceretur. Legiones ibi veterana sexta secum reducta ceteras reliquit, quo firmius esset eorum regum imperium, qui neque amorem suorum habere poterant, quod fideliter permanserant in Caesaris amicitia, neque vetustatis auctoritatem, paucis diebus reges constituti. Simul ad imperi nostri dignitatem utilitatemque publicam pertinere existimabat, si permanerent in fide reges, praesidiis eos nostris esse tutos; si essent ingrati, posse isdem praesidiis coerceri. Sic rebus omnibus confectis et collocatis ipse [1] profectus est in Syriam.

34 Dum haec in Aegypto geruntur, rex Deiotarus ad Domitium Calvinum, cui Caesar Asiam finitimasque provincias administrandas tradiderat, venit oratum ne Armeniam minorem, regnum suum, neve Cappadociam, regnum Ariobarzanis, possideri vastarique pateretur a Pharnace; quo malo nisi liberarentur, imperata se facere pecuniamque promissam Caesari non posse persolvere. Domitius, non tantum ad explicandos sumptus rei militaris cum pecuniam necessariam esse iudicaret, sed etiam turpe populo Romano et C. Caesari victori sibique infame esse statueret regna sociorum atque amicorum ab externo rege occupari, nuntios confestim ad Pharnacem misit,

---

[1] *The MSS. add* itinere terrestri, *which Nipperdey deleted.*

---

[1] The Twenty-Seventh, the Thirty-Seventh and a third whose identity is not certain—possibly the one despatched overland by Calvinus (see ch. 34).

[2] King of Pontus, son of Mithridates the Great.

prevent any renewed dissensions coming into being among factious folk before the dominion of the royal pair could be consolidated by the passage of time. The veteran Sixth legion he took away with him: all the others [1] he left there, the more to bolster up the dominion of the said rulers, who could enjoy neither the affection of their people, inasmuch as they had remained throughout staunch friends of Caesar, nor the authority of a long-established reign, it being but a few days since they came to the throne. At the same time he deemed it conducive to the dignity of our empire and to public expediency that, if the rulers remained loyal, they should be protected by our troops: whereas if they proved ungrateful, those same troops could hold them in check. Having thus completed all his dispositions, he set out in person for Syria.

34   While these events were taking place in Egypt, king Deiotarus came to Domitius Calvinus, to whom Caesar had assigned the government of Asia and the neighbouring provinces, to beg him not to allow Lesser Armenia, his own kingdom, or Cappadocia, the kingdom of Ariobarzanes, to be occupied and over-run by Pharnaces [2]: for unless they were liberated from this scourge, he could not carry out his instructions and pay out the money he had promised to Caesar. As Domitius not only considered the money to be indispensable for defraying military expenses, but also decided it was a shameful affront to the Roman people and to the triumphant C. Caesar as well as a slight to himself that the kingdoms of their allies and friends should be seized by a foreign king, he forthwith sent a deputation to Pharnaces, bidding him withdraw from Armenia and

Armenia Cappadociaque decederet neve occupatione belli civilis populi Romani ius maiestatemque temptaret. Hanc denuntiationem cum maiorem vim habituram existimaret, si propius eas regiones cum exercitu accessisset, ad legiones profectus unam ex tribus, XXXVI., secum ducit, duas in Aegyptum ad Caesarem mittit litteris eius evocatas; quarum altera bello Alexandrino non occurrit, quod itinere terrestri per Syriam erat missa. Adiungit Cn. Domitius legioni XXXVI. duas ab Deiotaro, quas ille disciplina atque armatura nostra compluris annos constitutas habebat, equitesque C, totidemque ab Ariobarzane sumit. Mittit P. Sestium ad C. Plaetorium quaestorem, ut legionem adduceret quae ex tumultuariis militibus in Ponto confecta erat, Quintumque Patisium in Ciliciam ad auxilia arcessenda. Quae copiae celeriter omnes iussu Domiti Comana convenerunt.

35 Interim legati a Pharnace responsa referunt: Cappadocia se decessisse, Armeniam minorem recepisse, quam paterno nomine iure obtinere deberet. Denique eius regni causa integra Caesari servaretur: paratum enim se facere quod is statuisset. Cn. Domitius cum animadverteret eum Cappadocia decessisse non voluntate adductum sed necessitate, quod facilius Armeniam defendere posset subiectam suo regno quam Cappadociam longius remotam, quodque omnis tris legiones adducturum Domitium

---

[1] See chapter 9 (arrival of the Thirty-Seventh) and chapter 33, note 1 on p. 64.
[2] A town in Pontus.

Cappadocia and not assail the rights and majesty
of the Roman people by resorting to civil war. In the
belief that this warning would have greater force if
he approached closer to that area with an army,
he set out for his legions; then, taking with him one
of the three, the Thirty-Sixth, he sent to Caesar in
Egypt the two[1] which the latter had called for in his
despatch. One of these two did not arrive in time
for the Alexandrian war, as it was sent by the overland route through Syria. Cn. Domitius reinforced
the Thirty-Sixth legion with two from Deiotarus,
which the latter had had for several years, having
built them up on our system of discipline and
armament; he also added to it 100 horsemen, and
took a like number from Ariobarzanes. He sent
P. Sestius to C. Plaetorius, the quaestor, with
instructions to bring the legion which had been
formed from the hastily improvised forces in Pontus;
and Quintus Patisius to Cilicia to muster auxiliary
troops. All these forces speedily assembled at
Comana[2] according to the orders of Domitius.

35   Meantime the envoys brought back this reply from
Pharnaces: 'he had withdrawn from Cappadocia,
but had recovered Lesser Armenia, which he ought
to possess by due right of inheritance from his father.
In short, the issue touching that kingdom should be
kept open for Caesar's decision; for he was ready to
do what Caesar should decide.' Now Cn. Domitius
observed that he had withdrawn from Cappadocia
not from free choice but of necessity, since he could
defend Armenia next door to his own kingdom more
easily than the more distant Cappadocia, and also
because he had supposed that Domitius would bring
up all three legions; and that when he heard that

67

putasset, ex quibus cum duas ad Caesarem missas
audisset, audacius in Armenia substitisse, per-
severare coepit, ut eo quoque regno decederet; neque
enim aliud ius esse Cappadociae atque Armeniae,
nec iuste eum postulare ut in Caesaris adventum res
integra differetur; id enim esse integrum quod ita
esset ut fuisset. His responsis datis cum eis copiis
quas supra scripsi profectus est in Armeniam locisque
superioribus iter facere instituit: nam ex Ponto a
Comanis iugum editum silvestre est, pertinens in
Armeniam minorem, quo Cappadocia finitur ab
Armenia; cuius itineris has esse certas opportuni-
tates vidit,[1] quod in locis superioribus nullus impetus
repentinus accidere hostium poterat, et quod Cappadocia his iugis subiecta magnam commeatus copiam
erat sumministratura.

36   Compluris interim legationes Pharnaces ad Domitium mittit quae de pace agerent regiaque munera
Domitio ferrent. Ea constanter omnia aspernabatur
nec sibi quicquam fore antiquius quam dignitatem
populi Romani et regna sociorum reciperare legatis
respondebat. Magnis et continuis itineribus confectis cum adventaret ad Nicopolim, quod oppidum
positum in Armenia minore est plano ipso loco,
montibus tamen altis ab duobus lateribus obiectis
satis magno intervallo ab oppido remotis, castra

---

[1] vidit *added by Forchhammer.*

---

[1] The conventional boundaries as marked in Map 2 are only
approximate: Armenia may well have extended further W.
and Cappadocia further N. Domitius may, as R. Holmes
suggested, have followed the ridge between the rivers Lycus
and Iris; and this would have been his most direct route.

two of those legions had been sent to Caesar, this had heightened his rash resolve to stay on in Armenia. Consequently Domitius proceeded to insist that Pharnaces should withdraw from that kingdom also: ' as far as legal right went, there was no difference between Cappadocia and Armenia, nor had he any right to demand that the question should be left open pending Caesar's arrival; a matter was ' open ' when it remained just as it had been.' Having given him this reply Domitius set out for Armenia with the forces I have recorded above, and began by marching along the higher ground. From Comana in Pontus there is, in fact, a lofty, wooded ridge which extends into Lesser Armenia and forms the boundary [1] between Cappadocia and Armenia. This route, as he saw, offered definite advantages, namely that on the higher ground no sudden enemy attack could develop, and that, as Cappadocia adjoined this ridge, it was likely to assist him by affording an abundance of supplies.

36   Meanwhile Pharnaces sent several embassies to Domitius to discuss peace and to take princely gifts for Domitius. All these he firmly rejected and replied to the envoys that as far as he was concerned nothing should take precedence over the prestige of the Roman people and the recovery of the kingdoms of its allies. Then, after completing an uninterrupted succession of long marches, he began to approach Nicopolis, a town in Lesser Armenia which is actually situated in the plain, though it is hemmed in on two sides by high mountains at a fairish distance. Here he pitched camp roughly seven

But he may have taken a more devious route further S. for the motives suggested in the text.

posuit longe a Nicopoli circiter milia passuum VII. Quibus ex castris cum locus angustus atque impeditus esset transeundus, Pharnaces in insidiis delectos pedites omnisque paene disposuit equites, magnam autem multitudinem pecoris intra eas fauces dissipari iussit paganosque et oppidanos in his locis obversari, ut sive amicus Domitius eas angustias transiret, nihil de insidiis suspicaretur, cum in agris et pecora et homines animum adverteret versari tamquam amicorum adventu, sive inimicus ut in hostium finis veniret, praeda diripienda milites dissiparentur dispersique caederentur.

37 Haec cum administraret, numquam tamen intermittebat legatos de pace atque amicitia mittere ad Domitium, cum hoc ipso crederet facilius eum decipi posse. At contra spes pacis Domitio in isdem castris morandi attulit causam. Ita Pharnaces, amissa proximi temporis occasione cum vereretur ne cognoscerentur insidiae, suos in castra revocavit. Domitius postero die propius Nicopolim accessit castraque oppido contulit. Quae dum muniunt nostri, Pharnaces aciem instruxit more suo atque instituto. In fronte enim simplici derecta acie cornua trinis firmabantur subsidiis; eadem ratione haec media collocabantur acie duobus dextra

miles from Nicopolis. From this camp he had to traverse a narrow and confined defile; and for this reason Pharnaces arrayed the pick of his infantry and practically all his cavalry in an ambush, giving orders, moreover, that a large number of cattle should be pastured at various points within this gorge, and that the peasants and burghers should go about openly in that area. His object in so doing was that, if Domitius should pass through that defile as a friend, he might have no suspicions of an ambush, as he would observe both men and beasts moving about the countryside, as if friends were in the offing; while if he should come in no friendly spirit, treating it as enemy territory, his troops might become scattered in the process of plundering and so be cut down piecemeal.

37 While making these dispositions he still constantly continued sending delegations to Domitius to talk of peace and friendship, as he believed that by these self-same tactics Domitius could the more readily be duped. But on the other hand Domitius' hopes of peace afforded him a motive for tarrying in the camp, where he was. Consequently, as Pharnaces had now lost his immediate opportunity and was afraid that his ambush might be discovered, he recalled his troops to camp. On the morrow Domitius advanced nearer Nicopolis and pitched his camp over against the town. While our troops were fortifying it, Pharnaces drew up his line of battle according to his own established custom. This, in fact, was formed with its front as a single straight line, with each of the wings reinforced by three supporting lines; and on the same principle support lines were also posted in the centre, while in the two spaces,

sinistraque intervallis simplicibus ordinibus instructis. Perfecit inceptum castrorum opus Domitius parte copiarum pro vallo constituta.

38 Proxima nocte Pharnaces interceptis tabellariis, qui de Alexandrinis rebus litteras ad Domitium ferebant, cognoscit Caesarem magno in periculo versari flagitarique ab Domitio ut quam primum Caesari subsidia mitteret propiusque ipse Alexandream per Syriam accederet. Qua cognita re Pharnaces victoriae loco ducebat, si trahere tempus posset, cum discedendum Domitio celeriter putaret. Itaque ab oppido, qua facillimum accessum et aequissimum ad dimicandum nostris videbat, fossas duas derectas non ita magno medio intervallo relicto IIII pedum altitudinis in eum locum deduxit quo longius constituerat suam non producere aciem. Inter has fossas aciem semper instruebat, equitatum autem omnem ab lateribus extra fossam collocabat; qui neque aliter utilis esse poterat et multum numero anteibat nostrum equitatum.

39 Domitius autem, cum Caesaris magis periculo quam suo commoveretur neque se tuto discessurum arbitraretur, si condiciones quas reiecerat rursus appeteret aut sine causa [1] discederet, ex propinquis castris in aciem exercitum eduxit; XXXVI. legionem in dextro cornu collocavit, Ponticam in sinistro, Deiotari legiones in mediam aciem contulit, quibus

[1] sine causa *MSS*. *Hoffmann conjectured* si negatis.

on the right hand and the left, single ranks were drawn up. Having once begun the task of fortifying his camp, Domitius completed it, with part of his forces posted in front of the rampart.

38 The following night Pharnaces intercepted some couriers who were carrying despatches to Domitius concerning the situation at Alexandria. From them he learned that Caesar was in a very dangerous position, and that an urgent request was being made to Domitius that he should send Caesar reinforcements as soon as possible and himself advance through Syria closer to Alexandria. On learning this, Pharnaces saw himself virtually victorious if he could spin out the time, as he thought that Domitius must speedily withdraw. Accordingly, from that side of the town which he saw offered our men the easiest and most favourable line of approach to do battle, he carried two straight trenches, four feet deep and spaced not so very far apart, as far as the point beyond which he had decided not to advance his own battle line. Between these trenches he consistently drew up his line, while posting all his cavalry on the flanks outside the trench; for otherwise they could not be of any use, and they far outnumbered our cavalry.

39 Domitius, however, was more disturbed by Caesar's peril than by his own; and as he thought that he would not be safe in withdrawing, if he made a fresh attempt to secure the terms he had rejected or if he withdrew for no good reason, he deployed his army from its nearby camp into battle formation. He posted the Thirty-Sixth legion on the right wing and the Pontic one on the left, while the legions of Deiotarus he concentrated in the centre, leaving

73

tamen angustissimum intervallum frontis reliquit
reliquis cohortibus in subsidiis collocatis. Sic utrimque acie instructa processum est ad dimicandum.

40 Signo sub idem tempus ab utroque dato concurritur: acriter varieque pugnatur. Nam XXXVI.
legio, cum extra fossam in equites regis impetum
fecisset, adeo secundum proelium fecit ut moenibus
oppidi succederet fossamque transiret aversosque
hostis aggrederetur. At Pontica ex altera parte
legio, cum paulum aversa hostibus cessisset, fossam
autem circumire ac transcendere [1] conata esset, ut
aperto latere aggrederetur hostem, in ipso transitu
fossae confixa et oppressa est. Deiotari vero legiones
vix impetum sustinuerunt. Ita victrices regiae
copiae cornu suo dextro mediaque acie converterunt
se ad XXXVI. legionem. Quae tamen fortiter
vincentium impetum sustinuit, magnis copiis hostium
circumdata praesentissimo animo pugnans in orbem
se recepit ad radices montium; quo Pharnaces
insequi propter iniquitatem loci noluit. Ita Pontica
legione paene tota amissa, magna parte Deiotari
militum interfecta XXXVI. legio in loca se superiora
contulit non amplius CCL desideratis. Ceciderunt eo proelio splendidi atque inlustres viri non
nulli, equites Romani. Quo tamen incommodo
Domitius accepto reliquias exercitus dissipati collegit

[1] acies secundo *MSS.*: ac transcendere *Nipperdey*.

---

[1] The text is corrupt and the manoeuvre is by no means
clear; but it would seem that part, if not all, the Pontic
legion—like the Thirty-Sixth—was posted outside the trench,
and so, to attack the enemy flank, they had either to cross the
trench (its width is not stated) or else retire far enough to work
round its end.

them, however, a very narrow frontage and posting his remaining cohorts behind them in support. The lines being thus arrayed on either side, they proceeded to battle.

40   The signal to attack was given almost simultaneously on both sides: then came the charge, with hotly contested and fluctuating fighting. Thus the Thirty-Sixth legion launched an attack on the king's cavalry outside the trench and fought so successful an action that it advanced up to the walls of the town, crossed the trench, and attacked the enemy in rear. The Pontic legion, however, on the other flank, drew back a little from the enemy, and attempted, moreover, to go round or cross the trench, so as to attack the enemy's exposed flank; but in the actual crossing of the trench it was pinned down and overwhelmed.[1] The legions of Deiotarus, indeed, offered scarcely any resistance to the attack. Consequently the king's forces, victorious on their own right wing and in the centre of the line, now turned upon the Thirty-Sixth legion. The latter, nevertheless, bore up bravely under the victors' attack and, though surrounded by large enemy forces, yet with consummate presence of mind formed a circle and so made a fighting withdrawal to the foothills, where Pharnaces was loth to pursue it owing to the hilly nature of the ground. And so, with the Pontic legion an almost total loss and a large proportion of the troops of Deiotarus killed, the Thirty-Sixth legion retired to higher ground with losses not exceeding 250 men. There fell in that battle not a few Roman knights—brilliant and distinguished men. After sustaining this defeat Domitius none the less collected the remnants of his scattered army and

itineribusque tutis per Cappadociam se in Asiam recepit.

41 Pharnaces rebus secundis elatus, cum de Caesare ea quae optabat speraret, Pontum omnibus copiis occupavit ibique et victor et crudelissimus rex, cum sibi fortunam paternam feliciore eventu destinaret, multa oppida expugnavit, bona civium Romanorum Ponticorumque diripuit, supplicia constituit in eos qui aliquam formae atque aetatis commendationem habebant ea quae morte essent miseriora, Pontumque nullo defendente paternum regnum glorians se recepisse obtinebat.

42 Sub idem tempus in Illyrico est incommodum acceptum, quae provincia superioribus mensibus retenta non tantum sine ignominia sed etiam cum laude erat. Namque eo missus aestate cum duabus legionibus Q. Cornificius, Caesaris quaestor, pro praetore, quamquam erat provincia minime copiosa ad exercitus alendos et finitimo bello ac dissensionibus confecta et vastata, tamen prudentia ac diligentia sua, quod magnam curam suscipiebat ne quo temere progrederetur, et recepit et defendit. Namque et castella complura locis editis posita, quorum opportunitas castellanos impellebat ad decursiones faciendas et bellum inferendum, ex-

---

[1] His hereditary kingdom, from which his father Mithridates had been driven by Lucullus.

[2] Mithridates the Great, a fugitive from Pompey the Great, took his own life in 63 B.C. as a result of the rebellion of his son Pharnaces.

[3] *viz.* castration, *cf.* ch. 70.

withdrew by safe routes through Cappadocia into Asia.

1   Elated by this success and confident that his wishes for Caesar's defeat would be granted, Pharnaces seized Pontus[1] with all his forces. There he played the role of victor and utterly ruthless tyrant and, promising himself his father's fortune though with a happier ending,[2] he took many towns by storm, plundered the property of Roman and Pontic citizens, and decreed for those who in respect of youth and beauty had anything to commend them such punishments[3] as proved more pitiful than death. Thus he held unchallenged sway over Pontus, boasting that he had recovered the kingdom of his father.

2   Round about the same time a set-back was sustained in Illyricum, a province which during the previous months had been firmly held not merely without incurring disgrace but even with distinction. To this province there had been sent out in the summer a quaestor of Caesar's, Q. Cornificius, as pro-praetor; 48 B.C. and although the province was not at all abundantly stocked for supporting armies and was exhausted and wasted by war upon its borders and by rebellions,[4] yet by his far-sighted and careful policy, taking great pains not to make an ill-considered advance in any quarter, he recovered and defended it. For example, he successfully stormed several mountain strongholds, the commanding position of which prompted their occupants to carry on a predatory warfare, and presented his troops with the resulting

----

[4] The Roman residents consistently supported Caesar, but the natives sided with Pompey. The heavy fighting at Dyrrhachium was just south of the border of the province.

pugnavit eaque praeda milites donavit, quae etsi
erat tenuis, tamen in tanta provinciae desperatione
erat grata, praesertim virtute parta, et cum Octavius
ex fuga Pharsalici proeli magna classe in illum se
sinum contulisset, paucis navibus Iadertinorum,
quorum semper in rem publicam singulare constiterat
officium, dispersis Octavianis navibus erat potitus, ut
vel classe dimicare posset adiunctis captivis navibus
sociorum. Cum diversissima parte orbis terrarum
Cn. Pompeium Caesar victor sequeretur complurisque
adversarios in Illyricum propter Macedoniae pro-
pinquitatem se reliquiis ex fuga collectis contulisse
audiret, litteras ad Gabinium mittit, uti cum legionibus tironum, quae nuper erant conscriptae, proficisceretur in Illyricum coniunctisque copiis cum
Q. Cornificio, si quod periculum provinciae in-
ferretur, depelleret; sin ea non magnis copiis tuta
esse posset, in Macedoniam legiones adduceret.
Omnem enim illam partem regionemque vivo Cn.
Pompeio bellum instauraturam esse credebat.

43 Gabinius ut in Illyricum venit hiberno tempore
anni ac difficili sive copiosiorem provinciam existimans
sive multum fortunae victoris Caesaris tribuens sive
virtute et scientia sua confisus, qua saepe in bellis

---

[1] See ch. 3. Caesar had recalled him from exile.

booty; which, paltry though it was, was none the less welcome—considering the very meagre prospects of the province—especially since it was the prize of valour. Again, when in the course of his flight from the battle of Pharsalia Octavius took refuge with a large fleet upon that coast, Cornificius, with the aid of a few ships of the men of Iadera—those devoted supporters of the commonwealth, who were unsurpassed in their constant loyalty—made himself master of Octavius' scattered ships, and was accordingly enabled by the addition of these vessels to those of his allies to go into action with something like a fleet. And when in quite a different quarter of the globe Caesar was victoriously pursuing Cn. Pompeius, and heard that several of his opponents had collected the remnants of the fugitives and taken refuge in Illyricum on account of its proximity to Macedonia, he sent despatches to Gabinius,[1] bidding him set out for Illyricum with the legions of recruits which had recently been raised: there he was to join forces with Q. Cornificius and repulse any dangerous move that might be made against the province: if on the other hand no large forces were needed to ensure the safety of the province, he was to lead his legions into Macedonia. It was in fact his belief that the whole of that neighbourhood and area would revive the war, so long as Cn. Pompeius was alive.

3   When Gabinius came to Illyricum in the difficult winter season,—whether it was he thought the province was more abundantly supplied, or whether he set great store by Caesar's winning luck, or whether he trusted in his own courage and skill, which had many a time enabled him, when sur-

79

periclitatus magnas res et secundas ductu ausuque
suo gesserat, neque provinciae facultatibus sub-
levabatur, quae partim erat exinanita partim
infidelis, neque navibus intercluso mari tempestatibus
commeatus supportari poterat; magnisque difficultatibus coactus non ut volebat sed ut necesse erat
bellum gerebat. Ita cum durissimis tempestatibus
propter inopiam castella aut oppida expugnare
cogeretur, crebro incommoda accipiebat adeoque est
a barbaris contemptus ut Salonam se recipiens in
oppidum maritimum, quod cives Romani fortissimi
fidelissimi incolebant, in agmine dimicare sit coactus.
Quo proelio duobus milibus militum amplius amissis,
centurionibus XXXVIII, tribunis IIII, cum reliquis
copiis Salonam se recepit summaque ibi difficultate
rerum omnium pressus paucis mensibus morbo periit.
Cuius et infelicitas vivi et subita mors in magnam
spem Octavium adduxit provinciae potiendae; quem
tamen diutius in rebus secundis et fortuna, quae
plurimum in bellis potest, diligentiaque Cornifici et
virtus Vatini versari passa non est.

44   Vatinius Brundisi cum esset, cognitis rebus quae
gesta erant in Illyrico, cum crebris litteris Cornifici
ad auxilium provinciae ferendum evocaretur et M.
Octavium audiret cum barbaris foedera percussisse
compluribusque locis nostrorum militum oppugnare
praesidia partim classe per se partim pedestribus

rounded by the hazards of war, to score great successes by his personal leadership and initiative—anyway he derived no support from the resources of the province, bled white as it partly was, and partly disloyal, nor could supplies be conveyed to him by ship, since stormy weather had interrupted navigation. As a result of these considerable difficulties he was forced to conduct the campaign, not as he wished, but as necessity dictated. And so, as lack of supplies forced him to storm towns or strongholds in very adverse weather, he frequently sustained reverses, and was held by the natives in such contempt that, while retreating on Salona, a coastal town occupied by very gallant and loyal Roman citizens, he was forced to fight an action on the march. In this battle Jan. 47. he lost more than two thousand soldiers, thirty-eight centurions and four tribunes : with what was left of his forces he retired to Salona, where, under the stress of overwhelming difficulties of every kind, he fell sick and died within a few months. His chequered fortune while alive and his sudden death inspired Octavius with high hopes of securing possession of the province; luck, however, which is a very potent factor in war, as well as the carefulness of Cornificius and the courage of Vatinius, did not allow Octavius to pursue his successful career much longer.

4   When Vatinius was at Brundisium he learned of what had been going on in Illyricum; moreover, frequent despatches from Cornificius kept summoning him to bring aid to the province, and he heard that M. Octavius had concluded treaties with the natives and in several places was attacking the garrisons of our troops, in some cases in person with his fleet, in others with land forces, employing

CAESAR

copiis per barbaros, etsi gravi valetudine adfectus vix
corporis viribus animum sequebatur, tamen virtute
vicit incommodum naturae difficultatesque et hiemis
et subitae praeparationis. Nam cum ipse paucas in
portu navis longas haberet, litteras in Achaiam ad
Q. Calenum misit, uti sibi classem mitteret. Quod
cum tardius fieret quam periculum nostrorum flagita-
bat, qui sustinere impetum Octavi non poterant,
navibus actuariis, quarum numerus erat satis magnus,
magnitudo nequaquam satis iusta ad proeliandum,
rostra imposuit. His adiunctis navibus longis et
numero classis aucto militibus veteranis impositis,
quorum magnam copiam habebat ex omnibus legionibus, qui numero aegrorum relicti erant Brundisi,
cum exercitus in Graeciam transportaretur, profectus est in Illyricum maritimasque non nullas
civitates, quae defecerant Octavioque se tradiderant,
partim recipiebat, partim remanentis in suo consilio
praetervehebatur nec sibi ullius rei moram necessi-
tatemque iniungebat quin quam celerrime posset
ipsum Octavium persequeretur. Hunc oppugnantem
Epidaurum terra marique, ubi nostrum erat praesidium, adventu suo discedere ab oppugnatione coegit
praesidiumque nostrum recepit.

45 Octavius cum Vatinium classem magna ex parte
confectam ex naviculis actuariis habere cognosset,
confisus sua classe substitit ad insulam Tauridem;

native troops. So, although he was afflicted by a serious illness and his bodily strength barely enabled him to obey his will, yet by courage he overcame his physical handicap, as well as the difficulties both of winter and the sudden mobilisation. Thus, as he himself had few warships in harbour, he sent despatches to Q. Calenus in Achaia, requesting him to send him a fleet; but as this proved too slow a business—our troops were in no position to withstand Octavius' attack, and their critical situation urgently demanded something speedier—he fitted beaks to some fast boats, of which he had a sufficient number, though their size was by no means adequate for fighting purposes. With these added to his warships, and his fleet thereby numerically increased, he put on board some veteran troops, of which he had an abundant supply from all the legions—they had been on the sick list and had been left behind at Brundisium when the army was being shipped to Greece—and so set out for Illyricum. Now there were not a few coastal communities there which had revolted and surrendered to Octavius: some of these he recovered, others he by-passed when they remained steadfast to their policy; nor would he allow anything, however pressing, to embarrass or delay him from pursuing Octavius himself with all the speed of which he was capable. While the latter was assaulting Epidaurus by land and sea, where there was a garrison of ours, Vatinius forced him by his approach to abandon his assault, and so relieved our garrison.

5   When Octavius learned that Vatinius had a fleet which was in the main made up of small, fast boats, having full confidence in his own fleet he hove to off the island of Tauris. In this area Vatinius was March 47.

83

qua regione Vatinius insequens navigabat, non quo
Octavium ibi restitisse sciret, sed quod eum longius
progressum insequi decreverat. Cum propius Tauridem accessisset distensis suis navibus, quod et
tempestas erat turbulenta et nulla suspicio hostis,
repente adversam ad se venientem navem antemnis
ad medium malum demissis instructam propugnatoribus animum advertit. Quod ubi conspexit,
celeriter vela subduci demittique antemnas iubet et
milites armari et vexillo sublato, quo pugnandi dabat
signum, quae primae naves subsequebantur idem ut
facerent significabat. Parabant se Vatiniani repente
oppressi; parati deinceps Octaviani ex portu pro-
cedebant. Instruitur utrimque acies, ordine disposita magis Octaviana, paratior militum animis
Vatiniana.

46 Vatinius cum animum adverteret neque navium se
magnitudine neque numero parem esse fortuitae
dimicationi, fortunae rem committere maluit. Itaque
primus sua quinqueremi in quadriremem ipsius
Octavi impetum fecit. Celerrime fortissimeque
contra illo remigante naves adversae rostris concurrerunt adeo vehementer ut navis Octaviana rostro
discusso ligno contineretur. Committitur acriter
reliquis locis proelium concurriturque ad duces
maxime: nam cum suo quisque auxilium ferret,
magnum comminus in angusto mari proelium factum

cruising in pursuit, not from any knowledge that
Octavius had hove to there, but because the latter
had gained a fairly good start, and he had resolved to
pursue him. On approaching closer to Tauris with
his ships strung out, since the weather was rough
and he had no suspicion of the enemy, he suddenly
observed a ship bearing down upon him, its yard-
arms lowered to mid-mast, and manned with combat
troops. When he saw this, he promptly ordered the
sails to be reefed, the yard-arms lowered, and the
troops to stand to; and then, by hoisting the pen-
nant, which was his method of giving the signal for
action, he signalled the leading ships astern of him
to do the same. The Vatinians being thus suddenly
taken unawares proceeded to man ship: the
Octavians, their ships already manned, came sailing
out of the harbour one after another. Line of
battle was formed on either side, that of Octavius
being superior in formation, that of Vatinius in the
morale of the troops.

6   When Vatinius observed that neither in the size
nor the number of his ships was he a match for a
chance engagement, he chose rather to trust to
luck. And so he attacked first, charging with his
own quinquereme the quadrireme which was the
flagship of Octavius. The latter rowed forward
against him with the utmost speed and bravery,
and the two ships ran together with their beaks
head-on so violently that Octavius' ship had its beak
smashed away and was locked to the other by its
timbers. Elsewhere a fierce engagement took place,
with particularly sharp fighting near the leaders;
for with each individual captain trying to support
his own leader, a great battle developed at close

est. Quantoque coniunctis magis navibus confligendi potestas dabatur, tanto superiores erant
Vatiniani; qui admiranda virtute ex suis navibus in
hostium navis transilire non dubitabant et dimica-
tione aequata longe superiores virtute rem feliciter
gerebant. Deprimitur ipsius Octavi quadriremis,
multae praeterea capiuntur aut rostris perforatae
merguntur; propugnatores Octaviani partim in
navibus iugulantur, partim in mare praecipitantur.
Ipse Octavius se in scapham confert; in quam plures
cum confugerent, depressa scapha vulneratus tamen
adnatat ad suum myoparonem. Eo receptus, cum
proelium nox dirimeret, tempestate magna velis
profugit. Sequuntur hunc suae naves non nullae,
quas casus ab illo periculo vindicarat.

47 At Vatinius re bene gesta receptui cecinit suisque
omnibus incolumibus in eum se portum victor
recepit, quo ex portu classis Octavi ad dimicandum
processerat. Capit ex eo proelio penterem unam,
triremis duas, dicrotas VIII complurisque remiges
Octavianos posteroque ibi die, dum suas captivasque
navis reficeret, consumpto post diem tertium contendit in insulam Issam, quod eo se recepisse ex
fuga credebat Octavium. Erat in ea[1] nobilissimum
regionum earum oppidum coniunctissimumque
Octavio. Quo ut venit, oppidani supplices se Vatinio

[1] *The MSS. vary between* eum *and* ea. *Possibly some
unfamiliar place name produced the present readings. Thus
Larsen conjectured* Ratineum.

range in the narrow sea. The more closely inter-
locked the ships—whenever the opportunity was
afforded for such fighting—the more marked was the
superiority of the Vatinians; for they displayed
admirable courage in leaping without hesitation
from their own ships on to those of the enemy, and
where the fighting was on equal terms their markedly
superior courage brought them success. Octavius'
own quadrireme was sunk, and many besides were
either captured or else rammed, holed and sunk:
some of his combat troops were cut down on the
ships, others dived overboard. Octavius himself took
refuge in a pinnace; and when too many others
sought safety in it and it capsized, wounded as he
was he swam to his own light galley. There he was
taken safely aboard and, when night put an end to
the action, took to flight, sailing in a stiff squall.
He was followed by not a few of his own ships, which
chance had delivered from that hazard.

47   Vatinius, on the other hand, rounded off this
success by sounding the retreat and withdrew
triumphantly with his entire force intact to the
harbour from which Octavius' fleet had advanced to
do battle. As a result of that action he captured one
quinquereme, two triremes, eight two-banked galleys
and a large number of Octavius' rowers. The next
day he spent there in refitting his own and the
captured vessels; and on the day following he
hastened to the island of Issa, in the belief that
Octavius had taken refuge there in the course of his
flight. In it there was a town—the best known one
in those parts, and one which was on the most
friendly terms with Octavius. On the arrival of
Vatinius there the townsfolk threw themselves upon

dediderunt, comperitque ipsum Octavium parvis paucisque navigiis vento secundo regionem Graeciae petisse, inde ut Siciliam, deinde Africam caperet. Ita brevi spatio re praeclarissime gesta, provincia recepta et Cornificio reddita, classe adversariorum ex illo toto sinu expulsa victor se Brundisium incolumi exercitu et classe recepit.

48 Eis autem temporibus quibus Caesar ad Dyrrachium Pompeium obsidebat et Palaepharsali rem feliciter gerebat Alexandreaeque cum periculo magno tum etiam maiore periculi fama dimicabat, Q. Cassius Longinus, in Hispania pro praetore provinciae ulterioris obtinendae causa relictus, sive consuetudine naturae suae sive odio quod in illam provinciam susceperat quaestor ex insidiis ibi vulneratus, magnas odi sui fecerat accessiones, quod vel ex conscientia sua, cum de se mutuo sentire provinciam crederet, vel multis signis et testimoniis eorum qui difficulter odia dissimulabant animum advertere poterat, et compensare offensionem provinciae exercitus amore cupiebat. Itaque, cum primum in unum locum exercitum conduxit, sestertios centenos militibus est pollicitus, nec multo post, cum in Lusitania Medobregam oppidum montemque Herminium expugnasset, quo Medobregenses con-

---

[1] In September 49 B.C. Caesar himself may have doubted the wisdom of this appointment, but Longinus had served him well in the past.

his mercy, and he learned that Octavius himself with
a few small vessels had set course with a following
wind in the direction of Greece, intending to make
for Sicily next and then Africa. Thus in a short
space of time Vatinius had achieved a most notable
success, recovering the province and restoring it to
Cornificius, and driving his opponents' fleet away
from the whole of that coast. Whereupon he withdrew in triumph to Brundisium with his army and
fleet unharmed.

48   Now during the period when Caesar was besieging
Pompeius at Dyrrachium, and achieving success at
Old Pharsalus, and was engaged at Alexandria in
operations which involved great risk, though rumour
made it out to be still greater, Q. Cassius Longinus
had been left behind in Spain as propraetor to
govern the further province.[1] Whether it was due
to his own natural disposition, or because he had
formed a hatred for that province from having as
quaestor been treacherously wounded there, he had
greatly added to his unpopularity; which fact he
was in a position to observe equally from his own
intuition—believing as he did that the province
reciprocated his own sentiments—and from the
manifold signs and indications afforded by those who
found difficulty in concealing their feelings of hate;
and now he was anxious to offset the dislike felt by
the province with the affection of his army. Consequently, as soon as he had mustered the army all
together, he promised the soldiers one hundred
sesterces apiece; and not long afterwards in Lusitania, after successfully storming the town of Medobrega and then Mount Herminius, on which the
townsfolk had taken refuge, and being hailed there

fugerant, ibique imperator esset appellatus, sestertiis centenis milites donavit. Multa praeterea et magna praemia singulis concedebat; quae speciosum reddebant praesentem exercitus amorem, paulatim tamen et occulte militarem disciplinam severitatemque minuebant.

49 Cassius legionibus in hiberna dispositis ad ius dicendum Cordubam se recepit contractumque in ea aes alienum gravissimis oneribus provinciae constituit exsolvere; et ut largitionis postulat consuetudo, per causam liberalitatis speciosam plura largitori quaerebantur. Pecuniae locupletibus imperabantur, quas Longinus sibi expensas ferri non tantum patiebatur sed etiam cogebat, in gregem locupletium simultatium causa tenues coiciebantur, neque ullum genus quaestus aut magni et evidentis aut minimi et sordidi praetermittebatur quo domus et tribunal imperatoris vacaret. Nemo erat, qui modo aliquam iacturam facere posset, quin aut vadimonio teneretur aut in reos referretur. Ita magna etiam sollicitudo periculorum ad iacturas et detrimenta rei familiaris adiungebatur.

50 Quibus de causis accidit ut, cum Longinus imperator eadem faceret quae fecerat quaestor, similia rursus de morte eius provinciales consilia inirent. Horum odium confirmabant non nulli familiares eius qui, cum in illa societate versarentur rapinarum,

---

[1] From the sequel described in ch. 56 such appears to be the most likely interpretation of this phrase. The sums were to be entered up in the ledgers as paid out to Longinus as loans.

[2] Or, adopting Schneider's conjecture *simulationis causa,* 'were included in the lists of the wealthy for the sake of appearances'.

as Imperator, he presented the soldiers each with 100 sesterces. In addition he granted many large rewards to individuals; and though these gifts inspired in the army a semblance of affection for the moment, yet they gradually and insidiously undermined strict military discipline.

Having settled his legions in winter quarters, Cassius proceeded to Corduba to administer justice, and resolved to lay a very heavy impost on the province and so defray the debts he had incurred in it. And so, as the habit of bribery necessitates, openhandedness was the plausible excuse for seeking yet further contributions to the source of bribery. Wealthy men were ordered to furnish sums of money, and these Longinus not merely allowed but even compelled to be debited to his own account:[1] poor men were precipitated into conflict with the wealthy class to promote dissensions;[2] and no kind of profit, either large and obvious, or quite insignificant and mean, was overlooked, none with which the commander-in-chief was not involved privately and officially. There was not one man—provided only he had something to lose—but he was either held on bail or duly entered in the lists of the accused. Thus there was also a very uneasy presentiment of danger in addition to the sacrifices and losses of personal possessions.

For these reasons it so fell out that, since Longinus as commander-in-chief was employing the same tactics he had used as quaestor, the provincials once again embarked upon similar plans for his assassination. Their hatred was intensified by some of his friends who, although they were employed in that plundering partnership, none the less hated the man

nihilo minus oderant eum cuius nomine peccabant,
sibique quod rapuerant acceptum referebant, quod
interciderat aut erat interpellatum Cassio assigna-
bant. Quintam legionem novam conscribit. Auge-
tur odium et ex ipso dilectu et sumptu additae
legionis. Complentur equitum III milia maximisque
ornantur impensis: nec provinciae datur ulla requies.

51   Interim litteras accepit a Caesare, ut in Africam
exercitum traiceret perque Mauretaniam ad finis
Numidiae perveniret, quod magna Cn. Pompeio
Iuba miserat auxilia maioraque missurus existimabatur. Quibus litteris acceptis insolenti voluptate
efferebatur, quod sibi novarum provinciarum et
fertilissimi regni tanta oblata esset facultas. Itaque
ipse in Lusitaniam proficiscitur ad legiones arces-
sendas auxiliaque adducenda; certis hominibus dat
negotium ut frumentum navesque C praepararentur
pecuniaeque describerentur atque imperarentur, ne
qua res cum redisset moraretur. Reditus eius fuit
celerior omnium opinione: non enim labor aut
vigilantia cupienti praesertim aliquid Cassio deerat.

52   Exercitu coacto in unum locum castris ad Cordubam positis pro contione militibus exponit quas res
Caesaris iussu gerere deberet, polliceturque eis, cum
in Mauretaniam traiecisset, sestertios centenos [1] se
daturum; quintam fore in Hispania legionem. Ex

---

[1] centenos *is omitted in all the MSS., which vary between*
sestertios, sestertia *and* sestertiorum.

---

[1] Caesar had allotted him four—the native legion and the
Second; and the Twenty-First and Thirtieth (sent from Italy).
Whether this Fifth is the same legion as that mentioned in the
African and Spanish Wars is a very vexed question.

[2] No mention is made of these in the list of Pompey's
forces given in *Civil Wars* III, chs. 3–5.

in whose name they did wrong, and so, while putting down to their own credit whatever they had gained by their plundering, attributed to Cassius whatever came to nothing or was foiled. He enrolled a new legion—the Fifth.[1] Hatred increased as a result of the actual levy and the expense of the extra legion. The cavalry were brought up to a strength of three thousand and equipped at the greatest expense. No respite was given to the province.

Meanwhile he received despatches from Caesar bidding him bring an army across to Africa and, passing through Mauretania, come to the territory of Numidia; for Juba had sent large reinforcements[2] for Cn. Pompeius and would, it was thought, send larger ones. When Cassius received these despatches he was in transports of immoderate delight at the thought of his being offered so magnificent a chance of new provinces and a highly fertile kingdom. And so he set out in person for Lusitania to summon the legions and fetch auxiliaries, allotting certain men the task of organising in advance supplies of corn and 100 ships, as well as assessing and levying contributions of money, so as to avoid any delay on his return. His return proved more expeditious than anyone expected; for there was no lack of energy or vigilance in Cassius, especially when he coveted something.

He then assembled his army at a single rendezvous and pitched camp near Corduba. There at a parade he explained to his troops the scheme it was his duty to carry out on Caesar's instructions, and promised to give them 100 sesterces apiece when he had crossed over into Mauretania. The Fifth legion, he explained, would be in Spain. Then, after the

contione se Cordubam recepit eoque ipso die tempore
postmeridiano, cum in basilicam iret, quidam
Minucius Silo cliens L. Racili libellum, quasi aliquid
ab eo postularet, ut miles ei tradit, deinde post
Racilium—nam is latus Cassi tegebat—, quasi
responsum peteret, celeriter dato loco cum se
insinuasset, sinistra corripit aversum dextraque bis
ferit pugione. Clamore sublato fit a coniuratis
impetus universis. Munatius Flaccus proximum
gladio traicit lictorem; hoc interfecto Q. Cassium
legatum vulnerat. Ibi T. Vasius et L. Mercello
simili confidentia Flaccum, municipem suum, adiu-
vant: erant enim omnes Italicenses. Ad ipsum
Longinum L. Licinius Squillus involat iacentemque
levibus sauciat plagis.

53 Concurritur ad Cassium defendendum: semper
enim Berones complurisque evocatos cum telis
secum habere consuerat. A quibus ceteri inter-
cluduntur qui ad caedem faciendam subsequebantur;
quo in numero fuit Calpurnius Salvianus et Manilius
Tusculus. Minucius inter saxa quae iacebant in
itinere fugiens opprimitur et relato domum Cassio ad
eum deducitur. Racilius in proximam se domum
familiaris sui confert, dum certum cognosceret con-
fectusne Cassius esset. L. Laterensis, cum id non

---

[1] cf. ch. 57 below, where the same man is mentioned again
as deputy to Longinus : the coincidence of names is confusing.

[2] A town in Baetica, N.W. of Hispalis, founded by Scipio
Africanus and the birthplace of Hadrian and Trajan.

[3] The Berones are mentioned in Livy, fragment 91 as a
powerful tribe in Hispania Tarraconensis.

[4] Presumably he tripped and his pursuers were luckier !
The alternative rendering ' in the course of flight was overwhelmed amid (a volley of) stones which littered the street '
seems barely justified by the Latin expression, though it

parade, he returned to Corduba. That same after-
noon, when he was entering the judgment hall, a
certain Minucius Silo, who was a client of L. Racilius
and was dressed as a soldier, handed him a note, as
if he had some petition to make of him; then,
following behind Racilius—who was walking beside
Cassius—as though he were waiting for an answer, he
quickly wormed his way in between them when the
chance offered, seized Longinus from behind with his
left hand and with his right stabbed him twice with a
dagger. No sooner was the alarm raised than all the
conspirators joined in the attack. Munatius Flaccus
ran the nearest lictor through with his sword, killed
him and then wounded Q. Cassius, Longinus'
deputy.[1] Thereupon T. Vasius and M. Mercello
displayed a like audacity in going to the help of
Flaccus, their fellow-townsman; for they all hailed
from Italica.[2] L. Licinius Squillus rushed up to
Longinus himself and inflicted minor wounds upon
him as he lay prostrate.

53   On all sides there was a rush to defend Cassius;
for it was his constant habit to have with him a
numerous armed bodyguard of Beronians [3] and ex-
soldiers. These intercepted all the other would-be
assassins who were following up behind, and among
them Calpurnius Salvianus and Manilius Tusculus.
Minucius was caught as he sought to escape through
the stones which were lying in the street,[4] and was
escorted to Cassius, who had now been carried home.
Racilius took refuge in a friend's house near by,
until he should learn for certain whether Cassius was
done for. L. Laterensis had no doubt about it, and

would perhaps account more satisfactorily for the mention of
the stones.

95

dubitaret, accurrit laetus in castra militibusque vernaculis et secundae legionis, quibus odio sciebat praecipue Cassium esse, gratulatur; tollitur a multitudine in tribunal, praetor appellatur. Nemo enim aut in provincia natus, ut vernaculae legionis milites, aut diuturnitate iam factus provincialis, quo in numero erat secunda legio, non cum omni provincia consenserat in odio Cassi: nam legionem XXX. et XXI. paucis mensibus in Italia scriptas Caesar attribuerat Longino, quinta legio nuper ibi erat confecta.

54 Interim nuntiatur Laterensi vivere Cassium. Quo nuntio dolore magis permotus quam animo perturbatus reficit se celeriter et ad Cassium visendum proficiscitur. Re cognita XXX. legio signa Cordubam infert ad auxilium ferendum imperatori suo. Facit hoc idem XXI. Subsequitur has V. Cum duae legiones reliquae essent in castris, secundani, veriti ne soli relinquerentur atque ex eo quid sensissent iudicaretur, secuti sunt factum superiorum. Permansit in sententia legio vernacula nec ullo timore de gradu deiecta est.

55 Cassius eos qui nominati erant conscii caedis iubet comprehendi; legiones in castra remittit quinque cohortibus tricesimae retentis.[1] Indicio

[1] legiones V in castra remittit cohortibus XXX retentis *MSS.*: *I have adopted Kuebler's conjecture.*

so hastened joyfully into the camp and congratulated the native troops and those of the Second legion, who, as he knew, cherished a particular hatred for Cassius; and there the mob hoisted him on to the platform and hailed him as praetor. There was in fact no man, either born in the province, like the troops of the native legion, or else by this time qualified as a provincial by virtue of long residence—and the Second legion came into this category—who had not shared in the hatred which the entire province felt towards Cassius; for the Thirtieth and Twenty-First legions, which Caesar had allotted to Longinus, had been enrolled in Italy within the last few months, while the Fifth legion had been raised in the province but recently.

54   Meanwhile the tidings reached Laterensis that Cassius was alive. Not so much disconcerted as grievously disappointed by these tidings, he quickly recovered himself and set out to visit Cassius. On learning of the facts the Thirtieth legion advanced to Corduba to bring aid to their commander-in-chief: the Twenty-First did likewise; and the Fifth followed their lead. Now that there were but two remaining legions in camp, the men of the Second were afraid that they might be the only ones left behind, and that the nature of their sentiments might be inferred from this circumstance: consequently they followed the example of the previous legions. The native legion remained steadfast in its attitude, and nothing could intimidate it or make it budge.

55   Cassius ordered the arrest of those who had been named as privy to the murderous plot and, retaining five cohorts of the Thirtieth legion, sent the rest back to camp. From the evidence of Minucius he

97

Minuci cognoscit L. Racilium et L. Laterensem et
Annium Scapulam, maximae dignitatis et gratiae
provincialem hominem sibique tam familiarem quam
Laterensem et Racilium, in eadem fuisse coniura-
tione, nec diu moratur dolorem suum quin eos interfici iubeat. Minucium libertis tradit excruciandum,
item Calpurnium Salvianum, qui profitetur indicium
coniuratorumque numerum auget, vere, ut quidam
existimant, ut non nulli queruntur, coactus. Isdem
cruciatibus adfectus L. Mercello.[1] . . . Squillus
nominat pluris; quos Cassius interfici iubet exceptis
eis qui se pecunia redemerunt. Nam palam HS
LX[2] cum Calpurnio paciscitur et cum Q. Sestio L.
Qui si maxime nocentes sunt multati, tamen periculum vitae dolorque vulnerum pecuniae remissus
crudelitatem cum avaritia certasse significabat.

56   Aliquot post diebus litteras a Caesare missas
accipit, quibus cognoscit Pompeium in acie victum
amissis copiis fugisse. Qua re cognita mixtam
dolore voluptatem capiebat: victoriae nuntius
laetitiam exprimebat, confectum bellum licentiam
temporum intercludebat. Sic erat dubius animus
utrum nihil timere an omnia licere mallet. Sanatis
vulneribus arcessit omnis qui sibi pecunias expensas
tulerant, acceptasque eas iubet referri; quibus

---

[1] *Nipperdey assumed a lacuna here.*
[2] s͞h͞i X *MSS.* : HS LX *Glandorp.*

---

[1] The interpretation 60,000 'great sesterces' (10 times the
sum), though permissible, seems less likely.

learned that L. Racilius and L. Laterensis and Annius Scapula—the last a provincial of the highest standing and influence, with whom he was on as intimate a footing as with Racilius and Laterensis—had all been involved in that same conspiracy; and it was not long before he gave expression to his indignation by ordering their execution. Minucius he handed over to his freedmen for torture; likewise Calpurnius Salvianus, who made a formal deposition in which he named a larger number of conspirators—truthfully, according to the belief of certain people; under duress, as some complain. Similar torture was applied to L. Mercello: . . . Squillus mentioned more names. Cassius ordered their execution, except for those who bought themselves off. For example, he openly made a bargain in fact with Calpurnius for sixty thousand sesterces,[1] and with Q. Sestius for fifty thousand. And if their extreme guilt earned them a corresponding fine, yet the fact that the peril of death and the pain of torture was remitted for cash showed how in Cassius cruelty had vied with greed.

6   Several days later he received despatches sent by Caesar, from which he learned that Pompeius had been beaten in the field, lost his forces, and fled. This intelligence inspired in him mixed feelings—of disappointment and pleasure: the news of victory could not but make him happy: the completion of the war put an end to the present licence. Consequently he could not make up his mind whether he would rather have nothing to fear or nothing barred. When his wounds were healed he summoned all those who had booked sums of money as debited to his account and ordered the said sums to be entered

99

parum videbatur imposuisse oneris, ampliorem
pecuniam imperat. Equitum autem Romanorum
dilectum instituit; quos ex omnibus conventibus
coloniisque conscriptos transmarina militia per-
territos ad sacramenti redemptionem vocabat.
Magnum hoc fuit vectigal, maius tamen creabat
odium. His rebus confectis totum exercitum lustrat;
legiones quas in Africam ducturus erat et auxilia
mittit ad traiectum. Ipse classem quam parabat ut
inspiceret, Hispalim accedit ibique moratur, propterea quod edictum tota provincia proposuerat,
quibus pecunias imperasset neque contulissent, se
adirent. Quae evocatio vehementer omnis turbavit.
57 Interim L. Titius, qui eo tempore tribunus militum
in legione vernacula fuerat, nuntiat eam a legione
XXX., quam Q. Cassius legatus simul ducebat, cum
ad oppidum Ilipam castra haberet, seditione facta
centurionibus aliquot occisis qui signa tolli non
patiebantur, discessisse et ad secundam legionem
contendisse, quae ad fretum alio itinere ducebatur.
Cognita re noctu cum V cohortibus unetvice-
simanorum egreditur, mane pervenit Naevam.[1] Ibi

[1] noctu *MSS*. Naevam *Schneider*.

---

[1] The sums here referred to appear to be those mentioned
in ch. 49, and the meaning seems to be that the outstanding
debts were written off in the ledgers as repaid, though in fact
Longinus kept the money. But as the two terms *expensas*
and *acceptas* denote the opposite sides of the ledger, the meaning might conceivably be that the outstanding debts were not
merely cancelled, but reversed; and that the sums were to
be entered up afresh as borrowed from (*acceptas*), not lent to
(*expensas*), Longinus. He would thus receive them twice
over. The following clause perhaps favours this latter
interpretation.

up as repaid;[1] and where he seemed to have imposed too light a burden, he ordered the man to pay a greater sum. Moreover, he held a levy of Roman knights. These were conscripted from all the corporations[2] and colonies and, as they were thoroughly scared of military service overseas, he invited them to purchase their discharge. This proved a great source of profit, but the hatred it produced was still greater. This done, he reviewed his entire army and then despatched to the point of embarkation the legions he intended to take into Africa, with their auxiliary troops. He himself proceeded to Hispalis to inspect the fleet he was building up; and there he tarried awhile, since he had published a decree throughout the province that those who had been ordered to contribute, but had not yet contributed sums of money, must come before him. This summons disturbed them all profoundly.

7 Meanwhile L. Titius brought tidings of the native legion, in which he had been at the time a military tribune: his report ran that while it was encamped near the town of Ilipa a mutiny had broken out, and several centurions who had refused to let them strike camp had been killed; the legion had then parted company with the Thirtieth legion—this was also under command of Q. Cassius, the governor's deputy—and made haste to join the Second legion, which was being taken to the straits by another route. On learning of the matter Longinus left by night with five cohorts of the Twenty-First legion, and early in the morning arrived at Naeva.[3] There

[2] These were guilds of Roman citizens associated for purposes of trade in the various provincial towns.

[3] Its exact location is unknown: see Index. Andrieu, however, identifies it with Villaverde, 27 km. from Seville.

eum diem, ut quid ageretur perspiceret, moratus Carmonem contendit. Hic, cum legio XXX. et XXI. et cohortes IIII ex V. legione totusque convenisset equitatus, audit IIII cohortis a vernaculis oppressas ad Obuculam cum his ad secundam pervenisse legionem omnisque ibi se coniunxisse et T. Thorium Italicensem ducem delegisse. Celeriter habito consilio M. Marcellum quaestorem Cordubam, ut eam in potestate retineret, Q. Cassium legatum Hispalim mittit. Paucis ei diebus affertur conventum Cordubensem ab eo defecisse Marcellumque aut voluntate aut necessitate adductum—namque id varie nuntiabatur—consentire cum Cordubensibus; duas cohortis legionis V., quae fuerant Cordubae in praesidio, idem facere. Cassius his rebus incensus movet castra et postero die Segoviam ad flumen Singiliense venit. Ibi habita contione militum temptat animos; quos cognoscit non sua sed Caesaris absentis causa sibi fidissimos esse nullumque periculum deprecaturos, dum per eos Caesari provincia restitueretur.

58   Interim Thorius ad Cordubam veteres legiones adducit ac, ne dissensionis initium natum seditiosa militum suaque natura videretur, simul ut contra Q.

---

¹ Its exact location is unknown : see Index.

he waited that day, in order to get a clear view of
what was taking place: then he marched to Carmo.
Here he was joined by the Thirtieth legion
and the Twenty-First, with four cohorts of the Fifth
and his entire cavalry force, and then heard that four
cohorts had been overpowered by the native troops,
and in company with the latter had made contact
with the second legion near Obucula,[1] where they
had all joined forces and chosen T. Thorius, a native
of Italica, as their leader. He promptly held a
consultation and despatched the quaestor, M.
Marcellus, to Corduba, to retain control of it, and
Q. Cassius, his deputy, to Hispalis. Within a few
days news was brought to him that the corporation of
Corduba had revolted from him, and that Marcellus,
either of his own free will, or under compulsion—
reports varied on this point—was hand in glove with
the men of Corduba; and that the two cohorts of the
Fifth legion which had formed the garrison force of
Corduba were taking a similar line. Incensed by
these reports Cassius struck camp, and on the morrow
came to Segovia[1] on the river Singilis. There he
held a parade and sounded the temper of his troops,
learning thereby that it was not for his own sake,
but for the sake of the absent Caesar that they were
entirely loyal to himself, and that there was no
hazard they would not face without a murmur, so be
they were the means of restoring the province to
Caesar.

58   Meanwhile Thorius led his veteran legions towards
Corduba. To avoid the impression that the quarrel
had originally arisen from any natural tendency to
mutiny on his own part or on that of his troops,
and at the same time to counter Q. Cassius—who, as

Cassium, qui Caesaris nomine maioribus viribus uti
videbatur, aeque potentem opponeret dignitatem,
Cn. Pompeio se provinciam reciperare velle palam
dictitabat. Et forsitan etiam hoc fecerit odio
Caesaris et amore Pompei, cuius nomen multum
poterat apud eas legiones quas M. Varro obtinuerat.
Sed id qua mente, communis erat coniectura:
certe hoc prae se Thorius ferebat; milites adeo
fatebantur, ut Cn. Pompei nomen in scutis inscriptum
haberent. Frequens legionibus conventus obviam
prodit, neque tantum virorum sed etiam matrum
familias ac praetextatorum, deprecaturque ne hostili
adventu Cordubam diriperent: nam se contra Cassium consentire cum omnibus; contra Caesarem ne
facere cogerentur orare.

59   Tantae multitudinis precibus et lacrimis exercitus
commotus cum videret ad Cassium persequendum
nihil opus esse Cn. Pompei nomine et memoria
tamque omnibus Caesarianis quam Pompeianis
Longinum esse in odio neque se conventum neque M.
Marcellum contra Caesaris causam posse perducere,
nomen Pompei ex scutis detraxerunt, Marcellum,
qui se Caesaris causam defensurum profitebatur,
ducem asciverunt praetoremque appellarunt et
conventum sibi adiunxerunt castraque ad Cordubam
posuerunt. Cassius eo biduo circiter IIII milia
passuum a Corduba citra flumen Baetim in oppidi

---

[1] Both the native and the second legion had served under
Varro.

it appeared, was operating in the name of Caesar with forces more powerful than his own—with no less weighty an authority, he kept openly asserting that it was for Cn. Pompeius that he wished to recover the province. And it may even be that he did so wish, owing to his hatred for Caesar and affection for Pompey, the latter's name carrying great weight with those legions which M. Varro had held.[1] But what his motive was in this was a matter for general conjecture. At any rate that was what Thorius gave out; and his troops acknowledged it to the extent that they had the name of Cn. Pompeius carved on their shields. A vast concourse of citizens came forth to meet the legions, not only of men but also of matrons and youths, beseeching them not to approach Corduba as enemies and plunder it: they themselves in fact shared in the universal antagonism against Cassius; and they prayed they might not be compelled to act against Caesar.

59 The tears and entreaties of this vast multitude had no little effect upon the army; it saw too that to punish Cassius it had no need of the name and memory of Cn. Pompeius; that Longinus was equally hateful to all the adherents of Caesar as he was to those of Pompey; and that it could induce neither the citizen corporation of Corduba nor Marcellus to act contrary to Caesar's interest. Accordingly they removed Pompey's name from their shields, adopted Marcellus, who professed his intention to champion Caesar's cause, as their leader and hailed him as praetor, made common cause with the citizen corporation, and pitched their camp near Corduba. Within two days Cassius pitched camp on his side of the river Baetis some four miles distant from Corduba,

conspectu loco excelso facit castra; litteras ad regem Bogudem in Mauretaniam et ad M. Lepidum proconsulem in Hispaniam citeriorem mittit, subsidio sibi provinciaeque Caesaris causa quam primum veniret. Ipse hostili modo Cordubensium agros vastat, aedificia incendit.

60 Cuius rei deformitate atque indignitate legiones quae Marcellum sibi ducem ceperant ad eum concurrerunt, ut in aciem educerentur orant, priusque confligendi sibi potestas fieret quam cum tanta contumelia nobilissimae carissimaeque possessiones Cordubensium in conspectu suo rapinis, ferro flammaque consumerentur. Marcellus cum confligere miserrimum putaret, quod et victoris et victi detrimentum ad eundem Caesarem esset redundaturum neque suae potestatis esset, legiones Baetim traducit aciemque instruit. Cum Cassium contra pro suis castris aciem instruxisse loco superiore videret, causa interposita, quod is in aequum non descenderet, Marcellus militibus persuadet ut se recipiant in castra. Itaque copias reducere coepit. Cassius, quo bono valebat Marcellumque infirmum esse sciebat, aggressus equitatu legionarios se recipientis compluris novissimos in fluminis ripis interfecit. Cum hoc detrimento quid transitus fluminis viti difficultatisque haberet cognitum esset, Marcellus castra Baetim transfert, crebroque uterque legiones

in a lofty position in sight of the town. He sent despatches to king Bogud in Mauretania and to M. Lepidus, the pro-consul, in Hither Spain, urging each to come as soon as possible to the aid of himself and the province, in the interest of Caesar. He himself laid waste in hostile fashion the territory of Corduba and set buildings ablaze.

The hideous and outrageous character of this action led the legions which had taken Marcellus for their leader to rush to him in a body and beg him that they might be led out to battle and granted an opportunity of engaging the enemy before those most illustrious and beloved possessions of the people of Corduba should suffer the grievous ignominy of being consumed before their very eyes by plunder, fire and sword. Though Marcellus thought it a thousand pities to engage, since the loss sustained by victor and vanquished alike would in either case have repercussions on Caesar, and it lay outside his power to control it, yet he took his legions across the Baetis and drew up his line. On seeing that Cassius had drawn up his line facing him on higher ground in front of his own camp, Marcellus prevailed upon his troops to withdraw to their camp, putting them off with the excuse that the enemy refused to come down into the plain. And so he proceeded to withdraw his forces. Cassius employed his excellent cavalry— in which arm he was strong, and knew Marcellus to be weak—to attack the retreating legionaries, and killed quite a number of their rearguard on the banks of the river. Made aware by this loss of the draw-back and difficulty involved in crossing the river, Marcellus transferred his camp to the other side of the Baetis. Now both commanders frequently led

in aciem educit; neque tamen confligitur propter locorum difficultates.

61 Erat copiis pedestribus multo firmior Marcellus; habebat enim veteranas multisque proeliis expertas legiones. Cassius fidei magis quam virtuti legionum confidebat. Itaque, cum castra castris collata essent et Marcellus locum idoneum castello cepisset quo prohibere aqua Cassianos posset, Longinus, veritus ne genere quodam obsidionis clauderetur in regionibus alienis sibique infestis, noctu silentio ex castris proficiscitur celerique itinere Uliam contendit, quod sibi fidele esse oppidum credebat. Ibi adeo coniuncta ponit moenibus castra ut et loci natura—namque Ulia in edito monte posita est—et ipsa munitione urbis undique ab oppugnatione tutus esset. Hunc Marcellus insequitur et quam proxime potest Uliam castra castris confert locorumque cognita natura, quo maxime rem deducere volebat, necessitate est deductus ut neque confligeret—cuius si rei facultas esset, resistere incitatis militibus non poterat— neque vagari Cassium latius pateretur, ne plures civitates ea paterentur quae passi erant Cordubenses. Castellis idoneis locis collocatis operibusque in circuitu oppidi continuatis Uliam Cassiumque munitionibus clausit. Quae prius quam perficerentur,

out their legions to battle; there was, however, no engagement owing to the difficult nature of the ground.

Marcellus was much stronger in infantry forces; for the legions he had were veteran ones, tested in many campaigns. Cassius relied on the loyalty rather than the valour of his legions. Consequently when the two camps had been pitched over against one another and Marcellus had selected a position suitable for a stronghold which might enable him to prevent the enemy troops from getting water, Longinus was afraid of being shut up by a virtual blockade in territory controlled by others and hostile to himself; and so he silently set out from his camp by night and marched swiftly to Ulia, a town which he believed to be loyal to himself. There he pitched his camp so close to the walls of the town that not only its natural position—for Ulia is situated on a lofty mountain—but also the actual fortification of the city made him safe on all sides from assault. Marcellus pursued him and pitched his camp over against the enemy camp as close to Ulia as he could. When he had appreciated the nature of the ground, he had inevitably to resort to the very tactics to which above all he wanted to resort, namely refraining from an engagement—and had there been an opportunity for engaging he could not have held in check his excited troops—and at the same time not allowing Cassius to roam too far afield, to prevent more communities from suffering the fate of the inhabitants of Corduba. By siting strongholds at suitable points and carrying his field-works in a continuous ring round the town, he hemmed in Ulia and Cassius with entrenchments. But before these

Longinus omnem suum equitatum emisit; quem
magno sibi usu fore credebat, si pabulari frumen-
tarique Marcellum non pateretur, magno autem fore
impedimento, si clausus obsidione et inutilis necessarium consumeret frumentum.

62 Paucis diebus Q. Cassi litteris acceptis rex Bogus
cum copiis venit adiungitque ei legioni quam secum
adduxerat compluris cohortis auxiliarias Hispanorum.
Namque ut in civilibus dissensionibus accidere consuevit, ita temporibus illis in Hispania non nullae
civitates rebus Cassi studebant, plures Marcellum
fovebant. Accedit cum copiis Bogus ad exteriores
Marcelli munitiones. Pugnatur utrimque acriter,
crebroque id accidit fortuna saepe ad utrumque
victoriam transferente; nec tamen umquam ab
operibus depellitur Marcellus.

63 Interim Lepidus ex citeriore provincia cum
cohortibus legionariis XXXV magnoque numero
equitum et reliquorum auxiliorum venit ea mente
Uliam, ut sine ullo studio contentiones Cassi Mar-
cellique componeret. Huic venienti sine dubitatione
Marcellus se credit atque offert; Cassius contra
suis se tenet praesidiis, sive eo quod plus sibi iuris
deberi quam Marcello existimabat, sive eo quod ne
praeoccupatus animus Lepidi esset obsequio adversarii verebatur. Ponit ad Uliam castra Lepidus
neque habet a Marcello quicquam divisi. Ne
pugnetur interdicit; ad exeundum Cassium invitat

could be completed, Longinus sent out his entire cavalry force, in the belief that it would stand him in very good stead if it stopped Marcellus from collecting fodder and corn, whereas it would prove a great handicap if, shut up by blockade and rendered useless, it used up precious corn.

2 Within a few days king Bogud, having received Q. Cassius' despatches, arrived with his forces; he had brought one legion with him, and to this he now added several auxiliary cohorts of Spanish troops. For, as usually happens in civil wars, some states in Spain at that time were supporters of Cassius, though a larger number warmly espoused the cause of Marcellus. Bogud and his forces came up to the outer entrenchments of Marcellus: sharp fighting broke out between the two sides, and this recurred at frequent intervals, with the tide of fortune often turning from one side to the other. Marcellus, however, was never dislodged from his field-works.

3 Meanwhile Lepidus came to Ulia from the nearer province with thirty-five legionary cohorts and a large number of cavalry and other auxiliary troops, his object being to resolve, quite impartially, the dispute between Cassius and Marcellus. On his arrival Marcellus without hesitation put himself confidently into Lepidus' hands. Cassius, on the other hand, remained within his own defences, either because he thought that a greater measure of justice was due to himself than to Marcellus, or else because he was afraid that Lepidus' attitude might have been biased by the deference shewn him by his opponent. Lepidus pitched his camp near Ulia, in complete accord with Marcellus. He refused to allow any fighting, invited Cassius to come out, and pledged

fidemque suam in re omni interponit. Cum diu
dubitasset Cassius quid sibi faciendum quidve Lepido
esset credendum, neque ullum exitum consili sui
reperiret si permaneret in sententia, postulat uti
munitiones disicerentur sibique liber exitus daretur.
Non tantum indutiis factis sed prope iam pace [1]
constituta opera cum [2] complanarent custodiaeque
munitionum essent deductae, auxilia regis in id
castellum Marcelli quod proximum erat regis castris,
neque opinantibus omnibus—si tamen in omnibus
fuit Cassius : nam de huius conscientia dubitabatur—,
impetum fecerunt complurisque ibi milites oppres-
serunt. Quod nisi celeriter indignatione et auxilio
Lepidi proelium esset diremptum, maior calamitas
esset accepta.

64   Cum iter Cassio patefactum esset, castra Marcellus
cum Lepido coniungit. Lepidus eodem tempore
Marcellusque Cordubam cum suis, Cassius proficiscitur Carmonem. Sub idem tempus Trebonius pro-
consul ad provinciam obtinendam venit. De cuius
adventu ut cognovit Cassius, legiones quas secum
habuerat equitatumque in hiberna distribuit; ipse
omnibus suis rebus celeriter correptis Malacam
contendit ibique adverso tempore navigandi navis
conscendit, ut ipse praedicabat, ne se Lepido et
Trebonio et Marcello committeret, ut amici eius
dictitabant, ne per eam provinciam minore cum

---

[1] pace *added by Nipperdey.*   [2] cum *added by Aldus.*

his word to every offer he made. For a long time
Cassius was in doubt as to what he should do or what
confidence he should place in Lepidus; but as he
could find no solution to his policy if he remained
steadfast in his decision, he demanded that the
entrenchments should be demolished and that he
himself should be granted leave to depart unmolested.
Not only had a truce been made, but by now a peace-
ful settlement had been all but arranged, and they
were dismantling the fieldworks and the sentries
manning the entrenchments had been withdrawn,
when, though nobody expected it—if indeed nobody
included Cassius, for there was some doubt as to his
complicity—the king's auxiliary forces launched an
attack upon the stronghold of Marcellus nearest the
king's camp, and overpowered a number of troops in
it. And had not Lepidus in righteous anger promptly
lent his assistance to break up that fray, a greater
disaster would have been sustained.

34   Now that the way lay open to Cassius, Marcellus
joined his camp to that of Lepidus. Lepidus and
Marcellus then set out with their forces simultaneously for Corduba, Cassius for Carmo. Round
about the same time Trebonius came to govern the Feb. 47.
province as pro-consul. When Cassius learned of his
coming he posted the legions under his command
and the cavalry to their various winter-quarters; as
for himself, he hurriedly grabbed all his belongings
and hastened to Malaca, where he embarked,
although the season was unfavourable for navigation.
His object, as he personally averred, was to avoid
committing himself to Lepidus, Trebonius and
Marcellus: as his friends asserted, to avoid the
relative humiliation of travelling through a province

113

dignitate iter faceret cuius magna pars ab eo
defecerat, ut ceteri existimabant, ne pecunia illa ex
infinitis rapinis confecta in potestatem cuiusquam
veniret. Progressus secunda ut hiberna tempestate
cum in Hiberum flumen noctis vitandae causa se
contulisset, inde paulo vehementiore tempestate,
nihilo periculosius se navigaturum credens, profectus,
adversis fluctibus occurrentibus ostio fluminis, in
ipsis faucibus, cum neque flectere navem propter vim
fluminis neque directam tantis fluctibus tenere posset,
demersa nave periit.

65   Cum in Syriam Caesar ex Aegypto venisset atque
ab eis qui Roma venerant ad eum cognosceret
litterisque urbanis animadverteret multa Romae
male et inutiliter administrari neque ullam partem
rei publicae satis commode geri, quod et conten-
tionibus tribuniciis perniciosae seditiones orirentur et
ambitione atque indulgentia tribunorum militum et
qui legionibus praeerant multa contra morem con-
suetudinemque militarem fierent, quae dissolvendae
disciplinae severitatisque essent, eaque omnia flagi-
tare adventum suum videret, tamen praeferendum
existimabat, quas in provincias regionesque venisset,
eas ita relinquere constitutas ut domesticis dissensionibus liberarentur, iura legesque acciperent,
externorum hostium metum deponerent. Haec in

---

[1] He touched first at Ace Ptolemais on the Syrian coast
about mid-June (Holmes), early July (Stoffel).

[2] The main causes of unrest were economic; in particular
Caesar's measures for the relief of debt were too mild for
extremists like Caelius and, later, Dolabella : see also Introduction to *Bell. Afr.*, p. 139.

a great part of which had revolted from him: as everyone else believed, to avoid letting that money of his—the proceeds of innumerable robberies—fall into the hands of anyone else. At first he made some headway in weather which, considering it was winter, was favourable; but after he had taken shelter in the river Ebro to avoid sailing by night, the weather then became somewhat stormier; believing, however, that he would run no greater risk if he sailed, he set forth: but what with the swell rolling in head on against the river mouth, and the strong current preventing him from putting about just as the huge waves made it impossible to hold on straight ahead, his ship sank in the very mouth of the river, and so he perished.

On his arrival in Syria [1] from Egypt Caesar learned from those who had joined him there from Rome, as well as from information contained in despatches from the city, that there was much that was bad and unprofitable in the administration at Rome, and that no department of the government was being really efficiently conducted [2]; for rivalries among the tribunes, it was said, were producing dangerous rifts, and the flattering indulgence shewn to their troops by the military tribunes and legionary commanders was giving rise to many practices opposed to military custom and usage which tended to undermine strict discipline. All this, as he saw, urgently demanded his presence: yet, for all that, he thought it more important to leave all the provinces and districts he visited organised in such a way that they would be immune from internal disagreements, would accept a legal constitution, and lay aside their fears of aggression from without. This he was

Syria, Cilicia, Asia celeriter se confecturum sperabat,
quod hae provinciae nullo bello premebantur; in
Bithynia ac Ponto plus oneris videbat sibi impendere.
Non excessisse enim Ponto Pharnacen audiebat
neque excessurum putabat, cum secundo proelio
vehementer esset inflatus quod contra Domitium
Calvinum fecerat. Commoratus fere in omnibus
civitatibus quae maiore sunt dignitate, praemia bene
meritis et viritim et publice tribuit, de controversiis
veteribus cognoscit ac statuit; reges, tyrannos,
dynastas provinciae finitimos, qui omnes ad eum con-
currerant, receptos in fidem condicionibus impositis
provinciae tuendae ac defendendae dimittit et sibi et
populo Romano amicissimos.

66 Paucis diebus in ea provincia consumptis Sextum
Caesarem, amicum et necessarium suum, legionibus
Syriaeque praeficit; ipse eadem classe qua venerat
proficiscitur in Ciliciam. Cuius provinciae civitates
omnis evocat Tarsum, quod oppidum fere totius
Ciliciae nobilissimum fortissimumque est. Ibi rebus
omnibus provinciae et finitimarum civitatium con-
stitutis cupiditate proficiscendi ad bellum gerendum
non diutius moratur, magnisque itineribus per
Cappadociam confectis biduum Mazacae commoratus
Comana venit,[1] vetustissimum et sanctissimum in
Cappadocia Bellonae templum, quod tanta religione

---

[1] venit *is read by two MSS., but is omitted by the rest.*

---

[1] He sailed from Seleucia, the port of Antioch, for Tarsus,
probably early in July, 47.

[2] This sentence, as the text stands, presents a difficulty;
for it implies that, despite his urgent haste, Caesar made a
detour of 60 miles S.E. from Mazaca to visit the Cappadocian
Comana. Strabo and Appian say that it was the Pontic,
not the Cappadocian, Comana that Caesar visited, and possibly
our author was confused.

confident he would speedily achieve in Syria, Cilicia
and Asia, as these provinces had no war afflicting
them: in Bithynia and Pontus he had, as he saw, a
heavier task impending. For he heard that Pharnaces had not evacuated Pontus, and he did not
expect him to do so, exceedingly puffed up as he was
by the successful battle he had fought against
Domitius Calvinus. He spent some time in practically all the more important states of Syria,
bestowing rewards both upon individuals and communities where they deserved them, and holding
official inquiries and giving his ruling in questions
of long-standing dispute; while as for the kings,
sovereigns and rulers who, as neighbours of the
province, had one and all flocked to him, he formally
took them under his protection and then, on condition that they undertook to watch over and guard
the province, he dismissed them as very loyal
friends both to himself and the Roman people.

66 After spending a few days in that province he
posted Sextus Caesar, his friend and kinsman, to
command the legions and govern Syria: he himself
set out [1] for Cilicia in the same fleet in which he had
arrived. He then summoned all the states of this
latter province to forgather at Tarsus—perhaps the
most famous and strongest township in the whole
of Cilicia. There he settled all the affairs of the
province and its neighbouring states; but when he
had done so, his eagerness to set out and prosecute
the war admitted no further delay; and so, after
traversing Cappadocia by forced marches and staying
two days at Mazaca, he reached Comana, where is
the shrine of Bellona—the most ancient and holiest
in Cappadocia.[2] This shrine is worshipped with such

CAESAR

colitur ut sacerdos eius deae maiestate, imperio,
potentia secundus a rege consensu gentis illius
habeatur. Id homini nobilissimo Lycomedi Bithyno
adiudicavit, qui regio Cappadocum genere ortus iure
minime dubio, vetustate tamen propter adversam
fortunam maiorum suorum mutationemque generis
intermisso sacerdotium id repetebat. Fratri autem
Ariobarzanis Ariarathi, cum bene meritus uterque
eorum de re publica esset, ne aut regni hereditas
Ariarathen sollicitaret aut heres regni terreret
Ariobarzanen, partem Armeniae minoris concessit,
eumque Ariobarzani attribuit qui sub eius imperio ac
dicione esset.[1] Ipse iter inceptum simili velocitate
conficere coepit.

67 Cum propius Pontum finisque Gallograeciae
accessisset, Deiotarus, tetrarches Gallograeciae tum
quidem paene totius, quod ei neque legibus neque
moribus concessum esse ceteri tetrarchae contende-
bant, sine dubio autem rex Armeniae minoris ab
senatu appellatus, depositis regiis insignibus neque
tantum privato vestitu sed etiam reorum habitu
supplex ad Caesarem venit oratum ut sibi ignosceret,
quod in ea parte positus terrarum quae nulla praesidia
Caesaris habuisset exercitibus imperiisque coactus [2]

[1] *this sentence is in great disorder in the MSS.: I have
adopted Nipperdey's reading.*
[2] coactus *added by Glandorp.*

---

[1] Better known as Galatia.
[2] For his assistance to the Romans against Mithridates
Deiotarus had been rewarded by Pompey with grants of
land in eastern Pontus and the title of king : Lesser Armenia
may have been given him at the same time. He was originally
tetrarch of western Galatia only, and his claim to central
Galatia as well is a matter of some obscurity.

reverence that the priest of that goddess is held by common consent of the nation to rank next to the king in majesty, dominion and influence. This priesthood he awarded to Lycomedes, a Bithynian of very noble descent, who sought it by right of inheritance; for he was sprung from the royal Cappadocian house, his claim in this respect being, in point of legal right, by no means in doubt, though, in long passing of time, because of the chequered fortunes of his ancestors and changes in the royal line of descent, continuity had been broken. As for Ariobarzanes and his brother Ariarathes, both of them had deserved well of the Republic; and so, to prevent Ariarathes from being tempted to claim his inheritance to the kingdom, or, as heir to it, from intimidating Ariobarzanes, Caesar granted him part of Lesser Armenia and allowed Ariobarzanes to treat him as his vassal. Whereupon Caesar himself proceeded to complete the remainder of his journey with similar despatch.

When Caesar approached closer to Pontus and the boundaries of Gallograecia,[1] he was met by Deiotarus. Although the latter's position at that time as tetrarch of practically the whole of Gallograecia was disputed by all his fellow tetrarchs as inadmissible both by law and by tradition, he was, however, indisputably hailed as king of Lesser Armenia by the Senate[2]; and now he laid aside his royal insignia and, dressed not merely as a private person but actually in the garb of defendants in the courts, he came to Caesar as a suppliant to beg his pardon for having been on the side of Cn. Pompeius. He explained that, situated as he was in a part of the world which had had no garrisons of Caesar's to protect

119

in Cn. Pompei castris fuisset: neque enim se debuisse iudicem esse controversiarum populi Romani, sed parere praesentibus imperiis.

68 Contra quem Caesar, cum plurima sua commemorasset officia quae consul ei decretis publicis tribuisset, cumque defensionem eius nullam posse excusationem eius imprudentiae recipere coarguisset, quod homo tantae prudentiae ac diligentiae scire potuisset quis urbem Italiamque teneret, ubi senatus populusque Romanus, ubi res publica esset, quis denique post L. Lentulum, C. Marcellum consul esset, tamen se concedere id factum superioribus suis beneficiis, veteri hospitio atque amicitiae, dignitati aetatique hominis, precibus eorum qui frequentes concurrissent hospites atque amici Deiotari ad deprecandum, de controversiis tetrarcharum postea se cogniturum esse dixit, regium vestitum ei restituit. Legionem autem eam quam ex genere civium suorum Deiotarus armatura disciplinaque nostra constitutam habebat equitatumque omnem ad bellum gerendum adducere iussit.

69 Cum in Pontum venisset copiasque omnis in unum locum coegisset, quae numero atque exercitatione bellorum mediocres erant—excepta enim legione sexta, quam secum abduxerat Alexandrea veteranam

---

[1] As consul in 59 B.C. Caesar had got the Senate to ratify the grants of land with which Pompey had rewarded him.

[2] Lentulus and Marcellus were consuls in 49 B.C.: Caesar and Servilius in 48.

[3] This appears to be the meaning of *superioribus suis beneficiis, viz.* ' past acts of kindness done by Deiotarus to Caesar '. Others interpret the words as meaning ' acts of kindness done by Caesar '; but though this would be the

it, he had been compelled to do so by orders backed by armed force; for it had been no business of his to act as judge in the disputes of the Roman people, but only to obey the commands of the moment.

8 In his reply Caesar reminded him of all the many loyal services he himself as consul had rendered to him by official decrees,[1] and went on to point out that his apology could not be accepted as any excuse for his unwisdom; a man, in fact, as wise and careful as he was could have known who was master of Rome and Italy, what was the attitude of the Senate and the Roman people and the position taken up by the government, who in short was consul after L. Lentulus and C. Marcellus.[2] 'Nevertheless,' he continued, 'I make allowance for that action of yours in view of your past generosity towards myself,[3] our long-standing ties of hospitality and friendship, your rank and age, and the entreaties of all those guests and friends of yours who have flocked in crowds to entreat for your pardon. As for the matters in dispute between the tetrarchs, I shall examine into them later.' He then bade Deiotarus resume his royal garb, but ordered him to bring that legion of his, which was raised from the ranks of his own countrymen but in equipment and training organised on our pattern, together with all his cavalry, for the prosecution of the war.

9 On his arrival in Pontus Caesar mustered his whole force at a single rendezvous. It was but a modest force both numerically and in practical experience in the field; for apart from the Sixth legion, which he had brought with him from Alexandria—and this,

more obvious and usual meaning of the phrase, it scarcely suits the present context.

multis laboribus periculisque functam multisque
militibus partim difficultate itinerum ac naviga-
tionum partim crebritate bellorum adeo deminutam,
ut minus mille hominibus in ea esset, reliquae erant
tres legiones, una Deiotari, duae quae in eo proelio
quod Cn. Domitium fecisse cum Pharnace scripsimus
fuerant—, legati a Pharnace missi Caesarem adeunt
atque imprimis deprecantur ne eius adventus hostilis
esset: facturum enim omnia Pharnacen quae
imperata essent. Maximeque commemorabant nulla
Pharnacen auxilia contra Caesarem Pompeio dare
voluisse, cum Deiotarus, qui dedisset, tamen ei
satisfecisset.

70 Caesar respondit se fore aequissimum Pharnaci, si
quae polliceretur repraesentaturus esset. Monuit
autem, ut solebat, mitibus verbis legatos, ne aut
Deiotarum sibi obicerent aut nimis eo gloriarentur
beneficio, quod auxilia Pompeio non misissent. Nam
se neque libentius facere quicquam quam supplicibus
ignoscere neque provinciarum publicas iniurias con-
donare eis posse qui fuissent in se officiosi. Quin [1] id
ipsum quod commemorarent officium fuisse utilius
Pharnaci, qui providisset ne vinceretur, quam sibi
cui di immortales victoriam tribuissent. Itaque se

[1] quam *MSS.*: quin *Nipperdey.*

being a veteran one with a long record of hazardous and strenuous achievements, had lost so many men, due partly to the difficulties of transit both by land and sea, partly to the frequency of its campaigns, and was now so much below strength as to comprise less than one thousand troops—apart from the Sixth, the remainder of the force consisted of three legions— one belonging to Deiotarus, and the two which had taken part in that engagement which Cn. Domitius fought with Pharnaces, as I have related. Where- upon envoys sent by Pharnaces approached Caesar and first and foremost entreated him not to approach their country in any hostile spirit, since Pharnaces would carry out all his instructions. In particular they reminded Caesar that Pharnaces had refused to provide Pompeius with any auxiliary troops for use against Caesar; whereas Deiotarus, who had pro- vided them, had none the less given him satisfaction.

70   Caesar replied that he would be scrupulously fair to Pharnaces if the latter intended to carry out his promises. He warned the envoys, however, in his usual tactful language, not to tax him with the case of Deiotarus or pride themselves unduly on their good services in having refused to send Pompeius auxiliary troops. For whereas nothing gave him greater pleasure than granting pardon when it was humbly entreated, yet it was impossible for him to condone public outrages against the provinces in the case of those who had been loyal towards himself. ' In point of fact,' he went on, ' that very act of loyalty which you call to mind proved more expedient to Pharnaces, who thereby had the foresight to avoid defeat, than to myself, for whose victory the immortal gods were responsible. As for the great and serious outrages

123

magnas et gravis iniurias civium Romanorum qui in
Ponto negotiati essent, quoniam in integrum restituere non posset, concedere Pharnaci. Nam neque
interfectis amissam vitam neque exsectis virilitatem
restituere posse; quod quidem supplicium gravius
morte cives Romani subissent. Ponto vero decederet
confestim familiasque publicanorum remitteret
ceteraque restitueret sociis civibusque Romanis quae
penes eum essent. Si fecisset, iam tunc sibi mitteret
munera ac dona quae bene rebus gestis imperatores
ab amicis accipere consuessent. Miserat enim
Pharnaces coronam auream. His responsis datis
legatos remisit.

71 At Pharnaces liberaliter omnia pollicitus, cum
festinantem ac praecurrentem Caesarem speraret
libentius etiam crediturum suis promissis quam res
pateretur, quo celerius honestiusque ad res magis
necessarias proficisceretur—nemini enim erat igno-
tum plurimis de causis ad urbem Caesarem revocari—,
lentius agere, decedendi diem postulare longiorem,
pactiones interponere, in summa frustrari coepit.
Caesar cognita calliditate hominis, quod aliis temporibus natura facere consueverat tunc necessitate
fecit adductus, ut celerius omnium opinione manum
consereret.

72 Zela est oppidum in Ponto positum, ipsum ut in
plano loco satis munitum: tumulus enim naturalis,

perpetrated against Roman citizens engaged in trade in Pontus, since it is not in my power to set them to rights, I accordingly forgive Pharnaces. I cannot, in fact, restore to murdered men the life they have lost, nor to the mutilated their manhood; and such indeed is the punishment—worse than death—that Roman citizens have undergone. Pharnaces, however, must withdraw forthwith from Pontus, release the household slaves of the tax-gatherers, and make all other such restitution as lies in his power to the allies and Roman citizens. If he does this, then—and not before—shall he send me the tributes and gifts which triumphant commanders are in the habit of receiving from their friends.' (Pharnaces had, in fact, sent him a golden crown.) Such was the reply with which the envoys were sent back.

71 All this Pharnaces graciously promised to do. However, as he hoped that Caesar's impetuous haste would lead him to trust his own assurances still more readily than the circumstances justified, so that he might tackle more urgent matters with the greater expedition and propriety—for everyone was aware that there were many reasons demanding Caesar's return to Rome—in this hope, then, he began to take a more leisurely line, to demand a later date for his withdrawal, to propose agreements by way of causing delay —in fine, he proceeded to cheat. Realising the fellow's cunning, Caesar was now of necessity constrained to adopt the very tactics which on other occasions it had been his natural habit to employ—namely to come to grips more promptly than anyone expected.

72 Zela is a town situated in Pontus, with adequate natural defences, considering its position in a plain: for its battlements are reared upon a hillock—a

velut manu factus, excelsiore undique fastigio sustinet murum. Circumpositi sunt huic oppido magni multique intercisi vallibus colles; quorum editissimus unus, qui propter victoriam Mithridatis et infelicitatem Triari detrimentumque exercitus nostri magnam in illis partibus habet nobilitatem, superioribus locis atque itineribus paene coniunctus est [1] oppido nec multo longius milibus passuum III abest ab Zela. Hunc locum Pharnaces veteribus paternorum felicium castrorum refectis operibus copiis suis omnibus occupavit.

73 Caesar cum ab hoste milia passuum V castra posuisset videretque eas vallis quibus regia castra munirentur eodem intervallo sua castra munituras, si modo ea loca hostes priores non cepissent, quae multo erant propiora regis castris, aggerem comportari iubet intra munitiones. Quo celeriter collato proxima nocte vigilia quarta legionibus omnibus expeditis impedimentisque in castris relictis prima luce neque opinantibus hostibus eum ipsum locum cepit, in quo Mithridates secundum proelium adversus Triarium fecerat. Huc omnem comportatum

---

[1] *I have adopted Vielhaber's restoration.*

---

[1] Lucullus' lieutenant, C. Triarius, was heavily defeated in 67.
[2] Its exact position is doubtful; the highest hill in the neighbourhood (now Altiagatch Dagh, about 2000 feet) being some eight Roman miles north of Zela.
[3] The reference of the two temporal expressions—*vigilia quarta* and *prima luce*—is not easy to decide. The rendering given is perhaps the most likely. Caesar had some four miles to march; and if he left camp early in the fourth watch (this would be quite short in June), he could have taken the position at dawn. Two other interpretations seem possible : (1) ' at the fourth watch as the dawn was (just) breaking he captured . . .' (2) ' When at the fourth watch on the following

natural one for all its artificial appearance—whose
summit is loftier than all the terrain surrounding it.
Encircling this town are many considerable hills,
intersected by valleys; and one of these—a very
lofty one—which enjoys no little fame in those parts
thanks to the victory of Mithridates, and the mis-
fortune of Triarius and defeat of our army,[1] is all but
linked to the town by tracks along the higher ground,
and is little more than three miles distant from Zela.[2]
Here Pharnaces repaired the ancient works of his
father's once prosperous camp, and occupied the
position with his entire forces.

73   Caesar pitched his camp five miles distant from the
enemy; and as he now saw that that valley by which
the king's camp was protected would, if its width
separated them, equally afford protection to a camp
of his own, provided only that the enemy did not
anticipate him in capturing the ground in question,
which was much nearer the king's camp, he ordered
materials for a rampart to be carted within the
entrenchments. This was speedily collected. The
following night he left camp at the fourth watch[3]
with all his legions in light order and the heavy
baggage left behind in camp, and surprised the
enemy at dawn by capturing that very position
where Mithridates once fought his successful action
against Triarius. To this spot[4] he ordered the slaves

night this material had been collected . . .'. But this would
more likely have been a daylight operation, unless motives
of security demanded otherwise.

[4] The site of Caesar's new camp appears to have been
immediately south of the valley, on the northern edge of which
Pharnaces was already encamped. The site seems to have
been dominated by—though not identical with—the hill
where Mithridates had once encamped.

CAESAR

aggerem ex castris per servitia aggeri [1] iussit, ne
quis ab opere miles discederet, cum spatio non
amplius passuum mille intercisa vallis castra hostium
divideret ab opere incepto Caesaris castrorum.

74 Pharnaces, cum id repente prima luce animadvertisset, copias suas omnis pro castris instruxit. Quas
interposita tanta locorum iniquitate consuetudine
magis pervulgata militari credebat instrui Caesar vel
ad opus suum tardandum, quo plures in armis tene-
rentur, vel ad ostentationem regiae fiduciae, ne
munitione magis quam manu defendere locum
Pharnaces videretur. Itaque deterritus non est quo
minus prima acie pro vallo instructa reliqua pars
exercitus opus faceret. At Pharnaces impulsus sive
loci felicitate sive auspiciis et religionibus inductus,
quibus obtemperasse eum postea audiebamus, sive
paucitate nostrorum qui in armis erant comperta,
cum more operis cotidiani magnam illam servorum
multitudinem quae aggerem portabat militem esse
credidisset, sive etiam fiducia veterani exercitus sui,

---

[1] agerentur *MSS.* : aggeri, *with* per *added before* servitia, *is
Kuebler's conjecture.*

128

to bring from the camp all the accumulated material for the rampart, so that none of his troops should quit their work of fortification, since the intervening valley which separated the enemy's camp from the emplacements which Caesar had begun was not more than a mile wide.

74   On suddenly observing this situation at dawn, Pharnaces drew up all his forces in front of his camp. In view of the highly uneven character of the intervening ground Caesar supposed that it was the king's normal military practice more than anything that occasioned this deployment; or else his object was to delay Caesar's own work of fortification, through the necessity of keeping more men standing to arms; or again it might be intended as a display of confidence on the king's part, to shew that it was not on fortification so much as on armed force that Pharnaces relied to defend his position. Accordingly, Caesar was not deterred from keeping the remainder of his army engaged on the work of fortification, deploying only the front line in front of the palisade. Pharnaces, however, took it into his head to engage. Whether it was the lucky associations of the spot that drove him to take this course, or whether it was his scrupulous observance of omens, to which, as we afterwards heard, he gave careful heed, that so prompted him; or maybe it was the small number of our troops which, according to his information, were standing to arms (for he had supposed that that vast gang of slaves which transported the material for the rampart, as though it was their daily employment, was in fact composed of troops); or maybe even it was his confidence in that veteran army of his, which, as his envoys boasted, had fought and

quem bis et vicies in acie conflixisse et vicisse legati
eius gloriabantur, simul contemptu exercitus nostri,
quem pulsum a se Domitio duce sciebat, inito
consilio dimicandi descendere praerupta valle coepit.
Cuius aliquamdiu Caesar irridebat inanem ostentationem et eo loco militum coartationem, quem in
locum nemo sanus hostis subiturus esset: cum
interim Pharnaces eodem gradu quo in praeruptam
descenderat vallem ascendere adversus arduum
collem instructis copiis coepit.

75 Caesar incredibili eius vel temeritate vel fiducia
commotus neque opinans imparatusque oppressus
eodem tempore milites ab opere revocat, arma
capere iubet, legiones opponit aciemque instruit;
cuius rei subita trepidatio magnum terrorem attulit
nostris.   Nondum ordinibus instructis falcatae regiae
quadrigae permixtos milites perturbant; quae tamen
celeriter multitudine telorum opprimuntur. Insequitur has acies hostium, et clamore sublato confligitur
multum adiuvante natura loci, plurimum deorum
immortalium benignitate; qui cum omnibus casibus
bellicis intersunt, tum praecipue eis quibus nihil
ratione potuit administrari.

76 Magno atque acri proelio comminus facto, dextro
cornu, quo veterana legio sexta erat collocata,

conquered upon two and twenty battle-fields, coupled
with a contempt for our army, which he knew had
been routed by himself when Domitius led it:
anyway, having decided to engage, he began the
descent down the steep ravine. For some little time
Caesar laughed contemptuously at this empty
bravado on the part of the king, and at his troops
packed closely on ground which no enemy in his
senses would be likely to set foot on; while in the
meantime Pharnaces with his forces in battle array
proceeded to climb the steep hill-side confronting
him at the same steady pace at which he had
descended the sheer ravine.

5   This incredible foolhardiness or confidence on the
part of the king disconcerted Caesar, who was not
expecting it and was caught unprepared. Simultaneously he recalled the troops from their work of
fortification, ordered them to stand to arms, deployed
his legions to meet the attack, and formed line of
battle; and the sudden excitement to which all this
gave rise occasioned considerable panic among our
troops. Disorganised as our men were, and as yet
in no regular formation, the king's chariots armed
with scythes threw them into confusion; but these
chariots were speedily overwhelmed by a mass of
missiles. In their wake came the enemy line: the
battle cry was raised and the conflict joined, our men
being greatly helped by the nature of the ground but
above all by the blessing of the immortal gods. For
just as the gods play a part in all the chance vicissi-
tudes of war, so above all do they do so in those where
human strategy has proved quite powerless to avail.

6   Heavy and bitter hand-to-hand fighting took place;
and it was on the right wing, where the veteran Sixth

initium victoriae natum est. Ab ea parte cum in
proclive detruderentur hostes, multo tardius, sed
tamen isdem dis adiuvantibus sinistro cornu mediaque
acie totae profligantur copiae regis. Quae quam facile
subierant iniquum locum, tam celeriter gradu pulsae
premebantur loci iniquitate. Itaque multis militibus
partim interfectis partim suorum ruina oppressis, qui
velocitate effugere poterant, armis tamen proiectis
vallem transgressi nihil ex loco superiore inermi proficere poterant. At nostri victoria elati subire
iniquum locum munitionesque aggredi non dubitarunt. Defendentibus autem eis cohortibus castra
quas Pharnaces praesidio reliquerat, celeriter castris
hostium sunt potiti. Interfecta multitudine omni
suorum aut capta Pharnaces cum paucis equitibus
profugit; cui nisi castrorum oppugnatio facultatem
attulisset liberius profugiendi, vivus in Caesaris
potestatem adductus esset.

77   Tali victoria totiens victor Caesar incredibili est
laetitia adfectus, quod maximum bellum tanta
celeritate confecerat, quodque subiti periculi re-
cordatione laetior victoria facilis ex difficillimis rebus

legion was posted that the first seeds of victory were
sown. As the enemy were being thrust back down
the slope on this wing, so too on the left wing and in
the centre—much more slowly, but thanks nevertheless to the same divine assistance—the entire
forces of the king were being crushed. The ease
with which they had climbed the uneven ground was
now matched by the speed with which, once dislodged from their footing, the unevenness of the
ground enabled them to be driven back. Consequently, after sustaining many casualties—some
killed, some knocked out by their comrades' falling
on top of them—those whose nimbleness did enable
them to escape none the less threw away their arms;
and so, after crossing the valley, they could not
make any effective stand from the higher ground,
unarmed as they now were. Our men, on the contrary, elated by their victory, did not hesitate to
climb the uneven ground and storm the entrenchments.
Moreover, despite the resistance of those enemy
cohorts which Pharnaces had left to guard his camp,
they promptly won possession of it. With his entire
forces either killed or captured Pharnaces took to
flight with a few horsemen; and had not our storming
of his camp afforded him a freer opportunity for
flight, he would have been brought alive into Caesar's
hands.

7   Such a victory transported Caesar—for all the
many past victories to his credit—with incredible
delight, inasmuch as he had brought a very serious
war to so speedy a conclusion, and because an easy
victory, which delighted him the more when he
recalled the sudden risk it had involved, had trans-
pired out of a very difficult situation. Having thus

acciderat. Ponto recepto praeda omni regia militibus condonata postero die cum expeditis equitibus ipse proficiscitur, legionem sextam decedere ad praemia atque honores accipiendos in Italiam iubet, auxilia Deiotari domum remittit, duas legiones cum Caelio Viniciano in Ponto relinquit.

78   Ita per Gallograeciam Bithyniamque in Asiam iter facit omniumque earum provinciarum de controversiis cognoscit et statuit; iura in tetrarchas, reges, civitates distribuit. Mithridaten Pergamenum, a quo rem feliciter celeriterque gestam in Aegypto supra scripsimus, regio genere ortum, disciplinis etiam regiis educatum—nam eum Mithridates, rex Asiae totius, propter nobilitatem Pergamo parvulum secum asportaverat in castra multosque retinuerat annos—regem Bosphori constituit, qui [1] sub imperio Pharnacis fuerat, provinciasque populi Romani a barbaris atque inimicis regibus interposito amicissimo rege munivit. Eidem tetrarchian Gallograecorum iure gentis et cognationis adiudicavit occupatam et possessam paucis ante annis a Deiotaro. Neque tamen usquam diutius moratus est quam necessitas urbanarum seditionum pati videbatur. Rebus felicissime celerrimeque confectis in Italiam celerius omnium opinione venit.

[1] quod *MSS.* : qui *Dinter.*

---

[1] Probably the tetrarchy of the Trocmi in East Galatia : *cf.* ch. 67.

recovered Pontus and made a present to his troops of all the royal plunder, he himself set out on the following day with his cavalry in light order; instructing the Sixth legion to leave for Italy to receive its rewards and honours, sending home the auxiliary troops of Deiotarus, and leaving two legions in Pontus with Caelius Vinicianus.

Thus he marched through Gallograecia and Bithynia into Asia, holding investigations and giving his formal ruling on matters of dispute in all those provinces, and assigning due prerogatives to tetrarchs, kings and states. Now Mithridates of Pergamum, whose speedy and successful action in Egypt I have described above, was not merely of royal birth but also of royal training and upbringing; for Mithridates, king of all Asia, had carried him off to camp with him from Pergamum on the score of his noble birth when he was quite young, and had kept him there for many years; for which reasons Caesar now appointed him king of Bosphorus, which had formerly been under control of Pharnaces, and, by thus creating a buffer state ruled by a most friendly king, he secured the provinces of the Roman people from barbarian and unfriendly kings. To the same Mithridates he awarded, by right of racial affinity and kinship, the tetrarchy of Gallograecia which had been seized and occupied a few years earlier by Deiotarus.[1] Nowhere, however, did he delay any longer than the urgency of unsettled conditions at Rome appeared to warrant; and when he had accomplished his tasks with the greatest success and expedition, he arrived in Italy more quickly than anyone expected.

THE AFRICAN WAR

INTRODUCTION

As soon as Caesar had crushed Pharnaces at Zela and temporarily reorganised the affairs of Asia, he might, if military strategy alone had governed his policy, have sailed straight to Africa, where his enemies had had a year already in which to consolidate their position. But Caesar was more than a mere general; and, as he well knew, the political situation in Rome was serious and urgently demanding his presence.[1]

Troubles there were in plenty. Economic problems such as the administration of the new law of debt gave scope to malcontents like Caelius and Dolabella, who had expected harsh reprisals against the defeated Pompeians and were disgusted with Caesar's leniency. Still more dangerous to public security were Caesar's veteran legions, who, having been sent home after Pharsalus, had now little to do save noisily demand their promised triumph and discharge. Antony, the absent dictator's deputy in the city, had found all this unrest beyond his powers effectively to check: no magistrates had as yet been elected for the current year, and those for 46 were shortly due for election.

Such was the situation which confronted Caesar in September. By November he had restored order:

[1] *Bell. Alex.* ch. 65.

the economic crisis had been temporarily mitigated:
the elections had been held: the mutinous legions
disciplined and some detailed for service in Africa.
But the additional delay was to cost him dear;
for not only was he to start his new campaign in the
winter, when every convoy from Sicily was at the
mercy of the winter gales, but, as he was soon to find
out, his opponents had made good use of the respite.

Since Curio's defeat in 49 the Roman province of
Africa had been in the hands of the Pompeians.
Its most powerful neighbour, king Juba of Numidia,
had no love for Caesar and could accordingly, if his
imperious temper were tactfully handled, be relied on
to support Caesar's enemies. His military resources
were reputed to be enormous and to outweigh by
far those of his two Mauretanian neighbours,
Bocchus and Bogud, who favoured Caesar, even if
the latter were backed up by Sittius, a Roman
adventurer who had for several years been operating
in those parts with his own private army. Attius
Varus, who had governed the province since 50, was
joined, after Pharsalus, by Scipio and Cato, each
with his own contingent of survivors from that battle.
Labienus, Petreius and Afranius had now also joined
them; and in Labienus the enemy had a tactician
hardly inferior to Caesar himself. In addition to
Juba's four legions and countless cavalry and light-
armed troops the Pompeians could muster ten
legions, though most of them were raised in Africa
and were of dubious quality. They possessed a
considerable fleet: they had fortified practically all

the coastal towns and concentrated in them abundant stocks of grain; and by calling up many of the native farmers they had curtailed the harvest of 47 and thus made it more difficult for Caesar to live off the land.

Caesar's tiny expeditionary force was thus beset with enormous difficulties, not only of supply and reinforcement, but of very existence; and within a week of its landing Labienus came very near to destroying it. The narrative of *de Bello Africo* bears striking testimony to Caesar's manifold qualities: the dogged patience which strategy demanded in the earlier stages: the outward buoyancy and cheerfulness with which, despite his inward anxiety, he maintained the morale of his troops: the unflagging determination with which he tempted Scipio to engage; and the brilliant tactics and opportunism thanks to which at Thapsus he finally turned the tables on his would-be ambusher.

Although the identity of the author of *de Bello Africo* is obscure, certain inferences may yet be drawn from his narrative.[1] The careful chronology and the faithful record of the feelings of the troops suggests a soldier—possibly a junior officer—who was on the spot. That he was young and inexperienced; an ardent, but not always a balanced, partisan; a keen observer of all that went on around him, but without access to the inner counsels of his

---

[1] For these remarks I have drawn freely on the wealth of material contained in Bouvet's excellent Introduction (pp. xvii–xxxix), to which the reader is referred for fuller detail in the way of illustration.

C.-in-C.—all these, I think, are reasonable inferences. His historical perspective was weak; for he sometimes gives unimportant, yet at other times withholds important, details.[1] However, apart from this and the errors into which his blind admiration for Caesar occasionally leads him,[2] his account on the whole rings true and leaves a distinct impression of sincerity and enthusiasm.

His literary style is distinctive. His vocabulary, though it includes a number of Greek words [3] and colloquial phrases [4] normally avoided by good prose writers, is nevertheless marked by a definite poverty of expression; [5] and his sentence structure, though not infrequently embellished by stock rhetorical flourishes,[6] is often ungainly and sometimes ungrammatical.[7] Yet, on the whole, his style is clear,

---

[1] *e.g.* the detailed order of battle given in ch. 59–60, though in fact no battle ensues; whereas at Thapsus much is left to the reader's imagination.

[2] *e.g.* in ch. 31 the various excuses made for Caesar's cautious tactics, especially the last.

[3] *e.g. catascopus*, ch. 26 : *epibata*, ch. 20.

[4] *e.g. convulnerare*, ch. 5, etc. : *rapsare*, ch. 73 : *magis suspensiore*, ch. 48.

[5] *e.g.* constant repetition of words such as *interim, praeterea*, etc.; in ch. 29–31, monotonous recourse to the relative pronoun as a link word (*quod . . . quod . . . quo facto . . . quod . . . quibus rebus*); in ch. 32 *non intermittere* in two consecutive sentences.

[6] *e.g.* alliteration : ch. 35 : *praemiis pollicitationibusque propositis pro perfugis*.
Chiasmus : ch. 37 : *singulae turres speculaeque singulae*.

[7] *e.g.* ch. 5, where *postquam* is followed by no less than seven imperfects; and ch. 19, last but one sentence, where *Labienus*, the subject, has no verb.

if frequently monotonous and, in places, mere-
tricious; and in the set speeches—in which respect
he is much more ambitious than the writer of *de
Bello Alexandrino*—he is quite effective in varying the
style to reflect the personality of the speaker.[1]

[1] *e.g.* the didactic tone of Cato's lecture in ch. 22; the forthright retort of the centurion in ch. 45; and Caesar's dis-
ciplinary harangue in ch. 54.

ANALYSIS OF THE BOOK

ANALYSIS OF THE BOOK

new camp opposite Uzitta.—Juba's arrogant
behaviour.—Order of battle on either side: only a
cavalry skirmish ensues.—Varus fires some of
Caesar's transports at Leptis: Caesar quits his
camp and personally leads a successful counter-
attack.—Foraging operations: Labienus vainly
lays another ambush.

67–78 Operations near Aggar

Lack of corn prompts Caesar to march to Aggar:
Scipio follows.—Caesar captures Zeta but is forced
to fight his way back under heavy attacks from
Numidian cavalry and light-armed units: he
adapts training methods to meet these new tactics:
his anxiety about the enemies' cavalry strength
and their elephants.—He twice offers battle:
captures Sarsura, approaches Thysdra, retires to
Aggar.—Cavalry engagement near Tegea.

79–86 Operations at Thapsus

Caesar advances to Thapsus and begins to invest
the town: Scipio follows and finally encamps close
to Thapsus.—Caesar's dispositions: his reluctance
to engage: the signal is finally given without his
orders.—Rout of Scipio's elephants: Caesar's
troops meet little resistance: sortie of the garrison
of Thapsus repulsed.—Savage vengeance by Caesar's
veterans on the fugitives.—Vergilius refuses to
surrender Thapsus: arrangements for blockading it
and Thysdra: Caesar proceeds to Utica.

87–98 Final stages of the campaign

Brutal sack of Parada by Scipio's cavalry: they
plunder Utica till Cato buys them off: he tries in
vain to organise resistance and then commits
suicide.—Caesar's clemency: he enters Utica and
punishes its Roman citizens by inflicting a heavy
fine.—Juba outlawed by his subjects takes refuge
with Petreius in a villa.—Caesar comes to Zama:
surrender of Thysdra and Thapsus: deaths of
Juba, Petreius, Afranius and Scipio.—Caesar returns
to Utica and fines Thapsus, Hadrumetum, Leptis
and Thysdra: embarks at Utica: calls at Caralis in
Sardinia: eventually arrives at Rome.

DE BELLO AFRICO

1 CAESAR itineribus iustis confectis nullo die intermisso a. d. XIIII. Kal. Ian. Lilybaeum pervenit statimque ostendit sese navis velle conscendere, cum non amplius legionem tironum haberet unam, equites vix DC. Tabernaculum secundum litus ipsum constituit, ut prope fluctus verberaret. Hoc eo consilio fecit ne quis sibi morae quicquam fore speraret et ut omnes in dies horasque parati essent. Incidit per id tempus ut tempestates ad navigandum idoneas non haberet; nihilo tamen minus in navibus remiges militesque continere et nullam praetermittere occasionem profectionis, cum praesertim ab incolis eius provinciae nuntiarentur adversariorum copiae equitatus infinitus, legiones regiae IIII, levis armaturae magna vis, Scipionis legiones X, elephanti CXX classesque esse complures; tamen non deterrebatur animoque et spe confidebat. Interim in dies et naves longae adaugeri et onerariae complures eodem

---

[1] It is not quite clear whether this means the complete journey from Rome (over 600 miles, via Rhegium and Messana), or merely the last stage from Messana (some 200 miles). But as it seems likely that he was not accompanied by any large number of troops—the legion of recruits may have been one already stationed at Lilybaeum—most commentators appear to assume that the reference is to the whole journey.

[2] = October 23rd, 47, if Le Verrier's rectified system be followed : October 1, according to Groebe's system. All the

THE AFRICAN WAR

1 AFTER completing a series of full day's marches [1] without pausing for a single day, Caesar arrived at Lilybaeum on December 17,[2] and shewed himself desirous of embarking forthwith, although he had no more than a single legion of recruits and barely six hundred cavalry. He had his tent pitched alongside the actual beach so that the waves all but beat upon it: his purpose in so doing was to prevent anyone from hoping he would enjoy any respite, and to ensure that everyone was in a state of daily and hourly readiness. During this time he was unlucky with the weather, which was unsuitable for sailing; but for all that he still kept his rowers and troops aboard the ships and let slip no opportunity for setting forth, despite, above all, the reports which were coming in from the local provincials about the forces of the enemy—innumerable cavalry, four royal legions, a great quantity of light-armed troops, ten legions under command of Scipio, a hundred-and-twenty elephants and several fleets: yet even so he was not deterred, but remained resolute and optimistic. Meanwhile every day saw an increase in the number of his warships, and numerous transports also

dates given in the text are according to the unreformed calendar, which was now some two months ahead owing to the failure of the *pontifices* to insert the necessary intercalary months.

concurrere et legiones tironum convenire IIII,[1]
veterana legio quinta, equitum ad II milia.

2 Legionibus collectis VI et equitum II milibus, ut
quaeque prima legio venerat in navis longas im-
ponebatur, equites autem in onerarias. Ita maiorem partem navium antecedere iussit et insulam
petere Aponianam, quae abest a Lilybaeo milia
passuum X: ipse paucos dies ibi [2] commoratus bona
paucorum vendit publice, deinde Alieno praetori,
qui Siciliam obtinebat, de omnibus rebus praecipit et
de reliquo exercitu celeriter imponendo. Datis
mandatis ipse navem conscendit a. d. VI. Kal. Ian. et
reliquas navis statim est consecutus. Ita vento
certo celerique navigio vectus post diem quartum cum
longis paucis navibus in conspectum Africae venit;
namque onerariae reliquae praeter paucas vento
dispersae atque errabundae diversa loca petierunt.
Clupeam classe praetervehitur, dein Neapolim;
complura praeterea castella et oppida non longe a
mari reliquit.

3 Postquam Hadrumetum accessit, ubi praesidium
erat adversariorum cui praeerat C. Considius, et a

[1] in his *MSS.*: IIII *R. Schneider.*
[2] milia . . . ibi *conjectured by R. Schneider to fill the lacuna of the MSS.*

---

[1] Probably the Fifth called *Alaudae*, formed in Gaul in
51 B.C.   There is much difficulty in identifying this veteran
Fifth legion with the Fifth raised by Cassius in Spain (*Bell.
Alex.* ch. 50).

[2] This apparently means Hadrumetum, and not Cape
Bon; for he must have landed at Hadrumetum on the 28th,
and 3–4 days' sail in a fast ship seems unduly long for the

assembled there : four legions of recruits, the veteran Fifth [1] legion, and some two thousand cavalry also joined the muster.

2   Six legions and two thousand cavalry had now been mustered. Each legion, as soon as it arrived, was embarked on the warships, while the cavalry were shipped aboard the transports. Accordingly, he ordered the greater part of the fleet to sail on ahead and make for the island of Aponiana, which is ten miles distant from Lilybaeum : he himself stayed behind there for a few days and sold up the property of a few persons for the profit of the state, and then gave full instructions to the praetor Alienus, who was governor of Sicily, in particular about the prompt embarkation of the rest of the army. Having given these instructions, he himself embarked on December 25 and immediately caught up with the remainder of his fleet. And so, sailing in a fast ship with a steady wind, three days later with a few warships he came into sight of Africa ; [2] for his transports, which comprised the rest of his fleet, had, with a few exceptions, been scattered by the wind and, losing their course, made for various points along the coast. He sailed on past Clupea with his fleet, and then past Neapolis ; and besides these places he passed by quite a number of strongholds and towns not far from the sea.

3   When Caesar reached Hadrumetum, where his opponents had a garrison commanded by C. Con-

passage of less than 100 miles (*cf.* ch. 34, where his second convoy makes Ruspina on the fourth day). Other apparent inconsistencies are the embarkation of all the legions aboard the warships and the capriciousness of the wind, which favoured the warships but scattered the transports.

CAESAR

Clupeis secundum oram maritimam cum equitatu Hadrumetum petens[1] Cn. Piso cum Maurorum circiter tribus milibus apparuit, ibi paulisper Caesar ante portum commoratus, dum reliquae naves convenirent, exponit exercitum, cuius numerus in praesentia fuit peditum III milia, equites CL, castrisque ante oppidum positis sine iniuria cuiusquam consedit cohibetque omnis a praeda. Oppidani interim muros armatis complent, ante portam frequentes considunt ad sese defendendum; quorum numerus duarum legionum instar erat. Caesar circum oppidum vectus natura loci perspecta rediit in castra. Non nemo culpae eius imprudentiaeque assignabat, quod neque circum loca gubernatoribus praefectisque quid peterent praeceperat neque, ut more ipsius consuetudo superioribus temporibus fuerat, tabellas signatas dediderat, ut in tempore his perlectis locum certum peterent universi. Quod minime Caesarem fefellerat; nam neque ullum portum terrae Africae quo classes decurrerent pro certo tutum ab hostium praesidio fore suspicabatur, sed fortuito oblatam occasionem egressus aucupabatur.

4 L. Plancus interim legatus petit a Caesare uti sibi daret potestatem cum Considio agendi, si posset aliqua ratione perduci ad sanitatem. Itaque data facultate litteras conscribit et eas captivo dat per-

---

[1] petens *added by Kiessling.*

sidius, Cn. Piso made his appearance there with approximately three thousand Moorish troops, approaching Hadrumetum with his cavalry along the sea coast from Clupea; whereupon Caesar paused for a little while in front of the port, waiting for the rest of his ships to assemble, and then landed his army, which numbered at present three thousand infantry and a hundred-and-fifty cavalry. He then pitched camp in front of the town and established himself without molesting anyone, looting being universally forbidden. Meanwhile the occupants of the town manned their battlements with armed troops, and massed in front of the gate to defend themselves: their numbers amounted to the equivalent of two legions. Caesar rode round the town carefully observing the lie of the land, and then returned to camp. Some blamed him for lack of foresight because he had not originally briefed his pilots and captains about what points on the coast they were to make for, and had not, as had been his own habitual practice on previous occasions, issued sealed instructions to be read at a specified time, so that they could all make for a given rendezvous together. But this was by no means an oversight on Caesar's part; in fact, he surmised that there was no port on African soil where his fleet could run ashore and which he could count on as immune from the enemy's protection; and failing that, he was on the watch for luck to present him with an opportunity to land.

4   Meanwhile one of his lieutenants, L. Plancus, asked Caesar to give him authority to treat with Considius, if by any means he could be brought to see reason. Permission being granted, he accordingly wrote a letter, which he gave to a prisoner to take to

ferendas in oppidum ad Considium. Quo simul
atque captivus cum pervenisset litterasque, ut erat
mandatum, Considio porrigere coepisset, prius quam
acciperet ille, ' Unde,' inquit, ' istas ? ' Tum captivus : ' Imperatore a Caesare.' Tum Considius,
' Unus est,' inquit, ' Scipio imperator hoc tempore
populi Romani '; deinde in conspectu suo statim
captivum interfici iubet litterasque nondum per-
lectas, sicut erant signatae, dat homini certo ad
Scipionem perferendas.

5 Postquam una nocte et die ad oppidum consumpta
neque responsum ullum a Considio dabatur, neque ei
reliquae copiae succurrebant neque equitatu abunda-
bat et ad oppidum oppugnandum non satis copiarum
habebat et eas tironum neque primo adventu con-
vulnerari exercitum volebat, et oppidi egregia
munitio et difficilis ad oppugnandum erat ascensus et
nuntiabatur auxilia magna equitatus oppidanis
suppetias venire, non est visa ratio ad oppugnandum
oppidum commorandi, ne, dum in ea re est Caesar
occupatus, circumventus a tergo ab equitatu hostium
laboraret.

6 Itaque castra cum movere vellet, subito ex oppido
erupit multitudo atque equitatus subsidio uno
tempore eis casu succurrit, qui erat missus a Iuba ad
stipendium accipiendum, castraque, unde Caesar
egressus iter facere coeperat, occupant et eius agmen

---

[1] This appears to mean the night of December 28th/29th
and (most of) the 29th ; for the fighting withdrawal to Ruspina
apparently took place on the 29th (the last day of the official
year, according to the unreformed calendar). Bouvet adopts
R. Schneider's insertion of *parte* before *die* ; but with a writer
like the present, whose accuracy is not always pedantic, the
MSS. reading may perhaps be retained.

Considius in the town. As soon as the prisoner had arrived there, and when he was in the very act of handing Considius the letter in accordance with his instructions, the latter remarked before accepting it: 'Where did you get this?' Whereupon the prisoner replied: 'From the commander-in-chief, Caesar.' Then Considius retorted: 'There is but one commander-in-chief of the Roman people at the moment, namely Scipio.' He then ordered the prisoner to be executed forthwith in his presence, and gave the letter—still unread and with its seals intact—to a reliable messenger to take to Scipio.

5 A night and a day [1] were spent under the walls of the town without any reply being given by Considius: moreover, the rest of Caesar's forces failed to arrive to reinforce him; he had no abundance of cavalry and insufficient forces to assault the town, and those he had were mere recruits; he was loath to let his army suffer heavy casualties immediately on its arrival; the defences of the town were remarkably strong, its lofty position rendering it difficult to attack; and reports were coming in that large reinforcements of cavalry were on their way to aid the occupants of the town. For these reasons there seemed no point in staying on for the purpose of attacking the town, lest, while engaged in that task, Caesar might be surrounded in the rear by the enemy cavalry and so find himself in difficulties.

6 Caesar therefore was minded to strike camp; and while he was doing so a large body of men suddenly sallied forth from the town, and were reinforced simultaneously, as it chanced, by some cavalry sent by Juba to collect their pay: they seized Caesar's camp, which he had just quitted to begin his march,

extremum insequi coeperunt. Quae res cum animadversa esset, subito legionarii consistunt et equites,
quamquam erant pauci, tamen contra tantam
multitudinem audacissime concurrunt. Accidit res
incredibilis, ut equites minus XXX Galli Maurorum
equitum II milia loco pellerent fugarentque in
oppidum. Postquam repulsi et coniecti erant intra
munitiones, Caesar iter constitutum ire contendit.
Quod cum saepius facerent et modo insequerentur,
modo rursus ab equitibus in oppidum repellerentur,
cohortibus paucis ex veteranis quas secum habebat in
extremo agmine collocatis et parte equitatus iter
leniter cum reliquis facere coepit. Ita quanto
longius ab oppido discedebatur, tanto tardiores ad
insequendum erant Numidae. Interim in itinere ex
oppidis et castellis legationes venire, polliceri frumentum paratosque esse quae imperasset facere.
Itaque eo die castra posuit ad oppidum Ruspinam.

7 Kal. Ianuariis [1] inde movit et pervenit ad oppidum
Leptim, liberam civitatem et immunem. Legati ex
oppido obviam veniunt, libenter se omnia facturos
quae vellet pollicentur. Itaque centurionibus ad
portas oppidi et custodiis impositis, ne quis miles in
oppidum introiret aut iniuriam faceret cuipiam
incolae, non longe ab oppido secundum litus facit
castra. Eodemque naves onerariae et longae non

---

[1] *I have followed Schneider in transferring this date from the
foot of chapter* 6. *cf. Ch.* 5, *Note* 1.

---

[1] Leptis was one of seven towns which in 146 B.C. had been
granted autonomy for failing to support Carthage in the
Second Punic War. *cf.* Acylla (ch. 33).

and began to pursue his rearguard. On seeing this
the legionary troops came to an abrupt halt, while the
cavalry, few as they were, nevertheless displayed the
utmost gallantry in charging against such vast
numbers. An incredible thing took place: less than
thirty Gallic cavalry dislodged two thousand Moorish
cavalry and drove them to take refuge in the town.
After they had been repulsed and hurled back within
their fortifications, Caesar made haste to proceed with
his projected march. But as the enemy repeated
these tactics all too frequently—now following in
pursuit, now once again driven back into the town by
the cavalry—Caesar posted in the rear of his column
a few cohorts of the veteran troops which he had
with him, as well as part of his cavalry, and so proceeded to march at a slow pace with the remainder
of his force. In this way the further they withdrew
from the town, the slower were the Numidians to
pursue them. Meanwhile in the course of his march
deputations arrived from towns and strongholds with
promises of corn and assurances of their readiness to
carry out any orders he might give them. And so on
that day he pitched camp near the town of Ruspina.

From there he moved camp on January 1st and
arrived at the town of Leptis, a free community,
immune from taxes.[1] Envoys came from the town to
meet him and promised they would readily do whatever he wished. Accordingly, he posted centurions
and picquets at the town gates, to prevent any soldier
from entering it or molesting any inhabitant, and
then made his camp adjoining the shore, not far
from the town. And it so chanced that some of his
transports and warships arrived at this same place:
as for the rest of them, it appeared from the reports

nullae casu advenerunt; reliquae, ut est ei nuntiatum, incertae locorum Uticam versus petere visae sunt. Interim Caesar a mari non digredi neque mediterranea petere propter navium errorem equitatumque in navibus omnem continere, ut arbitror, ne agri vastarentur; aquam in navis iubet comportari. Remiges interim, qui aquatum e navibus exierant, subito equites Mauri neque opinantibus Caesarianis adorti multos iaculis convulnerarunt, non nullos interfecerunt. Latent enim in insidiis cum equis inter convallis ut subito exsistant,[1] non ut in campo comminus depugnent.

8 Caesar interim in Sardiniam nuntios cum litteris et in reliquas provincias finitimas dimisit, ut sibi auxilia, commeatus, frumentum, simul atque litteras legissent, mittenda curarent, exoneratisque partim navibus longis Rabirium Postumum in Siciliam ad secundum commeatum arcessendum mittit. Vatinium[2] cum X navibus longis ad reliquas navis onerarias conquirendas quae deerrassent et simul mare tuendum ab hostibus iubet proficisci. Item C. Sallustium Crispum praetorem ad Cercinam insulam versus, quam adversarii tenebant, cum parte navium ire iubet, quod ibi magnum numerum frumenti esse audiebat. Haec ita imperabat unicuique, ita praecipiebat uti fieri possent necne locum excusatio nullum haberet nec moram tergiversatio. Ipse interea ex perfugis et incolis cognitis condicionibus

---

[1] et . . . exsistunt *MSS.* : ut . . . exsistant *Hoffmann*; *but the interpretation of the whole sentence is doubtful.*

[2] interim *MSS.* : Vatinium *Schneider.*

which reached him that owing to their uncertain knowledge of the district they were making towards Utica. For the time being Caesar would not leave the sea or strike inland on account of these wayward vessels, and kept all his cavalry aboard ship, his purpose being, I imagine, to prevent their pillaging the countryside: as for water, he ordered it to be carried aboard. Meanwhile Caesar's troops were taken by surprise when some rowers who had disembarked to fetch water were suddenly set upon by Moorish cavalry, who wounded many with their lances and killed some of them. These Moors in fact lurk in ambush with their horses in the wadis, so as to start up suddenly and not to fight it out hand to hand in the plain.

Meanwhile Caesar sent messengers to Sardinia and the other neighbouring provinces with despatches instructing them to take steps, immediately on reading the despatch, to send him reinforcements, supplies and corn. He also unloaded some of his warships and sent Rabirius Postumus to Sicily to fetch a second convoy. He ordered Vatinius to set out with ten warships to search for the remaining transports which had gone astray, and at the same time to keep the sea safe from enemy raiders. He likewise ordered the praetor C. Sallustius Crispus to proceed with a detachment of ships to the island of Cercina, which was under enemy occupation, as he heard that there was a great quantity of corn there. These orders and instructions he issued to each individual in such terms as to rule out any excuses as to whether or not they could be carried out, and to prevent any shuffling involving delay. Meanwhile he himself learned from deserters and the local

Scipionis et qui cum eo bellum contra se gerebant,
miserari—regium enim equitatum Scipio ex provincia Africa alebat—tanta homines esse dementia ut
malint regis esse vectigales quam cum civibus in
patria in suis fortunis esse incolumes.

9   Caesar a. d. IIII.[1] Non. Ian. castra movet; Lepti
sex cohortium praesidio cum Saserna relicto ipse
rursus unde pridie venerat Ruspinam cum reliquis
copiis convertit ibique sarcinis exercitus relictis ipse
cum expedita manu proficiscitur circum villas
frumentatum oppidanisque imperat ut plaustra
iumentaque omnia sequantur. Itaque magno numero
frumenti invento Ruspinam redit. Huc[2] eum idcirco existimo recepisse, ut maritima oppida post se
ne vacua relinqueret praesidioque firmata ad classim
receptacula muniret.

10   Itaque ibi relicto P. Saserna, fratre eius quem
Lepti in proximo oppido reliquerat, cum legione,
iubet comportari ligna in oppidum quam plurima;
ipse cum cohortibus VII, quae ex veteranis legionibus
in classe cum Sulpicio et Vatinio rem gesserant, ex
oppido Ruspina egressus proficiscitur ad portum,
qui abest ab oppido milia passuum duo, ibique
classem sub vesperum cum ea copia conscendit.

---

[1] III *MSS.*: IIII *Schneider.*
[2] hoc *MSS.*: huc *Davies.*

---

[1] Juba's cavalry, the payment of whom was alluded to in
ch. 6, above.
[2] This seems to be an attempt to account for Caesar's abrupt
withdrawal from Leptis, to which he had advanced without,
apparently, taking steps to secure Ruspina in his rear.
[3] *cf. Bell. Alex.* ch. 44.

inhabitants of the terms entered into by Scipio and his supporters who were engaged in hostilities against him—Scipio was in point of fact maintaining a royal [1] cavalry force at the expense of the province of Africa; and he felt sorry that men could be so mad as to prefer to be the hirelings of a king to being in their own country, in the company of their own citizens, secure in the possession of their own fortunes.

9   On January 2nd Caesar moved his camp. Leaving behind at Leptis a garrison of six cohorts with Saserna, he himself returned with his remaining forces back to Ruspina, whence he had come the previous day. There the army's baggage was left, and he himself set out with a force in light order to forage round the farms, issuing instructions to the townsfolk that all their carts and draught animals must go with him; and so, after finding a large quantity of corn, he returned to Ruspina. His object in returning to this town [2] was, I imagine, to avoid leaving the coastal towns behind him unoccupied, but rather, by securing them with garrisons, to fortify them as strongholds for the reception of his fleet.

10   And so, leaving behind a legion under command of P. Saserna—brother of the man he had left in the nearby town of Leptis—with instructions that as much wood as possible should be conveyed into the town, he left the town of Ruspina and made for its harbour, which is two miles distant. With him he took seven cohorts which were drawn from veteran legions and had seen service aboard the fleet with Sulpicius and Vatinius; [3] and having reached the harbour he went aboard his fleet with this force as evening was approaching. There was not a man in

CAESAR

Omnibus in exercitu insciis et requirentibus imperatoris consilium, magno metu ac tristimonia sollicita-
bantur. Parva enim cum copia et ea tironum,
neque omni exposita, in Africa contra magnas copias
et insidiosae nationis equitatum innumerabilem se
expositos videbant neque quicquam solati in praesentia neque auxili in suorum consilio animum
advertebant, nisi in ipsius imperatoris vultu, vigore
mirabilique hilaritate; animum enim altum et
erectum prae se gerebat. Huic adquiescebant
homines et in eius scientia et consilio omnia sibi
proclivia omnes fore sperabant.

11 Caesar una nocte in navibus consumpta iam caelo
albente cum proficisci conaretur, subito navium pars
de qua timebat ex errore eodem conferebatur. Hac
re cognita Caesar celeriter de navibus imperat
omnis egredi atque in litore armatos reliquos ad-
venientis milites exspectare. Itaque sine mora
navibus eis in portum receptis et advectis militum
equitumque copiis rursus ad oppidum Ruspinam
redit atque ibi castris constitutis ipse cum cohortibus
expeditis XXX frumentatum est profectus. Ex
eo est cognitum Caesaris consilium, illum cum classe
navibus onerariis quae deerrassent subsidio ire clam
hostibus voluisse, ne casu imprudentes suae naves in
classem adversariorum inciderent, neque eam rem

the army who knew the plans of the commander-in-chief, not a man but sought eagerly to know them; and in their ignorance they were all filled with anxiety, grave alarm and depression. For they saw themselves landed in Africa with a tiny force—and that too of recruits, and not all of it disembarked—pitted against large forces including the limitless cavalry of a treacherous race; nor could they discern anything to console them in their present plight, no help in the counsels of their comrades—no help at all, save in the expression of their commander himself, and his energy and remarkable cheerfulness; for he displayed a high and buoyant spirit. It was in him that his men found peace of mind: his skill and resolution would, they all hoped, make everything run smoothly for them.

1 After spending one night aboard his fleet Caesar was proceeding to set out at the first pale light of dawn, when suddenly the squadron about which he was apprehensive sought haven there from its wanderings. On learning of this, Caesar promptly ordered everyone to disembark and, drawn up under arms on the beach, to await the arrival of the rest of his troops. And so when these ships had been brought without delay into port, with their cargo of infantry and cavalry, Caesar once again returned to the town of Ruspina, drew up his camp there, and then set out himself with thirty cohorts in light order to forage. As a result of this Caesar's plan now became known: it had been his intention to go with his fleet to the assistance of those transports which had gone astray, but to do so without the enemy's knowing of it, lest by chance his own ships might run unawares against his opponents' fleet;

eos voluisse scire qui in praesidiis relicti sui milites fuissent, ne hi propter suorum paucitatem et hostium multitudinem metu deficerent.

12 Interim cum iam Caesar progressus esset a castris circiter milia passuum III, per speculatores et antecessores equites nuntiatur ei copias hostium haud longe ab sese visas. Et hercule cum eo nuntio pulvis ingens conspici coeptus est. Hac re cognita Caesar celeriter iubet equitatum universum, cuius copiam habuit in praesentia non magnam, et sagittarios, quorum parvus numerus, ex castris arcessi atque ordinatim signa se leniter consequi; ipse antecedere cum paucis armatis. Iamque cum procul hostis conspici posset, milites in campo iubet galeari et ad pugnam parari; quorum omnino numerus fuit XXX cohortium cum equitibus CCCC, sagittariis CL.

13 Hostes interim, quorum dux erat Labienus et duo Pacidei, aciem derigunt mirabili longitudine non peditum sed equitum confertam, et inter eos levis armaturae Numidas et sagittarios pedites interposuerant et ita condensaverant ut procul Caesariani pedestris copias arbitrarentur; dextrum ac sinistrum cornu magnis equitum copiis firmaverant. Interim Caesar aciem derigit simplicem, ut poterat propter paucitatem; sagittarios ante aciem constituit, equites dextro sinistroque cornu opponit et ita

---

¹ The number is strangely small in view of ch. 2 and the arrival of the missing troops recorded in ch. 11. Stoffel proposed to read ∞ ∞, i.e. 2000; the total force mentioned in ch. 2.

² The most brilliant and enterprising of Scipio's subordinate commanders; originally a staunch supporter of Caesar, he had joined Pompey's side early in 49 and, after Pharsalus, had crossed to Africa with Cato.

nor had he wanted his own troops left behind on guard to know of this plan, lest, on account of their own small numbers and the multitude of the enemy, fear should make them fail in their duty.

12　Meanwhile, when Caesar had now advanced about three miles from his camp, information obtained by his scouts and mounted patrols reached him that the enemy's forces had been sighted by them at no great distance. And indeed simultaneously with that information they began to see a great cloud of dust. On learning this, Caesar promptly gave orders for his entire cavalry force—of which arm he had no great abundance available at the moment—and his small contingent of archers to be summoned from the camp, and for the standards to follow him slowly in their regular order : he himself went on ahead with a small armed party. Now that the enemy could be seen in the distance, he ordered the troops to don their helmets and prepare for battle in the open plain : their total number comprised thirty cohorts, together with four hundred [1] cavalry and one hundred-and-fifty archers.

13　Meanwhile the enemy, led by Labienus [2] and the two Pacidei, deployed a straight line of remarkable length and closely packed, not with infantry, but with cavalry, interspersed with light-armed Numidians and unmounted archers in such close formation that at a distance Caesar's men supposed them to be infantry : the two wings—to right and left—were reinforced with strong detachments of cavalry. Meanwhile Caesar deployed a single straight line— the most his small numbers allowed ; he drew up his archers in front of the line and posted cavalry to cover his right and left wings, with instructions to

praecipit ut providerent ne multitudine equitatus hostium circumvenirentur : existimabat enim se acie instructa cum pedestribus copiis dimicaturum.

14 Cum utrimque exspectatio fieret neque Caesar sese moveret et cum suorum paucitate contra magnam vim hostium artificio magis quam viribus decernendum videret, subito adversariorum equitatus sese extendere et in latitudinem promovere collisque complecti et Caesaris equitatum extenuare simulque ad circumeundum comparare se coeperant. Caesariani equites eorum multitudinem aegre sustinebant. Acies interim mediae cum concurrere conarentur, subito ex condensis turmis pedites Numidae levis armaturae cum equitibus procurrunt et inter legionarios pedites iacula coiciunt. Hic cum Caesariani in eos impetum fecissent, illorum equites refugiebant ; pedites interim resistebant, dum equites rursus cursu renovato peditibus suis succurrerent.

15 Caesar novo genere pugnae oblato cum animum adverteret ordines suorum in procurrendo turbari— pedites enim, dum equites longius a signis persequuntur, latere nudato a proximis Numidis iaculis vulnerabantur ; equites autem hostium pilum militis cursu facile vitabant—edicit per ordines ne quis

take care they were not enveloped by the mass of the enemy's cavalry; for he supposed that he would be engaging infantry troops in the set battle line.

14 There was now on either side a growing feeling of expectancy; but Caesar made no move and saw that the smallness of his own forces called for the use of strategy rather than a trial of strength against the vast numbers of the enemy; when suddenly his opponents' cavalry began to deploy, extending towards the flanks and enveloping the high ground, causing Caesar's cavalry to lengthen and weaken their formation, and preparing simultaneously for an encircling movement. Caesar's cavalry found it difficult to bear up against their vast numbers. Meanwhile as the two centres were proceeding to charge one another, suddenly from out of the closely packed squadrons the light-armed Numidian infantry doubled forward alongside the cavalry and hurled their javelins among the infantry of the legions. Hereupon Caesar's men launched an attack upon them and their cavalry took to flight; but the infantry stood their ground meantime, until the cavalry should renew their charge and return to succour their own infantry.

5 Caesar was now confronted with novel tactics and observed that his men's formation was becoming disorganised as they ran forward to attack—the infantry in fact, exposing their flank as they advanced in pursuit of the cavalry too far from the standards, were suffering casualties from the javelins of the nearest Numidians; whereas the enemy cavalry easily eluded by their speed the heavy infantry javelin. Accordingly, he had the order passed down the ranks that no soldier should advance more

miles ab signis IIII pedes longius procederet. Equitatus interim Labieni suorum multitudine confisus
Caesaris paucitatem circuire conatur: equites Iuliani
pauci multitudine hostium defessi equis convulneratis
paulatim cedere; hostes magis magisque instare.
Ita puncto temporis omnibus legionariis ab hostium
equitatu circumventis Caesarisque copiis in orbem
compulsis intra cancellos omnes coniecti pugnare
cogebantur.

16 Labienus in equo capite nudo versari in prima acie;
simul suos cohortari, non numquam legionarios
Caesaris ita appellare: 'Quid tu,' inquit, 'miles
tiro? Tam feroculus es? Vos quoque iste verbis
infatuavit? In magnum mehercule vos periculum
impulit. Misereor vestri.' Tum miles, 'Non sum,'
inquit, 'tiro, Labiene, sed de legione X. veteranus.'
Tum Labienus, 'Non agnosco,' inquit, 'signa decu-
manorum.' Tum ait miles: 'Iam me qui sim
intelleges'; simul cassidem de capite deiecit, ut
cognosci ab eo posset, atque ita pilum viribus con-
tortum, dum in Labienum mittere contendit, equi
graviter adverso pectori adfixit et ait: 'Labiene,
decumanum militem qui te petit scito esse.'
Omnium tamen animi in terrorem coniecti, et
maxime tironum: circumspicere enim Caesarem
neque amplius facere nisi hostium iacula vitare.

than four feet from the standards. Meanwhile the cavalry of Labienus, relying on the large numbers on their own side, endeavoured to surround Caesar's scanty force; and the mere handful of Julian cavalry, worn out by the enemy hordes, their horses wounded, gave ground little by little, while the enemy pressed on them more and more. Thus in a moment all the legionaries were surrounded by the enemy cavalry, and Caesar's forces were compressed into a circle; and so they were all compelled to fight penned behind bars as it were.

16   Labienus rode bare-headed up and down the front line, encouraging his own men the while and occasionally accosting Caesar's legionaries in such terms as these: ' What are you up to, recruit? Quite the dashing little fellow, aren't you? Have all of you too been made fools of by that fellow's words? So help me, it's a very dangerous situation he has driven you into. I feel sorry for you.' ' I'm not a recruit, Labienus,' replied one soldier, ' but a veteran of the Tenth legion.' To this Labienus retorted: ' I don't recognise the standards of the Tenth.' Then said the soldier: ' You'll soon see what I'm made of.' As he spoke the words he flung the helmet from his head so that the other could recognise him and, thus uncovered, brandished his heavy javelin with all his force, as he aimed it at Labienus: then plunging it violently full in the horse's chest he said: ' That will teach you, Labienus, that it's a soldier of the Tenth who is attacking you.' All the troops, however, were demoralised, particularly the recruits; for they kept looking round for Caesar and contented themselves with dodging the enemy javelins.

17 Caesar interim consilio hostium cognito iubet aciem in longitudinem quam maximam porrigi et alternis conversis cohortibus, ut una post, altera ante signa tenderet, ita coronam hostium dextro sinistroque cornu mediam dividit et unam partem ab altera exclusam equitibus intrinsecus adortus cum peditatu telis coniectis in fugam vertit neque longius progressus veritus insidias se ad suos recipit; idem altera pars equitum peditumque Caesaris fecit. His rebus gestis ac procul hostibus repulsis convulneratisque ad sua praesidia sese, sicut erat instructus, recipere coepit.

18 Interim M. Petreius et Cn. Piso cum equitibus Numidis MDC[1] electis peditatuque eiusdem generis satis grandi ex itinere recta subsidio suis occurrunt. Atque hostes suis ex terrore firmatis rursusque renovatis animis legionarios conversis equitibus recipientes novissimos adoriri et impedire coeperunt quo minus se in castra reciperent. Hac re animadversa Caesar iubet signa converti et medio campo redintegrari proelium. Cum ab hostibus eodem modo pugnaretur nec comminus ad manus rediretur Caesarisque equites iumenta ex nausea recenti, siti, languore, paucitate, vulneribus defatigata ad insequendum hostem perseverandumque cursum tar-

---

[1] *The MSS. vary between* MC *and* CCC; *but cf. ch. 19.*

17   Meanwhile Caesar, aware of the enemy's tactics, gave orders for the line to be extended to its maximum length, and for every other cohort to turn about, so that one was facing to the rear of the standards, while the next one faced to their front. By this means with his right and left wing he split in half the encircling enemy force; and having isolated one half from the other with his cavalry, proceeded to attack it from inside with his infantry, turning it to flight with volleys of missiles: then, after advancing no great distance for fear of ambush, he retired to his own lines. The other half of Caesar's cavalry and infantry carried out the same tactics. This task accomplished and the enemy being driven far back with heavy casualties, Caesar began to retire to his own defence positions, maintaining battle formation.

18   Meanwhile M. Petreius and Cn. Piso arrived with Numidian troops—sixteen hundred picked cavalry and a fairly considerable force of infantry—and immediately on arrival hastened straight to the aid of their comrades. And so the enemy, putting their fears aside and taking fresh heart and courage, wheeled their cavalry round and began to attack the rear of the retreating legionaries and to hinder their withdrawal to camp. Observing this, Caesar ordered to turn about and renew the battle in the middle of the plain. As the enemy repeated the same manoeuvre, but without any return to hand-to-hand fighting, and as Caesar's cavalry found that their horses, worn out with the effects of recent sea-sickness, thirst and the fatigue and wounds sustained in their unequal contest, were now more reluctant to keep doggedly on the move in pursuit of the enemy,

diora haberent dieique pars exigua iam reliqua
esset, cohortibus equitibusque circumdatis cohortatur
ut uno ictu contenderent neque remitterent, donec
ultra ultimos collis hostis reppulissent atque eorum
essent potiti. Itaque signo dato cum iam hostes lan-
guide tela neglegenterque mitterent, subito immittit
cohortis turmasque suorum; atque puncto temporis
hostibus nullo negotio campo pulsis post collemque
deiectis nacti locum atque ibi paulisper commorati,
ita uti erant instructi leniter se ad suas recipiunt
munitiones. Itemque adversarii male accepti tum
demum se ad sua praesidia contulerunt.

19   Interim ea re gesta et proelio dirempto ex adversariis perfugere plures ex omni genere hominum,
et praeterea intercepti hostium complures equites
peditesque. Ex quibus cognitum est consilium
hostium, eos hac mente et conatu venisse ut novo
atque inusitato genere proeli tirones legionarii
paucique perturbati Curionis exemplo ab equitatu
circumventi opprimerentur, et ita Labienum dixisse
pro contione, tantam se multitudinem auxiliorum
adversariis Caesaris sumministraturum ut etiam
caedendo in ipsa victoria defatigati vincerentur atque
a suis superarentur, quippe qui sine illorum ope sibi

and as there was now but a little daylight left, Caesar urged his encircled cohorts and cavalry to make one vigorous thrust and not give up until they had driven the enemy back beyond the furthest high ground and gained possession of the latter. And so, waiting to give the signal until the enemy's volleys of missiles were half-hearted and inaccurate, he suddenly let loose some cohorts and squadrons of his own troops upon them. In a moment the enemy were driven without trouble off the plain and thrown back behind the high ground, and Caesar's men had gained the position; then, after a brief pause there, they retired slowly in battle formation to their own fortifications. Their opponents likewise, after this warm reception, then at length withdrew to their own positions.

9 Meanwhile after this engagement had taken place and when the action had been broken off, quite a number of all ranks of the opposing side deserted to Caesar, and in addition not a few of the enemy cavalry and infantry were taken prisoner. From them the enemy's plan became known. He had come with the intention of trying out new and un-familiar battle tactics upon Caesar's legionaries, in order that—raw recruits and few in numbers as they were—they should be demoralised thereby, and be enveloped and crushed by the cavalry, as Curio had been; and Labienus had spoken to this effect to his troops on parade, that he would furnish Caesar's opponents with so vast a number of auxiliaries that Caesar's men would be quite exhausted even with killing them, and so would be vanquished in the very hour of victory, and mastered by his forces. In fact, quite apart from the aid of those auxiliaries, he had reason for self-confidence: first because he had heard

confideret,[1] primum quod audierat Romae legiones
veteranas dissentire neque in Africam velle transire;
deinde quod triennio in Africa suos milites retentos
consuetudine fidelis sibi iam effecisset, maxima autem
auxilia haberet Numidarum equitum levisque armaturae, praeterea ex fuga proelioque Pompeiano
Labienus quos secum a Buthroto [2] transportaverat
equites Germanos Gallosque ibique postea ex hibri-
dis, libertinis servisque conscripserat, armaverat
equoque uti frenato condocuerat, praeterea regia
auxilia, elephantis CXX equitatuque innumerabili,[3]
deinde legiones conscriptas ex cuiusquemodi generis
amplius XII milibus. Hac spe atque ea audacia
inflammatus Labienus cum equitibus Gallis Ger-
manisque MDC, Numidarum sine frenis VIII milibus,
praeterea Petreiano auxilio adhibito equitibus MDC,
peditum ac levis armaturae quater tanto, sagittariis
ac funditoribus hippotoxotisque compluribus: his
copiis pridie Non. Ian., post diem VI. quam Africam
Caesar [4] attigit, in campis planissimis purissimisque
ab hora diei quinta usque ad solis occasum est decertatum. In eo proelio Petreius graviter ictus ex acie
recessit.

20   Caesar interim castra munire diligentius, praesidia
firmare copiis maioribus vallumque ab oppido Ruspina
usque ad mare ducere et a castris alterum eodem,

[1] quippe quis in illorum sibi confideret *is the general reading
of the MSS.*: *I have adopted Forchhammer's conjecture.*

[2] Brundisio *MSS.*: Buthroto *Frölich.*

[3] equitatusque innumerabilis *MSS.*: equitatuque innumerabili *Hoffmann.*

[4] Caesar *added by Dinter.*

that at Rome the veteran legions were mutinous and refusing to cross into Africa; next because he had kept his own troops in Africa for three years: they were acclimatised and he had now secured their loyalty to himself; he had, moreover, very large auxiliary forces composed of Numidian cavalry and light-armed troops and, besides these, the German and Gallic cavalry which, after the defeat and rout of Pompeius, he, Labienus, had brought across with him from Buthrotum, as well as those which he had levied later on in Africa from half-castes, freedmen and slaves, and had armed and taught to handle a bridled horse: he had in addition royal auxiliary forces, as well as a hundred and twenty elephants and innumerable cavalry; and finally, legions raised from more than twelve thousand men of every type. On such considerations was based the reckless confidence that fired Labienus, with his sixteen hundred Gallic and German cavalry, his eight thousand Numidians who rode without bridles, reinforced in addition by the cavalry contingent of Petreius, sixteen hundred strong, and with his infantry and light-armed force, four times as big, and with his numerous archers, slingers and mounted archers. These were the forces which on January 4th, five days after Caesar reached Africa, on a perfectly flat and unimpeded plain were engaged in a contest from the fifth hour of the day continuously till sundown. In that battle Petreius was gravely wounded and retired from the field.

Meanwhile Caesar fortified his camp with greater care, strengthened its defences by manning them with larger forces, and carried an entrenchment from the town of Ruspina right to the sea, and a second

quo tutius ultro citroque commeare auxiliaque sine periculo sibi succurrere possent, tela tormentaque ex navibus in castra comportare, remigum partem ex classe, Gallorum, Rhodiorum epibatarumque armare et in castra evocare uti, si posset, eadem ratione qua adversarii levis armatura interiecta inter equites suos interponeretur, sagittariisque ex omnibus navibus Ityreis, Syris et cuiusque generis ductis in castra compluribus frequentabat suas copias—audiebat enim Scipionem post diem tertium eius diei quo proelium factum erat appropinquare, copias suas cum Labieno et Petreio coniungere; cuius copiae legionum VIII et equitum III milium esse nuntiabantur —officinas ferrarias instruere, sagittas telaque ut fierent complura curare, glandis fundere, sudis comparare, litteras in Siciliam nuntiosque mittere, ut sibi cratis materiemque congererent ad arietes, cuius inopia in Africa esset, praeterea ferrum, plumbum mitteretur. Etiam animum advertebat frumento se in Africa nisi importaticio uti non posse : priore anno enim propter adversariorum dilectus, quod stipendiarii aratores milites essent facti, messem non esse factam ; praeterea ex omni Africa frumentum adversarios in pauca oppida et bene munita comportasse omnemque regionem Africae exinanisse frumento, oppida praeter ea pauca quae

from his camp likewise to the sea : his purpose was to ensure safer communication in both directions and to enable his reinforcements to come up to his support without danger. He brought missiles and artillery from the ships into his camp, and armed some of the Gallic and Rhodian rowers and marines from the fleet and summoned them to camp, in order that, if possible, on the same principle which his opponents had employed, light-armed troops should be interspersed at intervals among his cavalry. From all his ships he brought archers into camp—Ityreans, Syrians and men of divers races—and thronged his forces with numerous drafts of them; for he heard that on the second day after the battle was fought Scipio was approaching and uniting his forces—reported to comprise eight legions and three thousand cavalry—with those of Labienus and Petreius. He also established smithies, took steps to ensure a plentiful supply of arrows and missile-weapons, cast leaden bullets, collected stakes, and sent couriers with despatches to Sicily bidding them build up for his use stocks of hurdles and timber for battering-rams—timber was scarce in Africa—and in addition send him iron and lead. He realised, moreover, that no corn could be available for his use in Africa unless it was imported; for there had been no harvest the previous year on account of the levies held by his opponents and the fact that the farmers, being tributary subjects of Rome, had been called up for military service: moreover, his opponents had collected corn from the whole of Africa and conveyed it into a few well-fortified towns, and every corner of Africa was thus ransacked of corn; and apart from those few towns which his opponents

ipsi suis praesidiis tueri poterant reliqua dirui ac
deseri, et eorum incolas intra sua praesidia coegisse
commigrare, agros desertos ac vastatos esse.

21 Hac necessitate Caesar coactus privatos ambiendo
et blande appellando aliquantum numerum frumenti
in sua praesidia congesserat et eo parce utebatur.
Opera interim ipse cotidie circuire et alteras cohortis
in statione habere propter hostium multitudinem.
Labienus saucios suos, quorum numerus maximus
fuit, iubet in plaustris deligatos Hadrumetum depor-
tari. Naves interim Caesaris onerariae errabundae
male vagabantur incertae locorum atque castrorum
suorum; quas singulas scaphae adversariorum complures adortae incendebant atque expugnabant.
Hac re nuntiata Caesar classis circum insulas portus-
que disposuit, quo tutius commeatus supportari
posset.

22 M. Cato interim, qui Uticae praeerat, Cn. Pompeium filium multis verbis assidueque obiurgare non
desistebat, ' Tuus,' inquit, ' pater istuc aetatis cum
esset et animadvertisset rem publicam ab nefariis
sceleratisque civibus oppressam bonosque aut interfectos aut exsilio multatos patria civitateque carere,
gloria et animi magnitudine elatus privatus atque
adulescentulus paterni exercitus reliquiis collectis

were able to defend themselves with their own garrisons, the rest were being destroyed and abandoned: their inhabitants had been compelled to migrate to the shelter of the enemy garrisons, and their lands were now abandoned and laid waste.

1 Under stress of this emergency Caesar had, by soliciting private individuals with touching appeals, amassed a certain amount of corn in his garrisons, and this he was using sparingly. Meanwhile every day he went round the field-works in person, and doubled the number of cohorts on guard duty in view of the large numbers of the enemy. Labienus gave orders that his wounded, who were very numerous, should have their wounds dressed and then be carried in carts to Hadrumetum. Meanwhile some of Caesar's transports were cruising aimlessly about, badly off their course in their uncertain knowledge of the area and the position of his camp; and one by one they were set upon by a number of enemy pinnaces and set on fire or boarded. When this was reported to Caesar he posted squadrons round the islands and harbours to enable his supplies to be conveyed with greater safety.

2 Meanwhile M. Cato, who was in command at Utica, never left off assailing Cn. Pompeius, the son, with long and constant speeches of reproof. ' When your father was your age,' he said, ' he perceived that the state was oppressed by wicked and vicious citizens, and that loyal men had either been put to death or else, punished by exile, were deprived of their country and civic rights. Whereupon, carried away by his ambition and the nobility of his nature, though a mere private citizen and a callow youth, he mustered the remnants of his father's army and

177

paene oppressam funditus et deletam Italiam urbem-
que Romanam in libertatem vindicavit, idemque
Siciliam, Africam, Numidiam, Mauretaniam mirabili
celeritate armis recepit. Quibus ex rebus sibi eam
dignitatem quae est per gentis clarissima notissima-
que conciliavit adulescentulusque atque eques
Romanus triumphavit. Atque ille non ita amplis
rebus patris gestis neque tam excellenti dignitate
maiorum parta neque tantis clientelis nominisque
claritate praeditus in rem publicam est ingressus.
Tu contra et patris nobilitate et dignitate et per te
ipse satis animi magnitudine diligentiaque praeditus
nonne eniteris et proficisceris ad paternas clientelas
auxilium tibi reique publicae atque optimo cuique
efflagitatum? '

23   His verbis hominis gravissimi incitatus adulescentulus cum naviculis cuiusquemodi generis XXX, inibi
paucis rostratis, profectus ab Utica in Mauretaniam
regnumque Bogudis est ingressus expeditoque exercitu servorum, liberorum II milium numero, cuius
partem inermem, partem habuerat armatam, ad
oppidum Ascurum accedere coepit; in quo oppido
praesidium fuit regium. Pompeio adveniente oppidani, usque eo passi propius accedere donec ad ipsas
portas ac murum appropinquaret, subito eruptione
facta prostratos perterritosque Pompeianos in mare

emancipated Italy and the city of Rome when they were all but utterly overwhelmed and destroyed; and likewise he recovered Sicily, Africa, Numidia and Mauretania by force of arms with astonishing speed. By these achievements he won himself that prestige of his which in lustre and in fame is unequalled throughout the world, and, albeit a mere youth and a Roman knight, celebrated a triumph. And in his case his father had not the same imposing record as your father has, nor had he inherited from his ancestors the same position of eminent distinction, nor was he endowed with such influential ties of clientship or with a famous name, when he entered public life. Whereas in your case not only are you endowed with the fame and prestige of your father, but you yourself are also adequately endowed on your own account with nobility of nature and with earnestness. Will you not therefore make an effort and set out in quest of your father's clients to demand their assistance for yourself, for the state and for every loyal citizen?'

These words, coming from a man of the greatest authority, spurred on the youth. Taking with him thirty small ships of every type, including a few equipped with beaks, he set out from Utica and invaded Mauretania and the kingdom of Bogud. Dec. (?) 47. With an army in light order comprising two thousand slaves and freedmen, some with arms, some without, he proceeded to approach the town of Ascurum, where there was a royal garrison. As Pompeius drew near, the townsfolk allowed him to come closer and closer until he was actually approaching the very gates and the town wall: then suddenly they made a sally and drove the crushed and panic-stricken

navisque passim compulerunt. Ita re male gesta
Cn. Pompeius filius navis inde avertit neque postea
litus attigit classemque ad insulas Balearis versus
convertit.

24 Scipio interim cum eis copiis quas paulo ante
demonstravimus Uticae grandi praesidio relicto profectus primum Hadrumeti castra ponit, deinde ibi
paucos dies commoratus noctu itinere facto cum
Labieni et Petrei copiis coniungit, atque unis castris
factis III milia passuum longe considunt. Equitatus
interim eorum circum Caesaris munitiones vagari
atque eos qui pabulandi aut aquandi gratia extra
vallum progressi essent excipere: ita omnis adversarios intra munitiones continere. Qua re Caesariani
gravi annona sunt conflictati, ideo quod nondum
neque ab Sicilia neque ab Sardinia commeatus sup-
portatus erat neque per anni tempus in mari classes
sine periculo vagari poterant; neque amplius milia
passuum VI terrae Africae quoquo versus tenebant
pabulique inopia premebantur. Qua necessitate
coacti veterani milites equitesque, qui multa terra
marique bella confecissent et periculis inopiaque tali
saepe essent conflictati, alga e litore collecta et aqua
dulci eluta et ita iumentis esurientibus data vitam
eorum producebant.

25 Dum haec ita fierent, rex Iuba cognitis Caesaris
difficultatibus copiarumque paucitate—non est visum

---

[1] See Appendix A, p. 393.

[2] The figure VI, given by all MSS., is not easily reconciled
with the dimensions of the plateau of Ruspina : some editors
would amend it to III.

Pompeians back wholesale to the sea and their ships. After this reverse Cn. Pompeius, the son, withdrew his fleet from there and without touching land again set course with his fleet towards the Balearic Islands.

Meanwhile Scipio set out with the forces we enumerated a little earlier, leaving a considerable garrison behind at Utica, and pitched camp first at Hadrumetum. Then, after staying there a few days, he made a night march and joined up with the forces of Labienus and Petreius; whereupon they established themselves in a single camp three miles distant from Caesar.[1] Meanwhile their cavalry went roving round Caesar's entrenchments, intercepting all such troops as had advanced beyond the rampart to forage or fetch water; and this had the effect of keeping all their opponents confined within their defences. By these tactics Caesar's men were afflicted with a severe scarcity of corn, for this reason that supplies had not so far been conveyed to him either from Sicily or Sardinia, and, on account of the season of the year, fleets could not move freely about the seas without risk; moreover, they occupied no more than six[2] miles of African soil in any one direction, and were hard put to it for lack of fodder. The urgency of this situation drove the veteran troops—infantry and cavalry—men who had gone through many campaigns by land and sea and had often been afflicted by hazards and similar privation, to collect seaweed from the beach, cleanse it in fresh water, and give it in this state to their famished beasts, thereby prolonging their lives.

While these events were taking place, king Juba, who was aware of Caesar's difficulties and the small numbers of his forces, thought it advisable not to

dari spatium convalescendi augendarumque eius
opum: itaque comparatis equitum magnis peditumque copiis subsidio suis egressus e regno ire contendit.
P. Sittius interim et rex Bochus coniunctis suis copiis
cognito regis Iubae egressu propius eius regnum
copias suas admovere, Cirtamque, oppidum opulen-
tissimum eius regni, adortus paucis diebus pugnando
capit et praeterea duo oppida Gaetulorum. Quibus
cum condicionem ferret, ut oppido excederent idque
sibi vacuum traderent, condicionemque repudiassent,
postea ab eo capti interfectique sunt omnes. Inde
progressus agros oppidaque vexare non destitit.
Quibus rebus cognitis Iuba cum iam non longe ab
Scipione atque eius ducibus abesset, capit consilium
satius esse sibi suoque regno subsidio ire quam, dum
alios adiuturus proficisceretur, ipse suo regno
expulsus forsitan utraque re expelleretur. Itaque
rursus recipere atque auxilia etiam ab Scipione
abduxit sibi suisque rebus timens elephantisque
XXX relictis suis finibus oppidisque suppetias profectus est.

26   Caesar interim, cum de suo adventu dubitatio in
provincia esset neque quisquam crederet ipsum sed
aliquem legatum in Africam cum copiis venisse,
conscriptis litteris circum provinciam omnis civitates
facit de suo adventu certiores. Interim nobiles
homines ex suis oppidis profugere et in castra

---

[1] A Roman adventurer and soldier of fortune who since the
conspiracy of Catiline had been operating independently in
Africa with a body of troops raised in Spain. Bochus, king
of eastern Mauretania, sided with Caesar against Juba.

give him any respite for recruiting his strength or increasing his resources. And so, having got together large forces of cavalry and infantry, he departed from his kingdom and made haste to go to the assistance of his friends. Meanwhile P. Sittius [1] and king Bochus had united their forces and, learning of king Juba's departure, moved them closer to his kingdom. Sittius then attacked Cirta, the richest town of that kingdom, and after a few days' fighting captured it, as well as two Gaetulian towns. When he offered them terms, proposing that they should evacuate the town and surrender it unoccupied to him, they refused the terms and were subsequently captured by Sittius and all put to death. Thereupon he advanced, ravaging both countryside and towns without ceasing. Juba got to know of this when he was now not far away from Scipio and his lieutenants, and came to the conclusion that it was better to go to the aid of himself and his own kingdom, rather than that, in the course of setting out to help others, he should himself be driven out of his own kingdom, and perhaps be thwarted in both fields. Accordingly, he marched back again, withdrawing his auxiliary forces too from Scipio, in his alarm on account of himself and his own interests ; and leaving thirty elephants behind with Scipio, he set forth to the relief of his own territory and towns.

26   Meanwhile as there was some doubt in the province as to Caesar's arrival, and nobody believed it was Caesar in person that had come to Africa with the forces, but rather some one of his lieutenants, he sent written despatches round the province informing all the communities of his personal arrival. Meanwhile persons of note fled from their towns and sought

Caesaris devenire et de adversariorum eius crudelitate acerbitateque commemorare coeperunt. Quorum lacrimis querelisque Caesar commotus, cum antea constituisset e stativis castris aestate inita cunctis copiis auxiliisque accitis bellum cum suis adversariis gerere, hieme gerere [1] instituit, litteris celeriter in Siciliam ad Alienum et Rabirium Postumum conscriptis et per catascopum missis, ut sine mora ac nulla excusatione hiemis ventorumque quam celerrime exercitus sibi transportaretur: Africam provinciam perire funditusque everti ab suis inimicis; quod nisi celeriter sociis foret subventum, praeter ipsam Africam terram nihil, ne tectum quidem quo se reciperent, ab eorum scelere insidiisque reliquum futurum. Atque ipse erat in tanta festinatione et exspectatione ut postero die quam misisset litteras nuntiumque in Siciliam classem exercitumque morari diceret, dies noctesque oculos mentemque ad mare dispositos directosque haberet. Nec mirum: animadvertebat enim villas exuri, agros vastari, pecus diripi, trucidari, oppida castellaque dirui deserique, principes civitatum aut interfici aut in catenis teneri, liberos eorum obsidum nomine in servitutem abripi; eis se miseris suamque fidem implorantibus auxilio propter copiarum paucitatem esse non posse. Milites

[1] *The words* hieme gerere *were conjectured by Woelfflin.*

184

refuge in Caesar's camp and proceeded to quote instances of the cruelty and harshness of his opponents. Their tears and complainings had no little effect on Caesar; and though he had previously decided to wait for the beginning of summer to muster all his forces and auxiliaries from their permanent quarters and wage war on his opponents, he now resolved on a winter campaign, promptly drafting a despatch to Alienus and Rabirius Postumus in Sicily, which he sent by a reconnaissance vessel, to the effect that an army must be shipped across to him as quickly as possible: there must be no delay and no excuses on the ground of wintry weather or adverse winds. The province of Africa, he wrote, was in its death throes, in the process of utter destruction at the hands of his foes; and unless aid were promptly rendered to their allies, nothing save the very soil of Africa—not even a roof to give them shelter—would be left as the result of their enemies' treacherous crimes. Caesar himself was in such a ferment of impatient expectancy that on the day after he sent the messenger to Sicily with the despatch he kept saying that the fleet and army were dallying; and day and night he kept his eyes and attention bent and riveted upon the sea. And no wonder; for he perceived that farms were being burned to the ground, fields stripped, herds plundered or butchered, towns and strongholds destroyed and abandoned, and the principal citizens either murdered or held in chains, and their children haled off to slavery on the pretext of being hostages: yet to these folk, who in their misery implored his protection, he could give no assistance because his forces were so few. Meanwhile he kept his troops continuously at work on their training, proceeded

interim in opere exercere atque castra munire, turris, castella facere molesque iacere in mare non intermittere.

27 Scipio interim elephantos hoc modo condocefacere instituit. Duas instruxit acies, unam funditorum contra elephantos, quae quasi adversariorum locum obtineret et contra eorum frontem adversam lapillos minutos mitteret; deinde in ordinem elephantos constituit, post illos autem suam aciem instruxit ut, cum ab adversariis lapides mitti coepissent et elephanti perterriti se ad suos convertissent, rursus ab sua acie lapidibus missis eos converterent adversus hostem. Quod aegre tardeque fiebat; rudes enim elephanti multorum annorum doctrina usuque vetusto vix edocti tamen communi periculo in aciem producuntur.

28 Dum haec ad Ruspinam ab utrisque ducibus administrantur, C. Vergilius praetorius, qui Thapsi oppido maritimo praeerat, cum animum advertisset navis singulas cum exercitu Caesaris incertas locorum atque castrorum suorum vagari, occasionem nactus navem quam ibi habuit actuariam complet militibus et sagittariis et eidem scaphas de navibus adiungit ac singulas navis Caesarianas consectari coepit. Et cum pluris adortus esset pulsus fugatusque inde disces-

with the fortification of his camp, and went on without interruption constructing towers and redoubts and driving moles out into the sea.

Scipio meanwhile undertook the training of the elephants in the following manner. He drew up two lines of battle: one line of slingers, facing the elephants, to take the place of the enemy and to discharge small stones against the opposing front formed by the elephants; next he arranged the elephants in line, and behind them drew up his own line so that, when the enemy proceeded to sling their stones and the elephants in their consequent panic wheeled round upon their own side, his men should receive them with a volley of stones, and so make them wheel round again away from his own line in the direction of the enemy. This method worked, though it was a difficult and slow process; for elephants are uncouth creatures, and it is difficult to get them fully trained even with many years' training and long practice; and if they are led forth to battle, they are, for all their training, equally dangerous to both sides.

While these dispositions were being made at Ruspina by the leaders on either side, the ex-praetor C. Vergilius, who was in charge of the coastal town of Thapsus, observed that ships carrying Caesar's troops were sailing singly on no set course, due to their uncertain knowledge of the locality and of the position of his camp. He therefore seized the opportunity and manned with soldiers and archers a fast boat which he had there, to which he added some ship's pinnaces, and with these he set about the pursuit of Caesar's ships one by one. He had attacked several, only to be beaten off, put to flight and forced to quit the area, but even so was still

sisset nec tamen desisteret periclitari, forte incidit in
navem, in qua erant duo Titii, Hispani adulescentes,
tribuni legionis V., quorum patrem Caesar in senatum
legerat, et cum his T. Salienus, centurio legionis
eiusdem, qui M. Messallam legatum obsederat
Messanae seditiosissima oratione apud eum usus
idemque pecuniam et ornamenta triumphi Caesaris
retinenda et custodienda curarat et ob has causas
sibi timebat. Hic propter conscientiam peccatorum
suorum persuasit adulescentibus ne repugnarent
seseque Vergilio traderent. Itaque deducti a Vergilio ad Scipionem custodibus traditi et post diem
tertium sunt interfecti. Qui cum ducerentur ad
necem, petisse dicitur maior Titius a centurionibus
uti se priorem quam fratrem interficerent, idque ab
eis facile impetrasse atque ita esse interfectos.

29   Turmae interim equitum, quae pro vallo in stationibus esse solebant,[1] cotidie minutis proeliis inter
se depugnare non intermittunt; non numquam etiam
Germani Gallique Labieniani cum Caesaris equitibus
fide data inter se colloquebantur. Labienus interim
cum parte equitatus Leptim oppidum, cui praeerat
Saserna cum cohortibus VI, oppugnare ac vi irrum-
pere conabatur; quod ab defensoribus propter
egregiam munitionem oppidi et multitudinem tormentorum facile et sine periculo defendebatur.

---

[1] *After* solebant *the MSS. read* ab utrisque ducibus : *I
have followed Nipperdey in omitting them.*

---

[1] When Messalla and Sallust were sent by Caesar in August,
47, to order certain legions to concentrate in Sicily for the
African campaign, the legions mutinied and the Twelfth went
so far as to pelt them with stones.

persisting in his hazardous tactics, when chance led him to fall in with a ship which had on board two young Spaniards of the name of Titius—tribunes of the Fifth legion, whose father Caesar had caused to be elected to the Senate—as well as T. Salienus, a centurion of the same legion, who had laid siege to the house of M. Messalla,[1] Caesar's lieutenant, at Messana, employing in his presence the language of downright mutiny. This man had also been responsible for withholding under guard some money and trappings belonging to Caesar's triumph, and for these reasons viewed his own prospects with misgiving. His own guilty conscience led him to persuade the young men to put up no resistance, but to surrender to Vergilius. Accordingly they were escorted by Vergilius to Scipio, put under guard, and two days later put to death. As they were being led to execution, the elder Titius, it is said, besought the centurions to put him to death before his brother, and was readily granted that request, and they were put to death in that order.

Meanwhile the squadrons of cavalry whose regular duty it was to be on guard in front of the rampart were engaging daily in incessant skirmishes with one another; and there were also times when Labienus' Germans and Gauls and Caesar's cavalry exchanged pledges of good faith and conversed with one another. Meantime Labienus with part of his cavalry was endeavouring to assault and force his way into the town of Leptis, which was under command of Saserna with six cohorts; but its defenders, thanks to the excellent fortifications of the town and the large number of their engines of war, defended it easily and without danger. But Labienus' cavalry re-

Quod ubi saepius eius equitatus facere non intermittebat, et cum forte ante portam turma densa
adstitisset, scorpione accuratius misso atque eorum
decurione percusso et ad equum defixo reliqui perterriti fuga se in castra recipiunt.   Quo facto postea
sunt deterriti oppidum temptare.

30   Scipio interim fere cotidie non longe a suis castris
passibus CCC instruere aciem ac maiore parte diei
consumpta rursus in castra se recipere.   Quod cum
saepius fieret neque ex Caesaris castris quisquam
prodiret neque propius eius copias accederet,
despecta Caesaris patientia exercitusque eius,[1] universis copiis productis elephantisque turritis XXX
ante aciem instructis, quam latissime potuit porrecta
equitum peditumque multitudine uno tempore progressus haud ita longe a Caesaris castris constitit in
campo.

31   Quibus rebus cognitis Caesar iubet milites qui
extra munitiones processerant pabulandi lignandique
aut etiam muniendi gratia quique vallum petierant
quaeque ad eam rem opus erant,[2] omnis intra
munitiones minutatim modesteque sine tumultu aut
terrore se recipere atque in opere consistere.
Equitibus autem qui in statione fuerant praecipit ut

[1] *After* eius *all MSS. read* Iuba :   *most editors follow Aldus in
deleting it.*
[2] quique pabulandi aut lignandi aut etiam muniendi
gratia vallem petierant quique *most MSS.* : vallum quaeque
Aldus; quique *transposed by Forchhammer.*

---

[1] A small catapult.

peated these tactics fairly frequently and gave them no respite; and when it so chanced that a squadron had halted in massed formation in front of the gate, its captain was struck and pinned to his horse by a bolt discharged from a scorpion [1] with unusually accurate aim. This so unnerved the rest that they withdrew in flight to their camp, too much daunted by it to resume their attempt upon the town thereafter.

30   Meanwhile practically every day Scipio arrayed his line of battle at no great distance—three hundred paces—from his own camp, and then, when the greater part of the day was now spent, returned back again to camp. As this manoeuvre was carried out quite frequently without anyone's issuing forth from Caesar's camp or approaching closer to Scipio's forces, the latter, holding scorn of the forbearance shewn by Caesar and his army, led forth his entire force, with thirty elephants equipped with towers drawn up in front of his line: then, advancing and simultaneously deploying to the widest possible extent his vast numbers of cavalry and infantry, he halted in the plain not so very far from Caesar's camp.

31   When he learned of this Caesar gave orders that those troops who had gone forward outside the fortifications, whether to forage or fetch wood or even to work on the fortifications, as well as those who had been collecting stakes and what was needed for that work, should all retire within the fortifications—gradually and in a disciplined manner, without any fuss or alarm—and take their stand in the field-works. His instructions to the cavalry on guard were to go on holding the positions in which they had been

usque eo locum obtinerent in quo paulo ante consti-
tissent donec ab hoste telum missum ad se perveniret; quod si propius accederetur, quam honestis-
sime se intra munitiones reciperent. Alii quoque
equitatui edicit uti suo quisque loco paratus armatusque praesto esset. At haec non ipse per se coram,
cum de vallo prospecularetur, sed mirabili peritus
scientia bellandi in praetorio sedens per speculatores
et nuntios imperabat quae fieri volebat. Animadvertebat enim, quamquam magnis essent copiis
adversarii freti, tamen saepe a se fugatis, pulsis
perterritisque et concessam vitam et ignota peccata;
quibus rebus numquam tanta suppeteret ex ipsorum
inertia conscientiaque animi victoriae fiducia ut castra
sua adoriri auderent. Praeterea ipsius nomen
auctoritasque magna ex parte eorum exercitus
minuebat audaciam. Tum egregiae munitiones
castrorum atque valli fossarumque altitudo et extra
vallum stili caeci mirabilem in modum consiti vel
sine defensoribus aditum adversariis prohibebant:
scorpionum, catapultarum ceterorumque telorum
quae ad defendendum solent parari magnam copiam
habebat. Atque haec propter exercitus sui praesentis paucitatem et tirocinium praeparaverat, non

posted a little earlier, until they should come within range of the enemy's missiles: if the enemy advanced yet closer, they must then make as honourable a withdrawal as possible within the fortifications. As for the rest of the cavalry, they too had their orders— to be ready at hand, equipped and armed, each man in his proper place. These orders, however, he did not issue personally on the spot, surveying the situation for himself from the rampart; but so remarkable was his skill and knowledge of warfare that, making use of look-outs and orderlies, he issued the instructions necessary for his purpose as he sat in his head-quarters. For he observed that, although his opponents were relying on the great size of their forces, yet they were the very men whom he himself had often routed, beaten back and utterly demoralised, only to spare their lives and forgive their misdemeanours; in which circumstances, considering their own lack of initiative and their guilty conscience, they would never muster sufficient confidence in victory as to venture to attack his camp. Moreover, his own name and prestige had, to a great extent, a sobering effect upon the reckless spirit of their army. Then again the exceptional defences of the camp—the height of the rampart, the depth of the ditches, and the concealed stakes outside the rampart, marvellously well planted—all these, even without defenders, served to deter the enemy's approach; while as for scorpions, catapults and all the other normal weapons of defence, he had a plentiful supply of these. These he had prepared in advance in view of the small size and lack of experience of his army as it then was, and it was not because he was taken aback or dismayed at the

hostium vi et metu commotus patientem se timidumque hostium opinioni praebebat. Neque idcirco
copias, quamquam erant paucae tironumque, non
educebat in aciem qui victoriae suae diffideret, sed
referre arbitrabatur, cuiusmodi victoria esset futura ;
turpe enim sibi existimabat tot rebus gestis tantisque
exercitibus devictis, tot tam claris victoriis partis, ab
reliquis copiis adversariorum suorum ex fuga collectis
se cruentam adeptum existimari victoriam. Itaque
constituerat gloriam exsultationemque eorum pati,
donec sibi veteranarum legionum pars aliqua in
secundo commeatu occurrisset.

32   Scipio interim paulisper, ut antea dixi, in eo loco
commoratus, ut quasi despexisse Caesarem videretur,
paulatim reducit suas copias in castra et contione
advocata de terrore suo desperationeque exercitus
Caesaris facit verba et cohortatus suos victoriam
propriam se eis brevi daturum pollicetur. Caesar
iubet milites rursus ad opus redire et per causam
munitionum tirones in labore defatigare non intermittit. Interim Numidae Gaetulique diffugere cotidie ex castris Scipionis et partim in regnum se conferre, partim, quod ipsi maioresque eorum beneficio
C. Mari usi fuissent Caesaremque eius adfinem esse

---

[1] The famous soldier and democratic champion, who in 115
had married Julia, the sister of Caesar's father. There is no
mention in other writers of his beneficence towards the Gaetulians, who had presumably served him well as mercenaries in
his campaigns against Jugurtha (109–106). As some 60 years
had now elapsed, it would seem that very few, if any, of the
present Gaetulians could *themselves* have been kindly treated
by Marius. Chapters 35 and 56 below suggest rather that it
was their fathers or grandfathers who had been rewarded and

enemy's might that he showed himself—to the enemy's thinking—long-suffering and timid. The reason why he would not lead his forces on to the field, few and inexperienced though they were, was not that he lacked confidence in his victory, but he considered the important question was—what manner of victory it would prove; for he thought it a personal slur if after all his achievements, after all the many brilliant victories he had won over such massive armies, men should look upon this victory as one gained only with much bloodshed over such remnants as his opponents had mustered from their routed forces. And so he had resolved to endure their boastful triumph until his second convoy should join him, including some portion of his veteran legions.

2 Meanwhile Scipio lingered for a little while, as I mentioned earlier, in that postion, to create the impression that he had held Caesar virtually in contempt, and then gradually withdrew his forces to camp. There he paraded his troops and spoke to them of the dread which their own side inspired and the desperate attitude of Caesar's army; and with such words of encouragement to his men he promised them that he would shortly give them a lasting victory. Caesar ordered his troops to return once more to their duties and, on the pretext of the fortifications, kept his recruits constantly employed to the point of exhaustion. Meanwhile Numidians and Gaetulians were daily deserting from Scipio's camp: the former betook themselves to Juba's kingdom, while the latter, because they themselves and their ancestors had been kindly treated by C. Marius [1] and heard

made clients, and that the present generation had inherited this formal tie of clientship.

audiebant, in eius castra perfugere catervatim non intermittunt. Quorum ex numero electis hominibus inlustrioribus et litteris ad suos civis datis cohortatus uti manu facta se suosque defenderent, ne suis inimicis adversariisque dicto audientes essent, mittit.

33 Dum haec ad Ruspinam fiunt, legati ex Acylla, civitate libera et immuni,[1] ad Caesarem veniunt seque paratos quaecumque imperasset et libenti animo facturos pollicentur; tantum orare et petere ab eo ut sibi praesidium daret, quo tutius id et sine periculo facere possent; se et frumentum et quaecumque res eis suppeteret communis salutis gratia sumministraturos. Quibus rebus facile a Caesare impetratis praesidioque dato, C. Messium, aedilicia functum potestate, Acyllam iubet proficisci. Quibus rebus cognitis Considius Longus, qui Hadrumeti cum duabus legionibus et equitibus DCC praeerat, celeriter ibi parte praesidi relicta cum VIII cohortibus ad Acyllam ire contendit. Messius celerius itinere confecto prior Acyllam cum cohortibus pervenit. Considius interim cum ad urbem cum copiis accessisset et animadvertisset praesidium Caesaris ibi esse, non ausus periculum suorum facere nulla re gesta pro multitudine hominum rursus se Hadrumetum recepit; deinde, paucis post diebus eques-

---

[1] etiam undique *MSS.:* et immuni *Rubens.*

---

[1] See ch. 7, note 1. Its site is much disputed. I have marked it in Map 3—very tentatively—in accordance with its traditional identification with the Acholla mentioned by Strabo and Pliny. This satisfies the requirements of ch. 43. But it seems very doubtful whether C. would have detached precious troops to garrison a spot so far south; and this objection, together with its mention in ch. 67 in

that Caesar was a relation of his, swarmed constantly for refuge into Caesar's camp. From among their number Caesar chose certain more distinguished members, gave them letters for their fellow citizens, and so dismissed them, exhorting them to raise a force for the defence of themselves and their people, and not to submit passively to the dictates of their foes and opponents.

3   While these events were taking place at Ruspina, there came to Caesar envoys from Acylla, an independent state immune from taxes.[1] They assured him that they would readily and gladly do whatever he might bid: they merely prayed and besought him to give them a garrison to enable them to do his bidding with the greater safety and without peril: they would supply its members with corn and with all other adequate supplies for the sake of their common welfare. This request Caesar readily granted and gave them a garrison, ordering C. Messius, who had once held the office of aedile, to set out for Acylla. On learning this, Considius Longus, who was in command at Hadrumetum with two legions and seven hundred cavalry, left part of his garrison force behind and, taking eight cohorts with him, promptly hastened off to Acylla. Messius completed his march more rapidly and was the first to arrive at Acylla with his cohorts. Whereupon Considius approached the city with his forces and observed that Caesar's garrison was there; and not venturing to jeopardise his troops, retired back again to Hadrumetum without having achieved anything to warrant so large a force. Subsequently,

close conjunction with Leptis and Ruspina, led Veith to place it some 4 km. S.E. of Leptis.

tribus copiis a Labieno adductis, rursus Acyllitanos castris positis obsidere coepit.

34 Per id tempus C. Sallustius Crispus, quem paucis ante diebus missum a Caesare cum classe demonstravimus, Cercinam pervenit. Cuius adventu C. Decimius quaestorius, qui ibi cum grandi familiae suae praesidio praeerat commeatui, parvulum navigium nactus conscendit ac se fugae commendat. Sallustius interim praetor a Cercinitanis receptus magno numero frumenti invento navis onerarias, quarum ibi satis magna copia fuit, complet atque in castra ad Caesarem mittit. Alienus interim pro consule Lilybaeo in navis onerarias imponit legionem XIII. et XIIII. et equites Gallos DCCC, funditorum sagittariorumque mille ac secundum commeatum in Africam mittit ad Caesarem. Quae naves ventum secundum nactae quarto die in portum ad Ruspinam, ubi Caesar castra habuerat, incolumes pervenerunt. Ita Caesar duplici laetitia ac voluptate uno tempore auctus, frumento auxiliisque, tandem suis hilaratis annonaque levata sollicitudinem deponit, legiones equitesque ex navibus egressos iubet ex languore nauseaque reficere, dimissos in castella munitionesque disponit.

35 Quibus rebus Scipio quique cum eo essent comites mirari et requirere: C. Caesarem, qui ultro con-

when a few days later he had procured a contingent
of cavalry from Labienus, he returned, pitched his
camp and proceeded to lay siege to Acylla.

34   It was during this time that C. Sallustius Crispus,
who, as we have explained, had been despatched by
Caesar with a fleet a few days earlier, arrived at
Cercina. On his arrival the ex-quaestor C. Decimius,
who was controller of supplies there and was attended
by a large escort composed of his own household
slaves, went aboard a small boat he had got hold of
and took to flight. Meanwhile Sallustius, the
praetor, was welcomed by the inhabitants of Cercina;
and finding a large quantity of corn he loaded some
merchant vessels—there was quite a large number of
them there—and sent them to Caesar in his camp.
Meanwhile at Lilybaeum the pro-consul Alienus
embarked in transports the Thirteenth and Fourteenth legions, eight hundred Gallic cavalry and one
thousand slingers and archers, and sent to Caesar in
Africa his second convoy. With the wind behind
them these ships arrived safely three days later at the
harbour of Ruspina, the town where Caesar had his
camp. This heartened Caesar, who experienced
twofold pleasure and delight at thus simultaneously
receiving both corn and reinforcements; and now
that at last his troops were made cheerful and the
corn problem was eased, he laid aside his cares,
ordered his legions and cavalry to disembark and get
over the effects of their lassitude and seasickness, and
drafted them to the various forts and defended
positions.

35   All this filled Scipio and his colleagues with wonder
and curiosity; and they had a suspicion that some
deep purpose must underlie this sudden transforma-

suesset bellum inferre ac lacessere proelio, subito
commutatum non sine magno consilio suspicabantur.
Itaque ex eius patientia in magnum timorem coniecti
ex Gaetulis duos quos arbitrabantur suis rebus
amicissimos magnis praemiis pollicitationibusque propositis pro perfugis speculandi gratia in castra
Caesaris mittunt. Qui simul ad eum sunt deducti,
petierunt ut sibi liceret verba sine periculo proloqui.
Potestate facta, ' Saepenumero,' inquiunt, ' imperator, complures Gaetuli, qui sumus clientes C. Mari, et
propemodum omnes cives Romani qui sunt in legione
IIII. et VI., ad te voluimus in tuaque praesidia
confugere ; sed custodiis equitum Numidarum quo id
sine periculo minus faceremus impediebamur. Nunc
data facultate ad te cupidissime venimus, pro
speculatoribus missi ab Scipione ut perspiceremus
num quae fossae aut insidiae elephantis ante castra
portasque valli factae essent, simulque consilia
vestra contra easdem bestias comparationemque
pugnae cognosceremus atque eis renuntiaremus.'
Qui collaudati a Caesare stipendioque donati ad
reliquos perfugas deducuntur. Quorum orationem
celeriter veritas comprobavit : namque postero die
ex legionibus eis quas Gaetuli nominarunt milites
legionarii complures ab Scipione in castra Caesaris
perfugerunt.

36   Dum haec ad Ruspinam geruntur, M. Cato, qui
Uticae praeerat, dilectus cotidie libertinorum,

------

[1] *i.e.* by inheritance. See ch. 32, note 1.

tion in the C. Caesar who had habitually taken the offensive hitherto and was always spoiling for a fight. And so, thrown into no little panic as a result of his forbearance, they chose from the Gaetulians two men whom they considered to be the staunchest supporters of their cause; and after offering them large rewards and making them generous promises, sent them in the guise of deserters on a spying mission into Caesar's camp. No sooner had these men been escorted to Caesar than they sought leave to speak out frankly without danger. That leave being granted, they said: ' Many of us Gaetulians, Commander-in-Chief, who are clients [1] of C. Marius, and practically all the Roman citizens who are in the Fourth and Sixth legions have very often wanted to take refuge with you and resort to your protection; but we were prevented from doing so without hazard by the patrols of Numidian cavalry. But now that the chance has been given us we have come to you most eagerly. We were in fact sent by Scipio as spies to observe closely whether any trenches or traps had been made for the elephants in front of the camp and the gates of the rampart; and at the same time to ascertain your tactics against these same beasts and your dispositions for battle, and then report back to them.' Caesar highly commended them, furnished them with pay, and had them taken to join the other deserters. Their statement was speedily verified by actual events; for on the next day quite a number of legionary troops from the legions mentioned by the Gaetulians deserted from Scipio to Caesar's camp.

66 While this was going on at Ruspina, M. Cato, the commander of Utica, was holding a constant suc-

CAESAR

Afrorum, servorum denique et cuiusquemodi generis
hominum, qui modo per aetatem arma ferre poterant,
habere atque sub manum Scipioni in castra summittere non intermittit. Legati interim ex oppido
Thysdrae, in quod tritici modium milia CCC com-
portata fuerant a negotiatoribus Italicis aratoribus-
que, ad Caesarem venire, quantaque copia frumenti
apud se sit docent simulque orant ut sibi praesidium
mittat quo facilius et frumentum et copiae suae con-
serventur. Quibus Caesar in praesentia gratias egit
praesidiumque brevi tempore se missurum dixit
cohortatusque ad suos civis iubet proficisci. P.
Sittius interim cum copiis Numidiae finis ingressus
castellum in montis loco munito locatum, in quod
Iuba belli gerendi gratia et frumentum et res ceteras
quae ad bellum usui solent esse comportaverat, vi
expugnando est potitus.

37 Caesar postquam legionibus veteranis duabus,
equitatu levique armatura copias suas ex secundo
commeatu auxerat, navis exoneratas statim iubet
Lilybaeum ad reliquum exercitum transportandum
proficisci; ipse VI. Kal. Febr. circiter vigilia prima
imperat speculatores apparitoresque omnes ut sibi
praesto essent. Itaque omnibus insciis neque
suspicantibus vigilia tertia iubet omnis legiones
extra castra educi atque se consequi ad oppidum
Ruspinam versus, in quo ipse praesidium habuit et

---

[1] = approximately 71,000 bushels.
[2] *i.e.* early in the night of January 25/26.

cession of daily levies of freedmen, Africans, slaves even—any man, in fact, no matter of what class, so long as he was of an age to carry arms—and drafting them to Scipio's camp to be at his disposal. Meanwhile there came to Caesar envoys from the town of Thysdra, in which town three hundred thousand measures[1] of wheat had been collected by Italian merchants and farmers. These envoys now informed Caesar of the large quantity of corn they had and prayed him to send them a garrison whereby both their corn and all their stocks might the more readily be kept safe. For the present Caesar expressed his thanks to them, saying that, as for a garrison, he would send one shortly; he then dismissed them with words of encouragement, bidding them go back to their own countrymen. Meanwhile P. Sittius invaded the territory of Numidia with his forces and forcibly took by storm a stronghold, situated on a well-defended mountain height, in which Juba had collected both corn and all other regular munitions of war, for the sake of prosecuting his campaign.

Now that Caesar had reinforced his troops with two veteran legions, cavalry and light-armed forces from his second convoy, he gave orders that the ships, now unloaded, should set sail forthwith for Lilybaeum to bring across the rest of his army. On January 25, at approximately the first watch,[2] he personally issued orders that all his scouts and aides-de-camp should hold themselves at his disposal. Accordingly, without anyone's knowing or suspecting his plan, at the third watch he ordered all his legions to be led outside the camp and follow him in the direction of the town of Ruspina, where he had a garrison;

quod primum ad amicitiam eius accessit. Inde parvulam proclivitatem degressus sinistra parte campi propter mare legiones ducit. Hic campus mirabili planitie patet milia passuum XII; quem iugum cingens a mari ortum neque ita praealtum velut theatri efficit speciem. In hoc iugo colles sunt excelsi pauci, in quibus singulae turres speculaeque singulae perveteres erant collocatae, quarum apud ultimam praesidium et statio fuit Scipionis.

38   Postquam Caesar ad iugum de quo docui ascendit atque in unumquemque collem turremque, castella facere coepit atque ea minus semihora effecit; [1] et postquam non ita longe ab ultimo colle turrique fuit, quae proxima fuit castris adversariorum, in qua docui esse praesidium stationemque Numidarum, Caesar paulisper commoratus perspectaque natura loci equitatu in statione disposito legionibus opus attribuit bracchiumque medio iugo ab eo loco ad quem pervenerat usque ad eum unde egressus erat iubet derigi ac muniri. Quod postquam Scipio Labienusque animadverterant, equitatu omni ex castris educto acieque equestri instructa a suis munitionibus circiter passus mille progrediuntur pedestremque copiam in secunda acie minus passus CCCC a castris suis constituunt.

---

[1] turrem castellaque *MSS.* : turremque castella *Nipperdey.*

---

[1] See Maps 3 and 4. Presumably he kept close to the sea till he reached Sidi Messaoud, the north-easternmost height of the chain of hills, which lies approximately mid-way between Ruspina and Leptis, some two-thirds of a mile from the coast, and then struck inland.

it was also the first place to have joined his side. He then descended a gentle slope and, keeping to the left side of the plain, led his legions along close to the sea.[1] This plain is remarkably level and extends for twelve miles; and the chain of not so very lofty downs which encircles it right from the very sea gives it the appearance of a kind of amphitheatre. This chain includes a few high hills, on each of which were situated some very ancient turrets and watch-towers; and in the last [2] of these Scipio had a defence-post and picket.

After Caesar had climbed up to the ridge I have described and visited each individual hill and tower, he proceeded to construct redoubts and these he completed in less than half an hour; and when he was now not so very far away from the last hill and turret, which was nearest the enemy camp and where, as I have explained, there was a defence post and picket of Numidians, he paused for a little while; then, after studying the lie of the land, he posted his cavalry on guard and assigned to his legions their tasks, ordering them to carry a line of fortifications straight along the middle of the chain, from the point he had now reached right up to the point from where he had started. When Scipio and Labienus observed this, they led their entire cavalry force out of camp and, deploying it in battle line, advanced about a mile from their fortified positions and drew up their infantry forces in a second battle line less than four hundred paces from their camp.

[2] This would seem to mean the last, *i.e.* southernmost, hill which contained a turret: its possible identity, along with several other problems arising from the narrative of chs. 37–66, is discussed in Appendix A, p. 391.

39 Caesar in opere milites adhortari neque adversariorum copiis moveri. Iam cum non amplius
passus MD inter hostium agmen suasque munitiones
esse animadvertisset intellexissetque ad impediendos
milites suos et ab opere depellendos hostem propius
accedere necesseque haberet legiones a munitionibus
deducere, imperat turmae Hispanorum ut ad proximum collem propere occurrerent praesidiumque inde
deturbarent locumque caperent, eodemque iubet
levis armaturae paucos consequi subsidio. Qui missi
celeriter Numidas adorti partim vivos capiunt, non
nullos equites fugientis convulneraverunt locumque
sunt potiti. Postquam id Labienus animadvertit,
quo celerius eis auxilium ferret, ex acie instructa
equitatus sui prope totum dextrum cornu avertit
atque suis fugientibus suppetias ire contendit. Quod
ubi Caesar conspexit Labienum ab suis copiis longius
iam abscessisse, equitatus sui alam sinistram ad
intercludendos hostis immisit.

40 Erat in eo campo ubi ea res gerebatur villa per-
magna turribus IIII exstructa; quae Labieni pro-
spectum impediebat, ne posset animum advertere
ab equitatu Caesaris se intercludi. Itaque non prius
vidit turmas Iulianas quam suos caedi a tergo sentit.

39 Caesar kept encouraging the troops as they worked, quite unmoved by his opponents' forces. When he perceived that no more than a mile and a half now separated the enemy ranks from his own fortifications, and realised that the enemy were approaching closer for the purpose of obstructing his troops and forcing them to abandon their task, and as he considered that he must now perforce withdraw his legions from their work of building fortifications, he ordered a squadron of Spaniards to launch a speedy attack upon the adjacent hill, dislodge its enemy defenders, and capture the position; and he also instructed a small detachment of light-armed troops to follow them in support to the same objective. Thus despatched they speedily attacked the Numidians, capturing some of them alive and seriously wounding others of their troopers as they sought to escape, and so won the position. As soon as Labienus observed this, he detached practically the entire right wing of the line of cavalry he had deployed, so as the more speedily to render them assistance; and with this force he made haste to proceed to the relief of his retreating troops. But when Caesar saw that Labienus had now withdrawn some distance from his forces, he launched the left wing of his own cavalry, so as to cut the enemy off.

40 Now in the area where this action was going on there was a very large farm building, constructed with four lofty towers; and this impeded Labienus' field of view and prevented his observing that he was being cut off by Caesar's cavalry. Consequently it was only when he realised that his men were being cut down from the rear that he actually saw the Julian squadrons. As a result, triumph suddenly

Ex qua re subito in terrorem converso equitatu Numidarum recta in castra fugere contendit. Galli Germanique, qui restiterant, ex superiore loco et post tergum circumventi fortiterque restantes conciduntur universi. Quod ubi legiones Scipionis, quae pro castris erant instructae, animum adverterunt, metu ac terrore occaecatae omnibus portis in sua castra fugere coeperunt. Postquam Scipione eiusque copiis campo collibusque exturbatis atque in castra compulsis cum receptui Caesar cani iussisset equitatumque omnem intra suas munitiones recepisset, campo purgato animadvertit mirifica corpora Gallorum Germanorumque; qui partim eius auctoritatem erant ex Gallia secuti, partim pretio pollicitationibusque adducti ad eum se contulerant, non nulli, qui ex Curionis proelio capti conservatique parem gratiam in fide pariter tuenda[1] praestare voluerant. Horum corpora mirifica specie amplitudineque caesa toto campo ac prostrata diverse iacebant.

41 His rebus gestis Caesar postero die ex omnibus praesidiis cohortis deduxit atque omnis suas copias in campo instruxit. Scipio suis male acceptis, occisis convulneratisque intra suas continere se munitiones coepit. Caesar instructa acie secundum infimas iugi radices propius munitiones leniter accessit. Iamque

---

[1] partienda *MSS.* : pariter tuenda *Hoffmann.*

gave place to panic among the Numidian cavalry, and Labienus made haste to flee straight back to camp. As for the Gauls and Germans, they stood their ground; but hemmed in between the enemy on the higher ground and those in their rear, despite a gallant resistance they were slaughtered to a man. On observing this, Scipio's legions, which were drawn up in front of his camp, were seized with blind panic and began to flee by every gate into their camp. Now that Scipio and his forces had been swept in disorder from plain and hills and driven wholesale into their camp, Caesar ordered the retreat to be sounded and withdrew all his cavalry inside his own fortifications; and it was then, when the field had been cleared, that his attention was caught by the amazing bodies of the Gauls and Germans: some of whom had followed Labienus from Gaul in deference to his authority; others had been induced to join him by rewards and promises; and there were yet others who, having been made prisoners after Curio's defeat and their lives being spared, had been anxious to give proof of their unswerving gratitude by maintaining a correspondingly unswerving loyalty. These were the men whose bodies, amazing in their beauty and stature, were lying mutilated and prostrate here and there all over the battle-field.

On the day following this action Caesar withdrew his cohorts from all his defence posts and drew up all his forces in the plain: whereas Scipio, after the disastrous reception his troops had met with and their resulting heavy casualties in dead and wounded, proceeded to sit tight within his own fortifications. Caesar deployed his battle line along the lowest spurs of the chain of hills, and then slowly approached

minus mille passus ab oppido Uzitta, quod Scipio tenebat, aberant legiones Iulianae, cum Scipio veritus ne oppidum amitteret, unde aquari reliquisque rebus sublevari eius exercitus consuerat, eductis omnibus copiis quadruplici acie instructa ex instituto suo, prima equestri turmatim derecta elephantisque turritis interpositis armatisque, suppetias ire contendit—quod ubi Caesar animadvertit, arbitratus Scipionem ad dimicandum paratum ad se certo animo venire, in eo loco, quo paulo ante commemoravi, ante oppidum constitit—suamque aciem mediam eo oppido texit; dextrum sinistrumque cornu, ubi elephanti erant, in conspectu patenti adversariorum constituit.[1]

42   Cum iam prope solis occasum Caesar exspectavisset neque ex eo loco quo constiterat Scipionem progredi propius se animadvertisset locoque se magis defendere, si res coegisset, quam in campo comminus consistere audere, non est visa ratio propius accedendi eo die ad oppidum, quoniam ibi praesidium grande Numidarum esse cognoverat, hostisque mediam aciem suam oppido texisse et sibi difficile factu esse intellexit simul et oppidum uno tempore oppugnare et in acie in cornu dextro ac sinistro ex iniquiore loco pugnare, praesertim cum milites a mane diei ieiuni

---

[1] *I have followed Dinter's punctuation of this difficult sentence. Though either Caesar or Scipio could be the subject of* texit, *the clause* ubi elephanti erant *strongly suggests that Scipio is the subject of* constituit.

closer to Scipio's fortifications. And now the Julian legions were less than a mile away from the town of Uzitta, which Scipio held, when the latter, fearing that he would lose the town, on which his army had been accustomed to rely for its water supply and all other means of support, led out all his forces. These forces were drawn up, according to his custom, in four lines, the first consisting of cavalry deployed in line of squadrons, interspersed with elephants equipped with towers and armour. Thus deployed, Scipio marched to the relief of the town, while Caesar, observing this move and supposing that Scipio was advancing towards him prepared and fully resolved to fight, accordingly halted before the town in the position I described a little earlier. With his own centre covered by the town, Scipio drew up his right and left wings, where his elephants were, in full view of his opponents.

Caesar had now waited till nearly sunset without observing any signs of Scipio's leaving the position in which he had halted and advancing towards him; and his impression was that Scipio would rather remain on the defensive, utilising his position, if the circumstances demanded it, than venture to come to close grips on the plain. Accordingly, there seemed no sense in approaching closer to the town that day. For he was aware that it contained a large garrison force of Numidians, and he realised that the enemy had used the town to screen his centre, and that he himself was faced with a difficult task in simultaneously attacking the town and at the same time engaging in battle on his right and left wing from a disadvantageous position, the more especially so since his troops had been standing to since early

sub armis stetissent defatigati. Itaque reductis suis copiis in castra postero die propius eorum aciem instituit exporrigere munitiones.

43 Interim Considius, qui Acyllam VIII cohortibus et stipendiariis Numidis Gaetulisque obsidebat, ubi C. Messius cum III cohortibus praeerat,[1] diu multumque expertus magnisque operibus saepe admotis et his ab oppidanis incensis cum proficeret nihil, subito nuntio de equestri proelio allato commotus, frumento cuius in castris copiam habuerat incenso, vino, oleo ceterisque rebus quae ad victum parari solent corruptis, Acyllam, quam obsidebat, deseruit atque itinere per regnum Iubae facto copias cum Scipione partitus Hadrumetum se recepit.

44 Interea ex secundo commeatu, quem a Sicilia miserat Alienus, navis una, in qua fuerat Q. Cominius et L. Ticida, eques Romanus, ab residua classe cum erravisset delataque esset vento ad Thapson, a Vergilio scaphis naviculisque actuariis excepta est et adducta. Item altera navis trieris ex eadem classe errabunda ac tempestate delata ad Aegimurum a classe Vari et M. Octavi est capta, in qua milites veterani cum uno centurione et non nulli tirones fuerunt; quos Varus asservatos sine contumelia

---

[1] Acyllam et VIII cohortis stipendiarias Numidis Gaetulisque obsidebat ubi C. Messius qui cohortibus praeerat *MSS.* : VIII cohortibus et stipendiariis *Frölich* : cum III cohortibus praeerat *Kuebler.*

---

[1] It would seem that he marched west of the Sebkra de Sidi el Hani—thus entering Numidian territory—to give a wide berth to the fighting zone round Uzitta. But the site of Acylla is open to doubt.

morning without a bite of food, and were quite exhausted. Accordingly, he led his forces back to camp, deciding to wait till the following day and then extend his fortifications nearer the enemy's line.

In the meantime Considius with eight cohorts and some Numidian and Gaetulian mercenaries was besieging Acylla, where C. Messius was in command with three cohorts. He had made prolonged and manifold attempts, and had repeatedly approached the walls with siege-works on a large scale; but these the townsfolk had set on fire, and he was making no progress. So when the unexpected report of the cavalry engagement arrived, he was much disconcerted and set fire to the large stock of corn in his camp, rendered unusable his wine, oil and all the other victuals with which an army is normally provided, and raised the siege of Acylla. Then he marched through Juba's kingdom,[1] gave part of his forces to Scipio, and retired to Hadrumetum.

Meanwhile from the second convoy, which Alienus had despatched from Sicily,[2] one ship having aboard Q. Cominius and a Roman knight named L. Ticida had got astray from the rest of the fleet and had been carried by the wind towards Thapsus; and being intercepted by the pinnaces and light craft of Vergilius was escorted to that port. A second trireme from the same fleet likewise went astray, was carried by a gale towards Aegimurus, and captured by the fleet of Varus and M. Octavius. On board this vessel were some veteran soldiers, with one centurion and a few recruits; and these Varus kept under guard, though without any maltreatment,

[2] cf. ch. 34, where it is implied that all the ships arrived safely.

deducendos curavit ad Scipionem. Qui postquam ad eum pervenerunt et ante suggestum eius constiterunt, ' Non vestra,' inquit, ' sponte vos certo scio, sed illius scelerati vestri imperatoris impulsu et imperio coactos civis et optimum quemque nefarie consectari. Quos quoniam fortuna in nostram detulit potestatem, si, id quod facere debetis, rem publicam cum optimo quoque defendetis, certum est vobis vitam et pecuniam donare. Quapropter quid sentiatis proloquimini.'

45 Hac habita oratione Scipio cum existimasset pro suo beneficio sine dubio ab his gratias sibi actum iri, potestatem eis dicendi fecit. Ex eis centurio legionis XIIII. ' Pro tuo,' inquit, ' summo beneficio, Scipio, tibi gratias ago—non enim imperatorem te appello— quod mihi vitam incolumitatemque belli iure capto polliceris, et forsan isto uterer beneficio, si non ei summum scelus adiungeretur. Egone contra Caesarem imperatorem meum, apud quem ordinem duxi, eiusque exercitum, pro cuius dignitate victoriaque amplius XXXVI annos depugnavi, adversus armatusque consistam ? Neque ego istud facturus sum et te magnopere ut de negotio desistas adhortor. Contra cuius enim copias contendas, si minus antea expertus es, licet nunc cognoscas. Elige ex tuis cohortem unam quam putas esse firmissimam, et

---

[1] This, the MSS. reading, has often been queried. But thirty-six years' service was no impossibility; and the implied claim that it was all devoted to Caesar can, I think, be taken as a rhetorical overstatement prompted by that extreme loyalty which Caesar so often inspired in his troops.

and had them escorted to Scipio. When they came before him and stood in front of his tribunal, he said: ' It is not of your own free will—of that I am quite sure—but under the compulsion and at the behest of that villainous commander of yours, that you are iniquitously persecuting your own citizens and all true patriots. But now that fortune has delivered you into our hands, if you mean to do your duty and range yourselves on the side of all true patriots in the defence of the state, then I am resolved to grant you your lives and reward you with money. Now therefore declare your mind.'

45   After addressing them to this effect Scipio had little doubt that they would express their gratitude to him for his kindness, and accordingly gave them permission to speak. One of their number, a centurion of the Fourteenth legion, then spoke as follows: ' For your great kindness, Scipio—I refrain from calling you commander-in-chief—I thank you, inasmuch as you promise me, by rights a prisoner of war, my life and safety; and maybe I should now avail myself of that kind offer, but for the utterly iniquitous condition attached to it. Am I to range myself in armed opposition against Caesar, my commander-in-chief, under whom I have held my command, and against his army, to sustain the victorious reputation whereof I have been fighting for upwards of thirty-six years?[1] No, I am not likely to do that, and I strongly advise you to give up the attempt. For you now have the chance of appreciating—if you have not previously found it out sufficiently by experience—whose troops they are you are fighting. Choose from your men one cohort, the one you regard as your most reliable, and array

215

constitue contra me; ego autem ex meis com-
militonibus quos nunc in tua tenes potestate non
amplius X sumam. Tunc ex virtute nostra intelleges quid ex tuis copiis sperare debeas.'

46 Postquam haec centurio praesenti animo adversus
opinionem eius est locutus, ira percitus Scipio atque
animi dolore incensus innuit suis [1] centurionibus quid
fieri vellet, atque ante pedes centurionem interfecit
reliquosque veteranos a tironibus iubet secerni.
' Abducite istos,' inquit, ' nefario scelere contamina-
tos et caede civium saginatos.' Sic extra vallum
deducti sunt et cruciabiliter interfecti. Tirones
autem iubet inter legiones dispertiri et Cominium
cum Ticida in conspectum suum prohibet adduci.
Qua ex re Caesar commotus eos quos in stationibus
cum longis navibus apud Thapsum custodiae causa in
salo esse iusserat ut suis onerariis longisque navibus
praesidio essent, ob neglegentiam ignominiae causa
dimittendos ab exercitu gravissimumque in eos
edictum proponendum curavit.

47 Per id tempus fere Caesaris exercitui res accidit
incredibilis auditu. Namque vergiliarum signo confecto circiter vigilia secunda noctis nimbus cum
saxea grandine subito est exortus ingens. Ad hoc
autem incommodum accesserat quod Caesar non
more superiorum temporum [2] in hibernis exercitum

---

[1] suis *added by Warmington.*
[2] imperatorum *MSS.* : temporum *Glandorp.*

---

[1] The setting of the Pleiades in early November was
normally accompanied by stormy weather; but it was now
probably December, 47 (= February, 46, according to the
unreformed calendar).

it here over against me: I for my part will take no
more than ten men from my comrades whom you
now hold in your power. Then from our prowess
you shall realise what you ought to expect from your
own forces.'

6   This forthright and quite unlooked for retort on the
part of the centurion infuriated Scipio. Smarting
with resentment he signified his wishes to his own centurions by a nod, causing the centurion to be
executed in his presence, and issuing instructions
for the remaining veterans to be segregated from the
recruits. 'Away with these fellows,' said he,
'tainted as they are with unspeakable iniquities and
gorged with the blood of their own citizens.'
Accordingly, they were led outside the rampart and
tortured to death. As for the recruits, he ordered
them to be drafted among the legions, and would not
allow Cominius and Ticida to be brought into his
presence. This incident disquieted Caesar, who took
steps to punish those whom he had instructed to
be stationed with warships anchored out at sea on
guard off Thapsus, so as to give protection to his
transports and men-of-war: in view of their negli-
gence he had them dismissed the service with
ignominy, and had a general order published re-
primanding them most severely.

7   It was round about this time that an incredible
and unheard-of experience befell Caesar's army.
Although the constellation of the Pleiades had set,[1]
at about the second watch of the night a heavy rain-
storm suddenly broke, accompanied by a shower of
hail stones. Moreover, to make matters worse,
Caesar at the time was not, as was his custom on
previous occasions, keeping his army billeted in

continebat, sed in tertio quartoque die procedendo propiusque hostem accedendo castra communibat opereque faciendo milites se circumspiciendi non habebant facultatem. Praeterea ita ex Sicilia exercitum transportabat ut praeter ipsum militem et arma nec vas nec mancipium neque ullam rem quae usui militi esse consuevit in navis imponi pateretur. In Africa autem non modo sibi quicquam non adquisierant aut paraverant sed etiam propter annonae caritatem ante parta consumpserant. Quibus rebus attenuati oppido perquam pauci sub pellibus adquiescebant: reliqui ex vestimentis tentoriolis factis atque harundinibus scopisque contextis permanebant. Itaque subito imbre grandineque consecuta gravatis pondere tentoriis aquarumque vi subrutis disiectisque, nocte intempesta ignibus exstinctis, rebus quae ad victum pertinent omnibus corruptis per castra passim vagabantur scutisque capita contegebant. Eadem nocte V. legionis pilorum cacumina sua sponte arserunt.

48   Rex interim Iuba de equestri proelio Scipionis certior factus evocatusque ab eodem litteris praefecto Saburra cum parte exercitus contra Sittium relicto, ut secum ipse aliquid auctoritatis adderet exercitui Scipionis ac terrorem Caesaris, cum tribus legionibus equitibusque frenatis DCCC, Numidis sine frenis peditibusque levis armaturae grandi numero, ele-

---

[1] cf. ch. 54 for the flagrant infringement by Avienus, and ch. 85 where, by the time of the battle of Thapsus, there would seem to have been many slaves in Caesar's camp.

[2] Probably the electrostatic phenomenon called St. Elmo's fire.

winter quarters; but every other, or every third day, he would be advancing, moving up closer to the enemy and fortifying a camp, and in the course of doing this work his troops had no chance to look after themselves. Apart from this, his arrangements for transporting his army from Sicily were such as to allow only the troops themselves and their arms to be embarked, but no baggage, no slaves,[1] none of the soldier's normal comforts. In Africa, moreover, not only had they neither bought nor provided themselves with anything, but in addition the high price of corn had run away with all their savings. In these straitened circumstances very few men indeed were sleeping under proper tents: the rest bivouacked under tents of a sort improvised from clothing or woven with reeds and twigs. And so when the rain came down suddenly and the hail followed it, their tents sagged under the weight, and were undermined and swept away by the violence of the floods: in the dead of night the storm put out their fires: all their victuals were ruined; and they wandered aimlessly hither and thither about the camp, covering their heads with their shields. That same night the spear-points of the men of the Fifth legion spontaneously caught fire.[2]

Meanwhile king Juba had been informed of Scipio's cavalry battle; and in response to a written summons from the latter he left behind his general, Saburra, with part of his army, to keep Sittius in check, and quitting his kingdom set off to join Scipio. With him he took three legions, eight hundred bridled cavalry, a numerous contingent of Numidians who rode without bridles, and of light-armed infantry troops, and thirty elephants. His

phantis XXX egressus e regno ad Scipionem est profectus. Postquam ad eum pervenit, castris regiis
seorsum positis cum eis copiis quas commemoravi,
haud ita longe ab Scipione consedit.—Erat in castris
Caesaris superiore tempore magnus terror, et
exspectatione copiarum regiarum exercitus eius
magis suspensiore animo ante adventum Iubae com-
movebatur; postquam vero castra castris contulit,
despectis eius copiis omnem timorem deponit. Ita
quam antea absens habuerat auctoritatem, eam
omnem praesens dimiserat.—Quo facto cuivis facile
fuit intellectu Scipioni additum animum fiduciamque
regis adventu. Nam postero die universas suas
regisque copias cum elephantis LX productas in
aciem quam speciosissime potuit instruxit ac paulo
longius progressus ab suis munitionibus haud ita diu
commoratus se recipit in castra.

49 Caesar postquam animadvertit Scipioni auxilia fere
quae exspectasset omnia convenisse neque moram
pugnandi ullam fore, per iugum summum cum
copiis progredi coepit et bracchia protinus ducere et
castella munire propiusque Scipionem capiendo loca
excelsa occupare contendit, ne adversarii magnitudine copiarum confisi proximum collem occuparent

purpose in so doing was to add a certain prestige to Scipio's army by his personal appearance, and the more to intimidate Caesar's. On reaching Scipio he pitched a separate royal camp with the forces I have mentioned, and took up a position not so far distant from Scipio. Now hitherto there had been considerable apprehension in Caesar's camp: before Juba's arrival the feeling of suspense was greater, and it was this which unsettled Caesar's army as it was waiting for the royal forces; but as soon as the king pitched his camp close to theirs, they held his forces in contempt and all their fears were laid aside. And so all the prestige with which his previous absence had endowed the king he forfeited now that he was on the spot. That the king's arrival in this manner gave Scipio additional courage and confidence was a fact that anyone could readily appreciate; for on the following day he led out his own and the king's entire forces, including sixty elephants, and set them in battle array with as much pomp and circumstance as possible, and then, after advancing somewhat farther than usual from his fortified positions and pausing there a little while, withdrew to camp.

When Caesar observed that practically all the reinforcements that Scipio had been awaiting had now forgathered and that there was nothing to delay an engagement, he began to advance with his troops along the crest of the ridge, carrying forward his lines of fortification and building strong points. He also made strenuous efforts to seize the high ground closer to Scipio and, by capturing it, to forestall his opponents, lest, relying on their superiority in numbers, they should seize the nearby hill and so

atque ita longius sibi progrediendi eriperent facultatem.[1] Eiusdem collis occupandi Labienus consilium ceperat et quo propiore loco fuerat eo celerius
occurrerat.

50   Erat convallis satis magna latitudine, altitudine
praerupta, crebris locis speluncae in modum subrutis,
quae erat transgredienda Caesari, ante quam ad
eum collem quem capere volebat perveniretur;
ultraque eam convallem olivetum vetus crebris
arboribus condensum. Hic cum Labienus animadvertisset Caesarem, si vellet eum locum occupare,
prius necesse esse convallem olivetumque transgredi,
eorum locorum peritus in insidiis cum parte equitatus
levique armatura consedit et praeterea post montem
collesque[2] equites in occulto collocaverat ut, cum
ipse ex improviso legionarios adortus esset, ex colle
se equitatus ostenderet, ut re duplici perturbatus
Caesar eiusque exercitus neque retro regrediendi
neque ultra procedendi oblata facultate circumventus
concideretur. Caesar postquam equitatu ante praemisso inscius insidiarum cum ad eum locum venisset,
abusi sive obliti praeceptorum Labieni sive veriti ne
in fossa ab equitibus opprimerentur rari ac singuli de
rupe prodire et summa petere collis. Quos Caesaris
equites consecuti partim interfecerunt, partim vivorum sunt potiti; deinde protinus collem petere contenderunt atque eum decusso Labieni praesidio

---

[1] *I have followed Nipperdey's emendation, inserting* ne *and
altering the MSS. readings* occupaverunt *and* eripuerunt.

[2] *After* collesque *the MSS. read* Caesari subito se ostenderet
Aldus deleted these words.

deprive him of the opportunity of advancing farther. But Labienus too had made up his mind to seize this hill; and his closer proximity to it had enabled him to achieve the objective more rapidly.

50 There was a ravine, of a fair width and with high, precipitous sides, and honeycombed at many points with cave-like hollows; and Caesar had to cross it before he could reach the hill he wished to take. On the far side of this ravine there was an ancient olive grove, dense and thickly planted with trees. It was here that Labienus, perceiving that Caesar must first cross the ravine and olive grove if he wanted to seize that position, and availing himself of his local knowledge, took his stand in ambush with a detachment of cavalry and some light-armed troops. In addition he had posted some cavalry out of sight behind the range of hills, in order that, when he himself unexpectedly launched his attack upon the legionaries, this cavalry might make its appearance from behind the hill; thereby Caesar and his army were to be thrown into utter confusion by this double attack and, denied the opportunity either of retiring or advancing, were to be surrounded and cut to pieces. When Caesar, in ignorance of the ambush, but with a screen of cavalry thrown out in front, came up to this position, the troops of Labienus either misinterpreted or forgot his instructions, or maybe they were afraid of being caught in the trap by Caesar's cavalry; anyway, they came out from behind the rocks in small groups or singly, and made for the crest of the hill. Caesar's cavalry pursued them, killing some and capturing others alive, and then forthwith made all haste towards the hill, which they speedily seized after dislodging

celeriter occupaverunt. Labienus cum parte equitum vix fuga sibi peperit salutem.

51 Hac re per equites gesta Caesar legionibus opera distribuit atque in eo colle quo erat potitus castra munivit. Deinde ab suis maximis castris per medium campum e regione oppidi Uzittae, quod inter sua castra et Scipionis in planitie positum erat tenebaturque a Scipione, duo bracchia instituit ducere et ita dirigere ut ad angulum dextrum sinistrumque eius oppidi convenirent. Id hac ratione opus instruebat ut, cum propius oppidum copias admovisset oppugnareque coepisset, tecta latera suis munitionibus haberet, ne ab equitatus multitudine circumventus ab oppugnatione deterreretur, praeterea quo facilius colloquia fieri possent et, si qui perfugere vellent, id quod antea saepe accidebat magno cum eorum periculo, tum facile et sine periculo fieret. Voluit etiam experiri, cum propius hostem accessisset, haberetne in animo dimicare. Accedebat etiam ad reliquas causas quod is locus depressus erat puteique ibi non nulli fieri poterant: aquatione enim longa et angusta utebatur. Dum haec opera quae ante dixi fiebant a legione, interim pars acie ante opus instructa sub hoste stabat; equites barbari levisque armaturae proeliis minutis comminus dimicabant.

Labienus' holding force. Labienus and part of his cavalry barely managed to escape with their lives.

51 After this action fought by the cavalry Caesar fortified a camp on the hill of which he had gained possession, assigning each legion its share of the work. He then began to carry two fortified lines from his own principal camp across the centre of the plain in the direction of the town of Uzitta— which town was situated on flat ground between his camp and Scipio's and was occupied by the latter— their direction being such as to make them converge upon the right and left corners of the town. His purpose in constructing this field-work was as follows: when he advanced his forces closer to the town and proceeded to attack it, he should have his flanks covered by these fortifications of his and not be enveloped by the swarms of enemy cavalry and so be deterred from attacking; moreover, it should make it easier to hold conversations with the enemy, and if any of the latter wanted to desert—this had often occurred in the past, but at great risk to the deserters—it should now prove easy and devoid of risk. He was also anxious to discover, when he approached closer to the enemy, whether they intended to fight. Over and above these reasons was the additional fact that this was a low-lying tract, and quite a few wells could be sunk in it: water in fact was in short supply and had to be carried a long distance. While the legionaries were engaged in this work of fortification which I have mentioned above, a detachment of them took post in front of the work in battle formation close to the enemy; for the latter's foreign cavalry and part of his light-armed force kept skirmishing at close quarters.

52 Caesar ab eo opere cum iam sub vesperum copias in castra reduceret, magno incursu cum omni equitatu levique armatura Iuba, Scipio, Labienus in legionarios impetum fecerunt. Equites Caesariani vi universae subitaeque hostium multitudinis pulsi parumper cesserunt. Quae res aliter adversariis cecidit: namque Caesar ex medio itinere copiis reductis equitibus suis auxilium tulit; equites autem adventu legionum animo addito conversis equis in Numidas cupide insequentis dispersosque impetum fecerunt atque eos convulneratos usque in castra regia reppulerunt multosque ex eis interfecerunt. Quod nisi in noctem proelium esset coniectum pulvisque vento elatus omnium prospectui offecisset, Iuba cum I abieno capti in potestatem Caesaris venissent, equitatusque cum levi armatura funditus ad internecionem deletus esset. Interim incredibiliter ex legione IIII. et VI. Scipionis milites diffugere partim in castra Caesaris, partim in quas quisque poterat regiones pervenire; itemque equites Curioniani diffisi Scipioni eiusque copiis complures se eodem conferebant.

53 Dum haec circum Uzittam ab utrisque ducibus administrantur, legiones duae, X. et VIIII., ex Sicilia navibus onerariis profectae, cum iam non longe a portu Ruspinae abessent, conspicati navis

---

[1] After the battle of the Bagradas they had been pardoned by Juba and incorporated in his army: *cf.* ch. 40.

2   It was now nearly dusk, and Caesar was withdrawing his troops from this work to camp, when
Juba, Scipio and Labienus launched a violent attack
upon his legionaries, employing all their cavalry
and light-armed forces. Caesar's cavalry reeled and
gave ground momentarily under the sudden and
violent impact of the massed swarms of the enemy.
But the latter found that this manoeuvre did not go
according to plan; for Caesar halted in his tracks
and led his forces back to the assistance of his
cavalry. The arrival of the legions put fresh heart
into the cavalry, who wheeled round, charged the
Numidians in the middle of their eager, but scattered
pursuit, and drove them right back into the royal
camp, with heavy casualties and many of their
number killed. And had not nightfall speedily over-
taken this action, and a cloud of dust raised up by the
wind hampered everyone's vision, Juba and Labienus
would have been captured and have fallen into
Caesar's hands, and their cavalry and light-armed
troops would have been utterly and entirely an-
nihilated. Whereupon an incredible number of
Scipio's troops deserted from the Fourth and Sixth
legion—some to Caesar's camp, others to various
places wherever each individual managed to find
refuge. The cavalry who were once under Curio's
command [1] likewise lost confidence in Scipio and his
forces, and many of them took refuge with the
others.

While the leaders on either side were engaged in
these operations in the neighbourhood of Uzitta, two
legions, the Tenth and the Ninth, which had sailed
from Sicily in transports, were now not far from the
port of Ruspina. Here they sighted those ships of

Caesarianas quae in statione apud Thapsum stabant, veriti ne in adversariorum ut insidiandi gratia ibi commorantium classem inciderent imprudentes, vela in altum dederunt ac diu multumque iactati tandem multis post diebus siti inopiaque confecti ad Caesarem perveniunt.

54 Quibus legionibus expositis memor in Italia pristinae licentiae militaris ac rapinarum certorum hominum parvulam modo causulam nactus Caesar, quod C. Avienus, tribunus militum X. legionis, navem ex commeatu familia sua atque iumentis occupavisset neque militem unum ab Sicilia sustulisset, postero die de suggestu convocatis omnium legionum tribunis centurionibusque, ' Maxime vellem,' inquit, ' homines suae petulantiae nimiaeque libertatis aliquando finem fecissent meaeque lenitatis, modestiae patientiaeque rationem habuissent. Sed quoniam ipsi sibi neque modum neque terminum constituunt, quo ceteri dissimiliter se gerant egomet ipse documentum more militari constituam. C. Aviene, quod in Italia milites populi Romani contra rem publicam instigasti rapinasque per municipia fecisti quodque mihi reique publicae inutilis fuisti et pro militibus tuam familiam iumentaque in navis imposuisti tuaque opera militibus tempore necessario

Caesar's which were stationed on patrol off Thapsus;
and fearing they might be falling unawares upon an
enemy flotilla loitering there presumably with
treacherous designs, they made off out to sea.
Many days later, exhausted by thirst and privation
after a long and very storm-tossed voyage, they at
length reached Caesar.

4   These legions were then disembarked. Now
Caesar had in mind the lack of discipline of old among
the troops in Italy and the plundering exploits of
certain individuals; and he had now some ground for
complaint, though only a trifling one, in the fact that
C. Avienus, a military tribune of the Tenth legion,
had commandeered a vessel from the convoy and
filled it with his own household slaves and beasts
of burden, without transporting a single soldier from
Sicily. Accordingly, on the following day Caesar
paraded the tribunes and centurions of all his legions
and thus addressed them from the platform. ' I
could have wished above all things that people
would at some time or other have set bounds to their
wanton and highly irresponsible behaviour, and had
regard for my own leniency, moderation and forbearance. However, since they set themselves no
limit or boundary, I myself will set them a precedent
in accordance with military custom, so that the
remainder may behave somewhat differently. Inasmuch as you, C. Avienus, in Italy have stirred up
soldiers of the Roman people against the state and
have committed acts of plunder in various municipal
towns; inasmuch as you have proved useless to me
and to the state and have embarked, instead of
troops, your own household slaves and beasts of
burden, so that thanks to you the state is short of

res publica caret, ob eas res ignominiae causa ab exercitu meo removeo hodieque ex Africa abesse et quantum pote proficisci iubeo. Itemque te, A. Fontei, quod tribunus militum seditiosus malusque civis fuisti, te ab exercitu dimitto. T. Saliene, M. Tiro, C. Clusinas, cum ordines in meo exercitu beneficio non virtute consecuti ita vos gesseritis ut neque bello fortes neque pace boni aut utiles fueritis et magis in seditione concitandisque militibus adversum vestrum imperatorem[1] quam pudoris modestiaeque fueritis studiosiores, indignos vos esse arbitror qui in meo exercitu ordines ducatis, missosque facio et quantum pote abesse ex Africa iubeo.' Itaque tradit eos centurionibus et singulis non amplius singulos additos servos in navem imponendos separatim curavit.

55   Gaetuli interim perfugae, quos cum litteris mandatisque a Caesare missos supra docuimus, ad suos civis perveniunt. Quorum auctoritate facile adducti Caesarisque nomine persuasi a rege Iuba desciscunt celeriterque cuncti arma capiunt contraque regem facere non dubitant. Quibus rebus cognitis Iuba, distentus triplici bello necessitateque coactus, de suis copiis quas contra Caesarem adduxerat sex cohortis in finis regni sui mittit quae essent praesidio contra Gaetulos.

---

[1] adversariorum vestrorum imperatoris *MSS.*: adversum vestrum imperatorem *Ciacconius.*

troops at a critical time; for these reasons I hereby discharge you with ignominy from my army and direct that you leave as soon as possible and be quit of Africa this day. You also, A. Fonteius, I dismiss from my army, for having proved a mutinous military tribune and a disloyal citizen. T. Salienus, M. Tiro and C. Clusinas, you have attained your ranks in my army, not by merit, but by favour; your conduct has been such as to prove you neither brave in war, nor loyal nor competent in peace, and more eager to stir up mutiny among the troops against your commander-in-chief than to preserve respect and discipline: on these counts I deem you to be unworthy to hold rank in my army, and I hereby discharge you and direct that you be quit of Africa as soon as possible.' Accordingly he handed them over to the centurions, assigned them each no more than a single slave, and had them embarked separately in a ship.

55   Meanwhile the Gaetulian deserters who, as we have described above,[1] were sent by Caesar with despatches and instructions, arrived back among their own citizens. The authority they held readily induced their countrymen, who were also influenced by Caesar's reputation, to revolt from king Juba; and so they one and all promptly took up arms and did not hesitate to oppose the king. On learning of this situation king Juba, compelled as he now was by necessity to divide his energies between three fronts, detached six cohorts from the force which he had led against Caesar and sent them to his own royal domain to defend it against the Gaetulians.

---

[1] Ch. 32.

CAESAR

56 Caesar bracchiis perfectis promotisque usque eo
quo telum ex oppido adigi non posset castra munit,
ballistis scorpionibusque crebris ante frontem castrorum contra oppidum collocatis defensores muri
deterrere non intermittit eoque quinque legiones ex
superioribus castris deducit. Qua facultate oblata
inlustriores notissimique conspectum amicorum pro-
pinquorumque efflagitabant atque inter se colloquebantur. Quae res quid utilitatis haberet Caesarem
non fallebat: namque Gaetuli ex equitatu regio
nobiliores equitumque praefecti, quorum patres cum
Mario ante meruerant eiusque beneficio agris finibus-
que donati post Sullae victoriam sub Hiempsalis
regis erant dati potestatem, occasione capta nocte
iam luminibus accensis cum equis calonibusque suis
circiter mille perfugiunt in Caesaris castra quae
erant in campo proxime Uzittae locata.

57 Quod postquam Scipio quique cum eo erant cognoverunt, cum commoti ex tali incommodo essent, fere
per id tempus M. Aquinum cum C. Saserna collo-
quentem viderunt. Scipio mittit ad Aquinum, nihil
attinere eum cum adversariis colloqui. Cum nihilo
minus eius sermonem nuntius ad Scipionem[1] referret
sed restare ut reliqua quae sibi[2] vellet perageret,
viator praeterea ab Iuba ad eum est missus qui

---

[1] se *MSS.*: Scipionem *Davies.*
[2] si *MSS.*: sibi *Oudendorp.*

56   Caesar had now completed his lines of fortification and extended them right up to a point so as to be just out of range of spear-cast from the town. He then fortified a camp, ranging catapults and scorpions at close intervals in front of it and training them upon the town, and harrying without respite the defenders of its walls; he also detached five legions from his former camp and brought them down to the new one. Making use of the opportunity thus offered, certain more distinguished persons and those of the widest acquaintance kept demanding to see their friends and relations, and conversations ensued between them. Caesar was not blind to the expediency of this turn of events; and in fact some of the nobler Gaetulians among the royal cavalry, including captains of horse, whose fathers had previously served with Marius and had, by his good offices, been presented with farms and lands, but later on after Sulla's victory had been handed over as subjects to king Hiempsal, seized their chance and deserted, when it was night and the lamps were now lit, and came with their horses and grooms—roughly a thousand of them—to Caesar's camp which was situated in the plain close to Uzitta.

57   It was just about this time, after Scipio and his colleagues had come to learn of this disconcerting setback, that they saw M. Aquinus holding a conversation with C. Saserna. Scipio sent word to Aquinus saying that he had no business to be holding a conversation with the enemy. When none the less the messenger brought back to Scipio the other's answer, namely that on the contrary it remained for him to complete the rest of his business, Juba also sent him a courier, to say, in the hearing of Saserna:

diceret audiente Saserna: 'Vetat te rex colloqui.'
Quo nuntio perterritus discessit et dicto audiens
fuit regi. Usu venisse hoc civi Romano et ei qui ab
populo Romano honores accepisset, incolumi patria
fortunisque omnibus Iubae barbaro potius oboe-
dientem fuisse quam aut Scipionis obtemperasse
nuntio aut caesis eiusdem partis civibus incolumem
reverti malle! Atque etiam et superbius Iubae
factum non in M. Aquinum, hominem novum
parvumque senatorem, sed in Scipionem, hominem
illa familia, dignitate, honoribus praestantem. Namque cum Scipio sagulo purpureo ante regis adventum
uti solitus esset, dicitur Iuba cum eo egisse non
oportere illum eodem vestitu atque ipse uteretur.
Itaque factum est ut Scipio ad album sese vestitum
transferret et Iubae homini superbissimo inertissimo-
que obtemperaret.

58   Postero die universas omnium copias de castris
omnibus educunt et supercilium quoddam excelsum
nacti non longe a Caesaris castris aciem constituunt
atque ibi consistunt. Caesar item producit copias
celeriterque eis instructis ante suas munitiones quae
erant in campo consistit,[1] sine dubio existimans
ultro adversarios, cum tam magnis copiis auxiliisque
regis essent praediti promptiusque prosiluissent
ante, secum concursuros propiusque se accessuros.

---

[1] constituit *MSS.* : consistit *Davies.*

---

[1] This appears to imply that Labienus had a separate camp.

'The king forbids you to hold this conversation.' Alarmed by this message, Aquinus withdrew in deference to the king's injunction. To think that it had come to this, that a Roman citizen, one, moreover, who had received office at the hands of the Roman people, at a time when his country and all his fortunes stood secure, should rather have obeyed Juba, a foreigner, than deferred to Scipio's instructions or else, if he preferred, let his own partisans be massacred, while he himself returned home safe and sound! Still more arrogant even was Juba's behaviour, not towards M. Aquinus, a mere upstart and junior member of the Senate, but towards Scipio, whose family, rank and magistracies were such as to make him an outstanding man. For Scipio had been in the habit of wearing a purple cloak before the king arrived; and Juba—so it is said—took the matter up with him, saying that Scipio ought not to wear the same dress as he himself wore. And so it came about that Scipio changed to white dress in deference to Juba—that by-word of arrogance and indolence.

On the next day the enemy led out their entire combined forces from all[1] their camps and, gaining possession of a certain prominent knoll, arrayed their battle line not far from Caesar's camp, and took up their position there. Caesar likewise led forth his forces, speedily arrayed them and took up a position in front of his fortifications which were in the plain; for he thought, no doubt, that his opponents, seeing they were equipped with such substantial forces and the reinforcements supplied by the king, and had previously been quite prompt to sally forth, would now take the initiative, advance towards him and join battle. After riding round

Equo circumvectus legionesque cohortatus signo
dato accessum hostium aucupabatur. Ipse enim a
suis munitionibus longius non sine ratione non [1]
procedebat, quod in oppido Uzittae, quod Scipio
tenebat, hostium erant cohortes armatae; eidem
autem oppido ad dextrum latus eius cornu erat
oppositum, verebaturque ne, si praetergressus esset,
ex oppido eruptione facta ab latere eum adorti
conciderent. Praeterea haec quoque eum causa
tardavit, quod erat locus quidam perimpeditus ante
aciem Scipionis, quem suis impedimento ad ultro
occurrendum fore existimabat.

59   Non arbitror esse praetermittendum, quem ad
modum exercitus utriusque fuerint in aciem instructi.
Scipio hoc modo aciem derexit. Collocabat in fronte
suas et Iubae legiones, post eas autem Numidas in
subsidiaria acie ita extenuatos et in longitudinem
derectos ut procul simplex esse acies media ab
legionariis militibus videretur.[2] Elephantos dextro
sinistroque cornu collocaverat aequalibus inter eos
intervallis interiectis, post autem elephantos arma-
turas levis Numidasque auxiliaris substituerat.
Equitatum frenatum universum in suo dextro cornu
disposuerat: sinistrum enim cornu oppido Uzitta
claudebatur neque erat spatium equitatus explicandi.
Praeterea Numidas levisque armaturae infinitam
multitudinem ad dextram partem suae aciei oppo-
suerat fere interiecto non minus mille passuum
spatio et ad collis radices magis appulerat longiusque
ab adversariorum suisque copiis promovebat, id hoc
consilio ut, cum acies duae inter se concurrissent,

---

[1] non *added by Aldus.*
[2] *After* videretur *the MSS. add* in cornibus autem duplex
esse existimabatur. *Nipperdey deleted them.*

encouraging his legions he gave the signal and awaited the enemy's advance. For he himself had good reason not to advance too far from his fortifications, since the town of Uzitta, held by Scipio, contained enemy cohorts under arms; moreover, his right-hand wing lay opposite the said town, and he was afraid that, if he advanced beyond it, the enemy might make a sally from the town, attack him in flank, and maul him severely. Apart from this there was another reason too to make him pause, namely that in front of Scipio's line there was a patch of very broken ground, which he believed would prevent his troops from going over to the offensive.

I do not think I ought to pass over without mention the manner in which the armies of either side were deployed in battle formation. Scipio's order of battle was as follows. In front he placed his own and Juba's legions: behind these, in a support line, the Numidians, drawn out in so thin and long a formation as to give the impression at a distance that the centre was a single line composed of legionary troops. His elephants he had placed at regular intervals on his right and left wings, and behind the elephants his light-armed troops and Numidian auxiliaries were stationed in support. On his right wing he had posted his entire force of bridled cavalry; for his left wing was covered by the town of Uzitta, and there was no room to deploy cavalry. In addition he had posted some Numidians and a vast multitude of light-armed troops to cover the right flank of his line at a distance of at least a mile or so, pushing them more towards the foothills and so withdrawing them farther away both from the enemy and his own forces. His purpose in doing this was that when

237

initio certaminis paulo longius eius equitatus circumvectus ex improviso clauderet multitudine sua exercitum Caesaris atque perturbatum iaculis configeret. Haec fuit ratio Scipionis eo die proeliandi.

60 Caesaris autem acies hoc modo fuit collocata, ut ab sinistro eius cornu ordiar et ad dextrum perveniam. Habuit legionem X. et VIIII. in sinistro cornu, XXV., XXVIIII., XIII., XIV., XXVIII., XXVI. in media acie.[1] Ipso autem dextro cornu veteranarum legionum partem [2] cohortium collocaverat, praeterea ex tironum adiecerat paucas. Tertiam autem aciem in sinistrum suum cornu contulerat et usque ad aciei suae mediam legionem porrexerat et ita collocaverat uti sinistrum suum cornu esset triplex. Id eo consilio fecerat quod suum dextrum latus munitionibus adiuvabatur, sinistrum autem equitatus hostium multitudini uti resistere posset laborabat, eodemque suum omnem equitatum contulerat et, quod ei parum confidebat, praesidio his equitibus legionem V. praemiserat levemque armaturam inter equites interposuerat. Sagittarios varie passimque locis certis maximeque in cornibus collocaverat.

61 Sic utrorumque exercitus instructi non plus passuum CCC interiecto spatio, quod forsitan ante id

---

[1] *I have followed most editors in adopting Nipperdey's restoration of* X *and* XXV *in place of the MSS. readings* VIII *and* XXX.

[2] Fere ipsum dextrum cornu secundam autem aciem fere in earum legionum parte *most MSS.: I have followed Bouvet, who among other changes deletes* secundam autem aciem *and adopts Oudendorp's* veteranarum *in place of* fere in earum.

the two battle lines charged one another, his cavalry
would only have to continue their outflanking movement a little farther in the early stages of the action,
and then by sheer weight of numbers they could
surprise and envelop Caesar's army, throw it into
disorder, and riddle it with lances. Such was Scipio's
plan of battle that day.

30   Caesar's battle line, on the other hand, was disposed as follows, my description beginning with his
left wing and working round to his right. On his
left wing he had the Tenth and Ninth legions: in
the centre the Twenty-Fifth, Twenty-Ninth, Thirteenth, Fourteenth, Twenty-Eighth and Twenty-
Sixth. As for the actual right wing, he had posted
there some of the cohorts of his veteran legions as
well as a few cohorts from the legions of recruits
besides. His third line he had concentrated on his
left wing, extending it right up to the central legion
of his line, and had arranged it in such a formation
that his left wing was composed of three lines. His
motive for doing this was the fact that, whereas his
right flank was supported by his fortifications, he
was hard put to it to know how his left flank could
bear up under the hordes of enemy cavalry; and it
was on this same left flank that he had concentrated
the whole of his own cavalry and, not feeling too confident in it, had detached the Fifth legion to support
this cavalry, and drafted light-armed troops at
intervals among the horse. As for his archers, he
had posted them in various formations at definite
points throughout the line, but chiefly on the wings.

31   Such was the manner in which the armies on either
side were drawn up, with a distance of no more than
three hundred paces separating them—a situation

tempus acciderit numquam quin dimicaretur, a mane usque ad horam X. diei perstiterunt. Iamque Caesar dum exercitum intra munitiones suas reducere coepisset, subito universus equitatus ulterior Numidarum Gaetulorumque sine frenis ad dextram partem [1] se movere propiusque Caesaris castra quae erant in colle se conferre coepit, frenatus autem Labieni eques in loco permanere legionesque distinere: cum subito pars equitatus Caesaris cum levi armatura contra Gaetulos iniussu ac temere longius progressi paludemque transgressi multitudinem hostium pauci sustinere non potuerunt levique armatura deserta pulsi [2] convulneratique uno equite amisso, multis equis sauciis, levis armaturae XXVII occisis ad suos refugerunt. Quo secundo equestri proelio facto Scipio laetus in castra nocte copias reduxit. Quod proprium gaudium bellantibus fortuna tribuere non decrevit: namque postero die Caesar cum partem equitatus sui frumentandi gratia Leptim misisset, in itinere praedatores equites Numidas Gaetulosque ex improviso adorti circiter C partim occiderunt, partim vivorum potiti sunt. Caesar interim cotidie legiones in campum deducere atque opus facere vallumque et fossam per medium campum ducere adversariorumque excursionibus ita officere non

[1] ad dextram partem, *given by all MSS., is difficult, since the encircling manoeuvre (ch. 59) apparently required them to move to their left. The choice seems to lie between interpreting the phrase as denoting position rather than direction, or amending with Nipperdey to* ab dextra parte.

[2] ac *MSS.* : pulsi *Nipperdey.*

which had never, perhaps, arisen before without leading to an engagement; and there they remained continuously from early morning right until the tenth hour. And now, while Caesar was beginning to lead his army back within his fortifications, suddenly the entire force of cavalry—the more distant one, comprising Numidians and Gaetulians riding without bridles—began a movement on the right and to advance closer to Caesar's camp on the high ground, while Labienus' bridled cavalry maintained their positions and distracted the attention of the legions. Whereupon part of Caesar's cavalry together with the light-armed troops, acting without orders and without discretion, suddenly advanced too far, crossed a marshy tract and found themselves too far outnumbered to be able to contain the enemy. Abandoning the light-armed troops, the cavalry were driven back and fled to their own lines not without casualties—one horseman missing, many horses wounded and twenty-seven light-armed soldiers killed. It was now night when Scipio, delighted with this successful cavalry engagement, withdrew his forces into camp. But in vouchsafing him this triumph the fortunes of war saw fit to make it but short-lived. On the following day, in fact, a detachment of Caesar's cavalry which he had sent to Leptis on a foraging mission surprised in the course of their march and attacked about a hundred marauding Numidian and Gaetulian horse, killing some of them and taking the rest alive. Meanwhile Caesar made it his constant and daily practice to lead his legions down into the plain, proceed with his field-works, carry his rampart and trench across the middle of the plain, and thereby hinder his

intermittit. Scipio item munitiones contra facere et,
ne iugo a Caesare excluderetur, approperare. Ita
duces utrique et in operibus occupati esse et nihilo
minus equestribus proeliis inter se cotidie dimicabant.

62 Interim Varus classem, quam antea Uticae hiemis
gratia subduxerat, cognito legionis VII et VIII [1]
ex Sicilia adventu celeriter deducit ibique Gaetulis
remigibus epibatisque complet insidiandique gratia
ab Utica progressus Hadrumetum cum LV navibus
pervenit. Cuius adventus inscius Caesar L. Cispium
cum classe XXVII navium ad Thapsum versus in
stationem praesidi gratia commeatus sui mittit itemque Q. Aquilam cum XIII navibus longis Hadrumetum eadem de causa praemittit. Cispius quo
erat missus celeriter pervenit; Aquila tempestate
iactatus promunturium superare non potuit atque
angulum quendam tutum a tempestate nactus cum
classe se longius a prospectu removit. Reliqua classis
in salo ad Leptim egressis remigibus passimque in
litore vagantibus, partim in oppidum victus sui
mercandi gratia progressis, vacua a defensoribus
stabat. Quibus rebus Varus ex perfuga cognitis
occasionem nactus vigilia secunda Hadrumeto ex
cothone egressus primo mane Leptim cum universa
classe vectus navis onerarias, quae longius a portu

[1] *So most MSS. But it is strange that the author, who
elsewhere notes in detail the arrival of each convoy, should
nowhere else (except ch. 60 & ch. 81, where all MSS. read
VIII) have alluded to these two veteran legions. Accordingly*

opponents' sallies. Scipio likewise built counter-defences, pushing them forward in haste to prevent Caesar from barring him access to the ridge. Thus the generals on both sides were occupied with field-works, but none the less engaged one another daily in cavalry actions.

Meanwhile Varus, who had previously beached his flotilla at Utica for the winter, learned that the Seventh and Eighth legions were on the way from Sicily. Thereupon he promptly launched his flotilla, manned it on the spot with Gaetulian oarsmen and marines and, setting sail from Utica, arrived at Hadrumetum with fifty-five ships with the object of setting a trap for them. Caesar, who was unaware of his arrival, despatched L. Cispius with a squadron of twenty-seven ships to the area of Thapsus to patrol there and give cover to his convoy; and he also sent Q. Aquila with thirteen warships to Hadrumetum for the same purpose. Cispius speedily reached his destination, whereas Aquila, lashed by a storm and unable to double the headland, gained a certain cove which was sheltered from the storm and afforded him and his squadron a fairly inconspicuous retreat. The rest of the fleet stood at anchor out at sea off Leptis; and as the crews had disembarked and were roaming here and there about the beach, some of them having gone off to the town to buy themselves food, the fleet had no one to defend it. Learning of this situation from a deserter, Varus seized his opportunity: at the second watch he came out of the inner harbour of Hadrumetum and arrived off Leptis in the early morning with his entire squadron; and there he set

---

some editors conjecture IX *and* X, *assuming that the reference is to ch.* 53 : *others* XIII *and* XIV.

in salo stabant, vacuas a defensoribus [1] incendit et penteres duas nullo repugnante cepit.

63   Caesar interim celeriter per nuntios in castris, cum opera circumiret, certior factus, quae aberant a portu milia passuum VI, equo admisso omissis omnibus rebus celeriter pervenit Leptim ibique hortatur omnes ut se naves consequerentur; ipse parvulum navigiolum conscendit, in cursu Aquilam multitudine navium perterritum atque trepidantem nactus hostium classem sequi coepit.   Interim Varus celeritate Caesaris audaciaque commotus cum universa classe conversis navibus Hadrumetum versus fugere contendit.   Quem Caesar in milibus passuum IIII consecutus reciperata quinqueremi cum suis omnibus epibatis atque etiam hostium custodibus CXXX in ea nave captis triremem hostium proximam, quae in repugnando erat commorata, onustam remigum epibatarumque cepit.   Reliquae naves hostium promunturium superarunt atque Hadrumetum in cothonem se universae contulerunt.   Caesar eodem vento promunturium superare non potuit atque in salo in ancoris ea nocte commoratus prima luce Hadrumetum accedit ibique navibus onerariis quae erant extra cothonem incensis omnibusque reliquis ab eis aut subductis aut in cothonem compulsis paulisper

[1] *I have adopted Klotz's transposition of the words* vacuas a defensoribus, *which in the MSS. follow* duas; *for in the next chapter the words* reciperata quinqueremi cum suis omnibus epibatis *suggest that the penteremes had crews aboard.*

fire to the defenceless transports which were anchored
out at sea at some distance from the port, and
captured two five-banked warships, which offered no
resistance.

3   Meanwhile a message speedily acquainted Caesar
with the news as he was touring the defence works
in his camp, which was six miles distant from the
harbour. Putting everything else on one side and
giving his horse its head he speedily reached Leptis,
where he insisted that all the ships should follow his
lead: he himself then went aboard a small cutter.
As he sailed on he came up with Aquila, who was
filled with panic and confusion at the large number of
the enemy ships, and then set off in pursuit of the
enemy squadron. Meanwhile Varus, disconcerted
by Caesar's promptitude and boldness, had turned
about with his entire squadron and was now beating a
hasty retreat to Hadrumetum. In four miles' sail
Caesar overhauled him, recovered one of his quinqueremes, complete with all its crew, and capturing in
addition the enemy prize-crew aboard her, one
hundred-and-thirty strong, and then captured the
nearest enemy trireme, which in the course of the
action had lagged behind the rest, with its full
complement of rowers and marines. The rest of the
enemy fleet doubled the headland, and one and all
sought refuge in the inner harbour of Hadrumetum.
But the wind did not hold for Caesar also to be able
to double the headland; so after riding out that
night at anchor in deep water he approached Hadrumetum at dawn. There he set fire to the transports
which were outside the inner harbour and then, as
all the others had either been beached by the
enemy or massed inside the inner harbour, he waited

commoratus, si forte vellent classe dimicare, rursus se
recepit in castra.

64 In ea nave captus est P. Vestrius, eques Romanus,
et P. Ligarius, Afranianus, quem Caesar in Hispania
cum reliquis dimiserat, et postea se ad Pompeium
contulerat, inde ex proelio effugerat in Africamque
ad Varum venerat; quem ob periuri perfidiam
Caesar iussit necari. P. Vestrio autem, quod eius
frater Romae pecuniam imperatam numeraverat et
quod ipse suam causam probaverat Caesari, se a
Nasidi classe captum, cum ad necem duceretur,
beneficio Vari esse servatum, postea sibi facultatem
nullam datam transeundi, ignovit.

65 Est in Africa consuetudo incolarum ut in agris et in
omnibus fere villis sub terra specus frumenti con-
dendi gratia clam habeant atque id propter bella
maxime hostiumque subitum adventum praeparent.
Qua de re Caesar per indicem certior factus tertia
vigilia legiones duas cum equitatu mittit a castris
suis milia passuum X atque inde magno numero
frumenti onustos recipit in castra. Quibus rebus
cognitis Labienus progressus a suis castris milia
passuum VII per iugum et collem, per quem Caesar
pridie iter fecerat, ibi castra duarum legionum facit
atque ipse cotidie existimans Caesarem eadem saepe

---

[1] After the battle of Ilerda, in August 49 B.C.
[2] Perhaps S.E. to the fertile district round Moknine.

a little while to see if by chance the enemy were disposed to fight a naval action and then withdrew back to his camp.

Among those made prisoner aboard that trireme was P. Vestrius, a Roman knight, and P. Ligarius, once a supporter of Afranius. Caesar had set the latter free in Spain along with the other Afranians,[1] and he had later on joined Pompeius and then, as a fugitive after the battle (of Pharsalus), had come to Varus in Africa. In view of his falseness and treachery Caesar bade him be executed. P. Vestrius, on the other hand, he pardoned; for his brother had paid the stipulated ransom at Rome, and Vestrius himself had satisfied Caesar as to the honesty of his motives, explaining that he had been taken prisoner by the fleet of Nasidius, his life had been saved through the kindness of Varus just as he was being led off to execution, and after that he had been given no opportunity of going over to Caesar's side.

There is in Africa a custom among the natives whereby both in the open fields and in practically all their farm buildings they have a secret underground vault for the storage of corn, the main motive for this provision being wars and the sudden appearance of an enemy. When Caesar got to know of this custom through an informer, at the third watch of the night he sent two legions and some cavalry a distance of ten miles from his camp,[2] and later saw them return to camp laden with a large quantity of corn. When Labienus learned of this, he advanced seven miles from his camp across the hilly plateau across which Caesar had marched the day before, encamped two legions there and, supposing that Caesar would frequently pass along that same route for foraging

247

frumentandi gratia commeaturum cum magno equitatu levique armatura insidiaturus locis idoneis
considit.

66 Caesar interim de insidiis Labieni ex perfugis
certior factus paucos dies ibi commoratus, dum hostes
cotidiano instituto saepe idem faciendo in neglegentiam adducerentur, subito mane imperat porta
decumana legiones se III[1] veteranas cum parte
equitatus sequi atque equitibus praemissis neque
opinantis insidiatores subito in convallibus latentis
ex[2] levi armatura concidit circiter D, reliquos in
fugam turpissimam coniecit. Interim Labienus cum
universo equitatu fugientibus suis suppetias occurrit.
Cuius vim multitudinis cum equites pauci Caesariani
iam sustinere non possent, Caesar instructas legiones
hostium copiis ostendit. Quo facto perterrito Labieno ac retardato suos equites recepit incolumis.
Postero die Iuba Numidas eos qui loco amisso fuga
se receperant in castra in cruce omnis suffixit.

67 Caesar interim, quoniam inopia frumenti premebatur, copias omnis in castra conducit atque
praesidio Lepti, Ruspinae, Acyllae relicto, Cispio
Aquilaeque classe tradita ut alter Hadrumetum,
alter Thapsum mari obsiderent, ipse castris incensis
quarta noctis vigilia acie instructa impedimentis in
sinistra parte collocatis ex eo loco proficiscitur et
pervenit ad oppidum Aggar, quod a Gaetulis saepe

---

[1] VIII *MSS.* : III *Nipperdey.*
[2] ex *supplied by Nipperdey.*

purposes, established himself daily at suitable points to lie in wait for him with a large force of cavalry and light-armed troops.

In the meantime information reached Caesar from deserters about Labienus' trap. He waited in camp there a few days for the constant repetition of the same daily routine to lead the enemy into carelessness and then, early one morning, he suddenly gave the order that three veteran legions and a detachment of cavalry should follow him by way of the rear gate. Then, sending on the cavalry ahead, he suddenly surprised the enemy ambush lurking in the ravines, killing some five hundred of their light-armed troops and throwing the rest into a very unseemly rout. Whereupon Labienus dashed up with his entire cavalry force to the relief of his routed troops ; and as the odds were now too great for the Caesarian horse to contain their powerful onslaught, Caesar displayed to the enemy forces his legions in battle formation. This action utterly daunted and checked Labienus, and Caesar thereupon withdrew his own cavalry without loss. On the following day Juba crucified those Numidians who had quitted their posts and fled back to their camp.

Caesar meanwhile was embarrassed by lack of corn ; for which reason he mustered all his forces in camp and, leaving troops to garrison Leptis, Ruspina and Acylla, and assigning his fleet to Cispius and Aquila to maintain the naval blockade, the one of Hadrumetum and the other of Thapsus, he himself set fire to his camp and at the fourth watch of the night in battle formation with his baggage concentrated on the left wing evacuated that position and came to the town of Aggar. This town had pre-

antea oppugnatum summaque vi per ipsos oppidanos
erat defensum. Ibi in campo castris unis positis
ipse frumentatum circum villas cum parte exercitus
profectus magno invento hordei, olei, vini, fici
numero, pauco tritici, atque recreato exercitu redit
in castra. Scipio interim cognito Caesaris discessu
cum universis copiis per iugum Caesarem subsequi
coepit atque ab eius castris milia passuum VI longe
trinis castris dispertitis copiis consedit.

68   Oppidum erat Zeta, quod aberat a Scipione milia
passuum X, ad eius regionem et partem castrorum
collocatum, a Caesare autem diversum ac remotum,
quod erat ab eo longe milia passuum XIIII.[1] Huc
Scipio legiones duas frumentandi gratia misit.
Quod postquam Caesar ex perfuga cognovit, castris
ex campo in collem ac tutiora loca collatis atque ibi
praesidio relicto ipse quarta vigilia egressus praeter
hostium castra proficiscitur cum copiis et oppidum
potitur. Legiones Scipionis comperit longius in
agris frumentari et, cum eo contendere conaretur,
animadvertit copias hostium his legionibus occurrere
suppetias. Quae res eius impetum retardavit.
Itaque capto C. Minucio Regino, equite Romano,
Scipionis familiarissimo, qui ei oppido praeerat, et
P. Atrio, equite Romano de conventu Uticensi, et
camelis XXII regis abductis, praesidio ibi cum
Oppio legato relicto ipse se recipere coepit ad castra.

---

[1] The distances given in the MSS.—10 and 14 (or 18, or 19)
have been much disputed, and editors have amended to suit
their own identification of the towns. But the general
meaning seems clear—that Zeta lay closer to Scipio. I have
adopted Veith's identification of Aggar, Zeta and Tegea.

viously been repeatedly attacked by the Gaetulians
only to be very stoutly defended by the inhabitants
themselves. Here in the plain he pitched a single
camp and then set off in person with part of his army
on a foraging mission round the farmsteads; and
finding a large quantity of barley, oil, wine and figs,
and a little wheat, he returned to camp with his
army duly refreshed. Meanwhile Scipio, who had got
to know of Caesar's departure, proceeded to follow
him across the plateau with his entire forces and established himself six miles away from Caesar's camp,
with his forces divided among three separate camps.

68   There was a town called Zeta, which was ten miles
distant from Scipio but situated in the general
direction of his camp; whereas it was relatively
distant and remote—fourteen miles in fact—from
Caesar.[1] To this town Scipio sent two legions to
forage. When Caesar learned of this from a deserter
he moved his camp from the plain to a safer position
on the high ground; and leaving a covering force
there, he himself set out at the fourth watch, marched
on past the enemy's camp, and took possession of the
town. He then ascertained that Scipio's legions
were foraging farther afield; and he was just proceeding to march in their direction when he observed
enemy forces hastening up to support those legions.
This circumstance made him loath to attack. And so,
taking prisoner C. Minucius Reginus, the commandant of that town, who was a Roman knight and a
very intimate friend of Scipio, and P. Atrius, a
Roman knight and a member of the corporation of
Utica, and leading away twenty-two of the king's
camels, he proceeded to retire to camp, leaving his
lieutenant, Oppius, with a garrison in the town.

69 Cum iam non longe a castris Scipionis abesset,
quae eum necesse erat praetergredi, Labienus
Afraniusque cum omni equitatu levique armatura ex
insidiis adorti agmini eius extremo se offerunt atque
ex collibus proximis[1] exsistunt. Quod postquam
Caesar animum advertit, equitibus suis hostium vi
oppositis sarcinas legionarios in acervum iubet
comportare atque celeriter signa hostibus inferre.
Quod postquam coeptum est fieri, primo impetu
legionum equitatus et levis armatura hostium
nullo negotio loco pulsa et deiecta est de colle. Cum
iam Caesar existimasset hostis pulsos deterritosque
finem lacessendi facturos et iter coeptum pergere
coepisset, iterum celeriter ex proximis collibus
erumpunt atque eadem ratione qua ante dixi in
Caesaris legionarios impetum faciunt Numidae
levisque armatura mirabili velocitate praediti, qui
inter equites pugnabant et una pariterque cum
equitibus accurrere et refugere consueverant. Cum
hoc saepius facerent et proficiscentis Iulianos insequerentur, refugerent instantis, propius non accederent et singulari genere pugnae uterentur equosque[2] iaculis convulnerare satis esse existimarent,
Caesar intellexit nihil aliud eos conari nisi ut se
cogerent castra eo loco ponere ubi omnino aquae
nihil esset, ut exercitus ieiunus, qui a quarta vigilia

---

[1] primis *MSS.* : proximis *Schneider.*
[2] eosque *MSS.* : equosque *Hoffmann.*

THE AFRICAN WAR

69 When he was now not far away from Scipio's camp, which of necessity he had to pass, Labienus and Afranius with all their cavalry and light-armed troops sprang up and revealed themselves from behind the nearby hills where they had been lurking in ambush, and flung themselves upon his rear-guard. Seeing himself thus attacked, Caesar deployed his cavalry to bear the brunt of the enemy onslaught and ordered his legionaries to pile their packs and promptly deliver a counter-attack. As soon as this was under way the enemy cavalry and light-armed troops were without difficulty driven back and dislodged from the hill directly the legions charged. No sooner had Caesar come to the conclusion that the enemy, beaten back and demoralised as they were, would now stop their harrying, and no sooner had he begun to resume his march, than once again they promptly flung themselves from the cover of the nearby hills and attacked Caesar's legionaries, employing the same tactics as I described above—Numidians and light-armed troops they were, possessed of a marvellous turn of speed, fighting in the ranks of the cavalry and used to keeping pace with the horsemen and doubling forward or retreating at their side. As they repeated this manoeuvre quite frequently, chasing the Julians as they marched and taking to flight when their opponents turned to attack them, and as they would not approach at all close, but employed peculiar tactics and were content with wounding the horses with their javelins, Caesar realised that what they were trying to do was no less than force him to pitch camp at a spot where there was not a drop of water, so that his famished army, which had tasted nothing at all from

usque ad horam X. diei nihil gustasset, ac iumenta
siti perirent.

70 Cum iam ad solis occasum esset, et non totos C
passus in horis IIII esset progressus, equitatu suo
propter equorum interitum extremo agmine remoto
legiones in vicem ad extremum agmen evocabat.
Ita vim hostium placide leniterque procedens per
legionarium militem commodius sustinebat. Interim
equitum Numidarum copiae dextra sinistraque per
collis praecurrere coronaeque in modum cingere
multitudine sua Caesaris copias, pars agmen extremum insequi. Caesaris interim non amplius III aut
IIII milites veterani si se convertissent et pila viribus
contorta in Numidas infestos coniecissent, amplius
duum milium numero ad unum terga vertebant ac
rursus ad aciem passim conversis equis se colligebant
atque in spatio consequebantur et iacula in legionarios
coiciebant. Ita Caesar modo procedendo modo
resistendo tardius itinere confecto noctis hora prima
omnis suos ad unum in castra incolumis sauciis X
factis reduxit. Labienus circiter CCC amissis,
multis vulneratis ac defessis instando omnibus
ad suos se recepit. Scipio interim legiones productas cum elephantis, quos ante castra in acie

the fourth watch of the night right up till the tenth hour of the day, should die of thirst—both men and beasts.

70   It was now nearly sundown and less than a hundred paces had been covered all told in four hours, when Caesar withdrew his cavalry—in view of the casualties among their horses—from the rear-guard, and called on the legions to replace them. By employing the legionary troops in this manner and advancing calmly and at a gentle pace he found it less awkward to contain the enemy's violent onslaught. Meanwhile detachments of the Numidian cavalry kept charging ahead along the high ground to his right and left and availing themselves of their superior numbers to surround Caesar's forces with a kind of continuous circle of troops, while others of them pursued his rear-guard. Meanwhile on Caesar's part it needed no more than three or four of his veterans to wheel round and brandish and hurl amain their heavy javelins at the Numidians who menaced them for more than two thousand of the latter to turn tail to a man; and then, wheeling their horses round on all sides, they would regroup once more for battle and resume their pursuit at a set distance, hurling their javelins at the legionaries. In this manner, now advancing, now pausing to fight back, Caesar completed his march, albeit somewhat slowly; for it was the first hour of the night when he brought all his men back to camp, with not a single man lost and ten wounded. Labienus retired to his lines with roughly three hundred men missing, many wounded, and all his troops exhausted by their continuous offensive. Meanwhile Scipio, who had deployed his legions, with the elephants posted in

terroris gratia in conspectu Caesaris collocaverat,
reducit in castra.

71 Caesar contra eiusmodi hostium genera copias
suas non ut imperator exercitum veteranum victorem-
que maximis rebus gestis, sed ut lanista tirones
gladiatores condocefacere; quot pedes se reciperent
ab hoste et quem ad modum obversi adversariis et in
quantulo spatio resisterent, modo procurrerent modo
recederent comminarenturque impetum, ac prope
quo loco et quem ad modum tela mitterent, prae-
cipere. Mirifice enim hostium levis armatura
anxium exercitum nostrum atque sollicitum habebat,
quia et equites deterrebat proelium inire propter
equorum interitum, quod eos iaculis interficiebat,
et legionarium militem defatigabat propter velocitatem: gravis enim armaturae miles simul atque ab
eis insectatus constiterat in eosque impetum fecerat,
illi veloci cursu periculum facile vitabant.

72 Quibus ex rebus Caesar vehementer commove-
batur quod, quotienscunque proelium [1] erat commissum, equitatu suo sine legionario milite hostium
equitatui levique armaturae eorum nullo modo par
esse poterat. Sollicitabatur autem his rebus, quod
nondum legiones hostium cognoverat, et quonam
modo sustinere se posset ab eorum equitatu levique

---

[1] quodcumque proelium quotiens *most MSS*. quod, quotienscunque proelium *Woelfflin*.

battle array in front of his camp in full view of
Caesar to inspire terror, now led them back to camp.

71 Faced with an enemy of this kind Caesar proceeded to train his forces, not as a commander trains
a veteran army with a magnificent record of victorious achievements, but as a gladiatorial instructor
trains his recruits. How many feet they were to
retreat from the enemy; the manner in which they
must wheel round upon their adversary; the
restricted space in which they must offer him resistance—now doubling forward, now retiring and
making feint attacks; and almost the spot from
which, and the manner in which they must discharge
their missiles—these were the lessons he taught
them. For it was surprising the amount of worry
and anxiety the enemy's light-armed troops were
causing our army, what with their making the
cavalry chary of engaging for fear of losing their
mounts, since the light-armed troops kept killing
them with their javelins, and with their wearing
the legionaries out by their speediness; for no
sooner had a heavy-armed soldier, when pursued by
them, halted and then made an attack on them than
their speed of movement enabled them easily to
avoid the danger.

72 As a result of this Caesar was seriously perturbed,
since as often as an engagement had occurred he had
been quite unable to be a match with his own
cavalry, unsupported by legionary troops, for the
enemy cavalry and their light-armed units. Moreover, there was this other problem which worried
him: as yet he had had no experience of the enemy
legions; and how, he wondered, could he cope with
their cavalry and amazing light-armed troops if they

257

armatura, quae erat mirifica, si legiones quoque
accessissent. Accedebat etiam haec causa, quod
elephantorum magnitudo multitudoque animos militum detinebat in terrore. Cui uni rei tamen in-
venerat remedium: namque elephantos ex Italia
transportari iusserat, quos et miles nosset speciemque
et virtutem bestiae cognosceret et cui parti corporis
eius telum facile adigi posset, ornatusque ac loricatus
cum esset elephas, quae pars corporis eius sine
tegmine nuda relinqueretur, ut eo tela coicerentur;
praeterea ut iumenta bestiarum odorem, stridorem,
speciem consuetudine capta non reformidarent.
Quibus ex rebus largiter erat consecutus: nam et
milites bestias manibus pertrectabant earumque
tarditatem cognoscebant, equitesque in eos pila
praepilata coiciebant, atque in consuetudinem equos
patientia bestiarum adduxerat.

73   Ob has causas quas supra commemoravi sollicitabatur Caesar tardiorque et consideratior erat factus
et ex pristina bellandi consuetudine celeritateque
excesserat. Neque mirum: copias enim habebat in
Gallia bellare consuetas locis campestribus et contra
Gallos, homines apertos minimeque insidiosos, qui
per virtutem, non per dolum dimicare consuerunt;
tum autem erat ei laborandum ut consuefaceret
milites hostium dolos, insidias, artificia cognoscere et
quid sequi, quid vitare conveniret. Itaque, quo haec

were backed up by their legions too. He had yet another cause for anxiety—the panic with which the size and number of the elephants gripped the minds of his soldiers. Here, however, was one problem to which he had found an answer; for he had ordered elephants to be brought across from Italy to enable our troops not only to become familiar with them, but also to get to know both the appearance and capabilities of the beast, what part of its body was readily vulnerable to a missile and, when an elephant was accoutred and armoured, what part of its body was still left uncovered and unprotected, so that their missiles should be aimed at that spot. He had also this further object in mind, that his horses should learn by familiarity with these beasts not to be alarmed by their scent, trumpeting or appearance. From this experiment he had profited handsomely: for the troops handled the beasts and came to appreciate their sluggishness; the cavalry hurled dummy javelins at them; and the docility of the beasts had brought the horses to feel at home with them.

For the reasons mentioned above Caesar was worried, and his old habitual dashing tactics had now given place to a more sedate and deliberate policy. And no wonder: for the troops he now commanded had been used to fighting in the flat terrain of Gaul against Gauls—men of forthright character with barely a trace of deceit, whose habit it is to rely on valour, not on guile, in their fighting; whereas now he had to perform the arduous task of accustoming his troops to recognise the tricks, traps and stratagems of the enemy, and what tactics could fittingly be adopted, and what avoided. Accordingly, to speed up this training of theirs, he took pains not to

259

celerius conciperent, dabat operam ut legiones non in uno loco contineret sed per causam frumentandi huc atque illuc rapsaret, ideo quod hostium copias ab se suoque vestigio non discessuras existimabat. Atque post diem tertium productis accuratius suis copiis [1] sicut instruxerat, propter hostium castra praetergressus aequo loco invitat ad dimicandum. Postquam eos abhorrere videt, reducit sub vesperum legiones in castra.

74 Legati interim ex oppido Vaga, quod finitimum fuit Zetae, cuius Caesarem potitum esse demonstravimus, veniunt; petunt, obsecrant, ut sibi praesidium mittat; se res compluris quae utiles bello sint sumministraturos. Per id tempus deorum voluntate studioque erga Caesarem transfuga suos civis facit certiores [2] Iubam regem celeriter cum copiis suis, antequam Caesaris praesidium eo perveniret, ad oppidum accucurrisse atque advenientem multitudine circumdata eo potitum omnibusque eius oppidi incolis ad unum interfectis dedisse oppidum diripiendum delendumque militibus.

75 Caesar interim lustrato exercitu a. d. XII. Kal. April. postero die productis universis copiis progressus ab suis castris milia passuum V, a Scipionis circiter duum milium interiecto spatio, in acie constitit. Postquam satis diuque adversarios ab se ad dimicandum invitatos supersedere pugnae animadvertit, reducit copias posteroque die castra movet atque iter ad oppidum Sarsuram, ubi Scipio Numi-

---

[1] productas suas copias *MSS.* : *I have adopted Clark's conjecture.*
[2] *The MSS. text of the earlier part of this sentence is very probably corrupt : some MSS. read* de eorum *and* tranfugas.

keep the legions confined to one area, but to keep them constantly on the move, first to one spot, then to another, ostensibly for foraging purposes, for the very reason that he reckoned the enemy forces would not fail to follow in his tracks. And two days later, when he had led forth his forces duly and carefully deployed, he marched past close to the enemy's camp and challenged them to battle on level ground; but when he saw the enemy reluctant to accept, he led his legions back to camp as evening was approaching.

4   Meanwhile envoys arrived from the town of Vaga, which was near Zeta, the occupation of which by Caesar we have already described. They prayed and besought Caesar to send them a garrison, saying they would assist him by furnishing various supplies useful in war. At this point, by the good will of the gods and their favour towards Caesar, a deserter informed his compatriots that king Juba had speedily hastened to the town with his forces to forestall the arrival there of Caesar's garrison; that at his coming he had surrounded the town with vast forces, won control of it, slaughtered all the inhabitants to a man, and then given it over to his troops to plunder and destroy.

5   Meanwhile Caesar ceremonially purified his army on March 21st. On the following day he led forth his entire forces, advanced five miles from his own camp, and took his stand in battle array at a distance of some two miles from Scipio's camp. On perceiving that his opponents, despite this adequate and sustained challenge, declined his offer of battle, he led his forces back; and on the following day he struck camp and took the road to the town of Sarsura, where Scipio had posted a garrison of

darum habuerat praesidium frumentumque comportaverat, ire contendit. Quod ubi Labienus animadvertit, cum equitatu levique armatura agmen eius extremum carpere coepit atque ita lixarum mercatorumque qui plaustris merces portabant interceptis sarcinis addito animo propius audaciusque accedit ad legiones, quod existimabat milites sub onere ac sub sarcinis defatigatos pugnare non posse. Quae res Caesarem non fefellerat : namque expeditos ex singulis legionibus trecenos milites esse iusserat. Itaque eos in equitatum Labieni immissos turmis suorum suppetias mittit. Tum Labienus conversis equis signorum conspectu perterritus turpissime fugere contendit. Multis eius occisis, compluribus vulneratis milites legionarii ad sua se recipiunt signa atque iter inceptum ire coeperunt. Labienus per iugum summum collis dextrorsus procul subsequi non destitit.

76 Postquam Caesar ad oppidum Sarsuram venit, inspectantibus adversariis interfecto praesidio Scipionis, cum suis auxilium ferre non auderent, fortiter repugnante P. Cornelio, evocato Scipionis, qui ibi praeerat, atque a multitudine circumvento interfectoque oppido potitur atque ibi frumento exercitui dato postero die ad oppidum Thysdram pervenit; in quo Considius per id tempus fuerat cum grandi praesidio cohorteque sua gladiatorum. Caesar op-

Numidians and laid in a stock of corn. When Labienus perceived this he proceeded to harry Caesar's
rear-guard with his cavalry and light-armed troops;
and having by this means cut off the baggage trains
of the sutlers and merchants who were carrying their
wares in carts, he was thereby the more encouraged
to grow bolder and come closer to the legions, since
he supposed that the soldiers were worn out with
carrying their heavy packs and so in no condition to
fight. But this contingency had not escaped
Caesar's attention: he had in fact given instructions
that three hundred men out of each legion should
be in light order; and these he accordingly despatched against Labienus' cavalry to give support to
his own squadrons. Whereupon Labienus, dismayed
at the sight of the standards, wheeled round his
horses and beat a hasty and highly undignified
retreat. The legionary troops, having killed many
of his men and wounded not a few, retired to their
standards and proceeded to resume their march.
Labienus still kept up his pursuit at a distance,
moving along the crest of the ridge of hills upon the
right.

When Caesar came to the town of Sarsura he
massacred Scipio's garrison while his opponents
looked on, not daring to assist their friends. Its
commander, however, P. Cornelius, a reservist recalled by Scipio, offered a gallant resistance, but was
surrounded by overwhelming numbers and killed.
Then Caesar gained control of the town, distributed
corn to his army on the spot, and arrived next
day at the town of Thysdra. Considius was in the
town at this time with a considerable garrison
force and his own bodyguard of gladiators. Caesar

pidi natura perspecta aquae inopia ab oppugnatione
eius deterritus protinus profectus circiter milia
passuum IIII ad aquam facit castra atque inde quarta
vigilia egressus redit rursus ad ea castra quae ad
Aggar habuerat.   Idem facit Scipio atque in antiqua
castra copias reducit.

77   Thabenenses interim, qui sub dicione et potestate
Iubae esse consuessent in extrema eius regni regione
maritima locati, interfecto regio praesidio legatos ad
Caesarem mittunt, rem a se gestam docent, petunt
orantque ut suis fortunis populus Romanus, quod bene
meriti essent, auxilium ferret.   Caesar eorum consilio probato Marcium Crispum tribus cum cohortibus
et sagittariis tormentisque compluribus praesidio
Thabenam mittit.   Eodem tempore ex legionibus
omnibus milites qui aut morbo impediti aut commeatu dato cum signis non potuerant ante transire in
Africam ad milia IIII, equites CCCC, funditores
sagittariique mille uno commeatu Caesari occurrerunt.   Itaque cum his copiis et omnibus
legionibus eductis, sicut erat instructus, V milibus
passuum ab suis castris, ab Scipionis vero II milibus
passuum longe constitit in campo.

78   Erat oppidum infra castra Scipionis nomine Tegea,[1]
ubi praesidium equestre circiter II milium numero
habere consuerat.   Eo equitatu dextra sinistra
derecto ab oppidi lateribus ipse legiones ex castris

---

[1] Its site is unknown, and the suggested identification with
Thena, mentioned by Strabo and located by some editors
far south, opposite the islands of Cercina, seems dubious.

studied the characteristics of the town, and the lack of water discouraged him from attacking it: he then set out forthwith and pitched a camp some four miles away near water, only to quit it at the fourth watch and return once again to the camp he had occupied near Aggar. Scipio followed suit and led his forces back to his old camp.

Meanwhile the inhabitants of Thabena,[1] who dwelt on the coast at the extreme verge of Juba's kingdom and were his traditional lieges and subjects, had none the less massacred the royal garrison, and now sent envoys to Caesar informing him of their action and earnestly soliciting that the Roman people should give them succour in their present plight, as they had deserved well at their hands. Caesar approved their policy and sent Marcius Crispus with three cohorts and numerous archers and pieces of artillery to Thabena as a garrison force. It was at this same time that Caesar was reinforced by the troops from all his legions who, whether prevented by sickness or because they had been granted leave, had previously been unable to cross to Africa with the colours: these comprised about four thousand infantry, four hundred cavalry and a thousand slingers and archers, and all came in one convoy. And so, leading out all his legions, including these forces, he took up a position in battle array in the plain five miles away from his own camp and two miles distant from Scipio's.

Below Scipio's camp there was a town called Tegea, where he kept a standing garrison force of cavalry numbering some two thousand men. This cavalry he now deployed in line on the right- and left-hand flanks of the town, while he himself led his

eductas atque in iugo inferiore instructas non longius fere mille passus ab suis munitionibus progressus in acie constituit. Postquam diutius in uno loco Scipio commorabatur et tempus diei in otio consumebatur, Caesar equitum turmas suorum iubet in hostium equitatum qui ad oppidum in statione erant facere impressionem levemque armaturam, sagittarios funditoresque eodem summittit. Quod ubi coeptum est fieri et equis concitatis Iuliani impetum fecissent, Pacideius suos equites exporrigere coepit in longitudinem, ut haberent facultatem turmas Iulianas circumfundi et nihilo minus fortissime acerrimeque pugnare. Quod ubi Caesar animadvertit, CCC, quos ex legionibus habere expeditos consuerat, ex legione quae proxima ei proelio in acie constiterat iubet equitatui succurrere. Labienus interim suis equitibus auxilia equestria summittere sauciisque ac defatigatis integros recentioribusque viribus equites sumministrare. Postquam equites Iuliani CCCC vim hostium ad IIII milia numero sustinere non poterant et ab levi armatura Numidarum vulnerabantur minutatimque cedebant, Caesar alteram alam mittit qui satagentibus celeriter occurrerent. Quo facto sui sublati

legions out of camp and after advancing not much
more than about a mile from his defences drew them
up arrayed in battle formation on the lower slopes of
a ridge. After some little time had elapsed without Scipio's shifting his position, and as the daylight
hours were being frittered away in inaction, Caesar
ordered some squadrons of his own horse to make a
charge against the enemy cavalry which were posted
on guard near the town, and despatched some light-
armed units, archers and slingers to the same objective in support. When this manoeuvre was under
way and the Julians had delivered their attack at full
gallop, Pacideius began to deploy his horsemen on a
broader front, to enable them to swarm round the
flanks of the Julian cavalry and still fight with the
utmost gallantry and spirit. When Caesar observed
these tactics he instructed the three hundred men in
light order—it was his normal practice that this
number of men in each of his legions should be in
light order—from the legion which was posted in the
line nearest the scene of this action to hasten to the
assistance of the cavalry. Meanwhile Labienus sent
cavalry reinforcements to support his own horsemen,
furnishing unscathed troopers and those whose
strength was relatively unspent to take the place of
their wounded or exhausted comrades. Now that the
four hundred Julian cavalry were finding it impossible
to contain the violent onslaught of an enemy some
four thousand strong, and were suffering casualties at
the hands of the light-armed Numidians and giving
ground very slightly, Caesar despatched a second
wing of cavalry to dash speedily to the help of his
hard-pressed men. This action raised the spirits of
his troops, who delivered a massed charge against the

universi in hostis impressione facta in fugam adversarios dederunt; multis occisis, compluribus vulneratis insecuti per III milia passuum usque ad collem hostibus adactis se ad suos recipiunt. Caesar in horam X. commoratus, sicut erat instructus, se ad sua castra recepit omnibus incolumibus. In quo proelio Pacideius graviter pilo per cassidem caput ictus compluresque duces ac fortissimus quisque interfecti vulneratique sunt.

79 Postquam nulla condicione cogere adversarios poterat ut in aequum locum descenderent legionumque periculum facerent, neque ipse propius hostem castra ponere propter aquae penuriam se posse animadvertebat, adversarios non virtute eorum confidere sed aquarum inopia fretos despicere se intellexit, II. Non. Apr. tertia vigilia egressus ab Aggar XVI milia nocte progressus ad Thapsum, ubi Vergilius cum grandi praesidio praeerat, castra ponit oppidumque eo die circummunire coepit locaque idonea opportunaque complura praesidiis occupare, hostes ne intrare ad se ac loca interiora capere possent. Scipio interim cognitis Caesaris consiliis ad necessitatem adductus dimicandi, ne per summum dedecus fidissimos suis rebus Thapsitanos et Vergilium amitteret, confestim Caesarem per superiora loca consecutus milia passuum VIII a Thapso binis castris consedit.

---

[1] *i.e.* at about midnight on the night of April 3rd–4th. Thus *eo die* is still April 4th.

[2] See Map 5. I have assumed, with most editors, that Caesar approached Thapsus from the south, by way of the narrow coastal corridor east of the Marsh of Moknine; and that Scipio took the same route and encamped near its south-eastern fringe. The strategic points may well—as Veith suggested—have included El Faca and El Hafsa.

enemy and turned their opponents to flight; and after killing many and wounding not a few and chasing the enemy for three miles and driving them right up to the high ground they retired to their lines. Caesar waited till the tenth hour and then withdrew to his camp in battle order without any losses. In this engagement Pacideius was seriously wounded in the head by a heavy javelin which pierced his helmet; and several of the enemy leaders and all their bravest men were either killed or wounded.

9   Finding it impossible on any terms to induce his opponents to come down to level ground and risk their legions, and realising that it was equally impossible for him to pitch his own camp closer to the enemy owing to the poor supply of water, and perceiving that his opponents, so far from having any confidence in their own valour, were led to hold him in contempt by their reliance on the dearth of water, Caesar left Aggar on April 4th at the third watch.[1] Then, after advancing sixteen miles by night, he pitched camp near Thapsus,[2] where Vergilius was in command with a considerable garrison. That same day he began to invest the town, seizing and manning several suitable strategic points to prevent the enemy's being able to infiltrate and approach him, or capture any inner positions. Scipio had in the meantime got to know of Caesar's plans; and being now reduced to the necessity of fighting, if he was to avoid the utter humiliation of losing Vergilius and those most staunch supporters of his cause—the men of Thapsus, he forthwith followed Caesar along the high ground and established himself in two camps at a distance of eight miles from Thapsus.

80   Erat stagnum salinarum, inter quod et mare
angustiae quaedam non amplius mille et D passus
intererant; quas Scipio intrare et Thapsitanis
auxilium ferre conabatur. Quod futurum Caesarem
non fefellerat. Namque pridie in eo loco castello
munito ibique III cohortium [1] praesidio relicto ipse
cum reliquis copiis lunatis castris Thapsum operibus
circummunivit. Scipio interim exclusus ab incepto,
itinere supra stagnum postero die et nocte confecto,
caelo albente non longe a castris praesidioque quod
supra commemoravi MD passibus ad mare versus
consedit et castra munire coepit. Quod postquam
Caesari nuntiatum est, milite ab opere deducto,
castris praesidio Asprenate pro consule cum legionibus
duabus relicto ipse cum expedita copia in eum locum
citatim contendit, classisque parte ad Thapsum
relicta reliquas navis iubet post hostium tergum quam

---

[1] *The MSS. omit* cohortium, *which Woelfflin conjectured.*

---

[1] Apparently he marched round its western side. The
words *postero die et nocte* have been variously explained and
amended. Scipio's abortive attempt to penetrate the eastern
corridor was made, as *pridie* shews, on April 5th : *postero die*
is, I think, relative to *pridie* (April 4th) and denotes the
remainder of April 5th, *nocte* being the night of April 5th/6th.
The time involved—perhaps some eighteen hours is certainly
long for the distance of about 20 miles; but, as R. Holmes
has pointed out, Scipio may well have rested *en route* and
timed his march so as to begin his entrenchments under cover
of darkness.

[2] See Map 5. The defence area here alluded to may well
be that close to Thapsus mentioned in the previous chapter.
If the allusion is to the fort mentioned earlier in this chapter,
then the fort too must have been close to Thapsus. But the
only place where the corridor to-day is not more than a mile
and a half wide is at the S.E. corner of the lagoon.

THE AFRICAN WAR

80   There was a lagoon of salt water, separated from
the sea by a certain narrow strip of land not more
than a mile and a half wide; and this corridor Scipio
now attempted to enter to bring help to the men of
Thapsus. The likelihood of such a move had not
escaped Caesar's attention: in fact, the day before
he had built a fort at this spot and left behind a
force of three cohorts to hold it, while he himself
with the rest of his forces established a crescent-
shaped camp and invested Thapsus with a ring of
siege works. Meanwhile Scipio, foiled in his undertaking, by-passed the lagoon to the north by a march
which he completed in the ensuing day and night,[1]
and then, at the first pale light of dawn, took up a
position not far from the camp and the defence area
I mentioned above,[2] and a mile and a half from the
sea coast;[3] and there he began to fortify a camp.
When this was reported to Caesar, the latter withdrew his troops from their work of fortification, left
behind the pro-consul Asprenas to guard the camp
with two legions, and hurriedly marched to that
location with a force in light order. As for his fleet,
part of it was left behind off Thapsus, while the
remaining ships were ordered to advance as close as

[3] The words *MD passibus* present a difficulty. Bouvet
translates ' à quinze cents pas du côté de la mer,' though in a
later note he refers to Scipio's position as near Caesar (at 1500
paces), and in his map he marks Scipio's camp only 1 km.
distant from the sea. It seems possible to render the words
non longe . . . consedit by ' took up a position towards the sea,
not far distant—a mile and a half—from the camp . . .'.
According to this interpretation Scipio's camp would appear
on Map 5 not—as now marked—close to Bekalta, but some
1¼ Roman miles nearer the sea, behind the left wing of Scipio's
battle line. This is perhaps confirmed by the behaviour of the
routed elephants described below in ch. 83.

maxime ad litus appelli signumque suum observare,
quo signo dato subito clamore facto ex improviso
hostibus aversis incuterent terrorem, ut perturbati
ac perterriti respicere post terga cogerentur.

81 Quo postquam Caesar pervenit et animadvertit
aciem pro vallo Scipionis constitutam [1] elephantis
dextro sinistroque cornu collocatis, et nihilo minus
partem militum castra non ignaviter munire, ipse acie
triplici collocata, legione X. VII.que [2] dextro cornu,
VIII. et VIIII. sinistro oppositis, quintae legionis [3]
in quarta acie ad ipsa cornua quinis cohortibus
contra bestias collocatis, sagittariis, funditoribus
in utrisque cornibus dispositis levique armatura inter
equites interiecta, ipse pedibus circum milites con-
cursans virtutesque veteranorum proeliaque superiora
commemorans blandeque appellans animos eorum
excitabat. Tirones autem, qui numquam in acie
dimicassent, hortabatur ut veteranorum virtutem
aemularentur eorumque famam, locum, nomen
victoria parta cuperent possidere.

82 Itaque in circumeundo exercitu animadvertit hostis
circa vallum trepidare atque ultro citroque pavidos
concursare et modo se intra portas recipere, modo
inconstanter immoderateque prodire. Cum idem a
pluribus animadverti coeptum esset, subito legati

---

[1] contra *MSS.* : constitutam *R. Schneider.*

[2] secundaque *MSS.* : VII.que *Groebe* : *but it is open to
doubt whether the 7th & 8th legions were present : cf. note* 1 *on ch.*
62. *Nipperdey proposed* X. XIII.que . . . XIIII. et VIIII.;
Schneider X. VIIII.que . . . XIII. et XIIII.

[3] quinque legiones *MSS.* : quintae legionis *Vielhaber.*

possible inshore in rear of the enemy and to watch for a signal from Caesar; on the giving of which signal they were suddenly to raise a shout, surprise the enemy from the rear, and thus demoralise them, so that in their utter confusion and panic they would be obliged to look behind them.

1   When Caesar arrived there and observed Scipio's battle line arrayed in front of the rampart, with the elephants posted on the right and left wings, while none the less part of his troops were busily engaged in fortifying the camp, he himself disposed his army in three lines: the Tenth and Seventh legions he posted on the right wing, the Eighth and Ninth on the left, while five cohorts of the Fifth legion were stationed on each of the actual wings, forming a fourth line to contain the elephants; and his archers and slingers were deployed on either wing, and the light-armed units interspersed among the cavalry. Caesar himself hurriedly went the rounds of his troops on foot, reminding the veterans of their gallant bearing in previous combats and raising their morale by flattering appeals. As for the recruits, seeing they had never so far fought in pitched battle, he urged them to emulate the gallantry of the veterans and to make it their ambition by gaining a victory to enjoy a fame, status and renown equal to theirs.

Now in the course of making these rounds of his army he observed that the enemy in the neighbourhood of their rampart were excited, rushing hither and thither in alarm, now retiring inside the gates, now trooping out in a spasmodic and undisciplined fashion. Several others were beginning to observe the same symptoms when without more ado his

evocatique obsecrare Caesarem ne dubitaret signum
dare: victoriam sibi propriam a dis immortalibus
portendi. Dubitante Caesare atque eorum studio
cupiditatique resistente sibique eruptione pugnari
non placere clamitante, etiam atque etiam aciem
sustentante, subito dextro cornu iniussu Caesaris
tubicen a militibus coactus canere coepit. Quo
facto ab universis cohortibus signa in hostem coepere
inferri, cum centuriones pectore adverso resisterent
vique continerent milites, ne iniussu imperatoris
concurrerent, nec quicquam proficerent.

83   Quod postquam Caesar intellexit incitatis militum
animis resisti nullo modo posse, signo Felicitatis dato
equo admisso in hostem contra principes ire contendit. A dextro interim cornu funditores sagittariique concita tela in elephantos frequentes
iniciunt. Quo facto bestiae stridore fundarum,
lapidum plumbique iactatu [1] perterritae sese convertere et suos post se frequentis stipatosque pro-
terere et in portas valli semifactas ruere contendunt.
Item Mauri equites, qui in eodem cornu elephantis
erant, praesidio deserti principes fugiunt. Ita
celeriter bestiis circumitis legiones vallo hostium

[1] itata *MSS.*: iactatu *Kuebler*.

lieutenants and reservists implored Caesar not to hesitate to give the signal, saying that it was decisive victory that the immortal gods were thus foretelling them. Caesar still hesitated, opposing their impetuous eagerness, repeatedly protesting that a precipitate sally was not his approved way of fighting, and again and again holding his battle line in check; when suddenly on the right wing, without orders from Caesar but under coercion of the troops, a trumpeter began to sound the charge. Whereupon every single cohort began to attack the enemy, despite the resistance of the centurions, who planted themselves in the path of the troops and sought to hold them back by force to prevent their attacking without orders from the commander-in-chief, but all in vain.

When Caesar realised that it was quite out of the question to hold back his troops in their present state of excitement, he signalled ' Good Luck ' and giving his horse its head rode in hot haste against the enemy front ranks. Meanwhile on the right wing the slingers and archers in crowds launched rapid volleys of missiles against the elephants. Whereupon the beasts, terrified by the whizzing sound of the slings and by the stones and leaden bullets launched against them, speedily wheeled round, trampled under foot the massed and serried ranks of their own supporting troops behind them, and rushed towards the half-completed gates of the rampart. The Moorish cavalry, who were posted on the same wing as the elephants, followed suit and, abandoned by their protective screen, started the rout. Having thus speedily got round the elephants, the legions gained possession of the enemy's rampart;

sunt potitae, et paucis acriter repugnantibus inter-
fectisque reliqui concitati in castra unde pridie erant
egressi confugiunt.

84 Non videtur esse praetermittendum de virtute
militis veterani V. legionis. Nam cum in sinistro
cornu elephas vulnere ictus et dolore concitatus in
lixam inermem impetum fecisset eumque sub pede
subditum dein genu innixus pondere suo proboscide
erecta vibrantique stridore maximo premeret atque
enecaret, miles hic non potuit pati quin se armatus
bestiae offerret. Quem postquam elephas ad se telo
infesto venire animadvertit, relicto cadavere militem
proboscide circumdat atque in sublime extollit.
Armatus, qui in eiusmodi periculo constanter agendum sibi videret, gladio proboscidem qua erat
circumdatus caedere quantum viribus poterat non
destitit. Quo dolore adductus elephas milite abiecto
maximo cum stridore cursuque conversus ad reliquas
bestias se recepit.

85 Interim Thapso qui erant praesidio ex oppido
eruptionem porta maritima faciunt et, sive ut suis
subsidio occurrerent, sive ut oppido deserto fuga
salutem sibi parerent, egrediuntur atque ita per
mare umbilici fine ingressi terram petebant. Qui a
servitiis puerisque qui in castris erant lapidibus
pilisque prohibiti terram attingere rursus se in
oppidum receperunt. Interim Scipionis copiis pro-

---

[1] It would appear that Asprenas and his two legions (ch. 80)
had moved out, either to take part in the battle, or to seal off
the eastern corridor and menace Scipio's camps at its southern
end.

and when the few defenders who offered a spirited resistance had been killed, the remainder precipitately sought refuge in the camp from which they had issued the day before.

4   I ought not, I think, to omit to mention the gallantry of a veteran soldier of the Fifth legion. On the left wing an elephant, maddened by the pain of a wound it had received, had attacked an unarmed sutler, pinned him underfoot, and then knelt upon him; and now, with its trunk erect and swaying, and trumpeting loudly, it was crushing him to death with its weight. This was more than the soldier could bear; he could not but confront the beast, fully armed as he was. When it observed him coming towards it with weapon poised to strike, the elephant abandoned the corpse, encircled the soldier with its trunk, and lifted him up in the air. The soldier, perceiving that a dangerous crisis of this sort demanded resolute action on his part, hewed with his sword again and again at the encircling trunk with all the strength he could muster. The resulting pain caused the elephant to drop the soldier, wheel round, and with shrill trumpetings make all speed to rejoin its fellows.

5   Meanwhile the members of the garrison of Thapsus made a sortie from the town by way of the seaward gate and, whether their object was to hasten to the aid of their fellows, or to abandon the town and secure their own safety by flight, out they came and accordingly, wading waist-high into the sea, made for the land. They were, however, prevented from reaching land by stones and heavy javelins hurled by the slaves and lackeys in the camp;[1] and so they returned back into the town. Meanwhile Scipio's forces, now

stratis passimque toto campo fugientibus confestim
Caesaris legiones consequi spatiumque se non dare
colligendi. Qui postquam ad ea castra quae petebant perfugerunt, ut refecti [1] castris rursus sese
defenderent ducemque aliquem requirerent, quem
respicerent, cuius auctoritate imperioque rem ge-
rerent:—qui postquam animadverterunt neminem
ibi esse praesidio, protinus armis abiectis in regia
castra fugere contendunt. Quo postquam pervenerunt, ea quoque ab Iulianis teneri vident.
Desperata salute in quodam colle consistunt atque
armis demissis salutationem more militari faciunt.
Quibus miseris ea res parvo praesidio fuit. Namque
milites veterani ira et dolore incensi non modo ut
parcerent hosti non poterant adduci sed etiam ex suo
exercitu inlustris urbanos, quos auctores appellabant,
compluris aut vulnerarunt aut interfecerunt; in quo
numero fuit Tullius Rufus quaestorius, qui pilo
traiectus consulto a milite interiit; item Pompeius
Rufus bracchium gladio percussus, nisi celeriter ad
Caesarem accucurrisset, interfectus esset. Quo facto
complures equites Romani senatoresque perterriti ex
proelio se receperunt, ne a militibus, qui ex tanta
victoria licentiam sibi assumpsissent immoderate

---

[1] refectis *MSS.* : refecti *Daehn.*

thrown into utter confusion, were in wholesale retreat
in every sector of the field, and Caesar's legions
promptly pursued them without giving them any
respite in which to pull themselves together. When
the fugitives reached the camp they were making for,
with the object of making a recovery there and defending themselves once more, and of trying to find
someone to lead them—someone to look up to, under
whose authority and command they could carry on the
fight; when they got there and perceived that there
was nobody guarding it, they forthwith discarded
their armour and beat a hasty retreat to the royal
camp. This too on their arrival they saw to be in
the hands of the Julians. Abandoning all hope of
salvation, they now halted on a hill and gave the
military salute by lowering their arms. This
gesture, unhappily for them, stood them in but little
stead. For Caesar's veterans were filled with such
burning indignation and resentment that, so far
from any possibility of inducing them to spare the
enemy, they actually wounded or killed several men
of culture and distinction among the ranks of their
own side, calling them ringleaders. Among these
was Tullius Rufus, an ex-quaestor, who was mortally
wounded by a soldier who deliberately ran him
through with a heavy javelin; and similarly Pompeius Rufus was stabbed in the arm with a sword and
would have been done to death, had he not promptly
rushed to Caesar's side. This behaviour caused
grave alarm among quite a number of Roman knights
and senators, who retired from the battle lest they
themselves should also be massacred by the soldiers,
who after so resounding a victory had apparently
taken it for granted that they were free to perpetrate

peccandi impunitatis spe propter maximas res gestas, ipsi quoque interficerentur. Itaque ei omnes Scipionis milites cum fidem Caesaris implorarent, inspectante ipso Caesare et a militibus deprecante eis uti parcerent, ad unum sunt interfecti.

86 Caesar trinis castris potitus occisisque hostium X milibus fugatisque compluribus se recepit L militibus amissis, paucis sauciis in castra ac statim ex itinere ante oppidum Thapsum constitit elephantosque LXIIII ornatos armatosque cum turribus ornamentisque capit, captos ante oppidum instructos constituit, id hoc consilio, si posset Vergilius quique cum eo obsidebantur rei male gestae suorum indicio a pertinacia deduci. Deinde ipse Vergilium appellavit invitavitque ad deditionem suamque lenitatem et clementiam commemoravit. Quem postquam animadvertit responsum sibi non dare, ab oppido discessit. Postero die divina re facta contione advocata in conspectu oppidanorum milites collaudat totumque exercitum veteranorum donavit, praemia fortissimo cuique ac bene merenti pro suggestu tribuit, ac statim inde digressus Rebilo pro consule cum III ad Thapsum legionibus et Cn. Domitio cum duabus Thysdrae, ubi Considius praeerat, ad obsidendum

any excesses, on the assumption that they would go unpunished in view of their magnificent achievements. Accordingly, although all these troops of Scipio implored Caesar's protection, they were massacred to a man, despite the fact that Caesar himself was looking on and entreating his troops to spare them.

36   Having made himself master of three camps and killed ten thousand of the enemy and routed a large number, Caesar retired to camp with fifty soldiers missing and a few wounded. Immediately on his arrival he established himself in front of the town of Thapsus. He then took sixty-four elephants, equipped, armed and complete with towers and harness, and these he now drew up in array in front of the town: his object in so doing was to see if Vergilius and the others who were being besieged with him could be induced to abandon their obstinate resistance by the evidence of their comrades' failure. He then addressed a personal appeal to Vergilius inviting him to surrender and reminding him of his own leniency and clemency; but on failing to observe any response he withdrew from the town. On the following day, after offering sacrifice, he held a parade and in full view of the occupants of the town congratulated his troops, rewarding his entire veteran force and bestowing decorations publicly in front of the dais for conspicuous gallantry and meritorious service. Thereupon he immediately withdrew from the town, leaving behind the proconsul Rebilus in front of Thapsus with three legions and Cn. Domitius with two at Thysdra, where Considius was in command, to continue the blockades of these places; and then,

relictis, M. Messalla Uticam ante praemisso cum
equitatu ipse eodem iter facere contendit.

87 Equites interim Scipionis qui ex proelio fugerant,
cum Uticam versus iter facerent, perveniunt ad
oppidum Paradae. Ubi cum ab incolis non reciperentur, ideo quod fama de victoria Caesaris praecu-
currisset, vi oppido potiti in medio foro lignis coacervatis omnibusque rebus eorum congestis ignem
subiciunt atque eius oppidi incolas cuiusque generis
aetatisque vivos constrictosque in flammam coiciunt
atque ita acerbissimo adficiunt supplicio; deinde
protinus Uticam perveniunt. Superiore tempore M.
Cato, quod in Uticensibus propter beneficium legis
Iuliae parum suis partibus praesidi esse existima-
verat, plebem inermem oppido eiecerat et ante
portam bellicam castris fossaque parvula dumtaxat
muniverat ibique custodiis circumdatis habitare
coegerat; senatum autem oppidi custodia tenebat.
Eorum castra ei equites adorti expugnare coeperunt,
ideo quod eos Caesaris partibus favisse sciebant, ut
eis interfectis eorum pernicie dolorem suum ulcis-
cerentur. Uticenses animo addito ex Caesaris
victoria lapidibus fustibusque equites reppulerunt.
Itaque postea quam castra non potuerant potiri,

---

[1] Nothing is known of the details of this law, passed in his
consulship in 59 B.C., as affecting the citizens of Utica.

sending M. Messalla on ahead to Utica with the cavalry, he himself also proceeded with despatch to the same destination.

Meanwhile those horsemen of Scipio's who had escaped from the battle were proceeding in the direction of Utica when they came to the town of Parada. Being refused admittance by the inhabitants—for the tidings of Caesar's victory had preceded them—they gained possession of the town by force; then, making a pile of faggots in the middle of the market-place and heaping on top all the inhabitants' possessions, they set fire to it and then flung into the flames, alive and bound, the inhabitants of the town themselves, irrespective of rank or age, thereby meting out to them the most cruel of all punishments. Whereupon they came straight to Utica. Now earlier on M. Cato had come to the conclusion that on account of the benefit they had received from the Julian law [1] the men of Utica were but luke-warm supporters of his cause; and so he had expelled the unarmed mob from the town, built a concentration camp in front of the military gate, protected by quite a shallowish trench, and forced them to live there cordoned off by sentries. As for the town's senate, he kept it under restraint. This concentration camp of theirs Scipio's horsemen now attacked and began to storm, for the very reason that they knew that its occupants had been adherents of Caesar's side; and if they massacred them their destruction might serve to avenge their own sense of disappointment. But the people of Utica, emboldened as a result of Caesar's victory, drove back the horsemen with stones and clubs. And so, finding it impossible to gain possession of the camp, the

Uticam se in oppidum coniecerunt atque ibi multos
Uticensis interfecerunt domosque eorum expugna-
verunt ac diripuerunt. Quibus cum Cato persuadere
nulla ratione quiret ut secum oppidum defenderent
et caede rapinisque desisterent et quid sibi vellent
sciret, sedandae eorum importunitatis gratia singulis
C divisit. Idem Sulla Faustus fecit ac de sua pecunia
largitus est unaque cum his ab Utica proficiscitur
atque in regnum ire intendit.

88   Complures interim ex fuga Uticam perveniunt.
Quos omnis Cato convocatos una cum CCC, qui
pecuniam Scipioni ad bellum faciendum contulerant,
hortatur uti servitia manumitterent oppidumque
defenderent. Quorum cum partem assentire, partem
animum mentemque perterritam atque in fugam
destinatam habere intellexisset, amplius de ea re
agere destitit navisque his attribuit, ut in quas
quisque partis vellet proficisceretur. Ipse omnibus
rebus diligentissime constitutis, liberis suis L. Caesari,
qui tum ei pro quaestore fuerat, commendatis, et sine
suspicione, vultu atque sermone quo superiore
tempore usus fuerat, cum dormitum isset, ferrum
intro clam in cubiculum tulit atque ita se traiecit.
Qui dum anima nondum exspirata concidisset, et
impetu facto in cubiculum ex suspicione medicus
familiaresque continere atque vulnus obligare co-

---

[1] Wealthy Roman citizens—bankers and traders—organised
in an influential guild or corporation. Whether they formed
the whole *conventus* or only the council of a larger corporation
is not clear; nor is it certain, in view of the words *eos qu*
inter CCC in ch. 90, whether they had all contributed funds to
Scipio.

horsemen hurled themselves upon the town of Utica, where they massacred many of the inhabitants and stormed and looted their houses. As Cato could not persuade them by any means to join him in defending the town or cease from their butchery and pillaging, and as he was aware of their intentions, he distributed a hundred sesterces to each of them by way of appeasing their wanton attitude. Faustus Sulla followed suit and bribed them out of his own pocket; he then left Utica with them and proceeded on his way to Juba's kingdom.

Meanwhile a considerable number of the fugitives reached Utica. All these, together with the Three Hundred,[1] who had contributed money to Scipio for the prosecution of the war, Scipio now called together and urged them to set their slaves at liberty and defend the town. On perceiving that, while some of them agreed with him, others were thoroughly scared at heart and had set their minds on flight, he refrained from further mention of the subject and assigned ships to the latter to enable them to leave for the destination of their individual choice. As for himself, having made all arrangements with the greatest care and entrusted his children to L. Caesar, who at the time was acting as his quaestor, he retired to bed without arousing any suspicions, there being nothing unusual either about the way he looked or the way he talked; and then, having secretly smuggled a dagger into his bedroom, he accordingly stabbed himself. He had collapsed but was still breathing when his doctor and some members of his household, suspecting something amiss, forced their way into the bedroom and proceeded to staunch and bind up the wound; but with his own hands he

epissent, ipse suis manibus vulnus crudelissime divellit atque animo praesenti se interemit. Quem Uticenses quamquam oderant partium gratia, tamen propter eius singularem integritatem, et quod dissimillimus reliquorum ducum fuerat quodque Uticam mirificis operibus muniverat turrisque auxerat, sepultura adficiunt. Quo interfecto L. Caesar ut aliquid sibi ex ea re auxili pararet convocato populo contione habita cohortatur omnis ut portae aperirentur: se in C. Caesaris clementia magnam spem habere. Itaque portis patefactis Utica egressus Caesari imperatori obviam proficiscitur. Messalla, ut erat imperatum, Uticam pervenit omnibusque portis custodias ponit.

89 Caesar interim ab Thapso progressus Ussetam [1] pervenit, ubi Scipio magnum frumenti numerum, armorum, telorum ceterarumque rerum cum parvo praesidio habuerat. Id adveniens potitur, deinde Hadrumetum pervenit. Quo cum sine mora introisset, armis, frumento pecuniaque considerata Q. Ligario, C. Considio filio, qui tum ibi fuerant, vitam concessit. Deinde eodem die Hadrumeto egressus Livineio Regulo cum legione ibi relicto Uticam ire contendit. Cui in itinere fit obvius L. Caesar et subito se ad genua proiecit vitamque sibi neque amplius quicquam deprecatur. Cui Caesar facile et pro natura sua et pro instituto concessit, item

---

[1] *so most MSS.; but perhaps* Uzittam *should be read with Kuebler and Bouvet.*

tore it open with utter ruthlessness and resolutely made an end of himself. Despite their hatred of him on party grounds, yet, on account of his unique integrity, and because he had proved so very different from the other leaders and had fortified Utica with wonderful defences and extended its battlements, the men of Utica accorded him burial. After Cato's suicide L. Caesar, intending to turn this incident somehow to his personal advantage, delivered a speech to the assembled people in which he urged them all to open their gates, saying that he set great store by C. Caesar's clemency. Accordingly, the gates were thrown open and he came out from Utica and set forth to meet Caesar, the commander-in-chief. Messalla arrived at Utica in accordance with his instructions and posted guards at all the gates.

Caesar meanwhile advanced from Thapsus and arrived at Usseta, where Scipio had kept a large quantity of stores including, amongst other things, corn, arms and weapons: there was also a small garrison force. Of this arsenal he gained possession on his arrival, and then came to Hadrumetum. Entering this town without opposition, he made an inventory of the arms, corn and money in it, and spared the lives of Q. Ligarius and C. Considius, the son, both of whom were present at that time. Then, quitting Hadrumetum the same day and leaving Livineius Regulus behind there with a legion he hastened on to Utica. On the way he was met by L. Caesar, who incontinently threw himself at his feet and prayed him for one boon, for one alone—to spare him his life. Caesar readily granted him this boon—an act which accorded both with his natural temperament and principles; and in the same way

Caecinae, C. Ateio, P. Atrio, L. Cellae patri et
filio, M. Eppio, M. Aquino, Catonis filio Damasippi-
que liberis ex sua consuetudine tribuit circiterque
luminibus accensis Uticam pervenit atque extra
oppidum ea nocte mansit.

90   Postero die mane in oppidum introiit contioneque
advocata Uticensis incolas cohortatus gratias pro
eorum erga se studio egit, civis autem Romanos
negotiatores et eos qui inter CCC pecunias contulerant Varo et Scipioni multis verbis accusat[1] et
de eorum sceleribus longiore habita oratione ad
extremum ut sine metu prodirent edicit: se eis
dumtaxat vitam concessurum; bona quidem eorum
se venditurum, ita tamen, qui eorum ipse sua bona
redemisset, se bonorum venditionem inducturum et
pecuniam multae nomine relaturum, ut incolumitatem retinere posset.   Quibus metu exsanguibus de
vitaque ex suo promerito desperantibus subito oblata
salute libentes cupidique condicionem acceperunt
petieruntque a Caesare ut universis CCC uno nomine
pecuniam imperaret.   Itaque bis milies sestertio[2] his
imposito, ut per triennium sex pensionibus populo
Romano solverent, nullo eorum recusante ac se eo

---

[1] accusatos *MSS.* : accusat *R. Schneider.*
[2] sestertium *most MSS. :* sestertio *Oudendorp.*

he followed his normal procedure in sparing the
lives of Caecina, C. Ateius, P. Atrius, L. Cella (both
father and son), M. Eppius, M. Aquinus, as well as
Cato's son and the children of Damasippus. He then
arrived at Utica when it was just about dusk and
spent that night outside the town.

0 Early the following morning he entered the town
and summoned an assembly, at which he addressed
the citizens of Utica in a stirring speech and thanked
them for the zealous support they had given him.
As, however, for the Roman citizens who were
engaged in trade and those members of the Three
Hundred who had contributed sums of money to
Varus and Scipio, he brought a very detailed accusa-
tion against them and dilated at some length upon
their crimes, but finally announced that they could
come out into the open without fear: their lives at
any rate he would spare: their property indeed he
would sell, yet on the following condition, that if any
man among them personally bought in his own
property, he himself would duly register the sale of
the property and enter up the money paid under the
heading of a fine, so as to enable the man in question
to enjoy full security thereafter. For these men,
pale with fear and, considering their deserts, with
little hope of saving their lives, here was an unexpected offer of salvation. Gladly and eagerly they
accepted the terms and besought Caesar to fix a
lump sum of money to be paid by the entire Three
Hundred as a whole. Accordingly, he required them
to pay to the Roman people the sum of two hundred
million sesterces in six instalments spread over three
years; and this they accepted gladly and without
a single murmur, expressing their gratitude to

289

demum die natos praedicantes laeti gratias agunt
Caesari.

91 Rex interim Iuba, ut ex proelio fugerat, una cum
Petreio interdiu in villis latitando tandem nocturnis
itineribus confectis in regnum pervenit atque ad
oppidum Zamam, ubi ipse domicilium, coniuges
liberosque habebat, quo ex cuncto regno omnem
pecuniam carissimasque res comportaverat quodque
inito bello operibus maximis muniverat, accedit.
Quem antea oppidani rumore exoptato de Caesaris
victoria audito ob has causas oppido prohibuerunt,
quod bello contra populum Romanum suscepto in
oppido Zamae lignis congestis maximam in medio foro
pyram construxerat ut, si forte bello foret superatus,
omnibus rebus eo coacervatis, dein civibus cunctis
interfectis eodemque proiectis igne subiecto tum
demum se ipse insuper interficeret atque una cum
liberis, coniugibus, civibus cunctaque gaza regia
cremaretur. Postquam Iuba ante portas diu multumque primo minis pro imperio egisset cum Zamensibus,
dein cum se parum proficere intellexisset precibus
orasset uti se ad suos deos penates admitterent, ubi
eos perstare in sententia animadvertit nec minis nec
precibus suis moveri quo magis se reciperent, tertio
petit ab eis ut sibi coniuges liberosque redderent
290

Caesar and declaring that this day finally marked for them the start of a new life.

91   Meanwhile king Juba had fled from the battle and, accompanied by Petreius, by lying up in farms by day and travelling by night, arrived at length in his kingdom and came to the town of Zama. In this town he had his own residence and his wives and children; and it was here he had collected all his money and most precious possessions from all over his kingdom, having fortified the town at the outset of hostilities with very strong defences. But the townsfolk, who had already heard the much-desired tidings of Caesar's victory, refused him admittance on the following grounds: when he entered upon hostilities with the Roman people he had collected a mass of wooden billets and built a vast pyre in the town of Zama in the middle of the market-place, so that, should it so chance he was beaten in the war, he might pile all his possessions on it, then massacre all his citizens and fling them also on to it, set it alight, and then finally slay himself on top of it, and thus be consumed by fire along with his children, wives, citizens and the entire royal treasure. For a long time Juba earnestly treated with the men of Zama before the gates of the town, employing threats in the first place, as his authority warranted; secondly, realising that he was making but little headway, he besought them with entreaties to let him have access to his own hearth and home; and thirdly, when he observed that they persisted in their determination, and that neither threats nor entreaties on his part had any effect upon them or disposed them the more to admit him, he begged them to hand over to him his wives and children, so

ut secum eos asportaret.   Postquam sibi nihil omnino
oppidanos responsi reddere animadvertit, nulla re ab
his impetrata ab Zama discedit atque ad villam suam
se cum M. Petreio paucisque equitibus confert.

92   Zamenses interim legatos de his rebus ad Caesarem
Uticam mittunt petuntque ab eo uti antequam rex
manum colligeret seseque oppugnaret sibi auxilium
mitteret: se tamen paratos esse, sibi quoad vita
suppeteret, oppidum seque ei reservare. Legatos
collaudatos Caesar domum iubet antecedere ac suum
adventum praenuntiare. Ipse postero die Utica
egressus cum equitatu in regnum ire contendit.
Interim in itinere ex regiis copiis duces complures
ad Caesarem veniunt orantque ut sibi ignoscat.
Quibus supplicibus venia data Zamam pervenit.
Rumore interim perlato de eius lenitate clementiaque
propemodum omnes regni equites Zamam perveniunt
ad Caesarem ab eoque sunt metu periculoque liberati.

93   Dum haec utrobique geruntur, Considius, qui
Thysdrae cum familia sua, gladiatoria manu Gaetulisque praeerat, cognita caede suorum Domitique et
legionum adventu perterritus desperata salute
oppidum deserit seque clam cum paucis barbaris

that he could carry them away with him. On observing that the townsfolk vouchsafed him no answer at all he left Zama without gaining any satisfaction from them, and then betook himself to a country residence of his, attended by M. Petreius and a few horsemen.

Whereupon the men of Zama sent envoys to Caesar at Utica to discuss this situation, asking him to send them help before the king should collect a force and attack them: at all events, they said, they were prepared to preserve the town and themselves for him so long as the breath of life remained in them. Caesar congratulated the envoys and bade them return home: he would follow them, and they must make known his coming in advance. He himself left Utica the following day with his cavalry and proceeded with despatch into the royal territory. Meanwhile in the course of his march there came to Caesar several leaders of the royal forces, who begged him to forgive them. To these suppliants he granted pardon, and then came to Zama. Meanwhile the tidings of his leniency and clemency had spread abroad, with the result that practically all the horsemen in the kingdom came to Caesar at Zama; and there they were set free by him from their fears and the danger which involved them.

During the course of these proceedings on either side Considius, who was in command at Thysdra and was accompanied by his household slaves, a body-guard of gladiators and some Gaetulians, learned of the massacre of his comrades; and being seriously perturbed by the arrival of Domitius and his legions, and despairing of saving his life, he abandoned the town, made a secret withdrawal with a handful of his

pecunia onustus subducit atque in regnum fugere
contendit. Quem Gaetuli, sui comites, in itinere
praedae cupidi concidunt seque in quascumque
potuere partis conferunt. C. interim Vergilius,
postquam terra marique clausus se nihil proficere
intellexit suosque interfectos aut fugatos, M.
Catonem Uticae sibi ipsum manus attulisse, regem
vagum ab suisque desertum ab omnibus aspernari,
Saburram eiusque copias ab Sittio esse deletas,
Uticae Caesarem sine mora receptum, de tanto
exercitu reliquias esse nullas, ipse sibi suisque liberis
a Caninio pro consule, qui eum obsidebat, fide
accepta seque et sua omnia et oppidum proconsuli
tradit.

94   Rex interim ab omnibus civitatibus exclusus,
desperata salute, cum iam cenatus[1] esset cum
Petreio, ut per virtutem interfecti esse viderentur,
ferro inter se depugnant atque firmior imbecilliorem
Iuba Petreium[2] facile ferro consumpsit. Deinde
ipse sibi cum conaretur gladio traicere pectus nec
posset, precibus a servo suo impetravit ut se interficeret idque obtinuit.

95   P. Sittius interim pulso exercitu Saburrae, praefecti Iubae, ipsoque interfecto cum iter cum paucis
per Mauretaniam[3] ad Caesarem faceret, forte incidit

[1] conatus *MSS.*: cenatus *Rubenius.*

[2] Iuba Petreium *MSS.; but* Iubam Petreius *is a common
restoration which not only serves to improve the word order by
securing chiasmus, but also conforms to the traditional account
of the duel given both in* Livy, Epitome *and* Florus.

[3] *The MSS. reading appears corrupt: the phrase is barely
intelligible in this position, and Moelken may well be right in
placing it after* Hispaniam. *One MS. (M) gives* per marit-
timam, *whence* per maritima *or* per oram maritimam *have been
conjectured.*

foreign troops and a large sum of money, and beat a
hasty retreat to Juba's kingdom. But while he
was on the road the Gaetulians who bore him company cut him down in their impatience to loot his
treasure, and then made off, as best they could, in
various directions. Meanwhile C. Vergilius, who
was cut off alike by land and sea, perceived that he
was making no progress: that his comrades were
either killed or put to flight: that M. Cato had
taken his own life at Utica: that the king was a
wanderer at large, abandoned by his subjects and
held in universal contempt: that Saburra and his
troops had been destroyed by Sittius: that Caesar
had been received without opposition at Utica;
and that out of all that vast army there was nothing
left whatever. For his own part, therefore, he
accepted the safeguard for himself and his children
offered him by the pro-consul Caninius, who was
blockading him, and surrendered himself to the latter
with all his effects and the town.

94   Meanwhile king Juba, outlawed by all his townships, despaired of saving his life. And so finally,
after dining with Petreius, he fought a duel with him
with swords, so as to create the impression that both
had met a gallant death; and the sword of the
stronger man, Juba, easily put an end to Petreius,
his weaker adversary. Juba then endeavoured to
run himself through the chest with his sword; but
not being able to do it, he successfully entreated a
slave of his to kill him, and so achieved his purpose.

95   Meanwhile P. Sittius had routed the army of
Saburra, Juba's lieutenant, killing Saburra himself,
and was marching with a small force through
Mauretania to join Caesar when he happened to fall

in Faustum Afraniumque, qui eam manum habebant
qua Uticam diripuerant iterque in Hispaniam in-
tendebant et erant numero circiter mille. Itaque
celeriter nocturno tempore insidiis dispositis cum
prima luce adortus praeter paucos equites, qui ex
primo agmine fugerant, reliquos aut interfecit aut in
deditionem accepit, Afranium et Faustum cum
coniuge et liberis vivos capit. Paucis post diebus
dissensione in exercitu orta Faustus et Afranius
interficiuntur; Pompeiae cum Fausti liberis Caesar
incolumitatem suaque omnia concessit.

96 Scipio interim cum Damasippo et Torquato et
Plaetorio Rustiano navibus longis diu multumque
iactati, cum Hispaniam peterent, ad Hipponem
regium deferuntur, ubi classis P. Sitti id temporis
erat. A qua pauciora ab amplioribus circumventa
navigia deprimuntur, ibique Scipio cum illis quos[1]
paulo ante nominavi interiit.

97 Caesar interim Zamae auctione regia facta bonis-
que eorum venditis qui cives Romani contra populum
Romanum arma tulerant praemiisque Zamensibus,
qui de rege excludendo consilium ceperant, tributis
vectigalibusque regiis locatis[2] ex regnoque provincia
facta atque ibi C. Sallustio pro consule cum imperio
relicto ipse Zama egressus Uticam se recepit. Ibi
bonis venditis eorum qui sub Iuba Petreioque

---

[1] cum quos *or* cum illis quas *MSS. :* cum illis quos *Kuebler.*
[2] togatis *most MSS.* (irrogatis *in two inferior Dresden
codices*) : locatis *R. Schneider.*

in with Faustus and Afranius, who were in command
of the party—some thousand strong—with which
they had plundered Utica, and were now making
tracks for Spain. And so he promptly laid an ambush
by night and attacked them at dawn. A few of the
cavalry in their vanguard escaped; but all the rest
were either killed or else they surrendered, and
Sittius captured alive Afranius as well as Faustus
with his wife and children. A few days later some
disagreement arose in the army and Faustus and
Afranius were killed. As for Pompeia and the
children of Faustus, Caesar spared their lives and
allowed them to retain all their property.

96   Meanwhile Scipio, Damasippus, Torquatus and
Plaetorius Rustianus were making for Spain aboard
some warships; and after a long and very stormy
passage they were carried towards Royal Hippo,
where P. Sittius had his fleet at that time. Outnumbered as they were by the latter, Scipio's vessels
were surrounded and sunk; and Scipio and those I
have just named perished aboard them.

97   Meanwhile at Zama Caesar held an auction of the
royal property and sold the goods of those who,
albeit Roman citizens, had borne arms against the
Roman people. He bestowed rewards upon the
inhabitants of Zama, who had adopted the policy
of barring their gates to the king, farmed out the
collection of the royal taxes, and turned the kingdom
into a province. Then, leaving C. Sallustius behind
there in military command with the powers of pro-
consul, he himself left Zama and returned to Utica.
There he sold the property of those who had held
military commands under Juba and Petreius, and
exacted the following payments under the title of

ordines duxerant, Thapsitanis HS |XX̄, conventui
eorum HS XXX, itemque¹ Hadrumetinis HS |XX̄X̄,
conventui eorum HS L multae nomine imponit;
civitates bonaque eorum ab omni iniuria rapinisque
defendit. Leptitanos, quorum superioribus annis
bona Iuba diripuerat, et ad senatum questi per
legatos atque arbitris a senatu datis sua receperant,
XXX centenis milibus pondo olei in annos singulos
multat, ideo quod initio per dissensionem principum
societatem cum Iuba inierant eumque armis, militibus, pecunia iuverant. Thysdritanos propter
humilitatem civitatis certo numero frumenti multat.

98   His rebus gestis Idibus Iun. Uticae classem conscendit et post diem tertium Caralis in Sardiniam
pervenit. Ibi Sulcitanos, quod Nasidium eiusque
classem receperant copiisque iuverant, HS C multat
et pro decumis octavas pendere iubet bonaque
paucorum vendit et ante diem IIII Kal. Quint.
navis conscendit et a Caralibus secundum terram
provectus duodetricesimo die, ideo quod tempestatibus in portibus cohibebatur, ad urbem Romam
venit.

¹ itemque *appears in the MSS. before* Thapsitanis : *Nipperdey transposed it.*

fines: from the men of Thapsus—two million sesterces; from their corporation—three million; likewise from the men of Hadrumetum—three million; and from their corporation—five million. But he protected their cities and property from all injury and looting. As for the inhabitants of Leptis, whose property had been plundered in former years by Juba but had been restored to them after the Senate had appointed arbitrators on receiving a deputation of theirs lodging a formal complaint, Caesar now required them to pay by way of fine three million pounds weight of oil annually, because at the beginning of the war in the course of disagreements among their leaders they had entered into an alliance with Juba, and had assisted him with arms, troops and money. The men of Thysdra—not a well-to-do community—were fined a certain quantity of corn.

After making these arrangements he went aboard his fleet at Utica on June 13th, and arrived two days later at Caralis in Sardinia. There he fined the men of Sulci one hundred thousand sesterces for having harboured Nasidius and his fleet and assisted him by supplying troops, and directed that they should pay as tax one-eighth of their produce instead of one-tenth. He also sold up the property of a few individuals. Then he embarked on June 27th, and leaving Caralis, sailed along the coast. Twenty-seven days later—for bad weather kept holding him up in the various ports—he arrived at the city of Rome.

THE SPANISH WAR

INTRODUCTION

THE battle of Thapsus sealed the fate of the Pompeians' venture in Africa. Once again their army had been shattered: their main ally, Juba, was dead: Cato and Scipio had both perished by their own hands: Afranius, Petreius, Faustus Sulla and Considius had all been killed: of the leaders only Varus, Labienus and the two sons of Pompey survived. In Spain lay their last chance of regrouping and making another stand. But this time they were not to enjoy so long a respite in which to consolidate; for less than nine months after his victory at Thapsus Caesar was to set foot in Spain for the final reckoning.

For two months after the battle Caesar was occupied in reducing the remaining African strongholds, replenishing his finances by inflicting heavy fines upon the prosperous communities which had lately defied him, and reorganising the province and its neighbouring territories. On his return to Rome in July 46 conditions were outwardly more settled than on his previous visit. Honours and offices, including a third dictatorship and a fourth consulship for the ensuing year, were showered upon him, while preparations went ahead for his delayed triumphs. These he celebrated in August with unprecedented magnificence—over Gaul, Egypt, Pontus and Africa; and there appears to have been a general feeling that the last battle of the civil wars had already been

fought and that, with Cato's suicide, the struggle to maintain the old order was too futile to pursue.

Meanwhile the news from Further Spain was ominous. Since Caesar's brilliant victory at Ilerda in 49 much had happened to lessen his prestige and revive memories of Pompey's earlier feats of arms in the peninsula. The prolonged misgovernment of Q. Cassius had exasperated the Spaniards and driven several of the Roman legions to open mutiny [1]; and though this had been quelled with but little bloodshed and Cassius had fled, the mischief was done. The mutinous legions, fearing Caesar's retribution, expelled the new governor, Trebonius, and chose Scapula and Aponius as their leaders; and when, in the autumn of 46, Pompey's elder son, Gnaeus, landed in the province, he was at once elected as their commander. After Thapsus came the refugees—his younger brother, Sextus, and the remnants of the broken armies led by Labienus and Varus; while in Spain itself many of the troops who had once served with Afranius and had been disbanded by Caesar to their homes in Spain now joined his standards. By the end of 46 Gnaeus had thirteen legions, though only four were of proved worth; and though his own record ill fitted him for the supreme command, yet he had two valuable assets—the magic influence of his father's name and, in Labienus, at least one brilliant and experienced subordinate.

Caesar had not been blind to these ever-increasing dangers. Didius had been despatched with a fleet: Pedius and Fabius had been furnished initially with troops from Sardinia and, when these proved in-

[1] See *Bell. Alex.* chs. 48–64.

INTRODUCTION

sufficient, reinforced. But the situation had got out of their control: most of Baetica had gone over to the rebels, and the few remaining loyal communities like Ulia, unable to hold out much longer, kept sending him urgent appeals for help. Early in November 46 Caesar left Rome for Further Spain, where, with a force of eight legions and eight thousand cavalry, he now entered upon what was to prove the final campaign alike of the war and of his own career.

Of this campaign, the bloodiest of the war, we have one contemporary account, *de Bello Hispaniensi* —perhaps the most illiterate and exasperating book in classical literature. Who wrote it is unknown; but he appears to have been one of the combatants [1]; and Macaulay's guess that he was some ' sturdy old centurion who fought better than he wrote ' is possibly not far off the truth. In view of the sorry state of the MSS. tradition it is difficult to assess accurately his historical and literary merits: all that can be attempted here is a brief and general survey of his qualities.

As a military commentator he lacks a sense of proportion; for while he describes—often at some length—all kinds of engagements, including quite minor skirmishes,[2] as well as frequent atrocities,[3] desertions and even apparent trivialities,[4] yet he throws little light on problems of supply,[5] finance,

---

[1] *cf.* in ch. 29 the topographical details of the plain of Munda and the allusion to the weather.
[2] *e.g.* ch. 13, 21, 27.
[3] *e.g.* ch. 12, 15, 20, 21, 27.
[4] *e.g.* the appearance of the moon in ch. 27.
[5] The references in ch. 5, 11 and 26 are very vague.

INTRODUCTION

the number of troops engaged[1] and, above all, the tactical reasons for the various manoeuvres.[2] His grasp of tactics seems, in fact, negligible.[3]

His enumeration of casualties[4] sometimes reflects the partisan; but in other respects, wherever his narrative can be compared with the brief accounts of later writers, it appears in the main to be reasonably trustworthy.

His presentation of his material is not always effective. He tries hard to follow a chronological sequence and, when it occurs to him to do so, he quotes a date.[5] But this day-by-day system often involves a mere catalogue of disconnected incidents.[6] Nor is his chronology always accurate: not seldom he forgets to mention something in its proper place and so has to go back.[7]

His literary style is poor. Colloquial expressions[8] jostle with quotations from Ennius and reminiscences of Homer: his vocabulary is limited and dull repeti-

[1] Meagre details are given in ch. 7 and 30.

[2] Thus, while he accounts for Gnaeus's taking the field at Munda in ch. 28, he gives no reasons for the manoeuvres of ch. 27.

[3] *e.g.* in ch. 29 his strange assumption that the Caesarians expected the enemy to come down to fight in the plain.

[4] *e.g.* ch. 15 : 123 enemy dead, but only 3 Caesarians killed ; and ch. 23, where after desperate hand-to-hand fighting Caesarian casualties are two dead and several wounded.

[5] *e.g.* ch. 19, 27, 31, 39.

[6] *e.g.* ch. 10, 11, 13, 20.

[7] *e.g.* ch. 10 : ' I forgot to mention in its proper place ' ; moreover, he appears to have coined a special phrase for such emergencies, if the recurrent words *hoc praeterito tempore* mean, as they seem to, ' just before this time '.

[8] *e.g.* his constant use of *bene* in the sense of ' very ', which occurs in Cicero (but mainly in the letters) and the comic poets ; words like *loricatus*.

INTRODUCTION

tions of the same word or phrase are frequent.[1] His grammar is uncertain, often colloquial, sometimes barely intelligible.[2] But his chief failing is a want of clarity resulting from a habit of not stating clearly the subject of the sentence and frequently changing it without warning; and this often leads to serious ambiguities.[3]

Nevertheless, despite all its obvious failings, *de Bello Hispaniensi* has character. Its author appears as an honest man struggling with an unfamiliar task; and if fortune had not preserved his efforts, our knowledge of the campaign would be the poorer.

---

[1] *e.g.* his monotonous repetition of the relative pronoun as a connective in the middle of ch. 3, and the doubled *prope* in the last sentence; also, in ch. 9, *committere* twice in the same sentence. The repetition of *tripertito* in ch. 5 and of *itaque nostri procedunt* in ch. 29 is rather different and suggests the informal style of conversation.

[2] See ch. 22 for several examples of the subjunctive used in factual relative clauses : ch. 36 for *renuntiare* followed by a *quod* clause; and in ch. 27 the barely grammatical phrase ' *a. d. iii . . . factum est, ex eo tempore . . .*'.

[3] See note 1 at foot of ch. 27, and ch. 38.

ANALYSIS OF THE BOOK

ANALYSIS OF THE BOOK

DE BELLO HISPANIENSI

1 PHARNACE superato, Africa recepta, qui ex his
proeliis cum adulescente Cn. Pompeio profugissent,
cum . . . et ulterioris Hispaniae potitus esset, dum
Caesar muneribus dandis in Italia detinetur, . . .
quo facilius praesidia contra compararet, Pompeius
in fidem uniuscuiusque civitatis confugere coepit.[1]
Ita partim precibus partim vi bene magna comparata manu provinciam vastare. Quibus in rebus
non nullae civitates sua sponte auxilia mittebant,
item non nullae portas contra cludebant. Ex quibus
si qua oppida vi ceperat, cum aliquis ex ea civitate
optime de Cn. Pompeio meritus civis esset, propter
pecuniae magnitudinem alia qua ei inferebatur
causa, ut eo de medio sublato ex eius pecunia latro-
num largitio fieret. Ita paucis commoda ab hoste

---

[1] A. Klotz (Teubner, 1927) conjecturally restores the text as
follows :—Pharnace . . . proeliis ⟨superfuissent⟩ cum ⟨ad⟩
adulescente⟨m⟩ Cn. Pompeium profugissent, cum ⟨Baleares
appulisset⟩ et ulterioris . . . detinetur, ⟨magnas copias coege-
runt. Caesaris autem copiae nil profecerunt⟩. quo facilius . . .
'. . . and when those who had survived from these battles had
taken refuge with the young Cn. Pompeius, when he had put in
at the Balearic Islands and had gained possession of Further
Spain, . . . they collected large forces. Caesar's forces, however,
made no headway.'

---

[1] i.e. the elder of the two sons of Cn. Pompeius Magnus.
His departure from Africa before the decisive battle of Thapsus
is mentioned in Bell. Afr. ch. 23, where he is described as

THE SPANISH WAR

1 Now that Pharnaces had been overcome and Africa recovered, and those who had made good their escape from these battles with the young Cn. Pompeius [1] had . . . and he had gained possession of Further Spain, while Caesar was occupied in Italy exhibiting games, . . . to make it easier to gather together defensive forces for the purposes of resistance, Pompeius proceeded to throw himself upon the protection of each individual state. Having in this way mustered a good large force, partly by entreaties, partly by violent measures, he was now playing havoc with the province. In these circumstances some states sent reinforcements of their own accord, while on the other hand some shut their gates against him. And if, whenever he took any of their towns by force, there was any rich citizen of that township who had deserved well of Cn. Pompeius, yet in view of his great wealth some other charge would always be brought against him, in order that he might be done away with and his money used to provide a handsome share-out for the plunderers. This policy enabled a (Triumph: Sept. 46.)

setting course for the Balearic Islands. From references in Cicero and Dio it appears that he was ill in the summer of 46, but crossed to the mainland of Spain in the autumn and attacked New Carthage. Klotz's restoration of the sentence could, I think, imply that all the Pompeian survivors—including those from Thapsus—eventually joined the young Pompeius in Spain.

311

orta : eo[1] maiores augebantur copiae. Hoc crebrius[2] nuntiis in Italiam missis civitates contrariae Pompeio auxilia sibi depostulabant.

2   C. Caesar dictator tertio, designatus dictator quarto multis ante iter rebus confectis[3] cum celeri festinatione ad bellum conficiendum in Hispaniam cum venisset, legatique Cordubenses, qui a Cn. Pompeio discessissent, Caesari obviam venissent, a quibus nuntiabatur nocturno tempore oppidum Cordubam capi posse, quod nec opinantibus adversariis eius provinciae potitus esset, simulque quod tabellariis, qui a Cn. Pompeio dispositi omnibus locis essent, qui certiorem Cn. Pompeium de Caesaris adventu facerent, ipse suum eius adventus metum significasset,[4] multa praeterea veri similia proponebant. Quibus rebus adductus quos legatos ante exercitui praefecerat Q. Pedium et Q. Fabium Maximum de suo adventu facit certiores, utque sibi equitatus qui ex provincia fuisset praesidio esset. Ad quos celerius quam ipsi opinati sunt appropinquavit neque, ut ipse voluit, equitatum sibi praesidio habuit.

3   Erat idem temporis Sex. Pompeius frater qui cum praesidio Cordubam tenebat, quod eius provinciae caput esse existimabatur; ipse autem Cn. Pompeius adulescens Uliam[5] oppidum oppugnabat et fere iam aliquot mensibus ibi detinebatur. Quo ex oppido

[1] I have adopted Fleischer's emendation of the MSS. reading— ita pacis commoda hoste hortato.

[2] crebris MSS. : crebrius Nipperdey.

[3] multis iterante diebus coniectis MSS. : I have adopted Hoffmann's reading.

[4] ipse . . . significasset is Mommsen's conjectural restoration.

[5] ullam MSS. : Uliam most editors.

few men to reap profits on the enemy side, and their resources correspondingly increased; whereas its effect upon the states opposed to Pompeius was to make them send more frequent messages to Italy urgently requesting assistance to be sent to them.

2 C. Caesar, who was now in his third dictatorship and had been appointed to a fourth, had had much business to complete before he took to the road; but this was now disposed of, and he had come post haste to Spain to finish off the war. Envoys from those in Corduba who had deserted the cause of Cn. Pompeius had met Caesar and now reported that the town of Corduba could be captured by night, because it was by surprise that Pompeius had mastered his rivals in that province, and moreover, Pompeius himself had revealed his own fears of Caesar's arrival by the fact that he had posted couriers at all points to notify him of Caesar's coming. They also advanced many other plausible reasons besides this. Caesar was thereby encouraged and informed Q. Pedius and Q. Fabius Maximus, the two officers he had previously appointed to command his army, that he had arrived, adding instructions that the cavalry which had been raised in the province should support him. But he came up with them more expeditiously than they themselves anticipated, and so did not have the cavalry to support him as he himself had wished.

3 At the same time there was the brother, Sextus Pompeius, who was holding Corduba with a garrison force, that town being regarded as the capital of the province; whereas the young Cn. Pompeius himself was attacking the town of Ulia, and had now been engaged there for some months or so. On learning

313

cognito Caesaris adventu legati clam praesidia Cn.
Pompei Caesarem cum adissent, petere coeperunt
uti sibi primo quoque tempore subsidium mitteret.
Caesar—eam civitatem omni tempore optime de
populo Romano meritam esse—celeriter sex cohortis
secunda vigilia iubet proficisci, pari equites numero.
Quibus praefecit hominem eius provinciae notum et
non parum scientem, L. Vibium[1] Paciaecum. Qui
cum ad Cn. Pompei praesidia venisset, incidit idem
temporis ut tempestate adversa vehementique vento
adflictaretur; aditusque vis tempestatis ita obscura-
bat ut vix proximum agnoscere posset. Cuius
incommodum summam utilitatem ipsis praebebat.
Ita cum ad eum locum venerunt, iubet binos equites
conscendere, et recta per adversariorum praesidia ad
oppidum contendunt. Mediisque eorum praesidiis
cum essent, cum quaereretur qui essent, unus ex
nostris respondit, ut sileat verbum facere: nam id
temporis conari ad murum accedere, ut oppidum
capiant; et partim tempestate impediti vigiles non
poterant diligentiam praestare, partim illo responso
deterrebantur. Cum ad portam appropinquassent,
signo dato ab oppidanis sunt recepti, et pedites

---

[1] vivium *MSS.* : Vibium *Forchhammer.*

---

[1] Klotz, however, interprets :—' a man familiar with that
province and not without military knowledge.'

[2] Or possibly—' bade the infantry mount pillion '. The
subsequent rapid advance, as well as the mention of the
cavalry's being numerically equal to the infantry, tends,
I rather think, to support this interpretation. It would,
however, fit much better in the next chapter, where the
infantry undoubtedly took to the horses for a time. Perhaps

of Caesar's arrival, envoys left this town unbeknown
to Cn. Pompeius' outposts, came to Caesar, and proceeded to entreat him to send them help at the
earliest opportunity. Caesar, who was aware that
the township in question had always deserved well
of the Roman people, promptly gave orders that six
infantry cohorts and a corresponding number of
cavalry should set out at the second watch; and in
command of them he put L. Vibius Paciaecus, a well-
known member of that province, and one that knew
it pretty well.[1] Now it so chanced that at the very
time he came to Cn. Pompeius' outposts he was beset
by bad weather and a violent gale. So severe was
the storm and so dark did it make the approaches
to the town that they could scarcely recognise their
next-door neighbours. To them indeed this draw-
back proved of the utmost advantage. And so,
when they had got thus far, he bade the horsemen
go up in file,[2] and they pushed rapidly forward to
the town straight through their opponent's positions.
When they were in the middle of their positions someone asked who they were; and one of our men told
the questioner to hold his tongue: 'just at the
moment they were trying to come up to the wall so as
to capture the town.' It was in fact partly the disconcerting effect of this reply, partly the difficulties
of the storm, which prevented the sentries from displaying proper attention to their duties. When
they came up to the gate they gave the pass-word
and were admitted by the townsfolk: the infantry
were deployed in various sectors of the town and

the author was confused about the details of the two sorties,
and attributed somewhat allusively to both the tactics which
properly belonged only to one.

315

dispositi[1] partim ibi remanserunt, equites clamore
facto eruptionem in adversariorum castra fecerunt.
Sic in illo facto, cum inscientibus accidisset, existimabant prope magna pars hominum qui in his castris
fuissent se prope captos esse.

4 Hoc misso ad Uliam praesidio Caesar, ut Pompeium
ab ea oppugnatione deduceret, ad Cordubam contendit, ex quo itinere loricatos viros fortis cum
equitatu ante praemisit. Qui simul in conspectum
oppidi se dederunt, cum equis recipiuntur, hoc a Cordubensibus nequaquam poterat animadverti. Appro-
pinquantibus ex oppido bene magna multitudo ad
equitatum concidendum cum exissent, loricati, ut
supra scripsimus, ex equis descenderunt et magnum
proelium fecerunt, sic uti ex infinita hominum
multitudine pauci in oppidum se reciperent. Hoc
timore adductus Sex. Pompeius litteras fratri misit ut
celeriter sibi subsidio veniret, ne prius Caesar
Cordubam caperet quam ipse illo venisset. Itaque
Cn. Pompeius Ulia prope capta litteris fratris
excitus cum copiis ad Cordubam iter facere
coepit.

5 Caesar, cum ad flumen Baetim venisset neque
propter altitudinem fluminis transire posset, lapidibus
corbis plenos demisit: insuper ponit trabes; ita
ponte facto copias ad castra tripertito traduxit.
Tendebat adversum oppidum e regione pontis, ut

---

[1] pedites equites clamore facto dispositis *MSS.*: pedites
dispositi *Nipperdey.*

stayed inside, while the cavalry raised a shout and
sallied forth against the enemy camp. Thus, in the
course of this operation, which had taken the enemy
unawares, well nigh the majority of the troops in this
camp thought they were as good as captured.

4   Having despatched this relief force to Ulia, Caesar
marched to Corduba with the object of inducing
Pompeius to abandon his assault of Ulia; and while
on the march he sent on ahead some heavy-armed
infantry troops—brave soldiers—accompanied by
cavalry. No sooner had they come within sight of
the town than they all took to the horses; but this
manoeuvre it was quite impossible for the men of
Corduba to observe. Now as they were approaching
Corduba, a good large force came out of the town
to cut the cavalry to pieces, and the heavy-armed
infantry we have just mentioned now dismounted.
They then fought a great battle, to such effect that
out of that countless host but few men retired back
into the town. In his alarm at this reverse Sextus
Pompeius was constrained to send a despatch to his
brother urging him to come promptly to his aid, to
prevent Caesar's capturing Corduba before Gnaeus
himself could arrive there. Accordingly, though
Cn. Pompeius had almost captured Ulia, he was
disturbed by his brother's despatch and proceeded
to march to Corduba with his forces.

When Caesar came to the river Baetis he could not
cross it owing to the depth of the stream; so he
lowered into it wicker baskets filled with stones,
laid beams on top of them, and thus made a bridge,
by which he brought his forces across to a camp
divided into three sections. He was now encamped
over against the town in the area of the bridge, and

supra scripsimus, tripertito.[1] Huc cum Pompeius
cum suis copiis venisset, ex adverso pari ratione
castra ponit. Caesar, ut eum ab oppido commeatuque excluderet, bracchium ad pontem ducere
coepit: pari idem condicione Pompeius facit. Hic
inter duces duos fit contentio uter prius pontem
occuparet; ex qua contentione cotidiana minuta
proelia fiebant, ut modo hi, non numquam illi
superiores discederent. Quae res cum ad maiorem
contentionem venisset, ab utrisque comminus pugna
inita, dum cupidius locum student tenere, propter
pontem coagulabantur,[2] fluminis ripas appropin-
quantes coangustati praecipitabantur. Hic alternis[3]
non solum morti mortem exaggerabant, sed tumulos
tumulis exaequabant. Ita diebus compluribus consumptis cupiebat Caesar, si qua condicione posset,
adversarios in aequum locum deducere et primo
quoque tempore de bello decernere.

6   Id cum animadverteret adversarios minime velle,
quo eos quomodo ab Ulia[4] retraxerat in aequum

[1] *After* demisit *the MSS. give* :—ita insuper ponte facto
copias ad castra tripertito transduxit tenebat adversum
oppidum e regione ponit trabes pontis ut supra scripsimus
tripertito. *The reading here followed is that of Fleischer, but
with Kraner's* tendebat *in place of* tenebat.
[2] coagulabant *MSS.* : coagulabantur *Kuebler.*
[3] alterius *MSS.* : alternis *most editors.*
[4] quos quoniam a avia retraxerat ut *MSS. I have adopted
Nipperdey's restoration.*

---

[1] *viz.* the permanent bridge over the Baetis (*Guadalquivir*),
the northern end of which must have been in the hands of
Sextus : Caesar's object was to deny its use to Gnaeus.
Caesar's line presumably ran from his own bridgehead at the
southern end of his pile bridge to the southern end of the permanent bridge : Gnaeus' line must have been a contravallation.
[2] The exact import of this colourful expression is not easy to

his camp was, as we have just mentioned, divided into
three sections. When Pompeius arrived there with
his forces he pitched a camp on the same principle
on the opposite side. In order to cut him off from
the town and the supplies it afforded, Caesar began
to carry a line of fortifications to the bridge,[1] and
Pompeius adopted tactics on similar lines. Whereupon a race took place between the two commanders
as to which of them should seize the bridge first; and
this race gave rise to daily skirmishes on a small scale
in which now our troops, now theirs, would come out
on top. This situation had now developed into a
more intensive struggle, and both sides being more
passionately bent on holding their ground had embarked upon hand-to-hand fighting and formed a
solid mass near the bridge; and as they approached
the river's banks they were flung headlong into it,
packed tightly as they were. At this point the two
sides vied with each other not merely in piling one
death upon another but in matching mound of dead
with mound.[2] Several days were passed in this
fashion, and Caesar was anxious to bring his opponents down to favourable ground, if by any means he
could do so, and fight a decisive action at the earliest
opportunity.

3 Observing that his opponents were by no means
willing to do this, Caesar led his forces across the
river and ordered large fires to be lit at night, so as

decide. As it seems likely that the purpose of the whole
sentence is merely to emphasise the extent of the carnage, the
tumuli are probably the burial mounds, or possibly the piles of
corpses. The elaborate balance of expression suggests, I
think, that *tumulos tumulis* are the rival barrows. Klotz,
however, interprets the latter phrase as meaning ' they made
the barrows to look like hills.'

deduceret, copiis flumine traductis noctu iubet ignis
fieri magnos : ita firmissimum eius praesidium Ateguam proficiscitur. Id cum Pompeius ex perfugis
rescisset, qua die facultatem nactus est, relinquens
montis [1] et angustias, carra complura mulosque
onustos [2] retraxit et ad Cordubam se recepit.
Caesar munitionibus Ateguam [3] oppugnare et brac-
chiæ circumducere coepit. Cui de Pompeio cum nuntius esset allatus eo die proficisci,[4] cuius in adventu
praesidi causa Caesar complura castella occupasset,
partim ubi equitatus, partim ubi pedestres copiae in
statione et in excubitu [5] castris praesidio esse possent,
hic in adventu Pompei incidit ut matutino tempore
nebula esset crassissima. Ita illa obscuratione cum
aliquot cohortibus et equitum turmis circumcludunt
Caesaris equites et concidunt, sic ut vix in ea caede
pauci effugerent.

7 Insequenti nocte castra sua incendit Pompeius et
trans flumen Salsum per convallis castra inter duo
oppida Ateguam et Ucubim in monte constituit.
Caesar interim munitionibus ceterisque quae ad
oppugnandum opus fuerunt perfectis aggerem
vineasque agere instituit.[6] Haec loca sunt montuosa
et natura impedita [7] ad rem militarem ; quae planitie

---

[1] nactus . . . montis *was supplied by Mommsen.*
[2] multosque lanistas *MSS.*: mulosque onustos *Nipper-dey.*
[3] antequam *or* antiquas *MSS.*: Ateguam *Aldus.*
[4] proficiscitur *MSS.*: proficisci *Vahlen.*
[5] in stationes in excubitus *MSS.*: in statione et in excubitu
editors.
[6] Caesar in munitionibus ceterisque quae ad oppidum opus
fuerunt aggerem *MSS.*: interim *Fleischer*; oppugnandum
Kraner; perfectis *supplied by Nipperdey.*
[7] edita *MSS.*: impedita *Mommsen.*

to entice them into the plain just as he had drawn
them away from Ulia; and in this manner he set out
for Ategua, the strongest garrison of Pompeius. When
Pompeius got to know of this from deserters, on the
first day that afforded him the opportunity he quitted
the mountain passes and retired to Corduba with a
numerous train of carts and laden mules.[1] Caesar began to assault Ategua by surrounding it with siege
works and fortified lines. Now a message had been
brought to him concerning Pompeius to the effect that
he was setting out that day; and by way of safe-
guarding himself against Pompeius' coming Caesar
had occupied several forts where in some cases
cavalry, in others infantry forces could be posted as
outlying pickets and sentries to protect his camp:
yet, in these circumstances, it so chanced that
when Pompeius did arrive there was a very thick
mist in the early morning. And so in the resulting gloom the Pompeians surrounded Caesar's
cavalry with a number of infantry cohorts and
squadrons of horse, and cut them up so severely
that but few men barely managed to escape that
massacre.

The following night Pompeius burned his camp
and, passing through the valleys on the far side[2] of the
river Salsum, established a camp on a hill between the
two towns of Ategua and Ucubi. Meanwhile Caesar
had completed his emplacements and all his other
dispositions which were required for assaulting the
town, and proceeded to carry forward a ramp furnished with mantlets. Now this area is mountainous
and offers natural obstructions to military operations:
it is divided by a plain—the basin of the river

---

[1] See Appendix B, p. 397.   [2] i.e. S. of the river.

CAESAR

dividuntur, Salso flumine, proxime tamen Ateguam
ut flumen sit circiter passus duo milia. Ex ea
regione oppidi in montibus castra habuit posita
Pompeius in conspectu utrorumque oppidorum, neque
suis ausus est subsidio venire. Aquilas et signa
habuit XIII legionum; sed ex quibus aliquid
firmamenti se existimabat habere duae fuerunt
vernaculae, quae a Trebonio transfugerant; una
facta ex colonis qui fuerunt in his regionibus;
quarta fuit Afraniana ex Africa quam secum adduxerat; reliquae ex fugitivis auxiliariisve[1] con-
sistebant: nam de levi armatura et equitatu longe
et virtute et numero nostri erant superiores.

8   Accedebat huc, ut longius bellum duceret Pompeius, quod loca sunt edita et ad castrorum munitiones non parum idonea. Nam fere totius ulterioris
Hispaniae regio propter terrae fecunditatem et non
minus copiosam aquationem[2] inopem difficilemque

---

[1] auxiliares *MSS.* : auxiliariisve *Mommsen.*
[2] et . . . aquationem *follow* oppugnationem *in the MSS.* :
Nipperdey transposed them.

---

[1] Klotz, who puts a full stop after *sit*, takes this last phrase
as meaning ' Some two miles distant from the sector concerned
of the town Pompeius had his camp . . .' I have followed the
punctuation of Holmes and Du Pontet.

[2] It seems very difficult to identify these four reliable
legions with any certainty. The only Pompeian legions
definitely named in the narrative are :—the First (ch. 18);
the Second (ch. 13); and the Thirteenth (ch. 34). From *Bell.*
Alex. chs. 50–54 it is clear that Cassius, whom Trebonius
succeeded as governor of Further Spain, had five legions :
the Twenty-first and the Thirtieth (raised in Italy); the
Second (long quartered in Spain); the ' native legion '
(always thus named); and the Fifth (newly raised in Spain by
Cassius himself). Of these the Second, Fifth and the native
legion joined the mutiny against Cassius, and shewed Pom-

Salsum—in such a way, however, that the river is nearest Ategua, the distance being about two miles.[1] It was in this direction, namely that of Ategua, that Pompeius had his camp pitched in the mountains in sight of both towns, without, however, venturing to come to the aid of his comrades. He had the eagles and standards of thirteen legions; but among those which he thought afforded him any solid support two were native legions, having deserted from Trebonius; a third had been raised from the local Roman settlers; a fourth was one which was once commanded by Afranius and which Pompeius had brought with him from Africa[2]; while the rest were made up of runaways or auxiliaries. As for light-armed units and cavalry, our troops were in fact far superior both in quality and quantity.

8   Besides this, there was another factor which prompted Pompeius to protract hostilities[3]—the hilly type of country by no means unsuitable for the fortification of camps. In fact, practically the whole region of Further Spain, fertile as it is and correspondingly well watered, makes a siege a fruitless

peian sympathies; for which reason it would not seem surprising if they were opposing Caesar now. Holmes was satisfied that the other of the two native legions here mentioned was the Fifth; but he assumed, without accounting for the reference in ch. 13, that the Second had now joined Caesar. Klotz, on the other hand, asserting that there was never more than one native legion in Spain, adopts Mommsen's emendation and reads *vernacula e⟨t secunda⟩*. This drastic course seems indeed the only method of including the Second; and the Fifth might well be the one described as 'raised from the local Roman settlers'. But the whole problem is obscure. See also ch. 13, note 1 (trans.).

[3] *i.e.* his strategic decision not to relieve Ategua was influenced not only by his inferiority in troops, but also by the terrain.

habet oppugnationem. Hic etiam propter barbarorum crebras excursiones omnia loca quae sunt ab
oppidis remota turribus et munitionibus retinentur,
sicut in Africa, rudere, non tegulis teguntur; simulque in his habent speculas et propter altitudinem late
longeque prospiciunt. Item oppidorum magna pars
eius provinciae montibus fere munita et natura
excellentibus locis est constituta, ut simul aditus
ascensusque habeat difficilis. Ita ab oppugnationibus
natura loci distinentur, ut civitates Hispaniae non
facile ab hoste capiantur; id quod in hoc contigit
bello. Nam cum inter Ateguam et Ucubim, quae
oppida supra sunt scripta, Pompeius habuit castra
constituta in conspectu duorum oppidorum, ab suis
castris circiter milia passuum IIII grumus est excel-
lens natura, qui appellatur Castra Postumiana: ibi
praesidi causa castellum Caesar habuit constitutum.

9   Quod Pompeius, quod eodem iugo tegebatur loci
natura et remotum erat a castris Caesaris, animadvertebat [1] et, quia flumine Salso intercludebatur, non
esse commissurum Caesarem ut in tanta loci difficultate ad subsidium mittendum se committeret.[2]
Ita fretus opinione tertia vigilia profectus castellum
oppugnare coepit. Cum appropinquassent, clamore
repentino telorumque multitudine iactus facere
coeperunt, uti magnam partem hominum vulneribus

---

[1] animadvertebat loci difficultatem et *MSS.* : *Du Pontet
deleted* loci difficultatem.
[2] committendum se mitteret *MSS.* : mittendum se committeret *Nipperdey.*

---

[1] This is usually identified with the modern hill of Harinilla,
some 3 miles S.W. of Teba. It was probably named after L.
Postumius Albinus, propraetor of Further Spain in 180–179.

and difficult task. Here too, in view of the constant sallies of the natives, all places which are remote from towns are firmly held by towers and fortifications, as in Africa, roofed over with rough-cast, not tiles. Moreover, they have watch-towers in them, commanding a view far and wide by reason of their altitude. Again, a large proportion of the towns of this province are more or less protected by the mountains and are established in naturally elevated positions, with the result that the approach to them, involving as it does a simultaneous climb, proves a difficult task. Thus it is their natural position that holds them aloof from sieges, and as a result the townships of Spain are no easy prey to an enemy, as proved to be the case in this war. To take the present instance: Pompeius had his camp established between the above-mentioned towns of Ategua and Ucubi, in sight of both of them; and some four miles distant from his camp there lies a hillock—a natural elevation which goes by the name of the Camp of Postumius[1]; and there Caesar had established a fort for purposes of defence.

9   Now Pompeius observed that this fort was screened by its natural position on the same ridge of hills and was some distance away from Caesar's camp; and he further observed that Caesar, cut off as he was from it by the river Salsum, was not likely to let himself be committed to sending support, considering the very difficult character of the ground. Accordingly, with the courage of his convictions, he set out at the third watch and proceeded to attack the fort. On their approach they suddenly raised a shout and began to launch heavy volleys of missile weapons, with the result that they wounded a large proportion

325

CAESAR

adficerent. Quo peracto, cum ex castello repugnare
coepissent maioribusque castris Caesari nuntius
esset allatus, cum III legionibus est profectus, ut
laborantibus succurreret nostris;[1] et cum ad eos
appropinquasset, fuga perterriti multi sunt interfecti, complures capti, in quibus duo centuriones[2]:
multi praeterea armis exuti fugerunt, quorum scuta
sunt relata LXXX.

10 Insequenti luce Arguetius ex Italia cum equitatu
venit. Is signa Saguntinorum rettulit quinque,
quae ab oppidanis cepit. Suo loco praeteritum est[3]
quod equites ex Italia cum Asprenate ad Caesarem
venissent. Ea nocte Pompeius castra sua incendit
et ad Cordubam versus iter facere coepit. Rex
nomine Indo, qui cum equitatu suas copias adduxerat,
dum cupidius agmen adversariorum insequitur, a
vernaculis legionariis exceptus est et interfectus.

11 Postero die equites nostri longius ad Cordubam
versus prosecuti sunt eos qui commeatus ad castra
Pompei ex oppido portabant. Ex his capti L cum
iumentis ad nostra adducti sunt castra. Eo die Q.
Marcius, tribunus militum qui fuit Pompei, ad nos
transfugit; et noctis tertia vigilia in oppido acerrime

[1] ut . . . nostris (nostri *MSS.*) *transposed by Nipperdey. In
the MSS. they follow* coepit, 5 *lines above.*
[2] centuriones *supplied by Oudendorp.*
[3] praeterritus est *most MSS.* : praeteritum est *Davies.*

---

[1] or—' were panic-stricken by the ensuing rout, and many
were killed . . .'
[2] Possibly, the place mentioned by Pliny (III, 1, 15) in a
list of tributary Baeturian towns under the jurisdiction of
Cadiz. If so, he would seem to have come by sea. Klotz,
however, assumes the reference to be to Saguntum. *See*
Index.

of the defenders. Whereupon the latter began to fight back from the fort; and when the tidings were brought to Caesar in his main camp he set out with three legions to succour our hard-pressed troops. When he reached them the enemy retired in rout and panic,[1] with many killed and several captured, including two centurions. Many in addition threw away their arms and fled, and eighty of their shields were brought back by our men.

10 On the following day Arguetius arrived with cavalry from Italy. He brought with him five standards belonging to the men of Saguntia,[2] which he took from the inhabitants of that town. I omitted to mention in its proper place the arrival of the cavalry who came to Caesar from Italy with Asprenas. That night Pompeius burned his camp and proceeded to march towards Corduba.[3] A king named Indo, who had accompanied the cavalry, bringing with him troops of his own, pursued the enemy's column somewhat too eagerly, and in the process was cut off and killed by troops of the native legions.

11 On the next day our cavalry fared somewhat far afield in the direction of Corduba in pursuit of those who were carrying supplies from the town to Pompeius' camp. Fifty of the latter were captured and brought with their pack animals to our camp. That day Q. Marcius, who was one of Pompeius' military tribunes, deserted to us. At the third watch of the night there was very sharp fighting in the area of the

[3] Klotz plausibly suggests that Castra Postumiana was a serious threat to his lines of communication with Corduba; and that having failed to capture it, he now decided to withdraw farther West.

327

CAESAR

pugnatum est, ignemque multum miserunt.[1] Hoc
praeterito tempore C. Fundanius, eques Romanus,
ex castris adversariorum ad nos transfugit.

12   Postero die ex legione vernacula milites sunt capti
ab equitibus nostris duo, qui dixerunt se servos esse.
Cum venirent, cogniti sunt a militibus qui antea cum
Fabio[2] et Pedio fuerant, et a[3] Trebonio transfugerant.
Eis ad ignoscendum nulla facultas est data et a
militibus nostris interfecti sunt. Idem temporis
capti tabellarii, qui a Corduba ad Pompeium missi
erant perperamque ad nostra castra pervenerant,
praecisis manibus missi sunt facti. Pari consuetudine
vigilia secunda ex oppido ignem multum telorumque
multitudinem iactando bene magnum tempus con-
sumpserunt complurisque vulneribus adfecerunt.
Praeterito noctis tempore eruptionem ad legionem
VI. fecerunt, cum in opere nostri distenti essent,
acriterque pugnare coeperunt; quorum vis repressa a
nostris, etsi oppidani superiore loco defendebantur.
Hi[4] cum eruptionem facere coepissent, tamen virtute
militum nostrorum, etsi inferiore loco premebantur,

---

[1] *The MSS. add* : sicut omne genus quibus ignis per iactus
solitus est mitti. *I have followed Hoffmann in deleting them.*
[2] babio *or* babibio *or* habio *MSS.* : Fabio *Glandorp.*
[3] (a) *supplied by Kuebler, who assumed a lacuna after* fuerant.
[4] ·l· *MSS.* : Hi *Davies.*

---

[1] I think that Holmes was right in assuming that this
curious temporal phrase refers back to the past (literally—' *at
this past time* '); and that the author employs it whenever
his chronology has got out of hand. Thus, just as in ch. 10
the arrival of Arguetius reminds him to mention belatedly the
earlier arrival of Asprenas, so here the desertion of Q. Marcius
reminds him of that of Fundanius. Its use below in chs. 20

328

town, and many fire-brands were discharged. Just
before this time [1] a Roman knight named C. Fundanius deserted to us from the enemy lines.

12   On the next day two soldiers from one of the
native legions were captured by our cavalry: they
asserted they were slaves. Immediately on their
arrival they were recognised by troops who had
formerly been with Fabius and Pedius and had
deserted from Trebonius.[2] No opportunity was
afforded of reprieving them, and they were executed
by our troops. At the same time some couriers were
captured who had been sent from Corduba to
Pompeius and had come to our camp in error: their
hands were cut off and they were then let go. At
the second watch the enemy observed his usual
custom of hurling from the town a large quantity of
fire-brands and missiles, spending a good long time in
the process and wounding a large number. When
the night had now passed they made a sally against
the Sixth legion when our men were busily occupied
on a field-work,[3] and began a brisk engagement;
but their sharp attack was contained by our troops
despite the support which the townsmen derived
from the higher ground. Having once embarked
upon their sally, our opponents were none the less
repulsed by the gallantry of our troops, although the

and 22 seems similar. Klotz, however, apparently takes it
to mean ' *when this time had now gone past.*'
    [2] *cf.* p. 322 note 2 (trans.). It is clear that not all the troops
who had mutinied against Cassius and later deserted Trebonius
were now on Pompey's side. Some editors, however, suspect
the text.
    [3] In this phrase, which recurs below in ch. 27 the word *opus*
seems to have its technical meaning—' work of fortification.'
Klotz interprets : ' scattered among the fortifications.'

repulsi adversarii bene multis vulneribus adfecti in
oppidum se contulerunt.[1]

13   Postero die Pompeius ex castris suis bracchium
coepit ad flumen Salsum ducere;[2] et cum nostri
equites pauci in statione fuissent a pluribus reperti,
de statione sunt deiecti et occisi tres. Eo die A.
Valgius, senatoris filius, cuius frater in castris Pompei
fuisset, omnibus suis rebus relictis equum conscendit
et fugit. Speculator de legione II. Pompeiana
captus a militibus et interfectus est; idemque
temporis glans missa est inscripta: quo die ad
oppidum capiendum accederent, se scutum esse
positurum. Qua spe non nulli, dum sine periculo
murum ascendere et oppido potiri posse se sperant,
postero die ad murum opus facere coeperunt, et bene
magna prioris muri parte deiecta.[3] . . . Quo facto ab
oppidanis, ac si suarum partium essent, conservati . . .

    [1] *I have followed Kraner in deleting* qui *before* etsi *and* tamen
before repulsi *from the reading of the MSS.*
    [2] ducere *is omitted by all but two inferior MSS.*
    [3] *Klotz supplies* in oppidum intraverunt, *but considers it
probable that more than this is missing.*

---

    [1] cf. p. 322, note 2 (trans.). Klotz regards the addition of
Pompeiana as ' remarkable, since Caesar did not have a
Second legion.' It is true that in the narrative there is no
mention of the Second as fighting on Caesar's side. But
neither is there any mention of the Twenty-first, Twenty-
eighth, or Thirtieth, all of which may well have participated.
I am inclined to think that *Pompeiana* is no accidental
addition, but that it signified clearly one of two things :
either that there were two Second legions (just as there were
apparently two Fifth legions), and that this was not Caesar's
Second; *or*, if there was but one Second legion, that now,
after months of wavering loyalty, it was on Pompey's side.
To the author's contemporaries it was doubtless perfectly
clear which was the meaning intended.

latter were labouring under the disadvantage of a lower position; and after sustaining very heavy casualties they withdrew back into the town.

3 On the next day Pompeius began to carry a line of fortifications from his camp to the river Salsum; and when a few of our horsemen on outpost duty were discovered by the enemy, who were in greater strength, they were driven from their post, and three of them were killed. It was on that day that A. Valgius—his father was a senator and his brother was in Pompeius' camp—left all his kit behind, mounted his horse and deserted. A spy from the Second legion, on Pompeius' side,[1] was captured by our troops and put to death; and at the same time a sling-bullet was discharged which bore the following inscription: ' On the day you advance to capture the town I shall lay down my shield.'[2] This raised hopes in some of our men, who, feeling confident that they could now climb the wall and gain possession of the town without danger, proceeded on the next day to construct a field-work adjoining the wall; and having demolished a good large section of the first wall, . . . Whereupon, their lives being spared by the townsfolk as if they belonged to their own side,[3] . . . the latter begged Caesar to get

[2] Some editors render ' display a shield as a signal '; but the undertaking to offer no armed resistance seems to me to suit the context better. Though apparently in the singular number (Fleischer conjectured *posituros*), the message was no doubt interpreted as reflecting the attitude of many of the townsfolk.

[3] The mutilated state of the MSS. will permit no more than a disjointed rendering. It would seem that the storming party was captured, but that the townsfolk sent its members back unharmed, accompanied by a deputation to Caesar offering terms of surrender.

missos facere loricatos, qui praesidi causa praepositi
oppido a Pompeio essent, orabant. Quibus respondit
Caesar se condiciones dare, non accipere consuevisse.
Qui cum in oppidum revertissent, relato responso
clamore sublato omni genere telorum emisso pugnare
pro muro toto coeperunt; propter quod fere magna
pars hominum qui in castris nostris essent non
dubitarunt quin eruptionem eo die essent facturi.
Ita corona circumdata pugnatum est aliquamdiu
vehementissime, simulque ballista missa a nostris
turrem deiecit, qua adversariorum qui in ea turre
fuerant quinque deiecti sunt et puer, qui ballistam
solitus erat observare.

14   Eius diei praeterito tempore [1] Pompeius trans
flumen Salsum castellum constituit neque a nostris
prohibitus falsaque illa opinione gloriatus est quod
prope in nostris partibus locum tenuisset. Item
insequenti die eadem consuetudine dum longius
prosequitur, quo loco equites nostri stationem
habuerant, aliquot turmae cum levi armatura impetu
facto loco sunt deiecti et propter paucitatem nostrorum equitum simul cum levi armatura inter turmas
adversariorum protriti. Hoc in conspectu utrorumque castrorum gerebatur, et maiore Pompeiani
exsultabant gloria longius quod nostris cedentibus

---

[1] eius praeteriti temporis *MSS.* : eius diei praeterito
tempore *Nipperdey.*

---

[1] I interpret Nipperdey's restoration, on the analogy of the
phrase *hoc praeterito tempore* in ch. 11 above, as meaning
' in the past (earlier) period of that day.' Klotz retains the
MSS. reading, which he explains as a Genitive Absolute meaning ' that time having gone past.'

[2] *i.e.* N. of the river.

rid of the heavy-armed troops who had been put in charge of the defence of the town by Pompeius. Caesar's reply to them was that his habit was to impose conditions, not to accept them. On their return to the town with this reply, the inhabitants raised a shout, discharged volleys of missiles of all sorts, and went into action along the entire circuit of the battlements; and this led to a strong conviction among quite a large number of the men in our lines that they would make a sally that day. As a result a cordon of troops was thrown round the town and very violent fighting went on for some time; in the course of which a missile was discharged by our men from a piece of heavy artillery and demolished a tower, knocking out five members of the enemy crew who manned it, as well as a slave whose regular duty it was to keep watch on that piece of artillery.

Earlier on that day [1] Pompeius established a fort across [2] the river Salsum without meeting any opposition from our troops; and this put him under a misapprehension and led him to boast inasmuch as he had occupied a position which was as good as in our territory. Likewise on the following day he again pursued his usual tactics and made a fairly extensive sweep, in the course of which at one point where our cavalry were picketed several squadrons of ours with some light-armed troops were attacked and dislodged from their position; and then, because of their small numbers, both our horsemen and the light-armed troops were completely crushed amidst the squadrons of their opponents. This action took place in view of both camps, and now the Pompeians were boasting with yet greater triumph on the ground that they had begun to

prosequi coepissent. Qui cum aequo [1] loco a nostris
recepti essent, ut consuessent, eximia [2] virtute,
clamore facto aversati sunt proelium facere.

15 Fere apud exercitus haec est equestris proeli
consuetudo: cum eques ad dimicandum dimisso
equo cum pedite congreditur, nequaquam par
habetur; id quod contra [3] in hoc accidit proelio.
Cum pedites levi armatura lecti ad pugnam equitibus
nostris nec opinantibus venissent, idque in proelio
animadversum esset, complures ex equis descenderunt. Ita exiguo tempore eques pedestre [4] proelium
facere coepit, usque eo ut caedem proxime a vallo
fecerint. In quo proelio adversariorum ceciderunt
CXXIII, compluresque armis exuti, multi vulneribus
adfecti in castra sunt redacti. Nostri ceciderunt III;
saucii XII pedites et equites V. Eius diei insequenti

[1] aliquo *MSS.*: aequo Lipsius.
[2] ex simili *MSS.*: eximia *Mommsen.*
[3] contra *added by Hoffmann.*
[4] *The words* pedes equestre, *which follow here in all MSS.,*
were deleted by Nipperdey.

---

[1] Klotz, who retains the MSS. reading *ex simili*, assumes
qui to refer to the Caesarian cavalry mentioned above, the
subject changing abruptly to *Pompeiani* at *aversati sunt.*
His rendering would thus apparently be: 'When these
squadrons of ours had been received back on favourable
ground and, as usual, had raised the war cry with the same
bravery, the Pompeians refused battle.' But the sense seems
to me very strained; and the fact that *Pompeiani* is subject
of the clause which immediately precedes makes the repeated
change of subject exceptionally harsh. It is perhaps more
reasonable to assume that *Pompeiani* is subject throughout,
and that *recipio* is here used in the sense of *rursus excipio.*

[2] The reader may well be puzzled by the respective casualties resulting, apparently, from the outpost skirmish described
in ch. 14 above. It would seem that the figures are grossly

sweep further ahead while our men were retreating further back. But when on favourable ground our men took them on again with their customary outstanding gallantry, they cried out and refused to engage battle.[1]

5 With nearly all armies what normally happens in a cavalry battle is this: when a cavalryman is once dismounted and closes in with an infantryman to engage him, he is not by any means regarded as a match for the latter. However, it turned out quite otherwise in this battle. When picked light-armed infantry took our cavalry by surprise by coming forward to engage them, and when this manoeuvre was observed in the course of the fighting, quite a number of our horsemen dismounted. As a result, in a short time our cavalry began to fight an infantry action, to such good purpose that they dealt death right up close to the rampart. In this battle [2] on our opponents' side there fell one hundred and twenty-three men; and of those who were driven back to their camp not a few had been stripped of their arms and many were wounded. On our side there fell three men: twelve infantrymen and five horsemen were wounded. Later on that day the old routine

distorted if only three Caesarians were killed out of several squadrons and some light-armed troops overrun by the enemy cavalry! (cf. Introduction, p. 306, and, for official suppression of casualty figures, ch. 18.) But I rather suspect that cavalry reinforcements were despatched by Caesar and fought a second, and more evenly-matched action closer to Pompey's camp; and that brief details of this were originally given towards the end of ch. 14. If it is to this second action that the casualty figures relate, then it is not surprising that the Pompeians refused a third challenge on ground favourable to Caesar.

tempore pristina consuetudine pro muro pugnari coeptum est. Cum bene magnam multitudinem telorum ignemque nostris defendentibus iniecissent, nefandum crudelissimumque facinus sunt aggressi in conspectuque nostro hospites qui in oppido erant iugulare et de muro praecipites mittere coeperunt, sicuti apud barbaros; quod post hominum memoriam numquam est factum.

16 Huius diei extremo tempore a Pompeianis clam nostros[1] tabellarius est missus, ut ea nocte turris aggeremque incenderent et tertia vigilia eruptionem facerent. Ita igne telorumque multitudine iacta cum bene magnam partem noctis[2] consumpsissent, portam quae e regione et in conspectu Pompei castrorum fuerat aperuerunt copiaeque totae eruptionem fecerunt secumque extulerunt virgulta, cratis[3] ad fossas complendas et harpagones ad casas, quae stramenticiae ab nostris hibernorum causa aedificatae erant, diruendas et incendendas, praeterea argentum, vestimenta, ut, dum nostri in praeda detinentur, illi caede facta ad praesidia Pompei se reciperent: nam quod existimabat eos posse conatum[4] efficere, nocte tota ultra ibat flumen Salsum in acie. Quod factum licet nec opinantibus nostris esset gestum, tamen virtute freti repulsos multisque vulneribus adfectos oppido represserunt, praedam

---

[1] clam ad nostros *MSS.*: clam nostros *some editors*: clam nostros ad oppidum *Klotz.*
[2] muri *MSS.*: noctis *Fleischer.*
[3] cultatas *or* culc- *or* calc- *MSS.*: virgulta, cratis *Nipperdey.*
[4] conatu *MSS.*: conatum *or* -a *editors.*

---

[1] *i.e.* the Pompeian troops massacred those of the local townsfolk whom they suspected of siding with Caesar.
[2] Probably S. of the river.
[3] Or, if *oppido* is the adverb, ' completely drove them back.'

was observed and fighting broke out along the battlements. After discharging a very large number of
missile weapons and firebrands at our troops, who
were on the defensive, the enemy embarked upon an
abominable and completely ruthless outrage; for in
our sight they proceeded to massacre some of their
hosts [1] in the town, and to fling them headlong from
the battlements—a barbarous act, and one for which
history can produce no precedent.

6   In the closing hours of this day the Pompeians
sent a courier, without the knowledge of our men,
with instructions that in the course of that night
those in the town should set our towers and rampart
on fire and make a sally at the third watch. Accordingly, after they had hurled fire-brands and a quantity
of missile weapons and spent a very large part of the
night in so doing, they opened the gate which lay
directly opposite Pompeius' camp and was in sight
of it, and made a sally with their entire forces.
With them they brought out brushwood and hurdles
to fill up the trenches, as well as hooks for demolishing
and then burning the straw-thatched huts which had
been built by our men to serve as winter quarters;
they also brought silver and clothing besides, so that,
while our men were busily engaged in looting it,
they could wreak havoc upon them and then retire to
Pompeius' lines. For in the belief that they could
carry through their enterprise he spent the whole
night on the move in battle formation on the far
side [2] of the river Salsum. But although this operation had come as a surprise to our men, yet, relying
on their valour, they repulsed the enemy, inflicted
heavy casualties upon them, and drove them back to
the town,[3] taking possession of their booty and

armaque eorum sunt potiti vivosque aliquos ceperunt,
qui postero die sunt interfecti. Eodemque tempore
transfuga nuntiavit ex oppido Iunium, qui in
cuniculo fuisset, iugulatione oppidanorum facta
clamasse facinus se nefandum et scelus fecisse;
nam eos nihil meruisse quare tali poena adficerentur
qui eos ad aras et focos suos recepissent, eosque
hospitium scelere contaminasse; multa praeterea
dixisse : qua oratione deterritos amplius iugulationem
non fecisse.

17   Ita postero die Tullius legatus cum Catone et Antonio[1] venit et apud Caesarem verba fecit : ' Utinam
quidem di immortales fecissent ut tuus potius miles
quam Cn. Pompei factus essem et hanc virtutis
constantiam in tua victoria, non in illius calamitate
praestarem. Cuius funestae laudes quoniam ad
hanc fortunam reciderunt ut cives Romani indigentes
praesidi simus et propter patriae luctuosam perniciem
demur[2] hostium numero, qui neque in illius prospera
acie primam fortunam neque in adversa secundam
obtinuimus,[3] qui legionum tot impetus sustentantes,
nocturnis diurnisque operibus gladiorum ictus

---

[1] Lusitano *MSS. The arguments in support of this conjecture of mine and of* introiit *and* Catonem *in ch.* 18 *are set forth
in Appendix C, p.* 401.
[2] *I have followed Fleischer in supplying* simus *and reading*
demur *in place of* dedimur.
[3] *I have followed Nipperdey in deleting* victoriam *which the
MSS. give after* obtinuimus.

---

[1] This abrupt reference led Mommsen to conjecture *unum*
in place of *Iunium.* Klotz considers that, though no mine

equipment and capturing some alive, who were put to death the next day. It was at this same period that a deserter arrived from the town with the news that, after the massacre of the townsfolk, Junius, who had been in a mine,[1] protested that it was an abominable crime and outrage that his people had committed; for inasmuch as the burghers had given them the protection of their altars and hearths they had done nothing to deserve such punishment: rather had they themselves polluted hospitality by a crime. Junius had said a lot more besides, according to the deserter's account, and his words had frightened them and caused them to refrain from further massacres.

So the next day Tullius came as an envoy, accompanied by Cato and Antonius, and held talk with Caesar as follows: ' Would indeed that the immortal gods had caused me to have become a soldier of yours, rather than one of Pompeius', and vouchsafed that I should now display this unflinching valour of mine on your victorious side, and not at his debacle. Now that his prestige, fraught with disaster, has slumped so far that in this our present plight we, citizens of Rome, not only stand in need of protection, but on account of the grievous calamity of our country are accorded the status of public enemies; we, who alike won no success either when at first fortune smiled upon his deeds of arms or later when she frowned upon them; we, who have constantly borne up under so many attacks of legions and have as constantly, in operations by day and night, formed targets for the thrusts of swords and the flight of

has so far been mentioned, sapping was so constant in sieges that the apparent oversight is a natural one.

telorumque missus exceptantes, relicti[1] et deserti a
Pompeio, tua virtute superati salutem a tua clementia
deposcimus petimusque ut . . .'[2] ' qualem gentibus
me praestiti, similem in civium deditione praestabo.'
18   Remissis legatis, cum ad portam venissent, introiit[3]
Tib. Tullius ; et cum introeuntem Catonem[4] Antonius
insecutus non esset, revertit ad portam et hominem
apprehendit. Quod Tiberius cum fieri animadvertit,
simul pugionem eduxit et manum eius incidit. Ita
refugerunt ad Caesarem. Eodemque tempore signifer de legione prima transfugit et innotuit, quo die
equestre proelium factum esset, suo signo perisse
homines XXXV, neque licere castris Cn. Pompei
nuntiare neque dicere perisse quemquam.[5] Servus,
cuius dominus in Caesaris castris fuisset—uxorem et
filios in oppido reliquerat—dominum iugulavit et ita
clam a Caesaris praesidiis in Pompei castra discessit
. . . et indicium glande scriptum misit, per quod certior fieret Caesar quae in oppido ad defendendum
compararentur. Ita litteris acceptis, cum in oppidum
revertisset qui mittere glandem inscriptam sole-

[1] expectantes victi *MSS.* : exceptantes *Koch* : relicti
Nipperdey.
[2] *Klotz conjectures* vitam nobis concedas.' Quibus Caesar
respondit.
[3] *I have supplied* introiit.
[4] C. *MSS.* : *I have conjectured* Catonem.
[5] quamquam *or* quamque most *MSS.* : quemquam *editors.*

[1] grant us our lives.' To which Caesar replied : (according
to Klotz's conjecture).

missiles; we, who are now abandoned and forsaken by Pompeius and vanquished by your valour, do now earnestly entreat you in your mercy to save us, and beg you to . . .'[1] 'As I have shewn myself to foreign peoples, even so will I show myself to my fellow citizens when they surrender.'

The envoys were now sent back and on their arrival at the gate Tiberius Tullius went inside; and when, as Cato was going in, Antonius failed to follow him, Cato[2] turned back to the gate and grabbed the fellow. Observing this action, Tiberius immediately drew a dagger and stabbed Cato's hand. So they[3] fled back to Caesar. It was at this same time that a standard-bearer from the First legion deserted to us and it became known that on the day when the cavalry action was fought his own unit[4] lost thirty-five men, but that they were not allowed to report this in Cn. Pompeius' camp or to say that any man had been lost. A slave, whose master was in Caesar's camp—he had left his wife and sons behind in the town—murdered his master and then got away unobserved from Caesar's lines to Pompeius' camp . . . and he sent a message written on a bullet to apprise Caesar of the defence measures which were being taken in the town. Accordingly, when this message had been received, and the man who normally discharged the bullet bearing an inscription

[2] Klotz too assumes that Cato is the subject. He remarks that such abrupt changes of subject are not uncommon in the lively, colloquial style, and quotes parallel examples from Cicero, Livy and Seneca.

[3] sc. Tiberius and Antonius. See Appendix C, p. 401.

[4] here, probably, a *maniple*, nominally comprising 200 men.

341

bat.[1] . . . Insequenti tempore duo Lusitani fratres
transfugae nuntiarunt quam Pompeius contionem
habuisset: quoniam oppido subsidio non posset
venire, noctu ex adversariorum conspectu se dedu-
cerent ad mare versum; unum respondisse ut potius
ad dimicandum descenderent quam signum fugae
ostenderent; eum qui ita locutus esset iugulatum.
Eodem tempore tabellarii eius deprensi qui ad
oppidum veniebant: quorum litteras Caesar oppidanis obiecit et, qui vitam sibi peteret, iussit turrem
ligneam oppidanorum incendere; id si fecisset, ei se
promisit omnia concessurum. Quod difficile erat
factu, ut eam turrem sine periculo quis incenderet.
Ita fune crura deligatus,[2] cum propius accessisset, ab
oppidanis est occisus. Eadem nocte transfuga nuntiavit Pompeium et Labienum de iugulatione oppidanorum indignatos esse.

19 Vigilia secunda propter multitudinem telorum
turris lignea, quae nostra fuisset, ab imo vitium fecit
usque ad tabulatum secundum et tertium. Eodem
tempore pro muro pugnarunt acerrime et turrim
nostram ut superiorem incenderunt, idcirco quod
ventum oppidani secundum habuerunt. Insequenti

---

[1] solebant *MSS.*: solebat *Nipperdey, who first assumed a lacuna here.*
[2] crure de ligno *MSS.*: crura deligatus *Warmington.*

---

[1] I have followed Klotz in assuming two gaps in this
extraordinary narrative. For no likely explanation occurs to
me why the slave should have sent such a message to Caesar
from Pompey's camp. Whether it was his master or his
mistress he killed (in ch. 20 most MSS. read *dominam*), and
whether he was loyal to Caesar or to Pompey, it seems impossible to account consistently for his actions and subsequent
fate.

had returned to the town, . . .[1] At a later period two brothers, Lusitanians, deserted and reported a speech which Pompeius had delivered, to the effect that, since he could not come to the assistance of the town, they must withdraw by night out of sight of their opponents in the direction of the sea. One man, according to this account, retorted that they should rather go into battle than display the signal for retreat; whereupon the author of this remark had his throat cut. At the same time some of Pompeius' couriers were arrested on their way to the town. Caesar presented their despatches[2] to the townsfolk and directed that any of the couriers who wanted his life to be spared must set fire to a wooden tower belonging to the townsfolk, undertaking to grant him complete amnesty if he did so. But it was a difficult task for anyone to set fire to that tower without risking disaster; thus when any of them came close up to it, his legs were tied with a rope and he was killed by the townsfolk. That same night a deserter reported that Pompeius and Labienus had been filled with indignation at the massacre of the townsfolk.

9   At the second watch, as a result of a heavy salvo of missiles, a wooden tower of ours sustained damage which extended from its base up to the second and third storeys. Simultaneously there was very heavy fighting along the battlements, and the townsfolk, taking advantage of a favourable wind, set on fire our tower as aforementioned. The following day a

---

[2] Klotz believes that these despatches notified the commandant of Ategua that Pompey was withdrawing. This seems probable, and would explain why Caesar passed them on so promptly.

luce materfamilias de muro se deiecit et ad nos
transsiliit dixitque se cum familia constitutum
habuisse ut una transfugerent ad Caesarem; illam
oppressam et iugulatam. Hoc praeterea tempore
tabellae de muro sunt deiectae, in quibus scriptum
est inventum: ' L. Munatius Caesari. Si mihi
vitam tribues, quoniam ab Cn. Pompeio sum desertus,
qualem me illi praestiti tali virtute et constantia
futurum me in te esse praestabo.' Eodem tempore
oppidani legati qui antea exierant Caesarem adierunt:
si sibi vitam concederet, sese insequenti luce oppidum
esse dedituros. Quibus respondit se Caesarem
esse fidemque praestaturum. Ita ante diem XI.
Kal. Mart. oppido potitus imperator est appellatus.

20   Quod Pompeius ex perfugis cum deditionem
oppidi factam esse scisset, castra movit Ucubim
versus et circum ea loca castella disposuit et munitionibus se continere coepit: Caesar movit et
propius castra castris contulit. Eodem tempore
mane loricatus unus ex legione vernacula ad nos
transfugit et nuntiavit Pompeium oppidanos Ucu-
bensis convocasse eisque ita imperavisse, ut diligentia adhibita perquirerent qui essent suarum
partium itemque adversariorum victoriae fautores.
Hoc praeterito tempore in oppido quod fuit captum

344

mother of a family leapt down from the battlements
and slipped across to our lines and told us that she
had arranged with her household to desert to
Caesar all together; but her household, she said, had
been taken by surprise and massacred. It was at
this time also that a missive was thrown down from
the wall, which was found to contain the following
message: 'L. Munatius greets Caesar. If you
grant me my life, now that I am abandoned by Cn.
Pompeius, I will guarantee to display the same
unwavering courage in support of you as I have
shewn to him.' At the same time the envoys from
the townsfolk who had come out to Caesar before
now came to him, saying that, if he would spare their
lives, they would surrender the town the following
day. His reply to them ran thus: 'I am Caesar
and I will be as good as my word.' Accordingly, on
February 19th he took possession of the town and was
hailed as Imperator.

20   When Pompeius got to know from deserters that
the surrender of the town had taken place, he
moved his camp towards Ucubi, built forts at intervals in that locality, and proceeded to keep within
his emplacements. Caesar struck his camp and
moved it closer to that of Pompeius. It was at this
same time that early in the morning one of the
heavy-armed troops from a native legion deserted to
us and reported that Pompeius had assembled the
inhabitants of the town of Ucubi and given them
orders as follows, namely that they were to make
careful and searching enquiry who were in favour
of a victory for his side, and who on the contrary favoured victory for his enemies. Just before this the slave who, as we have described

345

servus est prensus in cuniculo quem supra demonstravimus dominum iugulasse : is vivus est combustus. Idemque temporis centuriones loricati VIII ad Caesarem transfugerunt ex legione vernacula, et equites nostri cum adversariorum equitibus congressi sunt, et saucii aliquot occiderunt levi armatura. Ea nocte speculatores prensi servi III et unus ex legione vernacula. Servi sunt in crucem sublati, militi cervices abscisae.

21 Postero die equites cum levi armatura ex adversariorum castris ad nos transfugerunt. Et eo tempore circiter XL equites ad aquatores nostros excucurrerunt, non nullos interfecerunt, item alios vivos abduxerunt ; e quibus capti sunt equites VIII. Insequenti die Pompeius securi percussit homines LXXIIII, qui dicebantur esse fautores Caesaris victoriae, reliquos rursus in[1] oppidum iussit deduci ; ex quibus effugerunt CXX et ad Caesarem venerunt.

22 Hoc praeterito tempore, qui in oppido Ategua Ursaonenses[2] capti sunt legati profecti sunt cum nostris uti rem gestam Ursaonensibus[2] referrent, quid sperarent de Cn. Pompeio, cum viderent hospites iugulari, praeterea multa scelera ab eis fieri qui praesidi causa ab eis reciperentur. Qui cum[3] ad oppidum venissent, nostri, qui fuissent equites Romani et senatores, non sunt ausi introire in oppidum, praeter quam qui eius civitatis fuissent. Quorum responsis ultro citroque acceptis et redditis

[1] versum *or* in *MSS.* : rursus in *Fleischer.*
[2] bursavonenses, -ibus *MSS.* : Ursaonenses, -ibus *Ciacconius.*
[3] cum *added by earlier editors.*

---

[1] *viz.* men of Ucubi : the author here resumes his narrative of chapter 20, which he interrupted to relate earlier incidents.

above, had murdered his master was arrested in a mine in the captured town: he was burned alive. At the same period eight heavy-armed centurions deserted to Caesar from a native legion; our cavalry came into conflict with the enemy cavalry and quite a number of our light-armed troops died of their wounds. That night some scouts were caught— three slaves and one soldier from a native legion. The slaves were crucified, the soldier beheaded.

On the next day some cavalry and light-armed troops came over to us from the enemy's camp. At that time too about forty of their horse dashed out upon a watering party of ours, killing some of its members and leading others off alive: eight of their horsemen were taken prisoner. The following day Pompeius beheaded seventy-four men [1] who were said to be in favour of a victory for Caesar: the remainder he ordered to be escorted back into the town; but a hundred and twenty of them escaped and came to Caesar.

[2] Just prior to this time the envoys from Ursao who had been captured in the town of Ategua set forth, accompanied by some of our men, to report to their fellow citizens of Ursao what had taken place and ask them what hopes they could entertain of Cn. Pompeius when they saw hosts being massacred and many other crimes too being perpetrated by those to whom the latter gave admittance as garrison troops. When the party reached Ursao, our men, who comprised Roman knights and senators, did not venture to enter the town, apart from those who were members of that community. An exchange of views then took place between the

[2] See Appendix D, p. 403, for a discussion of this chapter.

cum ad nostros se reciperent qui extra oppidum fuissent, illi praesidio insecuti ex aversione[1] legatos iugularunt. Duo reliqui ex eis fugerunt et Caesari rem gestam detulerunt . . .[2] et speculatores ad oppidum Ateguam miserunt. Qui cum certum comperissent legatorum responsa ita esse gesta quem ad modum illi retulissent, ab oppidanis concursu facto eum qui legatos iugulasset lapidare et ei manus intentare coeperunt: illius opera se perisse. Ita vix periculo liberatus petiit ab oppidanis ut ei liceret legatum ad Caesarem proficisci: illi se satisfacturum. Potestate data cum inde esset profectus, praesidio comparato, cum bene magnam manum fecisset et nocturno tempore per fallaciam in oppidum esset receptus, iugulationem magnam facit principibusque qui sibi contrarii fuissent interfectis oppidum in suam potestatem recepit.—Hoc praeterito tempore servi transfugae nuntiaverunt oppidanorum bona venire[3] neque extra vallum licere[4] exire nisi discinctum, idcirco quod ex quo die oppidum Ategua[1] esset captum metu conterritos compluris profugere in Baeturiam; neque sibi ullam spem victoriae propositam habere et, si qui ex nostris transfugeret, in

[1] adversione *MSS.* : aversione *Aldus.*
[2] *lacuna assumed by Nipperdey.*
[3] vendere *MSS.* : venire *Lipsius.*
[4] ne cui . . . liceret *MSS.* : neque . . . licere *Nipperdey*

[1] Of Ucubi, he may mean : see Appendix D, p. 404.

two sides; whereupon, as the envoys were rejoining our men who were outside the town, the townsmen followed them up from behind with an armed party and then massacred them. There were two survivors, who fled and reported the incident to Caesar . . . and the men of Ursao sent investigators to the town of Ategua. And when they had definitely established that the envoys' account was correct, and that the incidents had occurred just as they had related, a crowd of townsfolk quickly gathered, and they began to stone and shake their fists at the man who had massacred the envoys, shouting that he had been responsible for their own undoing. So when he had barely been rescued from his perilous plight, he besought the townsfolk for leave to go on a mission to Caesar, saying that he would satisfy the latter. Permission being granted, he set out from the town, collected a bodyguard and, when he had made it a good large force, contrived by treachery to be taken back into the town by night. Whereupon he carried out a wholesale massacre, killed the leading men who had been opposed to him, and took the town under his own control.—Just before this deserting slaves reported that the goods of the townsfolk [1] were being sold, and that it was forbidden to go out beyond the rampart except ungirt,[2] for the reason that, ever since the day when Ategua was captured, quite a number of people in their panic had been seeking asylum in Baeturia; that they had no prospects of success in view and that, if any man deserted from our side, he was shoved [3] into some

[2] *i.e.* without a belt, the wearing of which might enable them to conceal weapons.

[3] The use of *coicere* here appears to be disparaging.

levem armaturam coici eumque [1] non amplius XVII accipere.

23 Insequenti tempore Caesar castris castra contulit et bracchium ad flumen Salsum ducere coepit. Hic dum in opere nostri distenti essent, complures ex superiore loco adversariorum decucurrerunt nec desinentibus nostris [2] multis telis iniectis compluris vulneribus adfecere. Hic tum, ut ait Ennius, ' nostri cessere parumper.' Itaque praeter consuetudinem cum a nostris animadversum esset cedere, centuriones ex legione V. flumen transgressi duo restituerunt aciem, acriterque eximia virtute pluris cum agerent, ex superiore loco multitudine telorum alter eorum concidit. Ita cum eius comes impar [3] proelium facere coepisset, cum undique se circumveniri animum advertisset, regressus [4] pedem offendit. In huius concidentis centurionis ac viri [5] fortis insignia cum complures adversariorum concursum facerent, equites nostri transgressi inferiore [6] loco

[1] *The MSS. vary between* transfugerent *and* transfugerunt, eumque *and* eum qui. *I have adopted Fleischer's reading* transfugeret, *though possibly, in view of* qui, transfugerent ... eamque *should be read.*

[2] detinentibus nostros *MSS.* : desinentibus nostris *Vossius.*

[3] compar *MSS.* : comes *Warmington.* impar *added by Nipperdey, who also read* eius *for* eis *or is of MSS.*

[4] ingressus *MSS.* : regressus *Lipsius.*

[5] huius concidentis temporis aquari *MSS. I have adopted Nipperdey's conjecture.*

[6] interiori *MSS.* : inferiore *Heinsius.*

---

[1] This is the traditional interpretation, but the sense is far from satisfactory. Reckoning 10 *asses* = 1 *denarius* this would amount to over 600 *denarii* a year; whereas the legionaries' pay, as increased by Caesar, was only 225 *denarii*

light-armed unit and drew no more than seventeen
asses a day.[1]

23   In the period which followed Caesar moved up his
camp and proceeded to carry a line of fortifications to
the river Salsum. At this point, while our men were
busily engaged in the operation, a fair number of the
enemy swooped down upon them from higher
ground, as our men carried on with their work,
there were not a few casualties among them from the
heavy volleys of enemy missiles. Hereupon, as Ennius puts it, " our men gave ground for a brief space."
Consequently, when our men observed that they
were giving ground more than their wont, two
centurions from the Fifth legion crossed the river
and restored the battle line [2]; and as they drove
their more numerous enemies back, displaying dash
and gallantry of an exceptional order, one of them
succumbed to a heavy volley of missiles discharged
from higher ground. And so his colleague now
began an uphill fight; and when he observed that
he was being completely surrounded, he retreated
and lost his footing. As this gallant officer fell
not a few of the enemy made a rush to plunder his
decorations; but our cavalry crossed the river and
from lower ground proceeded to drive the enemy to

a year. Klotz's reading ·X·VII (sc. per mensem = 84 denarii
a year) is attractive.
    [2] It would seem that Caesar's main camp was still N. of the
river Salsum, whereas Pompeius was S. of it. But Caesar
may well have had detachments holding strong points across
the river (e.g. Castra Postumiana, ch. 8); and the present
context suggests, I think, that his sappers were working S.
of the river and that their desperate plight was observed
by their comrades, and relieved by the cavalry, from N. of
the river.

adversarios ad vallum agere coeperunt. Ita cupidius
dum intra praesidia illorum student caedem facere, a
turmis et levi armatura sunt interclusi. Quorum
nisi summa virtus fuisset, vivi capti essent: nam et
munitione praesidi ita coangustabantur ut eques
spatio intercluso vix se defendere posset. Ex
utroque genere pugnae complures sunt vulneribus
adfecti, in quis etiam Clodius Arquitius; inter quos
ita comminus est pugnatum ut ex nostris praeter duos
centuriones sit nemo desideratus gloria se efferentis.

24   Postero die ad Soricariam [1] utrorumque convenere
copiae. Nostri bracchia ducere coeperunt.   Pompeius cum animadverteret castello se excludi Aspavia,
quod est ab Ucubi milia passuum V, haec res necessario devocabat ut ad dimicandum descenderet;
neque tamen aequo loco sui potestatem faciebat,
sed ex grumo . . .[2] excelsum tumulum capiebant,
usque eo ut necessario cogeretur iniquum locum
subire. Quo de facto cum utrorumque copiae
tumulum excellentem petissent, prohibiti a nostris
sunt deiecti in planitiem.[3] Quae res secundum
nostris efficiebat proelium.   Undique cedentibus

[1] ab Soricaria *MSS.*: ad Soricariam *Glandorp*.
[2] *lacuna assumed by Nipperdey.*
[3] deiecti planitie *MSS. But the sense certainly seems to
require* in planitiem, *which I have accordingly conjectured.
(The plain dative* planitiei *or* planitiae *would be a simpler
correction and, syntactically, perhaps not impossible in the case
of this author.*)

---

[1] *i.e.* either infantry and cavalry, or, as Klotz suggests,
with the enemy cavalry and light-armed units.
[2] March 5th, as ch. 27 shews.
[3] Both Holmes and Klotz accept Stoffel's identification of
Soricaria with Castro del Rio, on the right bank of the Salsum,
6 miles S.E. of Ategua.

their rampart. And so, in their too eager anxiety
to carry destruction within the area of the latter's
defence positions, they were cut off by enemy squadrons and light-armed troops. Had not their gallantry been of the highest order, they would have been
captured alive; for they were, moreover, hemmed
in so tightly by the emplacements of the camp as to
make it well nigh impossible for a horseman to defend
himself in the restricted space. As a result of both
types of engagement [1]—quite a number of men
were wounded, including Clodius Arquitius; but
although both sides were engaged at such close
quarters, no-one was lost on our side apart from the
two centurions, who bore themselves with outstanding distinction.

4   On the next day [2] the forces of both sides con-
verged upon Soricaria.[3] Our men proceeded to build
fortified lines. When Pompeius observed that he
was in process of being cut off from the fortress of
Aspavia,[4] which is five miles distant from Ucubi,
this circumstance peremptorily demanded that he
should enter the lists; yet, for all that, he gave his
opponents no opportunity of engaging him on favourable ground, but from a hillock . . . they set
about capturing a lofty knoll, and made such good
progress that Caesar had no option but to approach
unfavourable ground. When accordingly the forces
of both sides had launched an attack upon this lofty
knoll, our men forestalled the enemy and hurled
them back on to the level ground. This led to a
successful action by our troops: on all sides their

---

[4] Stoffel sited it some 2 miles S.E. of Soricaria, and S. of
the river. Hence it would appear that Caesar had now—if not
before—crossed the Salsum.

adversariis non parum magna in caede versabantur.
Quibus mons, non virtus, saluti fuit. Quo subsidio
subnisi,[1] nisi advesperasset, a paucioribus nostris
omni auxilio privati essent. Nam ceciderunt ex levi
armatura CCCXXIII, ex legionariis CXXXVIII,
praeterquam quorum arma et spolia sunt ablata.
Ita pridie duorum centurionum interitio hac adversariorum poena est litata.

25 Insequenti die pari consuetudine cum ad eundem
locum eius praesidium venisset, pristino illo suo
utebantur instituto : nam praeter equites nullo loco
aequo se committere audebant. Cum nostri in
opere essent, equitum copiae concursus facere
coeperunt, simulque vociferantibus legionariis, cum
locum efflagitarent, ut consueti insequi—existimare
posses paratissimos esse ad dimicandum—nostri ex
humili convalle bene longe sunt egressi et planitie in
aequiore[2] loco constiterunt. Illi tamen procul dubio
ad congrediendum in aequum locum non sunt ausi
descendere praeter unum Antistium Turpionem; qui
fidens viribus ex adversariis sibi parem esse neminem

---

[1] quo subsidio ut nisi *most MSS.* : subnisi *is Dinter's conjecture.*
[2] inaequore *or* iniquiori *most MSS.* : in aequiore *Davies.*

---

[1] This appears, as Holmes has remarked, to be distinct
both from the *grumus* and the *tumulus* mentioned earlier.
No doubt it was some hill nearby to which the Pompeians had
been able to fight their way out.
[2] So Holmes : Caesar's, according to Klotz. But the
author normally uses *noster* to denote the Caesarians; and
the phrase *pari consuetudine* seems to me to refer rather to the

opponents gave ground, and our men were engaged in a massacre of no mean proportions. It was the high ground,[1] not the enemy's valour, which proved the latter's salvation; and even relying upon its aid they would, but for the approach of evening, have been deprived of all support by our less numerous forces. As it was, their casualties comprised three hundred and twenty-three light-armed and a hundred and thirty-eight legionaries, apart from those who were stripped of their arms and equipment. Thus by this present retribution did the enemy atone for his slaughter of our two centurions the day before.

On the following day Pompeius'[2] force followed a similar routine and returned to the same spot, where they employed those old established tactics of theirs; for with the exception of his cavalry at no point did his troops venture to commit themselves to favourable ground. While our men were engaged on their task of fortification, the enemy cavalry forces began to launch attacks; and simultaneously his legionary troops kept clamorously demanding to have their turn, seeing that their normal role was to support the cavalry— you might have supposed them to be straining madly at the leash; when our men advanced a good long way from a shallow valley and halted on more favourable ground in the plain. However, there was no doubt about it, the enemy all lacked the courage to come down into the plain to engage—all except one man, Antistius Turpio; and he, confident in his strength, began to indulge in taunts, claiming that there was nobody a match for him on the opposite side. Here-

third sentence of ch. 24. The 'same spot' would seem to be the neighbourhood of the lofty knoll, and not the high ground mentioned later.

355

CAESAR

agitare coepit. Hic, ut fertur Achillis Memnonisque
congressus, Q. Pompeius Niger, eques Romanus
Italicensis, ex acie nostra ad congrediendum progressus est. Quoniam ferocitas Antisti omnium
mentis converterat ab opere ad spectandum, acies
sunt dispositae : nam inter bellatores principes dubia
erat posita victoria, ut prope videretur finem bellandi
duorum dirimere pugna. * Ita avidi cupidique suarum
quisque ex partium virorum fautorumque voluntate
habebatur. Quorum virtute alacri, cum ad dimicandum in planitiem se contulissent, scutorumque
laudis insignia praefulgens opus caelatum . . .
quorum certamine [1] pugna esset prope profecto di-
rempta, nisi propter equitum congressum,[2] ut supra
demonstravimus . . . levem armaturam praesidi
causa non longe ab opere constituit.* [3]   Ut, nostri
equites in receptu dum ad castra redeunt, adversarii
cupidius sunt insecuti, universi clamore facto impetum dederunt. Ita metu perterriti, cum in fuga
essent multis amissis in castra se recipiunt.

26   Caesar ob virtutem turmae Cassianae donavit
milia ·X·III [4] et praefecto torques aureos V et levi
armaturae milia ·X·II.[5] Hoc die A. Baebius et C.
Flavius et A. Trebellius, equites Romani Astenses,
argento prope tectis equis [6] ad Caesarem transfuge-

---

* *The MSS. text of these two sentences appears to be highly
corrupt and so full of gaps as to defy any plausible reconstruction.
The English rendering is accordingly little more than an
approximation.*
    [1] certamine *added by Klotz.*
    [2] concessum *MSS.* : congressum *Nipperdey.*
    [3] castra constituit *MSS.* : *Klotz deletes* castra.
    [4] mil XIII *MSS.* : milia ·X·III *Dinter.*
    [5] mil ƆCCI *MSS.* : milia ·X·II *Dinter.*
    [6] tecti equites *MSS.* : tectis equis *Glandorp.*

upon, like the traditional encounter between Achilles and Memnon, Q. Pompeius Niger, a Roman knight from Italica, advanced from our ranks to encounter him. All men's minds were now distracted from their work and bent upon this spectacle —such was the effect of the dauntless spirit of Antistius—and the armies were arrayed over against one another; for the chances of victory were nicely balanced between the two warring champions, so that it almost seemed as if their duel meant the final decision and cessation of hostilities. So fanatically eager were they all, each man gripped by the enthusiasm of the champions and supporters of his own side. As for the two champions, what with their dashing courage, now that they had moved into the plain for the encounter, and the inwrought work of their shields—emblems of their fame—flashing in front of them . . . and their duel would almost certainly have put an end to the action, unless, owing to the attack of the enemy cavalry noted above, . . . Caesar posted some light-armed troops not far from the emplacement to give cover. While our cavalry were withdrawing to camp, the enemy pursued them too eagerly, whereupon the light-armed troops one and all raised a shout and charged them. This created a panic among them and they retired to their camp sustaining heavy losses in the course of their rout.

In recognition of the gallantry of the Cassian squadron Caesar awarded it three thousand denarii and its commander five golden collars; he also awarded the light-armed troops two thousand denarii. On this day A. Baebius, C. Flavius and A. Trebellius, who were Roman knights from the town of Asta, deserted to Caesar, with their

runt; qui nuntiaverunt equites Romanos coniurasse omnis qui in castris Pompei essent ut transitionem facerent; servi indicio omnis in custodiam esse coniectos, e quibus occasione capta se transfugisse. Item hoc die litterae sunt deprensae, quas mittebat Ursaonem Cn. Pompeius: ' S. V. G. E. V. Etsi, prout nostra felicitas, ex sententia adversarios adhuc propulsos habemus, si aequo loco sui potestatem facerent, celerius quam vestra opinio fert bellum confecissem; sed exercitum tironem non audent in campum deducere nostrisque adhuc fixi praesidiis bellum ducunt. Nam singulas civitates circumsederunt: inde sibi commeatus capiunt. Quare et civitates nostrarum partium conservabo et bellum primo quoque tempore conficiam. Cohortes . . . animo habeo ad vos mittere. Profectu[1] nostro commeatu privati necessario ad dimicandum descendent.'

27 Insequenti tempore cum nostri in opere distenti essent, equites in oliveto, dum lignantur, interfecti sunt aliquot. Servi transfugerunt, qui nuntiaverunt, a. d. III. Non. Mart. proelium ad Soricariam[2] quod factum est, ex eo tempore metum esse magnum, et

---

[1] profecto *MSS.* : profectu *Mommsen.*
[2] soriciam *or* siticiā *MSS.* : Soricariam *Clarke.*

---

[1] Presumably, as Klotz explains, they brought all their valuables with them. In the next sentence ' all the Roman knights ' must refer only to those from Asta.
[2] Yet from ch. 28 it appears that this despatch—or a copy of it—eventually got through. *cf.* ch. 18.

horses practically covered in silver.[1] They reported
that all the Roman knights in the camp of Pompeius had taken an oath to desert; but a slave
had informed against them, and they had all been
thrown into prison; they themselves were among
this number, but had seized their opportunity and
deserted. It was on this day too that a despatch
was intercepted [2] which Cn. Pompeius was sending to
Ursao: it read: ' If you are well, I am delighted:
I for my part am well.[3] Although, in accordance with
our usual good luck, we have so far kept the enemy
on the run to our satisfaction, yet, if they gave us
the chance of engaging them on favourable ground, I
should have finished the war sooner than your belief
suggests. But as it is, they lack the courage to
bring down their inexperienced army into the field,
and, pinned down so far by our forces,[4] they are prolonging hostilities. They have in fact laid siege to
individual townships, and it is from them that they
derive their supplies. I shall accordingly not only
protect the townships which belong to our side, but
shall finish the war at the first opportunity. I
intend to send you . . . cohorts. When we take
the field we shall deprive them of their vital supplies,
and they will then come down to fight.' [4]

27   Later on, when our men were busily engaged on
a field-work, a number of our cavalry were killed
while collecting wood in an olive grove. Some
slaves deserted to us, who reported that since
March 5th, the day when the battle took place at
Soricaria, there had been grave alarm, and Attius

---

[3] Abbreviation of—*Si valetis gaudeo, ego valeo.* This is
one of the conventional greetings with which many a Roman
letter began.   [4] See p. 405.

Attium Varum circum castella praeesse. Eo die
Pompeius castra movit et contra Spalim [1] in oliveto
constituit. Caesar prius quam eodem est profectus,
luna hora circiter sexta visa est. Ita castris motis
Ucubim [2] Pompeius praesidium quod reliquit iussit
incendere, ut deusto oppido in castra maiora se
reciperent. Insequenti tempore Ventiponem [3] oppidum cum oppugnare coepisset, deditione facta
iter fecit in Carrucam, contra Pompeium castra
posuit. Pompeius oppidum, quod contra sua praesidia portas claussiset, incendit; milesque, qui
fratrem suum in castris iugulasset, interceptus est a
nostris et fustibus percussus. Hinc itinere facto in
campum Mundensem cum esset ventum, castra
contra Pompeium constituit.

28   Sequenti die cum iter facere Caesar cum copiis
vellet, renuntiatum est a speculatoribus Pompeium
de tertia vigilia in acie stetisse. Hoc nuntio allato
vexillum proposuit. Idcirco enim copias eduxerat,

---

[1] *The MSS. give* Spalim *or* Sparim : *neither place is otherwise known. But the tempting conjecture* Hispalim *seems
geographically most improbable, as it lay some eighty miles
west of Soricaria and over forty miles distant from Ursao.*

[2] aucubim *or* accubim *MSS.* : Ucubim *editors.*

[3] ventiponte *MSS.* : Ventiponem *Nipperdey.*

---

[1] In this sentence and the following one the Latin presents
a striking example of the ambiguity mentioned in the Introduction, p. 307. Pompeius is almost certainly subject of
iussit, and the camp is presumably his; and so one expects—
in default of any indication to the contrary—Pompeius to be
subject in the following sentence too. But Caesar must
obviously be subject of *posuit* and is apparently also the
subject of *coepisset* and *fecit.*

[2] Carruca is not otherwise known : its general position can
thus be inferred only from this context—somewhere between
Ventipo (close to the modern *Casariche*) and Munda. Klotz,

Varus had been in command of the fortified zone. On that day Pompeius moved his camp and established it in an olive grove over against Spalis. Before Caesar set out for the same locality, the moon was observed at approximately the sixth hour. As Pompeius [1] had thus withdrawn his camp, he accordingly instructed his garrison force which he had left behind to set fire to Ucubi, so that, when the town was burned out, they should retire to his principal camp. Later on Caesar proceeded to assault the town of Ventipo; and when it capitulated he marched to Carruca,[2] and pitched camp over against Pompeius. Pompeius burned the town [3] for having barred its gates to his forces; and a soldier who had murdered his own brother in camp was intercepted by our troops and clubbed to death. From this area Caesar marched into the plain of Munda,[4] and on his arrival there established his camp over against Pompeius.

28   On the following day Caesar was minded to take the road with his forces when scouts came back with the news that Pompeius had been in battle formation since the third watch. On receipt of this news Caesar displayed the flag-signal for action. Now the reason why Pompeius had led out his forces was this:

however, who assumes throughout that operations were confined to a relatively small area, tentatively places Ventipo, Carruca and Spalis at distances respectively of only 7, 8 and 11 kilometres S. of Aspavia on the Salsum.

[3] *i.e.* Carruca.

[4] Its position is disputed : I have followed Holmes and Veith in locating it some six miles N.W. of Ursao (*Osuna*). Stoffel and Klotz place it at Montilla, some 35 miles N.E. of Ursao; while Hübner identifies it with a place known locally as Campo de Munda, about 30 miles S. of Ursao.

CAESAR

quod Ursaonensium[1] civitati, qui sui[2] fuissent
fautores, antea litteras miserat Caesarem nolle in
convallem descendere, quod maiorem partem exercitus tironem haberet. Hae litterae vehementer
confirmabant mentis oppidanorum. Ita hac opinione
fretus totum se[3] facere posse existimabat : etenim et
natura loci defendebatur et ipsius oppidi munitione,
ubi castra habuit constituta. Namque ut superius
demonstravimus, loca excellentia tumulis contineri
intervallo planitiei dividi[4]; id quod eo incidit
tempore.

29 Planities inter utraque castra intercedebat circiter
milia passuum V, ut auxilia Pompei duabus defen-
derentur rebus, oppido et excelsi[5] loci natura. Hinc
dirigens proxima planities aequabatur. Cuius de-
cursum antecedebat rivus, qui ad eorum accessum
summam efficiebat loci iniquitatem : nam palustri et
voraginoso solo currens erat ad dextram. Itaque[6]
Caesar cum aciem derectam vidisset, non habuit
dubium quin media planitie in aequum ad dimi-

[1] versaonensium *or* versoe- *or* verso- *MSS.* : Ursaonensium
Glandorp.
[2] qui sui *supplied by Nipperdey.*
[3] se *added by Oudendorp.*
[4] *I have adopted Nipperdey's conjecture. The MSS. give
variously* interim nulla planitia edividit : nullā planitiae
dividit : nullam planitie dividi.
[5] oppidi excelsi et *MSS.* : oppido et excelsi *Nipperdey.*
[6] id quod *MSS.* : itaque *Nipperdey.*

---

[1] Klotz takes this to mean the more confident attitude of
the men of Ursao. But would their increased confidence by
itself lead Pompey to think he could carry the whole thing
off ? It seems to me more likely that what the author
really meant was this : " The reason why Pompey had led
his forces out was that Caesar—so he had told the men of

he had previously sent a despatch to the citizens of
Ursao, who were supporters of his, saying that
Caesar was unwilling to come down into the valley
because the greater part of his army was inexperienced. This despatch stiffened the morale of
the townsfolk considerably. Pompeius therefore,
relying on this conviction,[1] supposed that he
could carry the whole thing off; for where he had
established his camp he was protected not only
by the natural conformation of the ground but also
by the fortifications of the town itself. For, as
we have pointed out earlier,[2] it is lofty country,
bastioned by hills with an occasional intervening
plain; and this, it so happened, was the case on the
present occasion.

Between the two camps ran a plain, extending for
some five miles, so that there were two factors which
made for the protection of Pompeius' troops—the
town, and the lofty nature of the ground. Extending
from the town the plain ground nearest to it levelled
out, and ran down to where a stream ran in front of
it, which made the ground there extremely awkward
for Caesar's troops to approach the Pompeians; for
the soil to the right of the river's course was marshy
and full of bog-holes. Consequently, when Caesar
saw their battle line deployed, he had no doubt that

Ursao in a despatch, which considerably encouraged them—
was unwilling to come down to engage. Pompey accordingly,
relying on this conviction (viz. that Caesar would decline
battle), supposed he could carry the whole thing off."

[2] The reference seems to me to be to the general description
of Baetica given in ch. 8 rather than to that of the Ategua–
Ucubi district in ch. 7. Stoffel assumes the latter on the
supposition that Munda was on the site of the modern *Montilla*, rather less than ten miles S.W. of Ucubi.

candum adversarii procederent. Hoc erat in omnium conspectu. Huc [1] accedebat ut locus illa planitie equitatum evocaret et diei solisque serenitate,[2] ut mirificum et optandum tempus prope ab dis immortalibus illud tributum esset ad proelium committendum. Nostri laetari, non nulli etiam timere, quod in eum locum res fortunaeque omnium deducerentur ut, quidquid post horam casus tribuisset, in dubio poneretur. Itaque nostri ad dimicandum procedunt, id quod adversarios existimabamus esse facturos; qui tamen a munitione oppidi longius non audebant procedere, immo se ibi prope murum adversarii [3] constituebant. Itaque nostri procedunt. Interdum aequitas loci adversarios efflagitabat ut tali condicione contenderent ad victoriam; neque tamen illi a sua consuetudine discedebant, ut aut ab excelso loco aut ab oppido discederent. Nostri pede presso propius rivum cum appropinquassent, adversarii patrocinari loco iniquo non desinunt.

30   Erat acies XIII aquilis constituta, quae lateribus equitatu tegebatur cum levi armatura milibus sex, praeterea auxiliares accedebant prope alterum tantum; nostra praesidia LXXX cohortibus, octo milibus equitum. Ita cum in extrema planitie iniquum in locum nostri appropinquassent, paratus hostis erat superior, ut transeundum superius iter

---

[1] hoc *MSS.*: huc *editors.*
[2] ornaret . . . serenitatem *MSS.*: evocaret . . . serenitate *Kraner.*
[3] in quo sibi . . . adversariis *MSS.*: immo se ibi . . . adversarii *Mommsen.*

---

[1] *i.e.* eight legions—4 veteran (III, V, VI and X) and 4 of recruits; the cavalry included a detachment of Numidians led by Bogud.

his opponents would advance to the level ground to
do battle in the middle of the plain. This area was
in full view of all. Moreover, with a level plain like
that and a calm, sunny day, it was a tempting
situation for cavalry—a wonderful, longed-for and
well-nigh heaven-sent opportunity for engaging
battle. Our men were delighted—though some also
had misgivings—at the thought that the welfare
and fortunes of everyone were being brought to the
point that no one could tell for certain what would
prove to be the luck vouchsafed them an hour later.
And so our men advanced to do battle; and we supposed that the enemy would do likewise: but our opponents would not venture to advance far from the
defences of the town: on the contrary, they were
establishing themselves in the town close to the wall.
And so our men advanced. From time to time the
favourable nature of the ground would sorely tempt
the enemy to press on to victory under such conditions; but, none the less, they would not depart
from their accustomed tactics so as to forsake either
the high ground or the town. And when our men,
advancing at a moderate pace, came up closer to the
stream, their opponents remained consistently on
the defensive on the steep ground.

Their battle line was composed of thirteen legions,
and was screened on the flanks by cavalry as well as
six thousand light-armed troops, while in addition
there were nearly as many again auxiliary troops
besides: our forces comprised eighty cohorts [1] and
eight thousand cavalry. So when our men, as they
approached, reached the unfavourable ground at the
farthest limit of the plain, the enemy were ready on
higher ground, making it extremely dangerous for our

vehementer esset periculosum. Quod cum a Caesare
esset animadversum, ne quid temere culpa secus
admitteretur, eum locum definire coepit. Quod cum
hominum auribus esset obiectum, moleste et acerbe
accipiebant se impediri quo minus proelium conficere possent. Haec mora adversarios alacriores
efficiebat : Caesaris copias timore impediri ad committendum proelium. Ita se efferentes iniquo loco
sui potestatem faciebant, ut magno tamen periculo
accessus eorum haberetur. Hic decumani suum
locum, cornum dextrum, tenebant, sinistrum III. et
V., itemque cetera auxilia et equitatus.[1] Proelium
clamore facto committitur.

31   Hic etsi virtute nostri antecedebant, adversarii
loco superiore se defendebant acerrime, et vehemens
fiebat ab utrisque clamor telorumque missu concursus, sic ut prope nostri diffiderent[2] victoriae.   Congressus enim et clamor, quibus rebus maxime hostis
conterretur, in collatu pari erat condicione.   Ita ex
utroque genere pugnae cum parem virtutem ad
bellandum contulissent, pilorum missu[3] fixa cumula-
tur et concidit adversariorum multitudo.   Dextrum ut
demonstravimus decumanos cornum tenuisse ; qui
etsi erant pauci, tamen propter virtutem magno
adversarios timore eorum opera adficiebant, quod a
suo loco hostis vehementer premere coeperunt, ut ad

---

[1] itemque et cetera auxilia equitatus *MSS.* : *most editors
either transpose or add* et *after* auxilia.
[2] different *or* -ferrent *or* deferunt *MSS.* : diffiderent *editors.*
[3] missus *MSS.* : missu *editors.*

---

[1] The phrase *locum definire* has been variously explained
by editors. But if it be assumed that Caesar's troops had
already crossed the stream, it may, I think, imply that
Caesar ordered a strictly limited advance up the slope,

men to pursue their passage to the higher level. When Caesar observed this, to avoid any blunder being perpetrated owing to rashness or faulty judgment, he began to restrict the operational area.[1] But when it came to the ears of the men that he was doing so, they were bitterly disgusted, as they took it to mean that their chance of deciding the conflict was being hampered. This delay made the enemy keener: it was fear, they thought, that was preventing Caesar's forces from joining battle: and although by displaying themselves they gave our men the opportunity of engaging them on steep ground, yet it was only at great risk that one could approach them. On our side the men of the Tenth legion held their proper post—the right wing; while the men of the Third and Fifth legions together with all the rest of our forces—the auxiliary troops and the cavalry—held the left wing. The shout was raised and the battle joined.

Hereupon, although our men were superior in point of valour, their opponents offered a very spirited resistance from their higher position; and so furious proved the shouting on both sides, so furious the charging with its attendant volley of missiles, that our men well nigh lost their confidence in victory. In fact, as regards attacking and shouting—the two chief methods of demoralising an enemy—both sides stood on equal terms of comparison. But, though they accordingly brought to the contest an equal fighting capacity in both these departments of battle, yet the enemy masses were pinned down by our volleys of heavy javelins, and fell in heaps. Our right wing,

since he was unaware as yet of the strength of the enemy's prepared positions on the heights.

subsidium, ne ab latere nostri occuparent, legio
adversariorum traduci coepta sit a dextro.[1] Quae
simul est mota, equitatus Caesaris sinistrum cornum
premere coepit ita uti eximia virtute proelium
facere possent,[2] locus in aciem ad subsidium veniendi
non daretur. Ita cum clamor esset intermixtus
gemitu gladiorumque crepitus auribus oblatus,
imperitorum mentis timore praepediebat. Hic, ut
ait Ennius, pes pede premitur, armis teruntur arma,
adversariosque vehementissime pugnantes nostri
agere coeperunt; quibus oppidum fuit subsidio. Ita
ipsis Liberalibus fusi fugatique non superfuissent,
nisi in eum locum confugissent ex quo erant egressi.
In quo proelio ceciderunt milia hominum circiter
XXX et si quid amplius, praeterea Labienus, Attius
Varus, quibus occisis utrisque funus est factum,
itemque equites Romani partim ex urbe partim ex
provincia ad milia III. Nostri desiderati ad
hominum mille partim equitum partim peditum;
saucii ad D. Adversariorum aquilae sunt ablatae
XIII et signa et fasces praeterea hos habuit . . .

[1] ad dextrum *MSS.* : a dextro *Glandorp. Klotz retains*
ad dextrum *as meaning to* Caesar's *right.*
[2] possent ut locus *MSS.* : *Du Pontet deleted* ut.

---

[1] I have retained the MSS. reading, although some emend
to give the sense ' from their own left wing ', *i.e.* on the
enemy's right. But as the Pompeian legion was already
crossing over, it seems to me that increased pressure by the
cavalry on the enemy's left wing might well have made
effective reinforcement impracticable.
[2] The festival in honour of Liber or Bacchus, celebrated on
March 17th.

as we have explained, was held by the men of the
Tenth legion; and despite their small numbers,
their gallantry none the less enabled them by their
exertions to inspire no little panic among their
opponents. They proceeded, in fact, to exert strong
pressure on the enemy, driving him back from his
positions, with the result that he began to transfer a
legion from his right, to give support and to prevent
our men from outflanking him. As soon as this
legion had been set in motion Caesar's cavalry
began to exert pressure on the enemy left wing,[1]
so that, no matter how gallantly the enemy might
fight, he was afforded no opportunity of reinforcing
his line. And so, as the motley din—shouts, groans,
the clash of swords—assailed their ears, it shackled
the minds of the inexperienced with fear. Hereupon, as Ennius puts it, "foot forces against foot and
weapons grind 'gainst weapons"; and in the teeth of
very strong opposition our men began to drive the
enemy back. The town, however, stood them in
good stead. And so they were routed and put to
flight on the very day of the Liberalia [2]; nor would
they have survived, had they not fled back to their
original starting point. In this battle there fell some
thirty thousand men—if anything, more—as well as
Labienus and Attius Varus, both of whom were
buried where they fell, and about three thousand
Roman knights besides, some from Rome, some from
the province. Our losses amounted to about a
thousand men, partly cavalry, partly infantry; while
our wounded totalled about five hundred. Thirteen
legionary eagles belonging to the enemy were
captured; and in addition he had the following
standards and rods of office . . .

32 . . . ex fuga hac qui oppidum Mundam sibi con-
stituissent praesidium, nostrique cogebantur necessario eos circumvallare. Ex hostium armis scuta et
pila pro vallo, pro caespite cadavera collocabantur,
insuper abscisa in gladiorum mucrone capita hominum ordinata ad oppidum conversa universa, ut et
ad hostium timorem virtutisque insignia proposita
viderent et vallo circumcluderentur adversarii.[1]
Ita Galli tragulis iaculisque oppidum ex hostium
cadaveribus circumplexi[2] oppugnare coeperunt. Ex
hoc proelio Valerius adulescens Cordubam cum
paucis equitibus fugit; Sex. Pompeio, qui Cordubae
fuisset, rem gestam refert. Cognito hoc negotio,
quos equites secum habuit, quod pecuniae secum
habuit eis distribuit et oppidanis dixit se de pace ad
Caesarem proficisci et secunda vigilia ab oppido
discessit. Cn. Pompeius cum equitibus paucis non
nullisque peditibus ad navale praesidium parte altera
Carteiam contendit, quod oppidum abest ab Corduba
milia passuum CLXX. Quo cum ad octavum
miliarium venisset, P. Caucilius,[3] qui castris antea
Pompei praepositus esset, eius verbis nuntium mittit
eum minus bellum habere: ut mitterent lecticam
qua in oppidum deferri posset. Lecticariis[4] missis
Pompeius Carteiam defertur. Qui illarum partium
fautores essent conveniunt in domum quo erat
delatus—qui arbitrati sunt clanculum venisse—, ut

[1] Ex hostium armis pro caespite cadavera collocabantur
scuta et pila pro vallo insuper occisi et gladio ut mucro et
capita. . . . *MSS. I have adopted:—Nipperdey's transposition of* scuta . . . vallo, *and his conjecture* in gladiorum
mucrone; *Oudendorp's* abscisa; *and Hoffmann's insertion of*
ut et ad *between* universa *and* hostium.

[2] sunt circumplexi *MSS.* : *Du Pontet deleted* sunt.

[3] caucili *MSS.* : Caucilius *Scaliger.*

[4] litteris *MSS.* : lecticariis *Fleischer.*

2 . . . those who, after surviving this rout, had made
the town of Munda their refuge, and our men were of
necessity compelled to blockade them. Shields and
javelins taken from among the enemy's weapons were
placed to serve as a palisade, dead bodies as a rampart; on top, impaled on sword points, severed
human heads were ranged in a row all facing the
town, the object being not merely to enclose the
enemy by a palisade, but to afford him an awe-
inspiring spectacle by displaying before him this
evidence of valour. Having thus encircled the town
with the javelins and spears taken from the corpses of
the enemy, the Gallic troops now proceeded to assault
it. From this battle the young Valerius escaped to
Corduba with a few horsemen, and delivered his
report of it to Sextus Pompeius, who was present
there. On learning of these events, the latter divided
what money he had with him among his present
cavalry force, told the townsfolk that he was setting
out for peace talks with Caesar, and left the town at
the second watch. Cn. Pompeius, attended by
a few horsemen and some infantry, pressed forward
on the other hand to the naval fortified base of
Carteia, a town which lies one hundred and seventy
miles away from Corduba. When he had reached
the eighth milestone from Carteia, P. Caucilius,
who had formerly been in command of Pompeius'
camp, sent a message dictated by Pompeius saying
that he was in a bad way, and they must send a litter
in which he could be carried into the town. A litter
and bearers were despatched, and Pompeius was
carried to Carteia. His partisans forgathered at the
house to which he had been brought—each supposing
his visit to have been a private one—to make enquiry

ab eo quae vellet[1] de bello requirerent. Cum
frequentia convenisset, de lectica Pompeius eorum in
fidem confugit.

33   Caesar ex proelio Munda munitione circumdata
Cordubam venit. Qui ex caede eo refugerant,
pontem occuparunt. Cum eo ventum esset, con-
viciari coeperunt: nos ex proelio paucos superesse;
quo fugeremus? Ita pugnare coeperunt de ponte.
Caesar flumen traiecit et castra posuit. Scapula,
totius seditionis, familiae et libertinorum caput, ex
proelio Cordubam cum venisset, familiam et libertos
convocavit, pyram sibi exstruxit, cenam adferri
quam optimam imperavit, item optimis insternendum
vestimentis: pecuniam et argentum in praesentia
familiae donavit. Ipse de tempore cenare; resinam[2]
et nardum identidem sibi infundit. Ita novissimo
tempore servum iussit et libertum, qui fuisset eius
concubinus, alterum se iugulare, alterum pyram
incendere.

[1] vellent *MSS. I have adopted* vellent—*conjectured by
Kraffert*—*assuming that* vellent *arose from the plural verb which
follows.*
[2] sitam *most MSS.* : resinam *some late MSS.* : stactam
(= *myrrh-oil*) *Oudendorp.*

---

[1] This seems to be the normal interpretation, though the
jeering remark seems rather pointless as addressed to Caesar.
I am inclined to believe that the words *Qui ex caede . . . de
ponte* are parenthetical and refer to the time when the
refugees first arrived. If so, the sense will be : *On their
arrival there they began to jeer, viz.* at the members of the
Caesarian faction, who wished them further, since their
presence would lessen the chances of reaching a composition

of him what were his intentions about the war; but when a crowd of them had forgathered, Pompeius left his litter and threw himself upon their protection.

3   After the battle Caesar invested Munda with a ring of emplacements and came to Corduba. The survivors of the carnage who had taken refuge there seized the bridge; and when Caesar [1] arrived there they proceeded to jeer, saying—' There are few of us survivors from the battle: where were we to seek refuge?' And so they fell to fighting from the bridge.[2] Caesar crossed the river and pitched camp. Now the ringleader of all this unrest, as well as the head of a gang of slaves and freedmen, was Scapula[3]; and when he came to Corduba as a survivor from the battle he summoned his slaves and freedmen, had himself built a lofty pyre, and ordered a banquet to be served on the most lavish possible scale and the finest tapestries likewise to be spread out; and then and there he presented his slaves with money and silver. As for himself, in due course he fell to upon the banquet, and ever and anon anointed himself with resin and nard. Accordingly, at the latest possible moment, he bade a slave and a freedman— the latter was his concubine—the one to cut his throat, the other to light the pyre.

with Caesar. The following chapter tends, I think, to confirm this interpretation.

[2] *i.e.* down from their position on it. If, however, the alternative interpretation given in the note above is accepted, the meaning might well be: ' And so they (*sc.* the refugees, who had seized the bridge, and the Caesarian partisans in the town) fell to fighting for control of the bridge.'

[3] Scapula and Aponius had been elected as leaders by the legions who had previously mutinied against Q. Cassius Longinus and later expelled his successor, Trebonius.

34 Oppidani autem, simul Caesar castra contra ad
oppidum posuit, discordare coeperunt usque eo ut
clamor in castra nostra perveniret rixae [1] inter
Caesarianos et inter Pompeianos.   Erant hic legiones
duae [2] ex perfugis conscriptae, partim oppidanorum
servi, qui erant a Sex. Pompeio manu missi; qui in
Caesaris adventum discedere [3] coeperunt.   Legio
XIII. oppidum defendere coepit, nonani [4] cum iam
depugnarent,[5] turris ex parte et murum occuparunt.
Denuo legatos ad Caesarem mittunt, ut sibi legiones
subsidio intromitteret.   Hoc cum animadverterent
homines fugitivi, oppidum incendere coeperunt.
Qui superati a nostris sunt interfecti hominum milia
XXII, praeter quam extra murum qui perierunt.   Ita
Caesar oppido potitur.   Dum hic detinetur, ex
proelio quos circummunitos superius demonstravimus, eruptionem fecerunt et bene multis interfectis
in oppidum sunt redacti.

35 Caesar Hispalim cum contendisset, legati depre-
catum venerunt.   Ita cum ad oppidum esset ventum,
Caninium cum praesidio legatum intromittit: ipse
castra ad oppidum ponit.   Erat bene magna manus [6]

---

[1] fere *MSS.*: rixae *Mommsen.*
[2] quae *MSS.*: duae *Madvig.*
[3] descendere *MSS.*: discedere *Duebner.*
[4] non *MSS.*: nonani *Hoffmann.*
[5] repugnarent *MSS.*: depugnarent *Nipperdey.*
[6] magnum *MSS.*: magna manus *Ciacconius.*

---

[1] *cf.* ch. 2.
[2] The state of the text makes the sketchy narrative still
harder to follow.   It looks rather as if the Thirteenth and the

34   Now as soon as Caesar pitched his camp over
against the town its occupants proceeded to quarrel; so
much so that the sound of the shouting and brawling
between the supporters of Caesar on the one hand,
and Pompeius on the other, reached our camp.
There were two legions in this town which had been
raised partly from deserters, while others were slaves
of the townsmen who had been set free by Sextus
Pompeius; and now in view of Caesar's approach
they began to desert. The Thirteenth legion proceeded to defend the town, whereas the men of the
Ninth, as soon as they became involved in the fray,
seized some of the towers and battlements. Once
again [1] they sent envoys to Caesar, requesting that he
should send in his legions to support them; and
when the refugees got to know of it they proceeded
to set fire to the town.[2] But they were overpowered
by our men and put to death, to the number of
twenty-two thousand men, not counting those who
lost their lives outside the battlements. Thus did
Caesar gain possession of the town. While he was
occupied here, the survivors of the battle who had
been shut up (in Munda), as we described above,[3]
made a sally, only to be driven back into the town
with very heavy losses.

35   On Caesar's marching to Hispalis envoys came to
him to entreat his pardon. So when he reached the
town, he sent in Caninius as his deputy, accompanied
by a garrison force, while he himself pitched camp
near the town. Now inside the town there was a

' refugees ' (survivors from Munda mentioned above in ch. 33?)
were still bent fanatically on resistance, while the Ninth (?) was
ready to surrender.
    [3] in ch. 32.

CAESAR

intra Pompeianarum partium, quae praesidium
receptum indignaretur clam quendam Philonem,
illum qui Pompeianarum partium fuisset defensor
acerrimus—is tota Lusitania notissimus erat—: hic
clam praesidia Lusitaniam proficiscitur et Caecilium
Nigrum, hominem [1] barbarum, ad Lennium convenit,
qui bene magnam manum Lusitanorum haberet.
Reversus Hispalim in [2] oppidum denuo noctu per
murum recipitur: praesidium, vigiles iugulant, portas
praecludunt, de integro pugnare coeperunt.

36   Dum haec geruntur, legati Carteienses renuntia-
verunt quod Pompeium in potestatem haberent.
Quod ante Caesari portas praeclusissent, illo beneficio
suum maleficium existimabant se lucri facere.
Lusitani Hispali pugnare nullo tempore desistebant.
Quod Caesar cum animadverteret, si oppidum
capere contenderet, timuit ne homines perditi
incenderent et moenia delerent; ita consilio habito
noctu patitur Lusitanos eruptionem facere; id quod
consulto non existimabant fieri. Ita erumpendo
navis, quae ad Baetim flumen fuissent, incendunt.
Nostri dum incendio detinentur, illi profugiunt et ab
equitibus conciduntur.   Quo facto oppido reciperato
Astam iter facere coepit; ex qua civitate legati ad
deditionem venerunt.   Mundenses, qui [3] ex proelio

---

[1] nomine *MSS.*: hominem *Glandorp.*
[2] in *added by Oudendorp.*
[3] mundensesque *MSS.*: Mundenses qui *Kraffert.*

good large group of supporters of Pompeius, who
thought it scandalous that a garrison should have
been admitted unbeknown to a certain Philo—the
man who had been the most ardent champion of the
Pompeian faction, and was a very well-known figure
throughout Lusitania. This man now set out for
Lusitania without the knowledge of our garrison
troops, and at Lennium met Caecilius Niger, a
foreigner, who had a good large force of Lusitanians.
Returning to Hispalis, he penetrated the fortifications
by night and thus gained re-admission to the town;
whereupon they massacred the garrison and sentries,
barred the gates, and renewed hostilities.

36   In the course of these proceedings envoys from
Carteia duly reported that they had Pompeius in
their hands. They thought they stood to gain by
this good deed, which might offset their previous
offence in having barred their gates to Caesar. At
Hispalis the Lusitanians kept up the fight without a
moment's pause; and when Caesar observed their
stubbornness he was afraid that, if he made strenuous
efforts to capture the town, these desperadoes might
fire the town and destroy the walls. So after holding
consultations he allowed the Lusitanians to make a
sally by night—a course which the latter never
supposed was deliberate policy. Accordingly, they
made a sally, and in the process fired some ships
which were alongside the river Baetis. While our men
were occupied with the fire, the Lusitanians took to
flight and were cut down by our cavalry. This led
to the recovery of the town; whereupon Caesar
proceeded to march to Asta, from which township
envoys came to him to surrender it. As for the
survivors of the battle who had taken refuge in the

in oppidum confugerant, cum diutius circumside-
rentur, bene multi deditionem faciunt et, cum essent
in legionem distributi, coniurant inter sese, ut noctu
signo dato qui in oppido fuissent eruptionem facerent,
illi caedem in castris administrarent. Hac re cognita
insequenti nocte vigilia tertia tessera data extra
vallum omnes sunt concisi.

37 Carteienses, dum Caesar in itinere reliqua oppida
oppugnat, propter Pompeium dissentire coeperunt.
Pars erat quae legatos ad Caesarem miserat, pars erat
qui Pompeianarum partium fautores essent. Seditione concitata portas [1] occupant; caedes fit magna;
saucius Pompeius navis XX occupat longas et profugit. Didius, qui Gadibus classi praefuisset, simul [2]
nuntius allatus est, confestim sequi coepit; Carteia
pedites [3] et equitatus ad persequendum celeriter iter
faciebant item confestim consequentes. Quarto die
navigationis,[4] quod imparati a Carteia profecti sine
aqua fuissent, ad terram applicant. Dum aquantur,
Didius classe accurrit, navis incendit, non nullas
capit.

[1] partes *MSS.*: portas *Vascosanus.*
[2] ad quem simul *MSS.*: ad quem *deleted by Vielhaber.*
[3] partim pedibus *MSS.*: Carteia pedites *Kuebler.*
[4] item quarto die navigatione confestim consequentes
MSS. I have adopted Nipperdey's conjecture.

---

[1] This rendering assumes that *tessera* refers to *signo*; that
the plot was allowed to take place by night, as originally
planned; but that the authorities, warned in advance,
intervened and cut down all the insurgents (*omnes* = both
groups ?) outside the rampart. Klotz, however, holds the
view that the conspirators were arrested as soon as the plot
was discovered, and then, very early next morning, led outside
the rampart and there executed. The fact that, as he observes,

town of Munda, a somewhat protracted siege led a good large number to surrender; and on being drafted to form a legion they swore a mutual oath that during the night at a given signal their comrades in the town should make a sally, while they carried out a massacre in the camp. But this plot was discovered; and when at the third watch on the following night the pass-word was given, they were all cut down outside the rampart.[1]

7 While Caesar was on the move and attacking the remaining towns, the men of Carteia began to fall out on the question of Pompeius. There was the party which had sent envoys to Caesar: there was another party which espoused the cause of Pompeius. Civil discord being thus stirred up, they seized the gates: much blood was shed: Pompeius, who was wounded,[2] seized twenty warships, and took to flight. As soon as the news of his escape reached Didius, who was at Gades in command of a squadron, he forthwith began to give chase; and from Carteia too the hunt was likewise taken up forthwith by infantry and cavalry marching in swift pursuit. On the fourth day of their voyage Pompeius' party put in to land, since they had been ill provided and without water when they sailed from Carteia. While they were getting water Didius hastened up with his fleet, captured some of their ships, and burned the rest.

such executions commonly took place around dawn and outside the rampart (cf. Bell. Afr. ch. 46) favours this view: against it it may perhaps be argued that the verb concidere is more appropriate to a surprise attack.

[2] That Pompey had been wounded at Munda seems implied in ch. 32, and details are given below in ch. 38. But whether he sustained further injuries on this occasion is by no means clear.

38 Pompeius cum paucis profugit et locum quendam munitum natura occupat. Equites et cohortes qui ad persequendum missi essent speculatoribus antemissis certiores fiunt: diem et noctem iter faciunt. Pompeius umero et sinistro crure vehementer erat saucius. Huc accedebat ut etiam talum intorsisset; quae res maxime impediebat. Ita lectica ad turrem cum esset ablatus in ea ferebatur. Lusitanus, more militari ex eius praesidio speculator missus, cum Caesaris praesidio [1] fuisset conspectus, celeriter equitatu cohortibusque circumcluditur. Erat accessus loci difficilis. Nam idcirco [2] munitum locum natura ceperat sibi Pompeius, ut quamvis magna multitudine adducta [3] pauci homines ex superiore loco defendere possent. Subeunt in adventu nostri, depelluntur telis. Quibus cedentibus cupidius insequebantur adversarii et confestim tardabant ab accessu. Hoc saepius facto animum advertebatur nostro magno id fieri periculo. Opere circummunire instituunt; [4] pares [5] autem ex celeri festinatione circummunitiones iugo derigunt, ut

[1] *I have adopted Hoffmann's conjecture; the MSS. reading—* Lusitanus more militari cum Caesaris praesidio fuisset conspectus—*seems very difficult.*

[2] *After* idcirco *the MSS. give—*propter suo praesidio fuisset conspectus celeriter ad. *I have omitted these words, following Dinter.*

[3] deducti *MSS.*: adducta *Madvig, who also supplied* ut *and* pauci.

[4] instituit *MSS.*: instituunt *Nipperdey.*

[5] pari *MSS.*: pares *Mommsen.*

THE SPANISH WAR

Pompeius took to flight with a few companions and occupied a certain spot which possessed natural defences. When the cavalry and infantry cohorts which had been despatched in his pursuit learned of this from scouts they had sent on ahead, they pushed on day and night. Now Pompeius was seriously wounded in the shoulder and left leg; added to which he had also sprained his ankle, which hampered him very much. So a litter was employed to carry him off to this redoubt and, once arrived there, he continued to be carried about in it. One of the Lusitanians who had been despatched from his escort on reconnaissance in accordance with normal military routine was now spotted by the Caesarian force, and Pompeius was promptly surrounded by the cavalry and cohorts. It was a difficult place to approach: that in fact was the very reason why Pompeius had chosen himself a naturally fortified position, so that, no matter how great a force was brought up to it, a handful of men might be able to defend it from higher ground. On their arrival our men came up close to it only to be driven back with javelins. As they gave ground the enemy pressed upon them the more eagerly and called an immediate halt to their advance. When this manoeuvre had been repeated several times it became obvious that it was a very risky business for our men. The enemy [1] then began to fortify his position with a circumvallation; our men, however, acting with speed and despatch, carried a similar circumvallation along the high ground, to enable them to

[1] In this and the following sentence all the subjects are left unspecified in the Latin: several interpretations are therefore possible.

aequo pede cum adversariis congredi possent. A
quibus cum animum adversum esset, fuga sibi
praesidium capiunt.

39   Pompeius, ut supra demonstravimus, saucius et
intorto talo idcirco tardabatur ad fugiendum, itemque propter loci difficultatem neque equo neque
vehiculo saluti suae praesidium parare poterat.
Caedes a nostris undique administrabatur. Exclusus [1] munitione amissisque auxiliis ad convallem
exesumque locum in speluncam Pompeius se occul-
tare coepit, ut a nostris non facile inveniretur nisi
captivorum indicio. Ita ibi interficitur. Cum Caesar
Gadibus fuisset, Hispalim prid. Id. April. caput
allatum et populo datum est in conspectum.

40   Interfecto Cn. Pompeio adulescente Didius, quem
supra demonstravimus, illa adfectus laetitia proximo
se recepit castello non nullasque navis ad reficiendum
subduxit et quodvis essent bracchium ex utrisque
partibus.[2] Lusitani qui ex pugna superfuerunt ad
signum se receperunt et bene magna manu comparata
ad Didium se reportant. Huic etsi non aberat
diligentia ad navis tuendas, tamen non numquam ex
castello propter eorum crebras excursiones eliciebatur,[3] et sic prope cotidianis pugnis insidias ponunt
et tripertito signa distribuunt. Erant parati qui
navis incenderent, incensisque qui subsidium repel-

---

[1] exclusa *MSS.* : exclusus *Fleischer.*

[2] *The last six words, as given by most MSS., are clearly
corrupt : no obvious emendation has been suggested, and
Nipperdey's assumption of a lacuna seems probable. Klotz
proposes* :—et quodvis essent ⟨periculum minaturi Lusitani
ut caveret⟩ bracchium ex utrisque partibus ⟨ad mare ducere
coepit⟩ ' *and, to guard against any danger likely to threaten from
the Lusitanians, proceeded to carry a line of fortifications to the
sea on either side.*'

[3] eiiciebatur *MSS.* : eliciebatur *Glandorp.*

encounter their opponents on an equal footing. When the latter observed this move they took refuge in flight.

Pompeius, as we have pointed out above, was wounded and had sprained his ankle, and this handicapped him in flight; moreover, the difficult nature of the ground made it impossible for him to have recourse to riding horseback or driving to assist his escape to safety. On all sides our troops were carrying on the work of slaughter. Cut off from his entrenchment and having lost his supporters, Pompeius now resorted to a ravine, to a spot where the ground was eaten away; and there in a cave he proceeded to hide himself, so that, short of his being given away by a prisoner, it was no easy matter for our men to find him. By such means in fact he was discovered there and put to death. When Caesar was at Gades, the head of Pompeius was brought to Hispalis on April 12th, and there publicly exhibited.

Filled with delight at the death of the young Pompeius, Didius, whom we mentioned above, withdrew to a nearby stronghold, beached some of his ships for a refit, and . . . Those Lusitanians who survived the battle rallied to their standard and, when a good large force had been mustered, duly proceeded against Didius. Although he displayed no lack of care in guarding his ships, yet their constant sallies enticed him on occasions to leave his stronghold, with the result that in the course of almost daily battles they laid a trap for him, dividing up their forces into three groups. There were some who were detailed to burn the ships; some to repel an enemy relief force, when the ships had once been

lerent [1] : hi sic dispositi erant, ut a nullo conspici
possent : reliqui in [2] conspectu omnium ad pugnam
contendunt. Ita cum ex castello Didius ad pro-
pellendum processisset cum copiis, signum a Lusi-
tanis tollitur, naves incenduntur, simulque qui ex
castello ad pugnam processerant, eodem signo
fugientis latrones dum persequuntur, a tergo insidiae
clamore sublato circumveniunt. Didius magna cum
virtute cum compluribus interficitur; non nulli ea
pugna scaphas quae ad litus fuerant occupant, item
complures nando ad navis quae in salo fuerunt se
recipiunt, ancoris sublatis pelagus remis petere
coeperunt; quae res eorum vitae fuit subsidio.
Lusitani praeda potiuntur. Caesar Gadibus rursus
ad Hispalim recurrit.

41 Fabius Maximus, quem ad Mundam praesidium
oppugnandum reliquerat, operibus assiduis diurnis
nocturnisque circumsedit : interclusi inter se decernere armis coeperunt, facta caede bene magna
eruptionem faciunt.[3] Nostri ad oppidum recipe-
randum occasionem non praetermittunt et reliquos
vivos capiunt, XIIII milia. Ursaonem proficiscuntur;
quod oppidum magna munitione continebatur, sic ut

[1] repeterent *MSS.* : repellerent *Glandorp.*
[2] conspici possent : reliqui in *added by Nipperdey.*
[3] operibus assiduis iurnis circum sese interclusi inter se
decernere facta caede bene magna faciunt *MSS.* : diurnis
nocturnisque *Dinter*; circumsedit *Fleischer*; armis coeperunt
added by Hoffmann; eruptionem *appears before* faciunt *in some
late MSS.*

---

[1] Klotz's punctuation (as followed here) whereby *eodem
signo* is taken with *fugientis*—the latter word apparently

fired: these parties were posted in such a way as to be entirely hidden from view, whereas the remainder marched into battle in full view of all. Accordingly, when Didius advanced with his forces from his stronghold to drive them back, the signal was displayed by the Lusitanians, the ships were set on fire, and simultaneously those who had advanced to battle from the stronghold—they were now pursuing the retreating bandits, who had turned tail on that same signal—were surprised by the ambushing party, which raised a shout and surrounded them from the rear.[1] Didius met a gallant death with many of his men; some in the course of the fighting seized some pinnaces which were close inshore, while quite a number, on the other hand, swam off to the ships moored in deep water, weighed anchor, and then began to row them out to sea, thereby saving their lives. The Lusitanians gained possession of the booty. Caesar left Gades and hastened back to Hispalis.

Fabius Maximus, who had been left behind by Caesar to attack the enemy garrison at Munda, besieged that town in a continuous series of operations by day and night. Now that they were cut off the enemy fell to fighting amongst themselves; and after a welter of bloodshed they made a sally. Our troops did not fail to take this opportunity of recovering the town and captured the remaining men alive, to the number of fourteen thousand. Our men now set out for Ursao, a town which was buttressed by massive fortifications, to such an extent that in itself the place seemed adapted to

implying both the initial act of turning about and the subsequent retreat—seems to yield the most satisfactory sense.

ipse locus non solum opere sed etiam natura datus [1]
ad oppugnandum hostem appareret. Huc accedebat
ut aqua praeter quam in ipso oppido unam circum-
circa nusquam reperiretur propius milia passuum
VIII; quae res magno erat adiumento oppidanis.
Tum praeterea accedebat ut aggerem, . . . materies-
que, unde soliti sunt turris ac vineas facere [2] propius
milia passuum VI non reperiebatur: ac Pompeius
ut se ad oppidi [3] oppugnationem tutiorem efficeret,
omnem materiem circum oppidum succisam intro
congessit. Ita necessario diducebantur nostri, ut a
Munda, quod proxime ceperant, materiem illo
deportarent.

42   Dum haec ad Mundam geruntur et Ursaonem,
Caesar, ad Hispalim cum Gadibus se recepisset,
insequenti die contione advocata commemorat:
initio quaesturae suae eam provinciam ex omnibus
provinciis peculiarem sibi constituisse et quae
potuisset eo tempore beneficia largitum esse; in-
sequente praetura ampliato honore vectigalia quae
Metellus inposuisset a senatu petisse et ea pecunia [4]
provinciam liberasse simulque patrocinio suscepto
multis legationibus ab se in senatum inductis simul

---

[1] aditus *MSS.*: datus *Hoffmann.*
[2] agi *MSS.*: ac vineas facere *Kraner.*
[3] hac Pompeius ad oppidum *MSS.*: *I have adopted Hoffmann's reading.*
[4] eius pecuniae or -a *MSS.*: ea pecunia *editors.*

---

[1] *ad oppugnandum hostem* appears to mean ' to assail a
(besieging) enemy ', the implication possibly being ' go over to
the offensive against '; but the text is very uncertain.
[2] 69 B.C. in Further Spain.
[3] 62 B.C.

assail[1] an enemy by virtue of its natural site as well as its artificial fortification. Added to this, apart from a single fountain in the town itself, there was no water to be found anywhere in the neighbourhood under eight miles from the town; and this was a great advantage to the townsfolk. Then again there was the additional circumstance that materials for a rampart, . . . and timber, which they habitually used for the construction of towers and mantlets, was not to be found under six miles' distance from the town; and in order the more to safeguard himself against an attack upon it, Pompeius had had all the timber in the neighbourhood felled and dumped inside it. Thus our troops were under the necessity of detaching men to carry timber thither from Munda, the town they had just recently captured.

2 While these operations were proceeding at Munda and Ursao, Caesar left Gades and returned to Hispalis, and on the day after his arrival there summoned an assembly of the people. He reminded them that at the outset of his quaestorship[2] he had made that province above all others his own special concern, and had liberally bestowed on it such benefits as lay in his power at that time; that when subsequently he had been promoted to the praetorship[3] he had asked the Senate to rescind the taxes which Metellus[4] had imposed, and had secured the province immunity from paying the money in question; that having once taken upon himself to champion the province he had defended it, not only introducing numerous deputations into the Senate

[4] Q. Caecilius Metellus Pius had, together with Cn. Pompeius Magnus, crushed the rebellion of Sertorius in Spain 80–72. The imposts mentioned here were probably punitory.

publicis privatisque causis multorum inimicitiis
susceptis defendisse ; suo item in consulatu absentem
quae potuisset commoda provinciae tribuisse : eorum
omnium commodorum et immemores [1] et ingratos in
se et in populum Romanum hoc bello et praeterito
tempore cognosse. ' Vos iure gentium civiumque
Romanorum institutis cognitis more barbarorum
populi Romani magistratibus sacrosancti manus
semel [2] et saepius attulistis et luce clara Cassium [3] in
medio foro nefarie interficere voluistis. Vos ita
pacem semper odistis ut nullo tempore legiones
desitae sint populi Romani in hac provincia haberi.
Apud vos beneficia pro maleficiis, maleficia pro
beneficiis habentur. Ita neque in otio concordiam
neque in bello virtutem ullo tempore retinere potuis-
tis. Privatus ex fuga Cn. Pompeius adulescens a
vobis receptus fascis imperiumque sibi arripuit,
multis interfectis civibus auxilia contra populum
Romanum comparavit, agros provinciamque vestro
impulsu depopulavit. In quo vos victores exstabatis ?
An me deleto non animum advertebatis habere
legiones populum Romanum, quae non solum vobis
obsistere sed etiam caelum diruere possent ? Quarum
laudibus et virtute . . .

---

[1] etiam memores *MSS.* : et immemores *editors.*

[2] magna trans aero (*or* ero *or* ore) sanctis Romanus *MSS.* :
magistratibus sacrosancti manus semel *Beroaldus.*

[3] captum *MSS.* : Cassium Aldus.

---

[1] 59 B.C. with Bibulus.

[2] *Bell. Alex.* ch. 52.

but also undertaking legal actions both public and private, and thereby incurring the enmity of many men. Similarly, during the period of his consulship[1] he had bestowed on the province in his absence such advantages as lay in his power. Yet both in the present war and in the period before it he was well aware that they had been unmindful of all these advantages, and ungrateful for them, both towards himself and towards the Roman people. ' You,' he went on, ' who are well acquainted with the law of nations and the established usages of Roman citizens, have none the less behaved like savages and have laid violent hands more often than once upon the inviolable magistrates of the Roman people, and designed the dastardly murder of Cassius[2] in broad daylight in the middle of the forum. You have always so hated peace that this province has never ceased to be occupied by the legions of the Roman people. With you good deeds count as misdeeds, and vice versa. Consequently you have never been able to maintain harmony in peace or high morale in war. It was you who harboured the young Cn. Pompeius after his flight; it was at your instigation that, albeit a private citizen, he seized the rods of office and usurped military command, put many citizens to death, raised armed forces to fight the Roman people, and laid waste the territories of the province. On what field did you come out victorious? Or didn't you take into consideration the fact that, if I were done away with, the Roman people possessed legions which could not only offer you resistance but could also cause the heavens to fall? By their glorious deeds of valour . . . '

APPENDIX A

THE OPERATIONS NEAR UZITTA
(*African War* chapters 37–66)

ALTHOUGH in general the narrative contained in these thirty chapters is clear, yet there remain not a few problems mainly concerned with the identification of positions mentioned in the text. Some of these problems are vital to the interpretation of the text; and as any adequate discussion of them is impossible in brief footnotes they are dealt with here in this appendix.

(1) *The Identity of the* ultimus collis *of chapters* 37–39

It is of some importance to identify this hill because it has a bearing not only upon the position of both Scipio's and Caesar's camps, but also upon the operations of chapters 49–51.

The first sentence of chapter 38 provides the main evidence for its identification. It was, apparently, not the southernmost hill in the chain (*Sidi Jeha*), but the southernmost of those hills only which contained ancient watch-towers. R. Holmes argued—convincingly, as I think—that the word *unumquemque* must imply that Caesar had visited at least three hills before he was not so far from the last one. This argument would suggest *Hamadet er Ressa* or one of its southern neighbours. To this it has been objected that Caesar could not possibly have covered the distance by night over rough ground; and in support of this objection great stress has been laid by some upon the word *semihora*. But to me it seems unnecessary to connect *semihora* with Caesar's preliminary reconnaissance: if

ea refers to *castella*, as it would seem to, may not the meaning be simply that, once the preliminary survey and briefing was completed, the temporary re-instatement of the old watch-towers—carried out simultaneously on all the hills by parties of sappers using in the main materials on the spot—was completed in half an hour?

As *Hamadet er Ressa* satisfies the other requirements— proximity to Scipio's camp and the operations described in chapter 49—I accordingly accept this identification.

(2) *Caesar's Camps and Fortified Lines*

Three distinct camps are referred to in the text—two main and one subsidiary. The latter is mentioned in the first sentence of chapter 51. It was apparently a redoubt, built on *Sidi Jeha*—possibly on the forward slopes—to command its southern and western approaches. It is marked on Map 4 (Uzitta) with the figure 2.

In the following sentence of chapter 51 the writer goes on : ' from his main [or possibly ' largest '] camp Caesar proceeded to carry two fortified lines across the centre of the plain towards Uzitta.' I have followed Stoffel and Holmes in locating this main camp (numbered 1 in map 4) on the western slopes of the ridge, rather than on the plateau farther east, where Veith and Bouvet place it. The former location agrees better with the statement in chapter 63 that the camp—apparently the main camp—was six miles from Leptis.

As to his third camp, there is little dispute about its position described in chapter 56. It was in the plain opposite Uzitta, just out of range of infantry weapons, but within artillery range of the town ; and it was large enough to hold five legions.

The approximate location of Caesar's main fortified lines is not seriously disputed. In Map 4 I have marked the initial field-works, described in chapter 38, as running along the crest of the ridge, though the phrase *medio iugo* might well imply ' half-way up (the western side of) the ridge '. Their prolongation S.W. to *Rhar ed Deba* is, I

APPENDIX A

think, implied in chapter 49, though the interpretation of this difficult chapter is much disputed. The words ' he began to advance along the crest of the ridge ' I interpret as a movement S.W. in the direction of *Sidi Jeha*, which I identify with *proximum collem*; and I interpret the phrase ' capturing the high ground closer to Scipio ' as implying the western slopes of *Rhar ed Deba*, which might otherwise provide Scipio with a springboard for an enflanking movement.

(3) *Scipio's Camp*

The position of this camp is a very vexed question. The main evidence in the text is as follows :

ch. 24 : Scipio, marching by night from Hadrumetum, joins forces with Labienus and Petreius, and they then establish themselves in a single camp three miles distant (presumably from Caesar's camp near Ruspina).

ch. 38 : ' from the last hill and turret, which was nearest the enemy's camp, . . .'

chs. 38, 39 : ' Scipio and Labienus advanced about a mile from their fortified positions. . . . When Caesar perceived that no more than a mile and a half now separated the enemy line from his own fortifications ; . . .' (*see* footnote on p. 396).

ch. 51 : ' the town of Uzitta, which was situated in the plain between his own (Caesar's) camp and Scipio's . . .'

Commentators have accordingly searched for a suitable site answering the following three requirements :

(*i*) three Roman miles distant from Ruspina;
(*ii*) roughly two and a half Roman miles from Caesar's emplacements on or near the ridge;
(*iii*) on the far (*i.e.* western) side of Uzitta.

Now it is fairly easy to select two sites which between them shall satisfy all these three conditions; but it is well nigh impossible to select one. Thus R. Holmes, differing

393

but slightly from Veith, places the camp about one and a half miles N.E. of Uzitta, not far from the modern village of *Mnara*. But this is nearly five Roman miles distant from Caesar's positions at Ruspina, and, moreover, it fails to satisfy the third condition. Bouvet, on the other hand, locates the camp about one mile N.W. of Uzitta, a location which satisfies the third condition but is four Roman miles from the ridge. I would place the camp somewhat closer to the town, though in Map 4 it may perhaps be marked too close, in view of the details—rather ambiguous ones—given in chapter 41 : some sort of compromise appears inevitable between these indications and the approximate distance of two and a half Roman miles mentioned above. But this location does not satisfy the first condition : it is about six Roman miles from Ruspina. Hence Bouvet somewhat arbitrarily amends the MSS. reading of *III* to *VI*.

It was Stoffel who, appreciating the difficulties of satisfying all the stated conditions in a single site, suggested that the camp mentioned in chapter 24 was not the same as the one close to Uzitta. Much scorn has been poured upon this theory, but even so I am inclined to accept it. What Scipio's reasons may have been for moving camp, if in fact he did so, are by no means apparent : a more serious objection to the theory is that the move is quite unmentioned. In this respect the question of Labienus' camp, discussed below, is somewhat parallel; and it is perhaps worth noting that more than one editor, while arguing on the one hand that Scipio could not have moved his camp because no mention is made of the fact, is quite disposed to believe on the other hand that Labienus latterly occupied a separate camp, even though this move too has gone unrecorded.

There is, I think, another point in favour of Stoffel's theory. In chapter 30 it is stated that Scipio made almost daily demonstrations in battle array at a distance of some 300 paces from his camp, Caesar being at that time still at Ruspina; and that finally Scipio halted his battle line not so far from Caesar's camp. That he made these

APPENDIX A

demonstrations in no serious spirit and took good care not to run any serious risk is no doubt true : he ran little enough risk in all conscience if his camp was then, as Stoffel suggests, near *Knais*, three miles away from Caesar at Ruspina; but if, even in those days, he was already encamped near Uzitta almost six miles distant, there would seem very little point in demonstrating at a range of some five and a half miles.

For these reasons I am inclined to accept Stoffel's theory in order to justify my location of Scipio's camp near Uzitta.

(4) *Juba's Camp*

There is little evidence in the text for its position, nor is the matter of any great moment. In chapter 48 it is stated that the king pitched a separate camp not far from Scipio. The statement in chapter 52 that Caesar's cavalry drove the Numidians right back to the royal camp seems to me inconclusive : Veith inferred from this that it was nearer than Scipio's camp to Uzitta; but the opposite conclusion might, I think, be drawn from the word *usque*.

(5) *Labienus' Camp*

Whereas it is clear from chapter 24 that while Caesar was still at Ruspina Labienus shared a single camp with Scipio and Petreius, there are certain indications that at a later period he was operating from a camp situated to the south of the plain. Thus in the last sentence of chapter 49 we read that ' Labienus too had made up his mind to seize this hill (probably *Sidi Jeha*), and his closer proximity to it had enabled him to achieve the goal more rapidly.' Chapter 50 implies that he was quite familiar with this southern area; while in chapter 58 it is stated that ' the enemy led forth their entire combined forces from all their camps.'

This evidence has led most editors to assume that Labienus latterly had an independent camp to the south-

395

APPENDIX A

ward. I have followed R. Holmes and Bouvet in locating it in the foothills east of the modern village of *Djemmal*. The battle dispositions described in chapters 59–60 make it difficult to assume that this camp was much farther north : I assume that the phrase ' closer proximity ' in chapter 49 refers, not to this main camp, but to some redoubt or advanced post which he occupied at the time.

(*Note.* On pp. 393–4 I have inferred from chs. 38 and 39 that Scipio's camp was ' roughly two and a half Roman miles from Caesar's emplacements '. But in fact the distance may have been greater, if it is assumed from the second sentence of ch. 39 that Scipio's cavalry, after *first* advancing about a mile, later *continued* to advance till they were now no more than a mile and a half from Caesar. On this assumption Bouvet's location of Scipio's camp some 4 miles distant from the ridge seems quite defensible so far as *this* evidence is concerned.)

APPENDIX B

CAESAR'S WITHDRAWAL FROM CORDUBA
(*Spanish War* chapter 6)

Many corruptions in the MSS. text of the earlier part of
this chapter make its interpretation very difficult. As the
text I have adopted varies considerably both from the
MSS. tradition and from the reading given by Klotz, all
three readings are here set out in full.

(i) *The MSS. Reading*

id cum animadverteret adversarios minime velle,
quos quoniam a avia retraxerat, ut in aequum
deduceret, copiis flumine traductis noctu iubet ignis
fieri magnos : ita firmissimum eius praesidium
Ateguam proficiscitur. id cum Pompeius ex perfugis
rescisset, qua die facultatem et angustias, carra complura multosque lanistas retraxit et ad Cordubam se
recepit. Caesar munitionibus antequam (*or* antiquas)
oppugnare et bracchia circumducere coepit. cui de
Pompeio cum nuntius esset allatus eo die proficiscitur.

(ii) *Klotz's Reading*

(ch. 5) id cum animadverteret adversarios minime
velle. . . .
(ch. 6) Quos quoniam ab Ulia retraxerat, ut in
aequum deduceret, copiis flumine traductis noctu
iubet ignes fieri magnos. ita firmissimum eius
praesidium Ateguam proficiscitur. id cum Pompeius ex perfugis rescisset, cum die facultatem
⟨liberam sequendi nactus inter montes⟩ et angustias

APPENDIX B

carra complura mulosque onustos retraxit et ad
Cordubam se recepit. Caesar munitionibus Ateguam
oppugnare et brachia circumducere coepit. cuius
re Pompeio cum nuntius esset adlatus, eo die proficiscitur.

(iii) *My Own Reading*

Id cum animadverteret adversarios minime velle,
quo eos quomodo ab Ulia retraxerat [ut] in aequum
deduceret, copiis flumine traductis noctu iubet ignis
fieri magnos : ita firmissimum eius praesidium
Ateguam proficiscitur. Id cum Pompeius ex perfugis
rescisset, qua die facultatem ⟨nactus est, relinquens
montis⟩ et angustias, carra complura mulosque
onustos retraxit et ad Cordubam se recepit. Caesar
munitionibus Ateguam oppugnare et bracchia circumducere coepit. Cui de Pompeio cum nuntius
esset allatus eo die proficisci[tur],

The two most puzzling problems involved in this
narrative seem to me to be these :—

(a) *The Purpose and Position of the Fires*

Holmes thought that they were left burning in Caesar's
camps at Corduba. But though that would doubtless
have been the orthodox manoeuvre, the author has
expressed himself very ambiguously, if that was his meaning. What he appears to say is that the order to light the
fires was given after the crossing of the river. To a rear
party perhaps ? Yet one would have expected the decoy
fires to have been most useful in misleading the enemy,
had they been alight during, not after, the crossing of the
river. The alternative occurs to me that they were lit
somewhere south of the river, and in the wrong direction,
so as to bring Pompey down from the high ground, but
none the less mislead him as to Caesar's route. Klotz
merely describes the fires as ' to cover the departure.'

APPENDIX B

(b) *How much did Pompey know of Caesar's plans, and why did he at first follow Caesar and then retire to Corduba ?*

Holmes took *id* in the phrase *id cum Pompeius ex perfugis rescisset* to refer to Caesar's destination, *viz.* Ategua, and not (as Stoffel, whom Klotz appears to follow) to the fact that Caesar had now left Corduba. In this I certainly think that Holmes is right; for even if the decoy fires were lit—as Holmes thinks—in Caesar's camps at Corduba, it seems almost incredible that Caesar's army should have crossed the river entirely unobserved by Pompey's outposts. Moreover, if the fires were lit subsequently, south of the river, it can fairly be assumed that Caesar never hoped to keep his departure secret, but only his destination; and that the latter was only now disclosed by deserters.

I assume that Pompey followed Caesar with the object of harassing his convoy, but without risking a general engagement. That he met with some success seems to be implied by the words *carra complura . . . retraxit*; for I accept Klotz's explanation that these were captured from Caesar's convoy. But the reason which Klotz suggests for Pompey's withdrawal to Corduba, *viz.* ' to protect his troops from the inclemency of the weather ', hardly seems adequate; it is more likely, I think, that Pompey had to return to Corduba to revictual his forces, since he was not sure whether his communications with Ategua—well stocked with corn, according to the account given by Dio Cassius—were still open.

The following points where my readings vary from those of Klotz are perhaps of less importance for the general interpretation of the narrative :—

> (1) In support of his reading *facultatem liberam sequendi nactus inter montes et angustias* Klotz remarks that the heights which surround the narrow places of the Guadajos valley are about 100 metres above the valley. On the other hand, my reading (based on Mommsen's conjecture) *facultatem nactus est, relinquens*

montis et angustias is, geographically speaking, perhaps no less possible, and seems more appropriate in view of Caesar's object of bringing Pompey down to the plain.

(2) As between Klotz's *cuius re Pompeio cum nuntius esset adlatus, eo die proficiscitur* and my *cui de Pompeio cum nuntius esset allatus eo die proficisci*, the latter admits a more emphatic interpretation of *eo die* which, to my mind, gives greater point to the following words; namely, that though Caesar was advised of the actual day when Pompey left Corduba, and though he had already made adequate dispositions against any surprise attack, yet a thick morning mist upset his calculations.

APPENDIX C

THE BEHAVIOUR OF THE ATEGUAN ENVOYS ON THEIR RETURN TO THE TOWN
(*Spanish War* chapter 18)

For the first three sentences of this chapter Klotz adopts the following reading :—

> Remissis legatis, cum ad portam venissent, ⟨constitit⟩ Tib. Tullius, et cum introeuntem Catonem [1] insecutus non esset, revertit ad portam et hominem adprehendit. quod Tiberius cum fieri animadvertit, simul pugionem eduxit et manum eius incidit. ita refugerunt ad Caesarem.

From the explanation which Klotz gives in his commentary he would seem to interpret as follows :—

> ' When the envoys had been sent back and had come to the gate, Tiberius Tullius stopped; and as, when Cato was going in, Tiberius did not follow him, Cato turned back to the gate and grabbed the fellow. Observing this action, Tiberius at once drew a dagger and stabbed the other's hand. So they fled back to Caesar.'

This reading, which is very close to the MSS., is in many ways attractive; but two serious objections can, I think, reasonably be made to the sense it gives.

(i) Why should both men flee back to Caesar ? Klotz suggests that ' they did not return to the town, probably because they were not sure of the comman-

---

[1] C. Antonius *MSS.*: Catonem *Mommsen*.

dant.' But when they had just fallen out—presumably over the question of the terms of surrender—and one had stabbed the other, it seems unlikely that *both* would flee to Caesar.

(ii) The phrase *quod Tiberius cum fieri animadvertit* seems to me inappropriate as applied to a man in the very act of being grabbed : on the contrary, it suggests a third party witnessing an action in which he is not immediately involved.

My own belief is that there were three envoys, not two; that the MSS. reading *C. Antonius* has partially preserved an original *Catonem Antonius*; and that at the beginning of ch. 17 *Lusitano* is a corruption of *et Antonio*.

On this assumption the narrative seems much easier to follow. Caesar had apparently rejected conditional terms of surrender. Tiberius and Antonius may have favoured unconditional surrender but have been overruled by Cato. By the time they reached the town they may have realised that Cato might denounce them to the commandant as traitors; and when he resorted to force, they sought safety with Caesar. That they later returned to the town and Cato was won over to their view is implied at the end of ch. 19.

APPENDIX D

THE EVENTS AT URSAO [1]
(*Spanish War* chapter 22)

PARTY strife seems to me to be the key to this difficult chapter. For though the existence of a Caesarian party in Ursao is nowhere mentioned, and in chapter 28 its inhabitants are described as supporters of Gnaeus, yet in view of the conditions at Ucubi (ch. 20–21), Corduba (ch. 34) and Carteia (ch. 37) this hypothesis appears reasonable. On this assumption the incidents described may, I think, be explained as follows.

The fall of Ategua—Gnaeus's strongest garrison—must have had important effects; for it strengthened the hand of Caesar's partisans in all the towns, and increased the strategic value of those in the south, particularly Ursao. The anxiety of Gnaeus is obviously reflected in his purge of the opposing faction at Ucubi.

Now Ursao was at this time divided in its allegiance and, as it lay some distance to the south, Gnaeus had not yet detached any troops to hold it, though he had in mind to do so (*cf.* ch. 26). Caesar was anxious that its inhabitants should learn how the Pompeian garrison at Ategua had behaved and accordingly had the envoys—clearly Caesarian partisans—escorted to the town; and the high

---

[1] Throughout the following argument it is assumed that the town referred to in the greater part of this chapter is Ursao (*Osuna*), mentioned later in the book in close connection with Munda. Madvig and Glandorp, among others, held this view. Klotz, however, who identifies Munda with *Montilla* (35 miles N.E. of *Osuna*), assumes (*Kommentar zum Bellum Hispaniense*, p. 80) that the reference here is to a town named Bursao, of unknown situation in Baetica.

rank of the members of this escorting party emphasises the importance of their mission. They may have been empowered to treat directly with the townsmen if the latter decided to join Caesar. But the Pompeian partisans seem to have persuaded their fellow-citizens as a whole that the envoys were liars in the pay of Caesar, and so procured the massacre of all but two of them before they could rejoin Caesar's deputation. Later on—no doubt at the instance of the Caesarian faction—a fact-finding commission was despatched to Ategua and on its return confirmed the envoys' report. A revulsion of feeling now set in and the Caesarians demanded vengeance on the Pompeian partisan who had misled them and, by butchering the envoys, ruined their chances of a composition with Caesar.

At this crisis the man appears to have duped his opponents very thoroughly. Affecting remorse, he sought to leave the town, pretending that he would explain to Caesar that the massacre was a genuine mistake committed in ignorance of the true facts of the case. But once clear of the town he collected sufficient reinforcements to enable him to massacre all his leading opponents and thus secure Ursao's allegiance to Gnaeus.

The last sentence of the chapter is particularly difficult to interpret. I myself believe that it refers, not to Ursao, but to Ucubi.[1] For Ursao lay forty-five miles south of the Salsum, where the fighting was then going on, and its distance from Baeturia was not much less. Deserters from Caesar's army would surely make for Ucubi; and Pompeian refugees from Ucubi would not have far to go to cross the Baetis.

It is not, I think, necessary to assume a gap in the text to account for the change in scene : harsh though it certainly is, it is perhaps not beyond the powers of the author. Elsewhere he uses the phrase *hoc praeterito tempore* to alter the scene as well as the time (*e.g.* the opening words of this same chapter; also ch. 20): his recurrence, in

---

[1] So also Klotz, *ibid.*, p. 81.

APPENDIX D

chapter 21, to events at Ucubi is quite sudden and *oppidum* is left unspecified; while in chapter 34 he switches harshly (*oppido . . . oppidum*) from Corduba to Munda.

If it is Ucubi to which he here refers, his narrative seems easier to follow. The goods being sold are those of Caesar's partisans in the town: all Pompey's troops are virtually confined to camp lest, following the example of the civilian refugees, they desert fully armed : morale in the town and camp is low and—if the text can be trusted— deserters from Caesar's side are discouraged to the extent of being embodied only in the low-paid light-armed units.

ADDITIONAL NOTE
(*Spanish War*, ch. 26, p. 359)

In two passages in this short despatch the interpretation given by Klotz in his commentary is as follows :—

> (i) Reading ' nostrisque adhuc *freti* praesidiis ', he renders ' relying on the strong places until now belonging to us ', explaining that the allusion is in particular to the provisions Caesar had captured at Ategua.
>
> (ii) Reading ' profecto nostro commeatu privati necessario ad dimicandum descendent ' he apparently renders ' assuredly, when they are deprived of the provisions we have collected (*sc.* and have fallen into their hands), they will of necessity come down to fight '.

This interpretation does, I admit, considerably improve the general sense; but whether the Latin text can in either case be fairly thus interpreted seems open to doubt.

INDEX OF PERSONS AND PLACES:
THE ALEXANDRIAN WAR

C.=Caesar, Caesarian; P.=Pompeius, Pompeian; R.=Roman;
cos.=consul, consulship.

*Figures in brackets denote dates B.C. : otherwise they refer to the chapters
of the Latin text.*

PERSONS AND PLACES (ALEX. WAR)

Calvinus, *see* Domitius.

Canopus, Egyptian coastal town at Canopic mouth of Nile, 25

Cappadoces, inhabitants of Cappadocia, 66

Cappadocia, eastern kingdom of Asia Minor adjoining Armenia, ruled by Ariobarzanes, 34, 35, 40, 66

Carfulenus, experienced C. officer prominent in Battle of Nile, 31

Carmo, Spanish town, now Carmona in Andalusia, E.N.E. of Seville, 57, 64

Cassius, (i) Q. Longinus, unpopular governor of Further Spain, appointed by C., 48–64. (ii) Q., deputy and military aide of the above, 52, 57

Chersonensus, Egyptian promontory, perhaps some 8 miles W. of Alexandrea, 14

Cilicia, district of Asia Minor between Taurus Mts. and sea, the coastal region being made a R. province by P. (66), 1, 25, 26, 34, 65, 66

Claudius, (i) C. Marcellus, cos. (49) with Lentulus, 68. (ii) M. Marcellus, quaestor of Cassius, sent to hold Corduba, but chosen as their leader by the mutinous legions, 57–64. (iii) Tiberius Nero, father of the emperor Tiberius, commanded a C. fleet, 25

Cleopatra, elder daughter of Ptolemaeus (Auletes), entrusted with the kingdom by C. jointly with her brother, 33

Comana, (i) town in Cappadocia, shrine of Bellona, 66. (ii) town in Pontus, used as a rendezvous by Domitius, 34, 35

Corduba, now Cordoba, Spanish town on river Baetis, capital of Further Spain, 49, 52, 54, 57–59, 64

Cordubenses, citizens of Corduba, 57, 59–61

Cornelius, L. Lentulus, cos. (49) with Marcellus, 68

Cornificius, Q., C. quaestor, governor of Illyricum as pro-praetor, 42–44, 47

Creta, Crete, 1

DEIOTARUS, king of Armenia Minor and a tetrarch of Galatia, supported

P., pardoned by C., 34, 39, 40, 67–70, 77, 78

Delta, the Delta of the Nile; sometimes used to refer to its S. apex, 27

Domitius, Cn. Calvinus, governor of Asia appointed by C., 9, 34–40, 65, 69, 74

Dyrrachium, now Durazzo in Albania, the Illyrian port linking with Brundisium, attacked by C. in July (48), 48

EPIDAURUS, town on Dalmatian coast besieged by Octavius, 44

Euphranor, Rhodian admiral killed in action off Canopus, 15, 25

FLACCUS, *see* Munatius.

GABINIUS, Aulus, had previously restored Ptolemaeus to Egyptian throne: defeated and died in Illyricum, 3, 42, 43

Galli equites, C. contingent of Gallic cavalry, 17

Gallograecia, otherwise Galatia, the central upland district of Asia Minor, divided into 3 tetrarchies, 67, 78

Ganymedes, an Egyptian eunuch, tutor to Arsinoe, to whom she delegated military command, 4, 5, 12, 23, 33

HERMINIUS mons, Spanish mountain range in W. Lusitania near Medobrega, 48

Hiberus flumen, river in E. Spain, now Ebro, 64

Hispalis, important Spanish town on river Baetis, now Seville, 56, 57

Hispania, Spain, as a whole, comprising 2 provinces, 48, 52, 62. Citerior (Hither Spain), roughly the E. half of the peninsula, 59, 63. Ulterior (Further Spain), the W. half with Portugal, 48–50, 53, 56–58, 64

IADERTINI, inhabitants of Iadera, an Illyrian town, now Zara, 42

Ilipa, Spanish town in Baetica, near modern Alcala del Rio on right bank of Guadalquivir, 57

Illyricum, R. province E. of Adriatic extending from Istria on N. to Epirus on S. and Macedonia on S.E., 42–44

Issa insula, now Lissa, an island off the Illyrian coast, 47

Italia, Italy, 53, 68, 77, 78

Italicensis, native of Italica, Spanish town in Baetica, now Santiponce, on right bank of river Baetis, 52, 57

Iuba, king of Numidia, ally of P., 51

Iulius, (i) C. Caesar, the dictator, rival of P. and most famous member of the Julian family, *passim.* (ii) Sextus Caesar, relation of the above, left by him as governor of Syria, 66

LATERENSIS, L., one of the conspirators against Cassius, 53–55

Lentulus, L., *see* Cornelius.

Lepidus, M., proconsular governor of Hither Spain, 59, 63, 64

Licinius, L. Squillus, one of the conspirators against Cassius, 52, 55

Longinus, *see* Cassius.

Lusitania, part of Further Spain, comprising Portugal S. of Oporto and part of W. Spain, 48, 51

Lyciae naves, ships from Lycia in S. Asia Minor, 13

Lycomedes, a noble Bithynian appointed by C. as priest of Bellona, 66

MACEDONIA, R. province N. of Thessaly and S.E. of Illyricum, 42

Malaca, Spanish town, now Malaga, some 70 miles N.E. of Gibraltar, 64

Malchus, king of the Nabataeans, 1

Manilius Tusculus, one of the conspirators against Cassius, 53

Marcellus, *see* Claudius.

Mauretania, country of the Mauri (Moors) on N. coast of Africa, opposite Spain and W. of Numidia, 51, 52, 59

Mazaca, chief town of Cappadocia, now Kaisariyeh, some 130 miles N. of Tarsus, 66

Medobrega, Spanish town in Lusitania, now Marvao, 48

Mercello, L., one of the conspirators against Cassius, 52, 55

Minucius Silo, leading conspirator against Cassius, 52, 53, 55

Mithridates, (i) the VIth, the ' Great ', king of Pontus and Bosphorus (120–63) who waged three wars against R. and was finally defeated by P., 72, 73, 78. (ii) Pergamenus, a well-born youth from Pergamum, adopted by the above, 26–28, 78

Munatius Flaccus, one of the conspirators against Cassius, 52

NABATAEI, Nabataeans, a people of Arabia Petraea, N.E. of the Red Sea, 1

Naeva (?), Spanish town, apparently between Hispalis and Carmo, exact position unknown, 57

Nero, T., *see* Claudius.

Nicopolis, town in Armenia Minor, where Pharnaces defeated Domitius, 36, 37

Nilus flumen, river Nile, 5, 13, 27–30

Numidia, N. African kingdom of Juba, between Mauretania and R. province of Africa, 51

OBUCULA, Spanish town probably lying between Carmo and Astigi, but exact position obscure, 57

Octavius, M., P. admiral operating off Illyrian coast, 42–47

PALAEPHARSALUS, Old Pharsalus in Thessaly, where C. defeated P. in August (48), 48

Paratonium, a place on the Egyptian coast W. of Alexandria ; of disputed position, but perhaps at the mouth of El Baradan some 20 miles W., 8

PERSONS AND PLACES (ALEX. WAR)

Patisius, Q., sent by Domitius into Cilicia for troops, 34

Pelusium, Egyptian coastal town near the E. mouth of the Nile, 26

Pergamenus, see Mithridates.

Pergamum, now Bergama, Mysian town on W. coast of Asia Minor, 78

Pharitae, inhabitants of island of Pharos, 17, 19

Pharnaces, son of Mithridates the Great, king of Bosphorus; overran Cappadocia, Armenia Minor and Pontus; finally defeated by C. at Zela, 34–41, 65, 69–78

Pharos, island off Alexandria, connected to it by mole, with famous lighthouse at E. tip, 14, 19, 26

Pharsalicum proelium, see Palaepharsalus.

Plaetorius, C., quaestor, to whom P. Sestius was sent in Pontus, 34

Pompeiani, troops or adherents of P., 9, 59

Pompeius, Cn. Magnus, Senatorial champion, defeated by C. at Pharsalus and later murdered in Egypt, 3, 42, 48, 51, 56, 58, 59, 67, 69, 70

Pontica legio, a legion hastily raised in Pontus, 34, 39, 40

Ponticae naves, C. squadron of ships from Pontus, 13, 14

Pontici cives, native population of Pontus plundered by Pharnaces, 41

Pontus, N.E. district of Asia Minor on Euxine (Black Sea), hereditary kingdom of Mithridates, 34, 35, 41, 65, 67, 69, 70, 72, 77

Ptolomaeus, more commonly Ptolemaeus, (i) Auletes, (father), restored to throne of Egypt (55) by Gabinius at instance of P.: appointed R. people to execute his will, 4, 33. (ii) rex, elder son of the above, 23–33

RACILIUS, L., one of the conspirators against Cassius, 52, 53, 55

Rhodiae naves, C. squadron of ships from Rhodes, 11, 13–15, 25

Rhodus, Rhodes, island in E. Mediterranean, 1

Roma (urbs), Rome, 65, 68, 71

Romani cives, R. citizens, 23, 25, 41, 43, 70

Romani equites, R. citizens of the equestrian order, the influential middle class, 40, 56

Romanus populus, the R. people in a political sense, 3, 24, 33, 34, 36, 65, 67, 68, 78

SALONA, town on Dalmatian coast near modern Spalato, 43

Salvianus, see Calpurnius.

Scapula, see Annius.

Segovia, Spanish town on river Singilis (Genil), exact position doubtful, probably between Astigi and Palma, 57

Sestius, (i) P., sent by Domitius to fetch the Pontic legion, 34. (ii) Q., conspirator against Cassius who bought his pardon, 55

Sicilia, Sicily, R. province, steppingstone to Africa, 47

Silo, see Minucius.

Singiliense flumen, river Singilis, now Genil, tributary of the Baetis, 57

Squillus, see Licinius.

Syria, R. province formed by P. (64), capital Antioch, 1, 25, 26, 33, 34, 38, 65, 66

TARSUS, chief town of Cilicia, on S. coast of Asia Minor, 66

Tauris insula, island off Illyrian coast, now Torcola, where Vatinius defeated Octavius, 45

Thorius, T., native of Italica, chosen as their leader by the troops who mutinied against Cassius, 57–58

Tiberius Nero, see Claudius.

Titius, L., tribune of the native legion who reported its mutiny, 57

Trebonius, C., succeeded Cassius as governor of Further Spain, 64

Triarius, C., lieutenant of Lucullus, defeated at Zela by Mithridates (67), 72, 73

Tusculus, see Manilius.

ULIA, Spanish town, now Monte Mayor, some 17 miles S. of Corduba 61, 63

INDEX OF PERSONS AND PLACES:
THE AFRICAN WAR

C. = Caesar, Caesarian ; P. = Pompeius, Pompeian ; R. = Roman ;
cos. = consul, consulship.

*Figures in brackets denote dates B.C. : otherwise they refer to the chapters
of the Latin text.*

PERSONS AND PLACES (AFR. WAR)

Cispius, L., officer sent by C. on naval patrol off Thapsus, 62, 67

Clupea, African coastal town near Cape Bon, now Kelibee, 2, 3

Clusinas, C., C. centurion cashiered for indiscipline, 54

Cominius, Q., C. officer captured at sea by Vergilius, 44, 46

Considius, (i) C. Longus (father), commanded P. garrison at Hadrumetum, and later at Thysdra, 3–5, 33, 43, 76, 86, 93. (ii) C. (son), spared by C., 89.

Cornelius, (i) L. Sulla, the dictator and rival of Marius, 56. (ii) L. Sulla Faustus, P. officer who fled with Afranius and was captured by Sittius, 87, 95; his wife and children pardoned by C., 95. (iii) P., reservist on P. side who commanded garrison at Sarsura, 76

Crispus, see Marcius and Sallustius.

Curioniani equites, cavalry once commanded by Curio who had joined Juba, 52

Curio, C. Scribonius, C. officer defeated and killed by Juba in Africa at river Bagrada (49), 19, 40

Damasippus, Licinius, R. senator, P. supporter, drowned off Hippo, 96; his children spared by C., 89

Decimius, C., controller of supplies at Cercina, 34

Domitius, Cn. Calvinus, entrusted by C. with siege of Thysdra, 86, 93

Eppius, M., supporter of P. pardoned by C., 89

Faustus, see Cornelius.

Fonteius, A, military tribune cashiered for mutinous conduct, 54

Gaetuli, Gaetulians, an inland Libyan people dwelling S. of Mauretania and Numidia, 25, 32, 35, 43, 55, 56, 61, 62, 67, 93

Galli equites, Gallic cavalry, contingents of which fought on both sides, 6, 19, 29, 34, 40

Galli remiges, Gallic rowers, 20

Gallia, Gaul, conquered by C. after eight years of campaigning (58–51), 40, 73

Germani equites, German cavalry, 19, 29, 40

Hadrumetini, inhabitants of Hadrumetum, 97

Hadrumetum, now Sousse on E. coast of Tunis, important P. stronghold, 3, 21, 24, 33, 43, 62, 63, 67, 89

Hiempsal, king of Numidia, father of Juba, expelled by Marians but restored by P., 56

Hippo regius, town on Numidian coast some 120 miles W. of Utica, 96

Hispani, Spaniards, 28, 39

Hispania, Spain, 64, 95, 96

Italia, Italy, 22, 54, 72

Ityrei, Ityreans, a people of Coelesyria (N. Palestine, El-Jeidoor) famed as archers, 20

Iuba, king of Numidia, adherent of P., 6, 25, 36, 43, 48, 52, 55, 57–59, 66, 74, 77, 91–97

Iuliani, C. troops, 15, 40, 41, 69, 78, 85

Iulius, (i) C. Caesar, the dictator and most famous member of the Julian family, passim. (ii) L. Caesar, acted as Cato's quaestor, surrendered Utica, pardoned by C., 88, 89

Labieniani, troops of Labienus, 29

Labienus, T., P. officer, 13, 15, 16, 19–21, 24, 29, 33, 38–40, 49–52, 61, 65, 66, 69, 70, 75, 78

Leptis, African coastal town between Ruspina and Thapsus, garrisoned by C., 7, 9, 10, 29, 61–63, 67

Leptitani, inhabitants of Leptis, fined by C., 97

Ligarius, (i) P., member of Afranius's army amnestied by C. in Spain, later executed for treachery, 64. (ii) Q., spared by C. at Hadrumetum, 89

Lilybaeum, embarkation port in extreme W. of Sicily, now Marsala, 1, 2, 34, 37

413

INDEX OF PERSONS AND PLACES:
THE SPANISH WAR

C. = Caesar, Caesarian; P. = Pompeius, Pompeian; R. = Roman;
cos. = consul, consulship.

Figures in brackets denote dates B.C.: otherwise they refer to the chapters of the
Latin text.

GENERAL SUBJECT INDEX

GENERAL SUBJECT INDEX

GENERAL SUBJECT INDEX

GENERAL SUBJECT INDEX

423

GENERAL SUBJECT INDEX

Punishments, military :
beating to death (murderer), S 27; beheading, S 20; burning alive (slave), S 20; crucifixion, Af 66, S 20 (slaves); dismissal with ignominy, Af 46, 54; execution of prisoners, Af 28, 64; S 12, 13, 16; mutilation, S 12

Pyre, funeral, Af 87, 91; S 33

Quaestor, Al 34, 42, 48, 50, 57; Af 88
Quaestorius, Af 34, 85
Quaestura, S 42

Ransom money, Af 64
Reconnaissance, Al 61; Af 3, 38, 76
Remiges, Al 10, 16, 20, 21, 47; Af 1, 7, 20, 62, 63
Rewards for loyalty, Al 65; Af 97
Rich men, victimised, Al 49
Rostra (beaks, rams), Al 44, 46

Sacramentum (military oath), Al 56
Sagittarii, Al 1, 30; Af 12, 13, 19, 20, 28, 34, 60, 77, 78, 81, 83
Salute, military, Af 85
Scalae, Al 18, 20
Scorpio (see tormenta)
Sea power, influence of, Al 8, 12
Sea-sickness, Af 18, 34
Seaweed, fed to animals, Af 24
Senator, Af 57, 85; S 13, 22
Senatus, Al 67, 68; Af 28, 87 (Utica), 97; S 42
Service, military overseas, Al 56; Af 19
Ships (for types see navis) :
firing of, Af 62, 63; S 36, 37, 40
capsizing when overloaded, Al 20, 21, 46
customs, at Nile mouths, Al 13
on tow, Al 11
off course, Af 2, 7, 8, 11, 21, 28, 44
refitting of, Al 12, 13, 47; S 40
rowing tests of, Al 13
Signa (standards of maniples), Al 20; Af 12, 15–17, 75, 77; S 7, 10, 18, 31, 40
convertere, Af 18
inferre, Al 54; Af 69, 82
tollere, Al 57

Signifer, S 18
Signum Felicitatis, Af 83
Slaves, recruiting, arming of, Al 2; Af 19, 22, 36, 88; S 34
used as pioneers, Al 73, 74; batmen, Af 54
in Scipio's camp at Thapsus, Af 85
Slingers (see funda).
Specula (watch-tower), Af 37; S 8
Speculatores, Af 12, 31, 35, 37; S 13, 20, 22, 28, 38
Statio, Al 19; Af 38, 62; S 14
in statione, Al 25; Af 21, 29, 31, 38, 46, 53, 78; S 6, 13
Stili caeci, Af 31
Stipendium, Af 35
Stores, destruction of, Af 43, 47
Sudes, Af 20

Tabellae, S 19
signatae (sealed sailing orders), Af 3
Tabellarii, Af 38; S 2, 12, 16, 18
Tabernaculum, Af 1
Taxes, imposts, Al 49; Af 97; S 42
Tentorium, tentoriolum, Af 47
Testamentum, Al 33
Testudo, Al 1
Tetrarches, tetrarchia, Al 67, 68, 78
Three Hundred, the, (body of R. traders at Utica), Af 88, 90
Tiro, tirones, Af 1, 5, 10, 16, 19, 31, 32, 44, 46, 60, 71, 81; S 26, 28
Tirocinium, Af 31
Tormenta (artillery), Al 1, 2, 9, 21; Af 20, 29, 77
on ships, Al 19
ballistum, Af 56; S 13
catapulta, Af 31
scorpio, Af 29, 31, 56
Torture, Af 46
examination under, Al 55
Tribuni plebis, rivalries among, Al 65
Tribunus militum, Al 43, 57, 65; Af 28, 54; S 11
Troops :
on leave, Af 77
on sick list, Al 44; Af 77
Tubicen, Af 82
Turma, Af 14, 18, 29, 39, 40, 75, 78; S 6, 14, 23, 26
Turmatim, Af 41

425

GENERAL SUBJECT INDEX

MAPS

PLAN OF ALEXANDRIA
(to illustrate Bellum Alexandrinum)

Map I

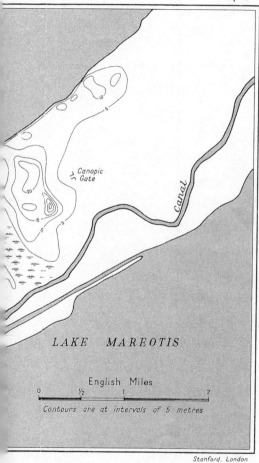

10

5

Canopic
Gate

canal

20

15

10   5

LAKE   MAREOTIS

English Miles

0   ½   1   2

Contours are at intervals of 5 metres

Stanford. London

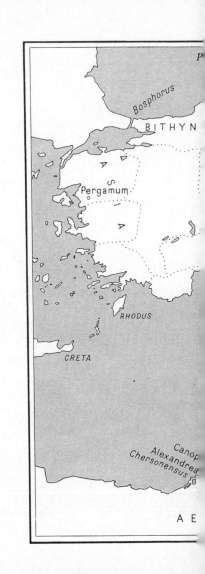

Map 2

CRUS EUXINUS

Halys Fl.

PONTUS

Comana

Zela

ARMENIA MINOR

ARMENIA MAJOR

Nicopolis

ATIA SIVE
OCRAECIA

Halys Fl.

Mazaca

CAPPADOCIA

Comana

CILICIA

Tarsus

Antioch

Seleuceia

Euphrates Flumen

SYRIA

CYPRUS

Ace
Ptolemais

ARABIA PETRAEA

NABATAEI

Pelusium

TUS

ASIA AND THE
EASTERN MEDITERRANEAN
to illustrate Bellum Alexandrinum

0   50   100   200
English Miles

Stanford, London.

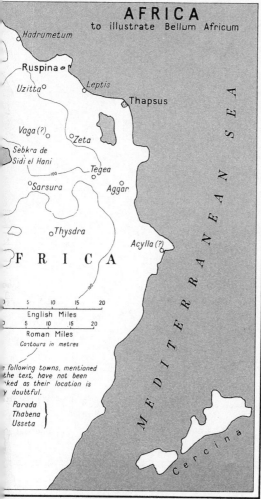

Map 3

AFRICA
to illustrate Bellum Africum

Hadrumetum

Ruspina

Uzitta

Leptis

Thapsus

Vaga (?)

Zeta

Sebkra de
Sidi el Hani

Tegea

Sarsura

Aggar

Thysdra

Acylla (?)

F R I C A

MEDITERRANEAN SEA

```
      5    10   15   20
    English Miles
      5    10   15   20
     Roman Miles
   Contours in metres
```

e following towns, mentioned
the text, have not been
·ked as their location is
y doubtful.

Parada
Thabena
Usseta

Cercina

Stanford. London.

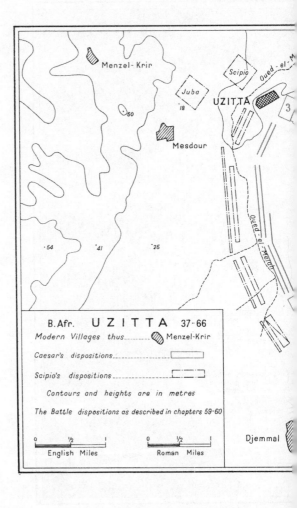

B. Afr. UZITTA 37–66

Modern Villages thus............ Menzel-Krir

Caesar's dispositions............. ⬜

Scipio's dispositions............. ⊏⊐⬜

Contours and heights are in metres

The Battle dispositions as described in chapters 59–60

0   ½   1   0   ½   1
English Miles   Roman Miles

Map 4

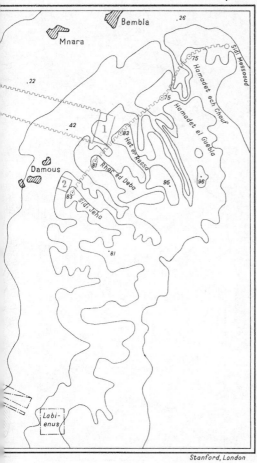

Bembla

.26

Mnara

Sidi Messaoud

.75

.22

Hamadet ech Chouf

.75

.42

1

.83

Hamadet el Guebla

Haî er Ressa

Damous

.81

Rhar ed Deba

95.

.98

2

.83

Sidi Jeha

.81

Labi-
enus

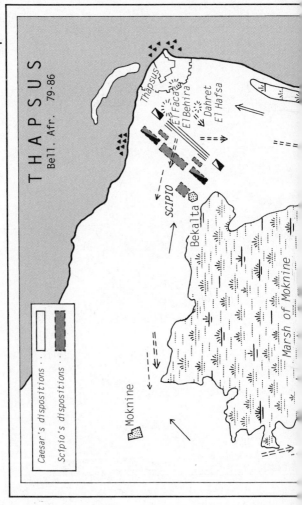

Map 5

THAPSUS
Bell. Afr. 79-86

Caesar's dispositions · ·
Scipio's dispositions · ·

Thapsus

El Faça
El Behira
Dahret
El Hafsa

SCIPIO

Bekalta

Moknine

Marsh of Moknine

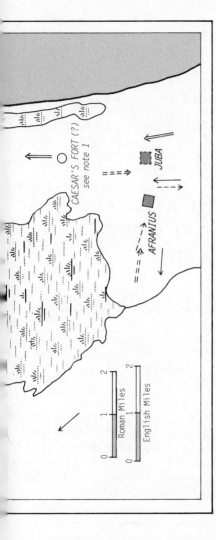

1. Some would place it further North on Dahret El Hafsa.
2. Double arrows indicate movement of Caesar's troops; single arrows, of Scipio's. Unbroken arrows indicate movements prior to the battle, broken ones movements after the battle.
3. Triangles off the coast indicate disposition of Caesar's ships.

CAESAR'S FORT (?)
see note 1

JUBA

AFRANIUS

Roman Miles
0   1   2

English Miles
0   1   2

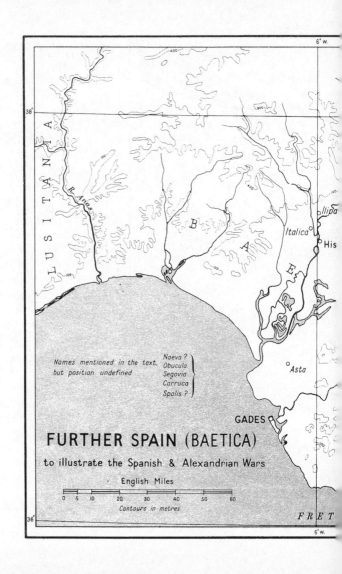

FURTHER SPAIN (BAETICA)

to illustrate the Spanish & Alexandrian Wars

English Miles

Contours in metres

Names mentioned in the text, but position undefined

Naeva?
Obucula
Segovia
Carruca
Spalis?

GADES

Asta

Italica

Ilipa

His

LUSITANIA

R. Anas

FRET

Map 6

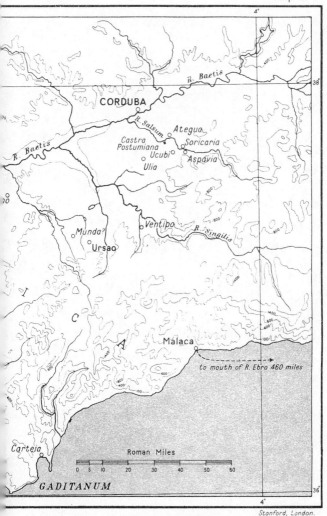

CORDUBA

R. Baetis

R. Salsum

Ategua

Castra Postumiana

Soricaria

Ucubi

Aspavia

Ulia

Ventipo

R. Singilis

Munda?

Ursao

Malaca

to mouth of R. Ebra 460 miles

Carteia

Roman Miles

0 5 10 20 30 40 50 60

GADITANUM